FREE Study Skills Videos/1

Dear Customer,

Thank you for your purchase from Mometrix! We consider it an honor and a privilege that you have purchased our product and we want to ensure your satisfaction.

As part of our ongoing effort to meet the needs of test takers, we have developed a set of Study Skills Videos that we would like to give you for <u>FREE</u>. These videos cover our *best practices* for getting ready for your exam, from how to use our study materials to how to best prepare for the day of the test.

All that we ask is that you email us with feedback that would describe your experience so far with our product. Good, bad, or indifferent, we want to know what you think!

To get your FREE Study Skills Videos, you can use the **QR code** below, or send us an **email** at studyvideos@mometrix.com with *FREE VIDEOS* in the subject line and the following information in the body of the email:

- The name of the product you purchased.
- Your product rating on a scale of 1-5, with 5 being the highest rating.
- Your feedback. It can be long, short, or anything in between. We just want to know your impressions and experience so far with our product. (Good feedback might include how our study material met your needs and ways we might be able to make it even better. You could highlight features that you found helpful or features that you think we should add.)

If you have any questions or concerns, please don't hesitate to contact me directly.

Thanks again!

Sincerely,

Jay Willis
Vice President
jay.willis@mometrix.com
1-800-673-8175

SCAN HERE

CHSPE

Preparation Book 2023-2024

3 Full-Length Practice Tests

Secrets Study Guide for the California High School Proficiency Exam with Step-by-Step Review Video Tutorials

3rd Edition

Written and edited by Matthew Bowling

Printed in the United States of America

This paper meets the requirements of ANSI/NISO Z39.48-1992 (Permanence of Paper).

Mometrix offers volume discount pricing to institutions. For more information or a price quote, please contact our sales department at sales@mometrix.com or 888-248-1219.

Paperback
ISBN 13: 978-1-5167-2174-0
ISBN 10: 1-5167-2174-8

DEAR FUTURE EXAM SUCCESS STORY

First of all, **THANK YOU** for purchasing Mometrix study materials!

Second, congratulations! You are one of the few determined test-takers who are committed to doing whatever it takes to excel on your exam. **You have come to the right place.** We developed these study materials with one goal in mind: to deliver you the information you need in a format that's concise and easy to use.

In addition to optimizing your guide for the content of the test, we've outlined our recommended steps for breaking down the preparation process into small, attainable goals so you can make sure you stay on track.

We've also analyzed the entire test-taking process, identifying the most common pitfalls and showing how you can overcome them and be ready for any curveball the test throws you.

Standardized testing is one of the biggest obstacles on your road to success, which only increases the importance of doing well in the high-pressure, high-stakes environment of test day. Your results on this test could have a significant impact on your future, and this guide provides the information and practical advice to help you achieve your full potential on test day.

Your success is our success

We would love to hear from you! If you would like to share the story of your exam success or if you have any questions or comments in regard to our products, please contact us at **800-673-8175** or **support@mometrix.com**.

Thanks again for your business and we wish you continued success!

Sincerely,
The Mometrix Test Preparation Team

Need more help? Check out our flashcards at:
http://MometrixFlashcards.com/CHSPE

TABLE OF CONTENTS

Introduction

Thank you for purchasing this resource! You have made the choice to prepare yourself for a test that could have a huge impact on your future, and this guide is designed to help you be fully ready for test day. Obviously, it's important to have a solid understanding of the test material, but you also need to be prepared for the unique environment and stressors of the test, so that you can perform to the best of your abilities.

For this purpose, the first section that appears in this guide is the **Secret Keys**. We've devoted countless hours to meticulously researching what works and what doesn't, and we've boiled down our findings to the five most impactful steps you can take to improve your performance on the test. We start at the beginning with study planning and move through the preparation process, all the way to the testing strategies that will help you get the most out of what you know when you're finally sitting in front of the test.

We recommend that you start preparing for your test as far in advance as possible. However, if you've bought this guide as a last-minute study resource and only have a few days before your test, we recommend that you skip over the first two Secret Keys since they address a long-term study plan.

If you struggle with **test anxiety**, we strongly encourage you to check out our recommendations for how you can overcome it. Test anxiety is a formidable foe, but it can be beaten, and we want to make sure you have the tools you need to defeat it.

1

Secret Key #1 – Plan Big, Study Small

There's a lot riding on your performance. If you want to ace this test, you're going to need to keep your skills sharp and the material fresh in your mind. You need a plan that lets you review everything you need to know while still fitting in your schedule. We'll break this strategy down into three categories.

Information Organization

Start with the information you already have: the official test outline. From this, you can make a complete list of all the concepts you need to cover before the test. Organize these concepts into groups that can be studied together, and create a list of any related vocabulary you need to learn so you can brush up on any difficult terms. You'll want to keep this vocabulary list handy once you actually start studying since you may need to add to it along the way.

Time Management

Once you have your set of study concepts, decide how to spread them out over the time you have left before the test. Break your study plan into small, clear goals so you have a manageable task for each day and know exactly what you're doing. Then just focus on one small step at a time. When you manage your time this way, you don't need to spend hours at a time studying. Studying a small block of content for a short period each day helps you retain information better and avoid stressing over how much you have left to do. You can relax knowing that you have a plan to cover everything in time. In order for this strategy to be effective though, you have to start studying early and stick to your schedule. Avoid the exhaustion and futility that comes from last-minute cramming!

Study Environment

The environment you study in has a big impact on your learning. Studying in a coffee shop, while probably more enjoyable, is not likely to be as fruitful as studying in a quiet room. It's important to keep distractions to a minimum. You're only planning to study for a short block of time, so make the most of it. Don't pause to check your phone or get up to find a snack. It's also important to **avoid multitasking**. Research has consistently shown that multitasking will make your studying dramatically less effective. Your study area should also be comfortable and well-lit so you don't have the distraction of straining your eyes or sitting on an uncomfortable chair.

 The time of day you study is also important. You want to be rested and alert. Don't wait until just before bedtime. Study when you'll be most likely to comprehend and remember. Even better, if you know what time of day your test will be, set that time aside for study. That way your brain will be used to working on that subject at that specific time and you'll have a better chance of recalling information.

Finally, it can be helpful to team up with others who are studying for the same test. Your actual studying should be done in as isolated an environment as possible, but the work of organizing the information and setting up the study plan can be divided up. In between study sessions, you can discuss with your teammates the concepts that you're all studying and quiz each other on the details. Just be sure that your teammates are as serious about the test as you are. If you find that your study time is being replaced with social time, you might need to find a new team.

Secret Key #2 – Make Your Studying Count

You're devoting a lot of time and effort to preparing for this test, so you want to be absolutely certain it will pay off. This means doing more than just reading the content and hoping you can remember it on test day. It's important to make every minute of study count. There are two main areas you can focus on to make your studying count.

Retention

It doesn't matter how much time you study if you can't remember the material. You need to make sure you are retaining the concepts. To check your retention of the information you're learning, try recalling it at later times with minimal prompting. Try carrying around flashcards and glance at one or two from time to time or ask a friend who's also studying for the test to quiz you.

To enhance your retention, look for ways to put the information into practice so that you can apply it rather than simply recalling it. If you're using the information in practical ways, it will be much easier to remember. Similarly, it helps to solidify a concept in your mind if you're not only reading it to yourself but also explaining it to someone else. Ask a friend to let you teach them about a concept you're a little shaky on (or speak aloud to an imaginary audience if necessary). As you try to summarize, define, give examples, and answer your friend's questions, you'll understand the concepts better and they will stay with you longer. Finally, step back for a big picture view and ask yourself how each piece of information fits with the whole subject. When you link the different concepts together and see them working together as a whole, it's easier to remember the individual components.

Finally, practice showing your work on any multi-step problems, even if you're just studying. Writing out each step you take to solve a problem will help solidify the process in your mind, and you'll be more likely to remember it during the test.

Modality

Modality simply refers to the means or method by which you study. Choosing a study modality that fits your own individual learning style is crucial. No two people learn best in exactly the same way, so it's important to know your strengths and use them to your advantage.

For example, if you learn best by visualization, focus on visualizing a concept in your mind and draw an image or a diagram. Try color-coding your notes, illustrating them, or creating symbols that will trigger your mind to recall a learned concept. If you learn best by hearing or discussing information, find a study partner who learns the same way or read aloud to yourself. Think about how to put the information in your own words. Imagine that you are giving a lecture on the topic and record yourself so you can listen to it later.

For any learning style, flashcards can be helpful. Organize the information so you can take advantage of spare moments to review. Underline key words or phrases. Use different colors for different categories. Mnemonic devices (such as creating a short list in which every item starts with the same letter) can also help with retention. Find what works best for you and use it to store the information in your mind most effectively and easily.

3

Secret Key #3 – Practice the Right Way

Your success on test day depends not only on how many hours you put into preparing, but also on whether you prepared the right way. It's good to check along the way to see if your studying is paying off. One of the most effective ways to do this is by taking practice tests to evaluate your progress. Practice tests are useful because they show exactly where you need to improve. Every time you take a practice test, pay special attention to these three groups of questions:

- The questions you got wrong
- The questions you had to guess on, even if you guessed right
- The questions you found difficult or slow to work through

This will show you exactly what your weak areas are, and where you need to devote more study time. Ask yourself why each of these questions gave you trouble. Was it because you didn't understand the material? Was it because you didn't remember the vocabulary? Do you need more repetitions on this type of question to build speed and confidence? Dig into those questions and figure out how you can strengthen your weak areas as you go back to review the material.

 Additionally, many practice tests have a section explaining the answer choices. It can be tempting to read the explanation and think that you now have a good understanding of the concept. However, an explanation likely only covers part of the question's broader context. Even if the explanation makes perfect sense, **go back and investigate** every concept related to the question until you're positive you have a thorough understanding.

As you go along, keep in mind that the practice test is just that: practice. Memorizing these questions and answers will not be very helpful on the actual test because it is unlikely to have any of the same exact questions. If you only know the right answers to the sample questions, you won't be prepared for the real thing. **Study the concepts** until you understand them fully, and then you'll be able to answer any question that shows up on the test.

It's important to wait on the practice tests until you're ready. If you take a test on your first day of study, you may be overwhelmed by the amount of material covered and how much you need to learn. Work up to it gradually.

On test day, you'll need to be prepared for answering questions, managing your time, and using the test-taking strategies you've learned. It's a lot to balance, like a mental marathon that will have a big impact on your future. Like training for a marathon, you'll need to start slowly and work your way up. When test day arrives, you'll be ready.

Start with the strategies you've read in the first two Secret Keys—plan your course and study in the way that works best for you. If you have time, consider using multiple study resources to get different approaches to the same concepts. It can be helpful to see difficult concepts from more than one angle. Then find a good source for practice tests. Many times, the test website will suggest potential study resources or provide sample tests.

Practice Test Strategy

If you're able to find at least three practice tests, we recommend this strategy:

UNTIMED AND OPEN-BOOK PRACTICE

Take the first test with no time constraints and with your notes and study guide handy. Take your time and focus on applying the strategies you've learned.

TIMED AND OPEN-BOOK PRACTICE

Take the second practice test open-book as well, but set a timer and practice pacing yourself to finish in time.

TIMED AND CLOSED-BOOK PRACTICE

Take any other practice tests as if it were test day. Set a timer and put away your study materials. Sit at a table or desk in a quiet room, imagine yourself at the testing center, and answer questions as quickly and accurately as possible.

Keep repeating timed and closed-book tests on a regular basis until you run out of practice tests or it's time for the actual test. Your mind will be ready for the schedule and stress of test day, and you'll be able to focus on recalling the material you've learned.

Secret Key #4 – Pace Yourself

Once you're fully prepared for the material on the test, your biggest challenge on test day will be managing your time. Just knowing that the clock is ticking can make you panic even if you have plenty of time left. Work on pacing yourself so you can build confidence against the time constraints of the exam. Pacing is a difficult skill to master, especially in a high-pressure environment, so **practice is vital**.

Set time expectations for your pace based on how much time is available. For example, if a section has 60 questions and the time limit is 30 minutes, you know you have to average 30 seconds or less per question in order to answer them all. Although 30 seconds is the hard limit, set 25 seconds per question as your goal, so you reserve extra time to spend on harder questions. When you budget extra time for the harder questions, you no longer have any reason to stress when those questions take longer to answer.

Don't let this time expectation distract you from working through the test at a calm, steady pace, but keep it in mind so you don't spend too much time on any one question. Recognize that taking extra time on one question you don't understand may keep you from answering two that you do understand later in the test. If your time limit for a question is up and you're still not sure of the answer, mark it and move on, and come back to it later if the time and the test format allow. If the testing format doesn't allow you to return to earlier questions, just make an educated guess; then put it out of your mind and move on.

On the easier questions, be careful not to rush. It may seem wise to hurry through them so you have more time for the challenging ones, but it's not worth missing one if you know the concept and just didn't take the time to read the question fully. Work efficiently but make sure you understand the question and have looked at all of the answer choices, since more than one may seem right at first.

Even if you're paying attention to the time, you may find yourself a little behind at some point. You should speed up to get back on track, but do so wisely. Don't panic; just take a few seconds less on each question until you're caught up. Don't guess without thinking, but do look through the answer choices and eliminate any you know are wrong. If you can get down to two choices, it is often worthwhile to guess from those. Once you've chosen an answer, move on and don't dwell on any that you skipped or had to hurry through. If a question was taking too long, chances are it was one of the harder ones, so you weren't as likely to get it right anyway.

On the other hand, if you find yourself getting ahead of schedule, it may be beneficial to slow down a little. The more quickly you work, the more likely you are to make a careless mistake that will affect your score. You've budgeted time for each question, so don't be afraid to spend that time. Practice an efficient but careful pace to get the most out of the time you have.

Secret Key #5 – Have a Plan for Guessing

When you're taking the test, you may find yourself stuck on a question. Some of the answer choices seem better than others, but you don't see the one answer choice that is obviously correct. What do you do?

The scenario described above is very common, yet most test takers have not effectively prepared for it. Developing and practicing a plan for guessing may be one of the single most effective uses of your time as you get ready for the exam.

In developing your plan for guessing, there are three questions to address:

- When should you start the guessing process?
- How should you narrow down the choices?
- Which answer should you choose?

When to Start the Guessing Process

Unless your plan for guessing is to select C every time (which, despite its merits, is not what we recommend), you need to leave yourself enough time to apply your answer elimination strategies. Since you have a limited amount of time for each question, that means that if you're going to give yourself the best shot at guessing correctly, you have to decide quickly whether or not you will guess.

Of course, the best-case scenario is that you don't have to guess at all, so first, see if you can answer the question based on your knowledge of the subject and basic reasoning skills. Focus on the key words in the question and try to jog your memory of related topics. Give yourself a chance to bring the knowledge to mind, but once you realize that you don't have (or you can't access) the knowledge you need to answer the question, it's time to start the guessing process.

It's almost always better to start the guessing process too early than too late. It only takes a few seconds to remember something and answer the question from knowledge. Carefully eliminating wrong answer choices takes longer. Plus, going through the process of eliminating answer choices can actually help jog your memory.

Summary: Start the guessing process as soon as you decide that you can't answer the question based on your knowledge.

7

How to Narrow Down the Choices

The next chapter in this book (**Test-Taking Strategies**) includes a wide range of strategies for how to approach questions and how to look for answer choices to eliminate. You will definitely want to read those carefully, practice them, and figure out which ones work best for you. Here though, we're going to address a mindset rather than a particular strategy.

Your odds of guessing an answer correctly depend on how many options you are choosing from.

Number of options left	5	4	3	2	1
Odds of guessing correctly	20%	25%	33%	50%	100%

You can see from this chart just how valuable it is to be able to eliminate incorrect answers and make an educated guess, but there are two things that many test takers do that cause them to miss out on the benefits of guessing:

- Accidentally eliminating the correct answer
- Selecting an answer based on an impression

We'll look at the first one here, and the second one in the next section.

To avoid accidentally eliminating the correct answer, we recommend a thought exercise called **the $5 challenge**. In this challenge, you only eliminate an answer choice from contention if you are willing to bet $5 on it being wrong. Why $5? Five dollars is a small but not insignificant amount of money. It's an amount you could afford to lose but wouldn't want to throw away. And while losing

$5 once might not hurt too much, doing it twenty times will set you back $100. In the same way, each small decision you make—eliminating a choice here, guessing on a question there—won't by itself impact your score very much, but when you put them all together, they can make a big difference. By holding each answer choice elimination decision to a higher standard, you can reduce the risk of accidentally eliminating the correct answer.

The $5 challenge can also be applied in a positive sense: If you are willing to bet $5 that an answer choice *is* correct, go ahead and mark it as correct.

Summary: Only eliminate an answer choice if you are willing to bet $5 that it is wrong.

8

Which Answer to Choose

You're taking the test. You've run into a hard question and decided you'll have to guess. You've eliminated all the answer choices you're willing to bet $5 on. Now you have to pick an answer. Why do we even need to talk about this? Why can't you just pick whichever one you feel like when the time comes?

The answer to these questions is that if you don't come into the test with a plan, you'll rely on your impression to select an answer choice, and if you do that, you risk falling into a trap. The test writers know that everyone who takes their test will be guessing on some of the questions, so they intentionally write wrong answer choices to seem plausible. You still have to pick an answer though, and if the wrong answer choices are designed to look right, how can you ever be sure that you're not falling for their trap? The best solution we've found to this dilemma is to take the decision out of your hands entirely. Here is the process we recommend:

Once you've eliminated any choices that you are confident (willing to bet $5) are wrong, select the first remaining choice as your answer.

Whether you choose to select the first remaining choice, the second, or the last, the important thing is that you use some preselected standard. Using this approach guarantees that you will not be enticed into selecting an answer choice that looks right, because you are not basing your decision on how the answer choices look.

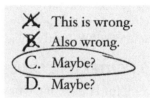

This is not meant to make you question your knowledge. Instead, it is to help you recognize the difference between your knowledge and your impressions. There's a huge difference between thinking an answer is right because of what you know, and thinking an answer is right because it looks or sounds like it should be right.

Summary: To ensure that your selection is appropriately random, make a predetermined selection from among all answer choices you have not eliminated.

Test-Taking Strategies

This section contains a list of test-taking strategies that you may find helpful as you work through the test. By taking what you know and applying logical thought, you can maximize your chances of answering any question correctly!

It is very important to realize that every question is different and every person is different: no single strategy will work on every question, and no single strategy will work for every person. That's why we've included all of them here, so you can try them out and determine which ones work best for different types of questions and which ones work best for you.

Question Strategies

⊘ READ CAREFULLY

Read the question and the answer choices carefully. Don't miss the question because you misread the terms. You have plenty of time to read each question thoroughly and make sure you understand what is being asked. Yet a happy medium must be attained, so don't waste too much time. You must read carefully and efficiently.

⊘ CONTEXTUAL CLUES

Look for contextual clues. If the question includes a word you are not familiar with, look at the immediate context for some indication of what the word might mean. Contextual clues can often give you all the information you need to decipher the meaning of an unfamiliar word. Even if you can't determine the meaning, you may be able to narrow down the possibilities enough to make a solid guess at the answer to the question.

⊘ PREFIXES

If you're having trouble with a word in the question or answer choices, try dissecting it. Take advantage of every clue that the word might include. Prefixes can be a huge help. Usually, they allow you to determine a basic meaning. *Pre-* means before, *post-* means after, *pro-* is positive, *de-* is negative. From prefixes, you can get an idea of the general meaning of the word and try to put it into context.

⊘ HEDGE WORDS

Watch out for critical hedge words, such as *likely, may, can, sometimes, often, almost, mostly, usually, generally, rarely,* and *sometimes.* Question writers insert these hedge phrases to cover every possibility. Often an answer choice will be wrong simply because it leaves no room for exception. Be on guard for answer choices that have definitive words such as *exactly* and *always.*

⊘ SWITCHBACK WORDS

Stay alert for *switchbacks.* These are the words and phrases frequently used to alert you to shifts in thought. The most common switchback words are *but, although,* and *however.* Others include *nevertheless, on the other hand, even though, while, in spite of, despite,* and *regardless of.* Switchback words are important to catch because they can change the direction of the question or an answer choice.

☑ FACE VALUE

When in doubt, use common sense. Accept the situation in the problem at face value. Don't read too much into it. These problems will not require you to make wild assumptions. If you have to go beyond creativity and warp time or space in order to have an answer choice fit the question, then you should move on and consider the other answer choices. These are normal problems rooted in reality. The applicable relationship or explanation may not be readily apparent, but it is there for you to figure out. Use your common sense to interpret anything that isn't clear.

Answer Choice Strategies

☑ ANSWER SELECTION

The most thorough way to pick an answer choice is to identify and eliminate wrong answers until only one is left, then confirm it is the correct answer. Sometimes an answer choice may immediately seem right, but be careful. The test writers will usually put more than one reasonable answer choice on each question, so take a second to read all of them and make sure that the other choices are not equally obvious. As long as you have time left, it is better to read every answer choice than to pick the first one that looks right without checking the others.

☑ ANSWER CHOICE FAMILIES

An answer choice family consists of two (in rare cases, three) answer choices that are very similar in construction and cannot all be true at the same time. If you see two answer choices that are direct opposites or parallels, one of them is usually the correct answer. For instance, if one answer choice says that quantity x increases and another either says that quantity x decreases (opposite) or says that quantity y increases (parallel), then those answer choices would fall into the same family. An answer choice that doesn't match the construction of the answer choice family is more likely to be incorrect. Most questions will not have answer choice families, but when they do appear, you should be prepared to recognize them.

☑ ELIMINATE ANSWERS

Eliminate answer choices as soon as you realize they are wrong, but make sure you consider all possibilities. If you are eliminating answer choices and realize that the last one you are left with is also wrong, don't panic. Start over and consider each choice again. There may be something you missed the first time that you will realize on the second pass.

☑ AVOID FACT TRAPS

Don't be distracted by an answer choice that is factually true but doesn't answer the question. You are looking for the choice that answers the question. Stay focused on what the question is asking for so you don't accidentally pick an answer that is true but incorrect. Always go back to the question and make sure the answer choice you've selected actually answers the question and is not merely a true statement.

☑ EXTREME STATEMENTS

In general, you should avoid answers that put forth extreme actions as standard practice or proclaim controversial ideas as established fact. An answer choice that states the "process should be used in certain situations, if…" is much more likely to be correct than one that states the "process should be discontinued completely." The first is a calm rational statement and doesn't even make a definitive, uncompromising stance, using a hedge word *if* to provide wiggle room, whereas the second choice is far more extreme.

✓ BENCHMARK

As you read through the answer choices and you come across one that seems to answer the question well, mentally select that answer choice. This is not your final answer, but it's the one that will help you evaluate the other answer choices. The one that you selected is your benchmark or standard for judging each of the other answer choices. Every other answer choice must be compared to your benchmark. That choice is correct until proven otherwise by another answer choice beating it. If you find a better answer, then that one becomes your new benchmark. Once you've decided that no other choice answers the question as well as your benchmark, you have your final answer.

✓ PREDICT THE ANSWER

Before you even start looking at the answer choices, it is often best to try to predict the answer. When you come up with the answer on your own, it is easier to avoid distractions and traps because you will know exactly what to look for. The right answer choice is unlikely to be word-for-word what you came up with, but it should be a close match. Even if you are confident that you have the right answer, you should still take the time to read each option before moving on.

General Strategies

✓ TOUGH QUESTIONS

If you are stumped on a problem or it appears too hard or too difficult, don't waste time. Move on! Remember though, if you can quickly check for obviously incorrect answer choices, your chances of guessing correctly are greatly improved. Before you completely give up, at least try to knock out a couple of possible answers. Eliminate what you can and then guess at the remaining answer choices before moving on.

✓ CHECK YOUR WORK

Since you will probably not know every term listed and the answer to every question, it is important that you get credit for the ones that you do know. Don't miss any questions through careless mistakes. If at all possible, try to take a second to look back over your answer selection and make sure you've selected the correct answer choice and haven't made a costly careless mistake (such as marking an answer choice that you didn't mean to mark). This quick double check should more than pay for itself in caught mistakes for the time it costs.

✓ PACE YOURSELF

It's easy to be overwhelmed when you're looking at a page full of questions; your mind is confused and full of random thoughts, and the clock is ticking down faster than you would like. Calm down and maintain the pace that you have set for yourself. Especially as you get down to the last few minutes of the test, don't let the small numbers on the clock make you panic. As long as you are on track by monitoring your pace, you are guaranteed to have time for each question.

✓ DON'T RUSH

It is very easy to make errors when you are in a hurry. Maintaining a fast pace in answering questions is pointless if it makes you miss questions that you would have gotten right otherwise. Test writers like to include distracting information and wrong answers that seem right. Taking a little extra time to avoid careless mistakes can make all the difference in your test score. Find a pace that allows you to be confident in the answers that you select.

⊘ Keep Moving

Panicking will not help you pass the test, so do your best to stay calm and keep moving. Taking deep breaths and going through the answer elimination steps you practiced can help to break through a stress barrier and keep your pace.

Final Notes

The combination of a solid foundation of content knowledge and the confidence that comes from practicing your plan for applying that knowledge is the key to maximizing your performance on test day. As your foundation of content knowledge is built up and strengthened, you'll find that the strategies included in this chapter become more and more effective in helping you quickly sift through the distractions and traps of the test to isolate the correct answer.

Now that you're preparing to move forward into the test content chapters of this book, be sure to keep your goal in mind. As you read, think about how you will be able to apply this information on the test. If you've already seen sample questions for the test and you have an idea of the question format and style, try to come up with questions of your own that you can answer based on what you're reading. This will give you valuable practice applying your knowledge in the same ways you can expect to on test day.

Good luck and good studying!

Mathematics

Numbers

CLASSIFICATIONS OF NUMBERS

Numbers are the basic building blocks of mathematics. Specific features of numbers are identified by the following terms:

Integer – any positive or negative whole number, including zero. Integers do not include fractions $\left(\frac{1}{3}\right)$, decimals (0.56), or mixed numbers $\left(7\frac{3}{4}\right)$.

Prime number – any whole number greater than 1 that has only two factors, itself and 1; that is, a number that can be divided evenly only by 1 and itself.

Composite number – any whole number greater than 1 that has more than two different factors; in other words, any whole number that is not a prime number. For example: The composite number 8 has the factors of 1, 2, 4, and 8.

Even number – any integer that can be divided by 2 without leaving a remainder. For example: 2, 4, 6, 8, and so on.

Odd number – any integer that cannot be divided evenly by 2. For example: 3, 5, 7, 9, and so on.

Decimal number – any number that uses a decimal point to show the part of the number that is less than one. Example: 1.234.

Decimal point – a symbol used to separate the ones place from the tenths place in decimals or dollars from cents in currency.

Decimal place – the position of a number to the right of the decimal point. In the decimal 0.123, the 1 is in the first place to the right of the decimal point, indicating tenths; the 2 is in the second place, indicating hundredths; and the 3 is in the third place, indicating thousandths.

The **decimal**, or base 10, system is a number system that uses ten different digits (0, 1, 2, 3, 4, 5, 6, 7, 8, 9). An example of a number system that uses something other than ten digits is the **binary**, or base 2, number system, used by computers, which uses only the numbers 0 and 1. It is thought that the decimal system originated because people had only their 10 fingers for counting.

Rational numbers include all integers, decimals, and fractions. Any terminating or repeating decimal number is a rational number.

Irrational numbers cannot be written as fractions or decimals because the number of decimal places is infinite and there is no recurring pattern of digits within the number. For example, pi (π) begins with 3.141592 and continues without terminating or repeating, so pi is an irrational number.

Real numbers are the set of all rational and irrational numbers.

THE NUMBER LINE

A number line is a graph to see the distance between numbers. Basically, this graph shows the relationship between numbers. So a number line may have a point for zero and may show negative numbers on the left side of the line. Any positive numbers are placed on the right side of the line. For example, consider the points labeled on the following number line:

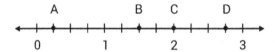

We can use the dashed lines on the number line to identify each point. Each dashed line between two whole numbers is $\frac{1}{4}$. The line halfway between two numbers is $\frac{1}{2}$.

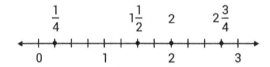

NUMBERS IN WORD FORM AND PLACE VALUE

When writing numbers out in word form or translating word form to numbers, it is essential to understand how a place value system works. In the decimal or base-10 system, each digit of a number represents how many of the corresponding place value—a specific factor of 10—are contained in the number being represented. To make reading numbers easier, every three digits to the left of the decimal place is preceded by a comma. The following table demonstrates some of the place values:

Power of 10	10^3	10^2	10^1	10^0	10^{-1}	10^{-2}	10^{-3}
Value	1,000	100	10	1	0.1	0.01	0.001
Place	thousands	hundreds	tens	ones	tenths	hundredths	thousandths

For example, consider the number 4,546.09, which can be separated into each place value like this:

4: thousands
5: hundreds
4: tens
6: ones
0: tenths
9: hundredths

This number in word form would be *four thousand five hundred forty-six and nine hundredths.*

Review Video: <u>Place Value</u>
Visit mometrix.com/academy and enter code: 205433

ABSOLUTE VALUE

A precursor to working with negative numbers is understanding what **absolute values** are. A number's absolute value is simply the distance away from zero a number is on the number line. The absolute value of a number is always positive and is written $|x|$. For example, the absolute value of 3, written as $|3|$, is 3 because the distance between 0 and 3 on a number line is three units. Likewise, the absolute value of −3, written as $|−3|$, is 3 because the distance between 0 and −3 on a number line is three units. So $|3| = |−3|$.

Review Video: <u>Absolute Value</u>
Visit mometrix.com/academy and enter code: 314669

Operations

OPERATIONS

An **operation** is simply a mathematical process that takes some value(s) as input(s) and produces an output. Elementary operations are often written in the following form: *value operation value*. For instance, in the expression $1 + 2$ the values are 1 and 2 and the operation is addition. Performing the operation gives the output of 3. In this way we can say that $1 + 2$ and 3 are equal, or $1 + 2 = 3$.

ADDITION

Addition increases the value of one quantity by the value of another quantity (both called **addends**). Example: $2 + 4 = 6$ or $8 + 9 = 17$. The result is called the **sum**. With addition, the order does not matter, $4 + 2 = 2 + 4$.

When adding signed numbers, if the signs are the same simply add the absolute values of the addends and apply the original sign to the sum. For example, $(+4) + (+8) = +12$ and $(-4) + (-8) = -12$. When the original signs are different, take the absolute values of the addends and subtract the smaller value from the larger value, then apply the original sign of the larger value to the difference. Example: $(+4) + (-8) = -4$ and $(-4) + (+8) = +4$.

SUBTRACTION

Subtraction is the opposite operation to addition; it decreases the value of one quantity (the **minuend**) by the value of another quantity (the **subtrahend**). For example, $6 - 4 = 2$ or $17 - 8 = 9$. The result is called the **difference**. Note that with subtraction, the order does matter, $6 - 4 \neq 4 - 6$.

For subtracting signed numbers, change the sign of the subtrahend and then follow the same rules used for addition. Example: $(+4) - (+8) = (+4) + (-8) = -4$

MULTIPLICATION

Multiplication can be thought of as repeated addition. One number (the **multiplier**) indicates how many times to add the other number (the **multiplicand**) to itself. Example: $3 \times 2 = 2 + 2 + 2 = 6$. With multiplication, the order does not matter, $2 \times 3 = 3 \times 2$ or $3 + 3 = 2 + 2 + 2$, either way the result (the **product**) is the same.

If the signs are the same, the product is positive when multiplying signed numbers. Example: $(+4) \times (+8) = +32$ and $(-4) \times (-8) = +32$. If the signs are opposite, the product is negative. Example: $(+4) \times (-8) = -32$ and $(-4) \times (+8) = -32$. When more than two factors are multiplied together, the sign of the product is determined by how many negative factors are present. If there are an odd number of negative factors then the product is negative, whereas an even number of negative factors indicates a positive product. Example: $(+4) \times (-8) \times (-2) = +64$ and $(-4) \times (-8) \times (-2) = -64$.

DIVISION

Division is the opposite operation to multiplication; one number (the **divisor**) tells us how many parts to divide the other number (the **dividend**) into. The result of division is called the **quotient**. Example: $20 \div 4 = 5$. If 20 is split into 4 equal parts, each part is 5. With division, the order of the numbers does matter, $20 \div 4 \neq 4 \div 20$.

The rules for dividing signed numbers are similar to multiplying signed numbers. If the dividend and divisor have the same sign, the quotient is positive. If the dividend and divisor have opposite signs, the quotient is negative. Example: $(-4) \div (+8) = -0.5$.

> **Review Video: Mathematical Operations**
> Visit mometrix.com/academy and enter code: 208095

PARENTHESES

Parentheses are used to designate which operations should be done first when there are multiple operations. Example: $4 - (2 + 1) = 1$; the parentheses tell us that we must add 2 and 1, and then subtract the sum from 4, rather than subtracting 2 from 4 and then adding 1 (this would give us an answer of 3).

> **Review Video: Mathematical Parentheses**
> Visit mometrix.com/academy and enter code: 978600

EXPONENTS

An **exponent** is a superscript number placed next to another number at the top right. It indicates how many times the base number is to be multiplied by itself. Exponents provide a shorthand way to write what would be a longer mathematical expression, Example: $2^4 = 2 \times 2 \times 2 \times 2$. A number with an exponent of 2 is said to be "squared," while a number with an exponent of 3 is said to be "cubed." The value of a number raised to an exponent is called its power. So 8^4 is read as "8 to the 4th power," or "8 raised to the power of 4."

The properties of exponents are as follows:

Property	Description
$a^1 = a$	Any number to the power of 1 is equal to itself
$1^n = 1$	The number 1 raised to any power is equal to 1
$a^0 = 1$	Any number raised to the power of 0 is equal to 1
$a^n \times a^m = a^{n+m}$	Add exponents to multiply powers of the same base number
$a^n \div a^m = a^{n-m}$	Subtract exponents to divide powers of the same base number
$(a^n)^m = a^{n \times m}$	When a power is raised to a power, the exponents are multiplied
$(a \times b)^n = a^n \times b^n$ $(a \div b)^n = a^n \div b^n$	Multiplication and division operations inside parentheses can be raised to a power. This is the same as each term being raised to that power.
$a^{-n} = \dfrac{1}{a^n}$	A negative exponent is the same as the reciprocal of a positive exponent

Note that exponents do not have to be integers. Fractional or decimal exponents follow all the rules above as well. Example: $5^{\frac{1}{4}} \times 5^{\frac{3}{4}} = 5^{\frac{1}{4}+\frac{3}{4}} = 5^1 = 5$.

> **Review Video: Introduction to Exponents**
> Visit mometrix.com/academy and enter code: 600998
>
> **Review Video: Properties of Exponents**
> Visit mometrix.com/academy and enter code: 532558

ROOTS

A **root**, such as a square root, is another way of writing a fractional exponent. Instead of using a superscript, roots use the radical symbol ($\sqrt{}$) to indicate the operation. A radical will have a number underneath the bar, and may sometimes have a number in the upper left: $\sqrt[n]{a}$, read as "the nth root of a." The relationship between radical notation and exponent notation can be described by this equation:

$$\sqrt[n]{a} = a^{\frac{1}{n}}$$

The two special cases of $n = 2$ and $n = 3$ are called square roots and cube roots. If there is no number to the upper left, the radical is understood to be a square root ($n = 2$). Nearly all of the roots you encounter will be square roots. A square root is the same as a number raised to the one-half power. When we say that a is the square root of b ($a = \sqrt{b}$), we mean that a multiplied by itself equals b: ($a \times a = b$).

A **perfect square** is a number that has an integer for its square root. There are 10 perfect squares from 1 to 100: 1, 4, 9, 16, 25, 36, 49, 64, 81, 100 (the squares of integers 1 through 10).

> **Review Video: Roots**
> Visit mometrix.com/academy and enter code: 795655
>
> **Review Video: Square Root and Perfect Squares**
> Visit mometrix.com/academy and enter code: 648063

ORDER OF OPERATIONS

The **order of operations** is a set of rules that dictates the order in which we must perform each operation in an expression so that we will evaluate it accurately. If we have an expression that includes multiple different operations, the order of operations tells us which operations to do first. The most common mnemonic for the order of operations is **PEMDAS**, or "Please Excuse My Dear Aunt Sally." PEMDAS stands for parentheses, exponents, multiplication, division, addition, and subtraction. It is important to understand that multiplication and division have equal precedence, as do addition and subtraction, so those pairs of operations are simply worked from left to right in order.

For example, evaluating the expression $5 + 20 \div 4 \times (2 + 3)^2 - 6$ using the correct order of operations would be done like this:

- **P:** Perform the operations inside the parentheses: $(2 + 3) = 5$
- **E:** Simplify the exponents: $(5)^2 = 5 \times 5 = 25$
  - The equation now looks like this: $5 + 20 \div 4 \times 25 - 6$
- **MD:** Perform multiplication and division from left to right: $20 \div 4 = 5$; then $5 \times 25 = 125$
  - The equation now looks like this: $5 + 125 - 6$
- **AS:** Perform addition and subtraction from left to right: $5 + 125 = 130$; then $130 - 6 = 124$

> **Review Video: Order of Operations**
> Visit mometrix.com/academy and enter code: 259675

SUBTRACTION WITH REGROUPING

A great way to make use of some of the features built into the decimal system would be regrouping when attempting longform subtraction operations. When subtracting within a place value, sometimes the minuend is smaller than the subtrahend, **regrouping** enables you to 'borrow' a unit from a place value to the left in order to get a positive difference. For example, consider subtracting 189 from 525 with regrouping.

> **Review Video: <u>Subtracting Large Numbers</u>**
> Visit mometrix.com/academy and enter code: 603350

First, set up the subtraction problem in vertical form:

$$\begin{array}{r} 525 \\ -\ 189 \\ \hline \end{array}$$

Notice that the numbers in the ones and tens columns of 525 are smaller than the numbers in the ones and tens columns of 189. This means you will need to use regrouping to perform subtraction:

$$\begin{array}{cccc} & 5 & 2 & 5 \\ - & 1 & 8 & 9 \\ \hline \end{array}$$

To subtract 9 from 5 in the ones column you will need to borrow from the 2 in the tens columns:

$$\begin{array}{cccc} & 5 & 1 & 15 \\ - & 1 & 8 & 9 \\ \hline & & & 6 \end{array}$$

Next, to subtract 8 from 1 in the tens column you will need to borrow from the 5 in the hundreds column:

$$\begin{array}{cccc} & 4 & 11 & 15 \\ - & 1 & 8 & 9 \\ \hline & & 3 & 6 \end{array}$$

Last, subtract the 1 from the 4 in the hundreds column:

$$\begin{array}{cccc} & 4 & 11 & 15 \\ - & 1 & 8 & 9 \\ \hline & 3 & 3 & 6 \end{array}$$

WORD PROBLEMS AND MATHEMATICAL SYMBOLS

When working on word problems, you must be able to translate verbal expressions or "math words" into math symbols. This chart contains several "math words" and their appropriate symbols:

Phrase	Symbol
equal, is, was, will be, has, costs, gets to, is the same as, becomes	$=$
times, of, multiplied by, product of, twice, doubles, halves, triples	$\times$
divided by, per, ratio of/to, out of	$\div$
plus, added to, sum, combined, and, more than, totals of	$+$
subtracted from, less than, decreased by, minus, difference between	$-$
what, how much, original value, how many, a number, a variable	x, n, etc.

EXAMPLES OF TRANSLATED MATHEMATICAL PHRASES

- The phrase four more than twice a number can be written algebraically as $2x + 4$.
- The phrase half a number decreased by six can be written algebraically as $\frac{1}{2}x - 6$.
- The phrase the sum of a number and the product of five and that number can be written algebraically as $x + 5x$.
- You may see a test question that says, "Olivia is constructing a bookcase from seven boards. Two of them are for vertical supports and five are for shelves. The height of the bookcase is twice the width of the bookcase. If the seven boards total 36 feet in length, what will be the height of Olivia's bookcase?" You would need to make a sketch and then create the equation to determine the width of the shelves. The height can be represented as double the width. (If x represents the width of the shelves in feet, then the height of the bookcase is $2x$. Since the seven boards total 36 feet, $2x + 2x + x + x + x + x + x = 36$ or $9x = 36$; $x = 4$. The height is twice the width, or 8 feet.)

Rational Numbers

FRACTIONS

A **fraction** is a number that is expressed as one integer written above another integer, with a dividing line between them $\left(\frac{x}{y}\right)$. It represents the **quotient** of the two numbers "x divided by y." It can also be thought of as x out of y equal parts.

The top number of a fraction is called the **numerator**, and it represents the number of parts under consideration. The 1 in $\frac{1}{4}$ means that 1 part out of the whole is being considered in the calculation. The bottom number of a fraction is called the **denominator**, and it represents the total number of equal parts. The 4 in $\frac{1}{4}$ means that the whole consists of 4 equal parts. A fraction cannot have a denominator of zero; this is referred to as "*undefined*."

Fractions can be manipulated, without changing the value of the fraction, by multiplying or dividing (but not adding or subtracting) both the numerator and denominator by the same number. If you divide both numbers by a common factor, you are **reducing** or simplifying the fraction. Two fractions that have the same value but are expressed differently are known as **equivalent fractions**. For example, $\frac{2}{10}, \frac{3}{15}, \frac{4}{20},$ and $\frac{5}{25}$ are all equivalent fractions. They can also all be reduced or simplified to $\frac{1}{5}$.

When two fractions are manipulated so that they have the same denominator, this is known as finding a **common denominator**. The number chosen to be that common denominator should be the least common multiple of the two original denominators. Example: $\frac{3}{4}$ and $\frac{5}{6}$; the least common multiple of 4 and 6 is 12. Manipulating to achieve the common denominator: $\frac{3}{4} = \frac{9}{12}; \frac{5}{6} = \frac{10}{12}$.

PROPER FRACTIONS AND MIXED NUMBERS

A fraction whose denominator is greater than its numerator is known as a **proper fraction**, while a fraction whose numerator is greater than its denominator is known as an **improper fraction**. Proper fractions have values *less than one* and improper fractions have values *greater than one*.

A **mixed number** is a number that contains both an integer and a fraction. Any improper fraction can be rewritten as a mixed number. Example: $\frac{8}{3} = \frac{6}{3} + \frac{2}{3} = 2 + \frac{2}{3} = 2\frac{2}{3}$. Similarly, any mixed number can be rewritten as an improper fraction. Example: $1\frac{3}{5} = 1 + \frac{3}{5} = \frac{5}{5} + \frac{3}{5} = \frac{8}{5}$.

> **Review Video: Improper Fractions and Mixed Numbers**
> Visit mometrix.com/academy and enter code: 211077
>
> **Review Video: Overview of Fractions**
> Visit mometrix.com/academy and enter code: 262335

ADDING AND SUBTRACTING FRACTIONS

If two fractions have a common denominator, they can be added or subtracted simply by adding or subtracting the two numerators and retaining the same denominator. If the two fractions do not already have the same denominator, one or both of them must be manipulated to achieve a common denominator before they can be added or subtracted. Example: $\frac{1}{2} + \frac{1}{4} = \frac{2}{4} + \frac{1}{4} = \frac{3}{4}$.

> **Review Video: Adding and Subtracting Fractions**
> Visit mometrix.com/academy and enter code: 378080

MULTIPLYING FRACTIONS

Two fractions can be multiplied by multiplying the two numerators to find the new numerator and the two denominators to find the new denominator. Example: $\frac{1}{3} \times \frac{2}{3} = \frac{1 \times 2}{3 \times 3} = \frac{2}{9}$.

DIVIDING FRACTIONS

Two fractions can be divided by flipping the numerator and denominator of the second fraction and then proceeding as though it were a multiplication problem. Example: $\frac{2}{3} \div \frac{3}{4} = \frac{2}{3} \times \frac{4}{3} = \frac{8}{9}$.

> **Review Video: Multiplying and Dividing Fractions**
> Visit mometrix.com/academy and enter code: 473632

MULTIPLYING A MIXED NUMBER BY A WHOLE NUMBER OR A DECIMAL

When multiplying a mixed number by something, it is usually best to convert it to an improper fraction first. Additionally, if the multiplicand is a decimal, it is most often simplest to convert it to a fraction. For instance, to multiply $4\frac{3}{8}$ by 3.5, begin by rewriting each quantity as a whole number plus a proper fraction. Remember, a mixed number is a fraction added to a whole number and a decimal is a representation of the sum of fractions, specifically tenths, hundredths, thousandths, and so on:

$$4\frac{3}{8} \times 3.5 = \left(4 + \frac{3}{8}\right) \times \left(3 + \frac{1}{2}\right)$$

Next, the quantities being added need to be expressed with the same denominator. This is achieved by multiplying and dividing the whole number by the denominator of the fraction. Recall that a whole number is equivalent to that number divided by 1:

$$= \left(\frac{4}{1} \times \frac{8}{8} + \frac{3}{8}\right) \times \left(\frac{3}{1} \times \frac{2}{2} + \frac{1}{2}\right)$$

When multiplying fractions, remember to multiply the numerators and denominators separately:

$$= \left(\frac{4 \times 8}{1 \times 8} + \frac{3}{8}\right) \times \left(\frac{3 \times 2}{1 \times 2} + \frac{1}{2}\right)$$
$$= \left(\frac{32}{8} + \frac{3}{8}\right) \times \left(\frac{6}{2} + \frac{1}{2}\right)$$

Now that the fractions have the same denominators, they can be added:

$$= \frac{35}{8} \times \frac{7}{2}$$

Finally, perform the last multiplication and then simplify:

$$= \frac{35 \times 7}{8 \times 2} = \frac{245}{16} = \frac{240}{16} + \frac{5}{16} = 15\frac{5}{16}$$

DECIMALS

Decimals are one way to represent parts of a whole. Using the place value system, each digit to the right of a decimal point denotes the number of units of a corresponding *negative* power of ten. For example, consider the decimal 0.24. We can use a model to represent the decimal. Since a dime is worth one-tenth of a dollar and a penny is worth one-hundredth of a dollar, one possible model to represent this fraction is to have 2 dimes representing the 2 in the tenths place and 4 pennies representing the 4 in the hundredths place:

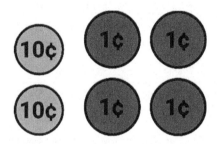

To write the decimal as a fraction, put the decimal in the numerator with 1 in the denominator. Multiply the numerator and denominator by tens until there are no more decimal places. Then simplify the fraction to lowest terms. For example, converting 0.24 to a fraction:

$$0.24 = \frac{0.24}{1} = \frac{0.24 \times 100}{1 \times 100} = \frac{24}{100} = \frac{6}{25}$$

Review Video: Decimals
Visit mometrix.com/academy and enter code: 837268

OPERATIONS WITH DECIMALS
ADDING AND SUBTRACTING DECIMALS

When adding and subtracting decimals, the decimal points must always be aligned. Adding decimals is just like adding regular whole numbers. Example: $4.5 + 2.0 = 6.5$.

If the problem-solver does not properly align the decimal points, an incorrect answer of 4.7 may result. An easy way to add decimals is to align all of the decimal points in a vertical column visually. This will allow you to see exactly where the decimal should be placed in the final answer. Begin adding from right to left. Add each column in turn, making sure to carry the number to the left if a column adds up to more than 9. The same rules apply to the subtraction of decimals.

Review Video: Adding and Subtracting Decimals
Visit mometrix.com/academy and enter code: 381101

MULTIPLYING DECIMALS

A simple multiplication problem has two components: a **multiplicand** and a **multiplier**. When multiplying decimals, work as though the numbers were whole rather than decimals. Once the final product is calculated, count the number of places to the right of the decimal in both the multiplicand and the multiplier. Then, count that number of places from the right of the product and place the decimal in that position.

For example, 12.3×2.56 has a total of three places to the right of the respective decimals. Multiply 123×256 to get 31,488. Now, beginning on the right, count three places to the left and insert the decimal. The final product will be 31.488.

> **Review Video: How to Multiply Decimals**
> Visit mometrix.com/academy and enter code: 731574

DIVIDING DECIMALS

Every division problem has a **divisor** and a **dividend**. The dividend is the number that is being divided. In the problem $14 \div 7$, 14 is the dividend and 7 is the divisor. In a division problem with decimals, the divisor must be converted into a whole number. Begin by moving the decimal in the divisor to the right until a whole number is created. Next, move the decimal in the dividend the same number of spaces to the right. For example, 4.9 into 24.5 would become 49 into 245. The decimal was moved one space to the right to create a whole number in the divisor, and then the same was done for the dividend. Once the whole numbers are created, the problem is carried out normally: $245 \div 49 = 5$.

> **Review Video: How to Divide Decimals**
> Visit mometrix.com/academy and enter code: 560690
>
> **Review Video: Dividing Decimals by Whole Numbers**
> Visit mometrix.com/academy and enter code: 535669

PERCENTAGES

Percentages can be thought of as fractions that are based on a whole of 100; that is, one whole is equal to 100%. The word **percent** means "per hundred." Percentage problems are often presented in three main ways:

- Find what percentage of some number another number is.
  - Example: What percentage of 40 is 8?
- Find what number is some percentage of a given number.
  - Example: What number is 20% of 40?
- Find what number another number is a given percentage of.
  - Example: What number is 8 20% of?

There are three components in each of these cases: a **whole** (W), a **part** (P), and a **percentage** (%). These are related by the equation: $P = W \times \%$. This can easily be rearranged into other forms that may suit different questions better: $\% = \frac{P}{W}$ and $W = \frac{P}{\%}$. Percentage problems are often also word problems. As such, a large part of solving them is figuring out which quantities are what. For example, consider the following word problem:

In a school cafeteria, 7 students choose pizza, 9 choose hamburgers, and 4 choose tacos. What percentage of student choose tacos?

To find the whole, you must first add all of the parts: $7 + 9 + 4 = 20$. The percentage can then be found by dividing the part by the whole $\left(\% = \frac{P}{W} \right)$: $\frac{4}{20} = \frac{20}{100} = 20\%$.

> **Review Video: Computation with Percentages**
> Visit mometrix.com/academy and enter code: 693099

26

CONVERTING BETWEEN PERCENTAGES, FRACTIONS, AND DECIMALS

Converting decimals to percentages and percentages to decimals is as simple as moving the decimal point. To *convert from a decimal to a percentage*, move the decimal point **two places to the right**. To *convert from a percentage to a decimal*, move it **two places to the left**. It may be helpful to remember that the percentage number will always be larger than the equivalent decimal number. Example:

$$0.23 = 23\% \quad 5.34 = 534\% \quad 0.007 = 0.7\%$$
$$700\% = 7.00 \quad 86\% = 0.86 \quad 0.15\% = 0.0015$$

To convert a fraction to a decimal, simply divide the numerator by the denominator in the fraction. To convert a decimal to a fraction, put the decimal in the numerator with 1 in the denominator. Multiply the numerator and denominator by tens until there are no more decimal places. Then simplify the fraction to lowest terms. For example, converting 0.24 to a fraction:

$$0.24 = \frac{0.24}{1} = \frac{0.24 \times 100}{1 \times 100} = \frac{24}{100} = \frac{6}{25}$$

Fractions can be converted to a percentage by finding equivalent fractions with a denominator of 100. Example:

$$\frac{7}{10} = \frac{70}{100} = 70\% \quad \frac{1}{4} = \frac{25}{100} = 25\%$$

To convert a percentage to a fraction, divide the percentage number by 100 and reduce the fraction to its simplest possible terms. Example:

$$60\% = \frac{60}{100} = \frac{3}{5} \quad 96\% = \frac{96}{100} = \frac{24}{25}$$

> **Review Video: Converting Decimals, Improper Fractions, and Mixed Numbers**
> Visit mometrix.com/academy and enter code: 696924
>
> **Review Video: Converting Fractions to Percentages and Decimals**
> Visit mometrix.com/academy and enter code: 306233
>
> **Review Video: Converting Percentages to Decimals and Fractions**
> Visit mometrix.com/academy and enter code: 287297
>
> **Review Video: Converting Decimals to Fractions and Percentages**
> Visit mometrix.com/academy and enter code: 986765

RATIONAL NUMBERS

The term **rational** means that the number can be expressed as a ratio or fraction. That is, a number, r, is rational if and only if it can be represented by a fraction $\frac{a}{b}$ where a and b are integers and b does not equal 0. The set of rational numbers includes integers and decimals. If there is no finite way to represent a value with a fraction of integers, then the number is **irrational**. Common examples of irrational numbers include: $\sqrt{5}$, $\left(1 + \sqrt{2}\right)$, and π.

> **Review Video:** <u>**Rational and Irrational Numbers**</u>
> Visit mometrix.com/academy and enter code: 280645

Proportions and Ratios

PROPORTIONS

A proportion is a relationship between two quantities that dictates how one changes when the other changes. A **direct proportion** describes a relationship in which a quantity increases by a set amount for every increase in the other quantity, or decreases by that same amount for every decrease in the other quantity. Example: Assuming a constant driving speed, the time required for a car trip increases as the distance of the trip increases. The distance to be traveled and the time required to travel are directly proportional.

An **inverse proportion** is a relationship in which an increase in one quantity is accompanied by a decrease in the other, or vice versa. Example: the time required for a car trip decreases as the speed increases and increases as the speed decreases, so the time required is inversely proportional to the speed of the car.

> **Review Video: Proportions**
> Visit mometrix.com/academy and enter code: 505355

RATIOS

A **ratio** is a comparison of two quantities in a particular order. Example: If there are 14 computers in a lab, and the class has 20 students, there is a student to computer ratio of 20 to 14, commonly written as 20: 14. Ratios are normally reduced to their smallest whole number representation, so 20: 14 would be reduced to 10: 7 by dividing both sides by 2.

> **Review Video: Ratios**
> Visit mometrix.com/academy and enter code: 996914

CONSTANT OF PROPORTIONALITY

When two quantities have a proportional relationship, there exists a **constant of proportionality** between the quantities. The product of this constant and one of the quantities is equal to the other quantity. For example, if one lemon costs $0.25, two lemons cost $0.50, and three lemons cost $0.75, there is a proportional relationship between the total cost of lemons and the number of lemons purchased. The constant of proportionality is the **unit price**, namely $0.25/lemon. Notice that the total price of lemons, t, can be found by multiplying the unit price of lemons, p, and the number of lemons, n: $t = pn$.

WORK/UNIT RATE

Unit rate expresses a quantity of one thing in terms of one unit of another. For example, if you travel 30 miles every two hours, a unit rate expresses this comparison in terms of one hour: in one hour you travel 15 miles, so your unit rate is 15 miles per hour. Other examples are how much one ounce of food costs (price per ounce) or figuring out how much one egg costs out of the dozen (price per 1 egg, instead of price per 12 eggs). The denominator of a unit rate is always 1. Unit rates are used to compare different situations to solve problems. For example, to make sure you get the best deal when deciding which kind of soda to buy, you can find the unit rate of each. If soda #1 costs $1.50 for a 1-liter bottle, and soda #2 costs $2.75 for a 2-liter bottle, it would be a better deal to buy soda #2, because its unit rate is only $1.375 per 1-liter, which is cheaper than soda #1. Unit rates can also help determine the length of time a given event will take. For example, if you can paint 2 rooms in 4.5 hours, you can determine how long it will take you to paint 5 rooms by solving for the unit rate per room and then multiplying that by 5.

SLOPE

On a graph with two points, (x_1, y_1) and (x_2, y_2), the **slope** is found with the formula $m = \frac{y_2-y_1}{x_2-x_1}$; where $x_1 \neq x_2$ and m stands for slope. If the value of the slope is **positive**, the line has an *upward direction* from left to right. If the value of the slope is **negative**, the line has a *downward direction* from left to right. Consider the following example:

A new book goes on sale in bookstores and online stores. In the first month, 5,000 copies of the book are sold. Over time, the book continues to grow in popularity. The data for the number of copies sold is in the table below.

# of Months on Sale	1	2	3	4	5
# of Copies Sold (In Thousands)	5	10	15	20	25

So, the number of copies that are sold and the time that the book is on sale is a proportional relationship. In this example, an equation can be used to show the data: $y = 5x$, where x is the number of months that the book is on sale. Also, y is the number of copies sold. So, the slope of the corresponding line is $\frac{\text{rise}}{\text{run}} = \frac{5}{1} = 5$.

FINDING AN UNKNOWN IN EQUIVALENT EXPRESSIONS

It is often necessary to apply information given about a rate or proportion to a new scenario. For example, if you know that Jedha can run a marathon (26.2 miles) in 3 hours, how long would it take her to run 10 miles at the same pace? Start by setting up equivalent expressions:

$$\frac{26.2 \text{ mi}}{3 \text{ hr}} = \frac{10 \text{ mi}}{x \text{ hr}}$$

Now, cross multiply and solve for x:

$$26.2x = 30$$
$$x = \frac{30}{26.2} = \frac{15}{13.1}$$
$$x \approx 1.15 \text{ hrs } or \text{ 1 hr 9 min}$$

So, at this pace, Jedha could run 10 miles in about 1.15 hours or about 1 hour and 9 minutes.

Expressions

TERMS AND COEFFICIENTS

Mathematical expressions consist of a combination of one or more values arranged in terms that are added together. As such, an expression could be just a single number, including zero. A **variable term** is the product of a real number, also called a **coefficient**, and one or more variables, each of which may be raised to an exponent. Expressions may also include numbers without a variable, called **constants** or **constant terms**. The expression $6s^2$, for example, is a single term where the coefficient is the real number 6 and the variable term is s^2. Note that if a term is written as simply a variable to some exponent, like t^2, then the coefficient is 1, because $t^2 = 1t^2$.

LINEAR EXPRESSIONS

A **single variable linear expression** is the sum of a single variable term, where the variable has no exponent, and a constant, which may be zero. For instance, the expression $2w + 7$ has $2w$ as the variable term and 7 as the constant term. It is important to realize that terms are separated by addition or subtraction. Since an expression is a sum of terms, expressions such as $5x - 3$ can be written as $5x + (-3)$ to emphasize that the constant term is negative. A real-world example of a single variable linear expression is the perimeter of a square, four times the side length, often expressed: $4s$.

In general, a **linear expression** is the sum of any number of variable terms so long as none of the variables have an exponent. For example, $3m + 8n - \frac{1}{4}p + 5.5q - 1$ is a linear expression, but $3y^3$ is not. In the same way, the expression for the perimeter of a general triangle, the sum of the side lengths $(a + b + c)$ is considered to be linear, but the expression for the area of a square, the side length squared (s^2) is not.

Equations

LINEAR EQUATIONS

Equations that can be written as $ax + b = 0$, where $a \neq 0$, are referred to as **one variable linear equations**. A solution to such an equation is called a **root**. In the case where we have the equation $5x + 10 = 0$, if we solve for x we get a solution of $x = -2$. In other words, the root of the equation is –2. This is found by first subtracting 10 from both sides, which gives $5x = -10$. Next, simply divide both sides by the coefficient of the variable, in this case 5, to get $x = -2$. This can be checked by plugging –2 back into the original equation $(5)(-2) + 10 = -10 + 10 = 0$.

The **solution set** is the set of all solutions of an equation. In our example, the solution set would simply be –2. If there were more solutions (there usually are in multivariable equations) then they would also be included in the solution set. When an equation has no true solutions, it is referred to as an **empty set**. Equations with identical solution sets are **equivalent equations**. An **identity** is a term whose value or determinant is equal to 1.

Linear equations can be written many ways. Below is a list of some forms linear equations can take:

- **Standard Form**: $Ax + By = C$; the slope is $\frac{-A}{B}$ and the y-intercept is $\frac{C}{B}$
- **Slope Intercept Form**: $y = mx + b$, where m is the slope and b is the y-intercept
- **Point-Slope Form**: $y - y_1 = m(x - x_1)$, where m is the slope and (x_1, y_1) is a point on the line
- **Two-Point Form**: $\frac{y - y_1}{x - x_1} = \frac{y_2 - y_1}{x_2 - x_1}$, where (x_1, y_1) and (x_2, y_2) are two points on the given line
- **Intercept Form**: $\frac{x}{x_1} + \frac{y}{y_1} = 1$, where $(x_1, 0)$ is the point at which a line intersects the x-axis, and $(0, y_1)$ is the point at which the same line intersects the y-axis

> **Review Video: Slope-Intercept and Point-Slope Forms**
> Visit mometrix.com/academy and enter code: 113216
>
> **Review Video: Linear Equations Basics**
> Visit mometrix.com/academy and enter code: 793005

SOLVING ONE-VARIABLE LINEAR EQUATIONS

Multiply all terms by the lowest common denominator to eliminate any fractions. Look for addition or subtraction to undo so you can isolate the variable on one side of the equal sign. Divide both sides by the coefficient of the variable. When you have a value for the variable, substitute this value into the original equation to make sure you have a true equation. Consider the following example:

Kim's savings are represented by the table below. Represent her savings, using an equation.

X (Months)	Y (Total Savings)
2	$1,300
5	$2,050
9	$3,050
11	$3,550
16	$4,800

The table shows a function with a constant rate of change, or slope, of 250. Given the points on the table, the slopes can be calculated as $\frac{(2,050-1300)}{(5-2)}$, $\frac{(3,050-2,050)}{(9-5)}$, $\frac{(3,550-3,050)}{(11-9)}$, and $\frac{(4,800-3,550)}{(16-11)}$, each of which equals 250. Thus, the table shows a constant rate of change, indicating a linear function. The slope-intercept form of a linear equation is written as $y = mx + b$, where m represents the slope and b represents the y-intercept. Substituting the slope into this form gives $y = 250x + b$. Substituting corresponding x- and y-values from any point into this equation will give the y-intercept, or b. Using the point, $(2, 1,300)$, gives $1,300 = 250(2) + b$, which simplifies as $b = 800$. Thus, her savings may be represented by the equation, $y = 250x + 800$.

RULES FOR MANIPULATING EQUATIONS
LIKE TERMS

Like terms are terms in an equation that have the same variable, regardless of whether or not they also have the same coefficient. This includes terms that *lack* a variable; all constants (i.e., numbers without variables) are considered like terms. If the equation involves terms with a variable raised to different powers, the like terms are those that have the variable raised to the same power.

For example, consider the equation $x^2 + 3x + 2 = 2x^2 + x - 7 + 2x$. In this equation, 2 and –7 are like terms; they are both constants. $3x$, x, and $2x$ are like terms, they all include the variable x raised to the first power. x^2 and $2x^2$ are like terms, they both include the variable x, raised to the second power. $2x$ and $2x^2$ are not like terms; although they both involve the variable x, the variable is not raised to the same power in both terms. The fact that they have the same coefficient, 2, is not relevant.

> **Review Video: Rules for Manipulating Equations**
> Visit mometrix.com/academy and enter code: 838871

CARRYING OUT THE SAME OPERATION ON BOTH SIDES OF AN EQUATION

When solving an equation, the general procedure is to carry out a series of operations on both sides of an equation, choosing operations that will tend to simplify the equation when doing so. The reason why the same operation must be carried out on both sides of the equation is because that leaves the meaning of the equation unchanged, and yields a result that is equivalent to the original equation. This would not be the case if we carried out an operation on one side of an equation and not the other. Consider what an equation means: it is a statement that two values or expressions are equal. If we carry out the same operation on both sides of the equation—add 3 to both sides, for example—then the two sides of the equation are changed in the same way, and so remain equal. If we do that to only one side of the equation—add 3 to one side but not the other—then that wouldn't be true; if we change one side of the equation but not the other then the two sides are no longer equal.

ADVANTAGE OF COMBINING LIKE TERMS

Combining like terms refers to adding or subtracting like terms—terms with the same variable—and therefore reducing sets of like terms to a single term. The main advantage of doing this is that it simplifies the equation. Often, combining like terms can be done as the first step in solving an equation, though it can also be done later, such as after distributing terms in a product.

For example, consider the equation $2(x + 3) + 3(2 + x + 3) = -4$. The 2 and the 3 in the second set of parentheses are like terms, and we can combine them, yielding $2(x + 3) + 3(x + 5) = -4$.

Now we can carry out the multiplications implied by the parentheses, distributing the outer 2 and 3 accordingly: $2x + 6 + 3x + 15 = -4$. The $2x$ and the $3x$ are like terms, and we can add them together: $5x + 6 + 15 = -4$. Now, the constants 6, 15, and –4 are also like terms, and we can combine them as well: subtracting 6 and 15 from both sides of the equation, we get $5x = -4 - 6 - 15$, or $5x = -25$, which simplifies further to $x = -5$.

> **Review Video: Solving Equations by Combining Like Terms**
> Visit mometrix.com/academy and enter code: 668506

CANCELING TERMS ON OPPOSITE SIDES OF AN EQUATION

Two terms on opposite sides of an equation can be canceled if and only if they *exactly* match each other. They must have the same variable raised to the same power and the same coefficient. For example, in the equation $3x + 2x^2 + 6 = 2x^2 - 6$, $2x^2$ appears on both sides of the equation and can be canceled, leaving $3x + 6 = -6$. The 6 on each side of the equation *cannot* be canceled, because it is added on one side of the equation and subtracted on the other. While they cannot be canceled, however, the 6 and –6 are like terms and can be combined, yielding $3x = -12$, which simplifies further to $x = -4$.

It's also important to note that the terms to be canceled must be independent terms and cannot be part of a larger term. For example, consider the equation $2(x + 6) = 3(x + 4) + 1$. We cannot cancel the x's, because even though they match each other they are part of the larger terms $2(x + 6)$ and $3(x + 4)$. We must first distribute the 2 and 3, yielding $2x + 12 = 3x + 12 + 1$. Now we see that the terms with the x's do not match, but the 12s do, and can be canceled, leaving $2x = 3x + 1$, which simplifies to $x = -1$.

PROCESS FOR MANIPULATING EQUATIONS

ISOLATING VARIABLES

To **isolate a variable** means to manipulate the equation so that the variable appears by itself on one side of the equation, and does not appear at all on the other side. Generally, an equation or inequality is considered to be solved once the variable is isolated and the other side of the equation or inequality is simplified as much as possible. In the case of a two-variable equation or inequality, only one variable needs to be isolated; it will not usually be possible to simultaneously isolate both variables.

For a linear equation—an equation in which the variable only appears raised to the first power— isolating a variable can be done by first moving all the terms with the variable to one side of the equation and all other terms to the other side. (*Moving* a term really means adding the inverse of the term to both sides; when a term is *moved* to the other side of the equation its sign is flipped.) Then combine like terms on each side. Finally, divide both sides by the coefficient of the variable, if applicable. The steps need not necessarily be done in this order, but this order will always work.

> **Review Video: Solving One-Step Equations**
> Visit mometrix.com/academy and enter code: 777004

EQUATIONS WITH MORE THAN ONE SOLUTION

Some types of non-linear equations, such as equations involving squares of variables, may have more than one solution. For example, the equation $x^2 = 4$ has two solutions: 2 and –2. Equations with absolute values can also have multiple solutions: $|x| = 1$ has the solutions $x = 1$ and $x = -1$.

It is also possible for a linear equation to have more than one solution, but only if the equation is true regardless of the value of the variable. In this case, the equation is considered to have infinitely many solutions, because any possible value of the variable is a solution. We know a linear equation has infinitely many solutions if when we combine like terms the variables cancel, leaving a true statement. For example, consider the equation $2(3x + 5) = x + 5(x + 2)$. Distributing, we get $6x + 10 = x + 5x + 10$; combining like terms gives $6x + 10 = 6x + 10$, and the $6x$-terms cancel to leave $10 = 10$. This is clearly true, so the original equation is true for any value of x. We could also have canceled the 10s leaving $0 = 0$, but again this is clearly true—in general if both sides of the equation match exactly, it has infinitely many solutions.

EQUATIONS WITH NO SOLUTION

Some types of non-linear equations, such as equations involving squares of variables, may have no solution. For example, the equation $x^2 = -2$ has no solutions in the real numbers, because the square of any real number must be positive. Similarly, $|x| = -1$ has no solution, because the absolute value of a number is always positive.

It is also possible for an equation to have no solution even if does not involve any powers greater than one, absolute values, or other special functions. For example, the equation $2(x + 3) + x = 3x$ has no solution. We can see that if we try to solve it: first we distribute, leaving $2x + 6 + x = 3x$. But now if we try to combine all the terms with the variable, we find that they cancel: we have $3x$ on the left and $3x$ on the right, canceling to leave us with $6 = 0$. This is clearly false. In general, whenever the variable terms in an equation cancel leaving different constants on both sides, it means that the equation has no solution. (If we are left with the *same* constant on both sides, the equation has infinitely many solutions instead.)

FEATURES OF EQUATIONS THAT REQUIRE SPECIAL TREATMENT
LINEAR EQUATIONS

A linear equation is an equation in which variables only appear by themselves: not multiplied together, not with exponents other than one, and not inside absolute value signs or any other functions. For example, the equation $x + 1 - 3x = 5 - x$ is a linear equation; while x appears multiple times, it never appears with an exponent other than one, or inside any function. The two-variable equation $2x - 3y = 5 + 2x$ is also a linear equation. In contrast, the equation $x^2 - 5 = 3x$ is *not* a linear equation, because it involves the term x^2. $\sqrt{x} = 5$ is not a linear equation, because it involves a square root. $(x - 1)^2 = 4$ is not a linear equation because even though there's no exponent on the x directly, it appears as part of an expression that is squared. The two-variable equation $x + xy - y = 5$ is not a linear equation because it includes the term xy, where two variables are multiplied together.

Linear equations can always be solved (or shown to have no solution) by combining like terms and performing simple operations on both sides of the equation. Some non-linear equations can be solved by similar methods, but others may require more advanced methods of solution, if they can be solved analytically at all.

SOLVING EQUATIONS INVOLVING ROOTS

In an equation involving roots, the first step is to isolate the term with the root, if possible, and then raise both sides of the equation to the appropriate power to eliminate it. Consider an example equation, $2\sqrt{x + 1} - 1 = 3$. In this case, begin by adding 1 to both sides, yielding $2\sqrt{x + 1} = 4$, and then dividing both sides by 2, yielding $\sqrt{x + 1} = 2$. Now square both sides, yielding $x + 1 = 4$. Finally, subtracting 1 from both sides yields $x = 3$.

Squaring both sides of an equation may, however, yield a spurious solution—a solution to the squared equation that is *not* a solution of the original equation. It's therefore necessary to plug the solution back into the original equation to make sure it works. In this case, it does: $2\sqrt{3+1} - 1 = 2\sqrt{4} - 1 = 2(2) - 1 = 4 - 1 = 3$.

The same procedure applies for other roots as well. For example, given the equation $3 + \sqrt[3]{2x} = 5$, we can first subtract 3 from both sides, yielding $\sqrt[3]{2x} = 2$ and isolating the root. Raising both sides to the third power yields $2x = 2^3$; i.e., $2x = 8$. We can now divide both sides by 2 to get $x = 4$.

Review Video: <u>Solving Equations Involving Roots</u>
Visit mometrix.com/academy and enter code: 297670

SOLVING EQUATIONS WITH EXPONENTS

To solve an equation involving an exponent, the first step is to isolate the variable with the exponent. We can then take the appropriate root of both sides to eliminate the exponent. For instance, for the equation $2x^3 + 17 = 5x^3 - 7$, we can subtract $5x^3$ from both sides to get $-3x^3 + 17 = -7$, and then subtract 17 from both sides to get $-3x^3 = -24$. Finally, we can divide both sides by –3 to get $x^3 = 8$. Finally, we can take the cube root of both sides to get $x = \sqrt[3]{8} = 2$.

One important but often overlooked point is that equations with an exponent greater than 1 may have more than one answer. The solution to $x^2 = 9$ isn't simply $x = 3$; it's $x = \pm 3$ (that is, $x = 3$ or $x = -3$). For a slightly more complicated example, consider the equation $(x - 1)^2 - 1 = 3$. Adding 1 to both sides yields $(x - 1)^2 = 4$; taking the square root of both sides yields $x - 1 = 2$. We can then add 1 to both sides to get $x = 3$. However, there's a second solution. We also have the possibility that $x - 1 = -2$, in which case $x = -1$. Both $x = 3$ and $x = -1$ are valid solutions, as can be verified by substituting them both into the original equation.

Review Video: <u>Solving Equations with Exponents</u>
Visit mometrix.com/academy and enter code: 514557

SOLVING EQUATIONS WITH ABSOLUTE VALUES

When solving an equation with an absolute value, the first step is to isolate the absolute value term. We then consider two possibilities: when the expression inside the absolute value is positive or when it is negative. In the former case, the expression in the absolute value equals the expression on the other side of the equation; in the latter, it equals the additive inverse of that expression—the expression times negative one. We consider each case separately and finally check for spurious solutions.

For instance, consider solving $|2x - 1| + x = 5$ for x. We can first isolate the absolute value by moving the x to the other side: $|2x - 1| = -x + 5$. Now, we have two possibilities. First, that $2x - 1$ is positive, and hence $2x - 1 = -x + 5$. Rearranging and combining like terms yields $3x = 6$, and hence $x = 2$. The other possibility is that $2x - 1$ is negative, and hence $2x - 1 = -(-x + 5) = x - 5$. In this case, rearranging and combining like terms yields $x = -4$. Substituting $x = 2$ and $x = -4$ back into the original equation, we see that they are both valid solutions.

Note that the absolute value of a sum or difference applies to the sum or difference as a whole, not to the individual terms; in general, $|2x - 1|$ is not equal to $|2x + 1|$ or to $|2x| - 1$.

SPURIOUS SOLUTIONS

A **spurious solution** may arise when we square both sides of an equation as a step in solving it or under certain other operations on the equation. It is a solution to the squared or otherwise modified equation that is *not* a solution of the original equation. To identify a spurious solution, it's useful when you solve an equation involving roots or absolute values to plug the solution back into the original equation to make sure it's valid.

CHOOSING WHICH VARIABLE TO ISOLATE IN TWO-VARIABLE EQUATIONS

Similar to methods for a one-variable equation, solving a two-variable equation involves isolating a variable: manipulating the equation so that a variable appears by itself on one side of the equation, and not at all on the other side. However, in a two-variable equation, you will usually only be able to isolate one of the variables; the other variable may appear on the other side along with constant terms, or with exponents or other functions.

Often one variable will be much more easily isolated than the other, and therefore that's the variable you should choose. If one variable appears with various exponents, and the other is only raised to the first power, the latter variable is the one to isolate: given the equation $a^2 + 2b = a^3 + b + 3$, the b only appears to the first power, whereas a appears squared and cubed, so b is the variable that can be solved for: combining like terms and isolating the b on the left side of the equation, we get $b = a^3 - a^2 + 3$. If both variables are equally easy to isolate, then it's best to isolate the independent variable, if one is defined; if the two variables are x and y, the convention is that y is the independent variable.

37

Inequalities

WORKING WITH INEQUALITIES

Commonly in algebra and other upper-level fields of math you find yourself working with mathematical expressions that do not equal each other. The statement comparing such expressions with symbols such as < (less than) or > (greater than) is called an *inequality*. An example of an inequality is $7x > 5$. To solve for x, simply divide both sides by 7 and the solution is shown to be $x > \frac{5}{7}$. Graphs of the solution set of inequalities are represented on a number line. Open circles are used to show that an expression approaches a number but is never quite equal to that number.

> **Review Video: Solving Multi-Step Inequalities**
> Visit mometrix.com/academy and enter code: 347842
>
> **Review Video: Solving Inequalities Using All 4 Basic Operations**
> Visit mometrix.com/academy and enter code: 401111

Conditional inequalities are those with certain values for the variable that will make the condition true and other values for the variable where the condition will be false. **Absolute inequalities** can have any real number as the value for the variable to make the condition true, while there is no real number value for the variable that will make the condition false. Solving inequalities is done by following the same rules for solving equations with the exception that when multiplying or dividing by a negative number the direction of the inequality sign must be flipped or reversed. **Double inequalities** are situations where two inequality statements apply to the same variable expression. Example: $-c < ax + b < c$.

> **Review Video: Conditional and Absolute Inequalities**
> Visit mometrix.com/academy and enter code: 980164

DETERMINING SOLUTIONS TO INEQUALITIES

To determine whether a coordinate is a solution of an inequality, you can substitute the values of the coordinate into the inequality, simplify, and check whether the resulting statement holds true. For instance, to determine whether $(-2,4)$ is a solution of the inequality $y \geq -2x + 3$, substitute the values into the inequality, $4 \geq -2(-2) + 3$. Simplify the right side of the inequality and the result is $4 \geq 7$, which is a false statement. Therefore, the coordinate is not a solution of the inequality. You can also use this method to determine which part of the graph of an inequality is shaded. The graph of $y \geq -2x + 3$ includes the solid line $y = -2x + 3$ and, since it excludes the point $(-2,4)$ to the left of the line, it is shaded to the right of the line.

> **Review Video: Graphing Linear Inequalities**
> Visit mometrix.com/academy and enter code: 439421

FLIPPING INEQUALITY SIGNS

When given an inequality, we can always turn the entire inequality around, swapping the two sides of the inequality and changing the inequality sign. For instance, $x + 2 > 2x - 3$ is equivalent to $2x - 3 < x + 2$. Aside from that, normally the inequality does not change if we carry out the same operation on both sides of the inequality. There is, however, one principal exception: if we *multiply* or *divide* both sides of the inequality by a *negative number*, the inequality is flipped. For example, if we take the inequality $-2x < 6$ and divide both sides by –2, the inequality flips and we are left with

$x > -3$. This *only* applies to multiplication and division, and only with negative numbers. Multiplying or dividing both sides by a positive number, or adding or subtracting any number regardless of sign, does not flip the inequality.

COMPOUND INEQUALITIES

A **compound inequality** is an equality that consists of two inequalities combined with *and* or *or*. The two components of a proper compound inequality must be of opposite type: that is, one must be greater than (or greater than or equal to), the other less than (or less than or equal to). For instance, "$x + 1 < 2$ or $x + 1 > 3$" is a compound inequality, as is "$2x \geq 4$ and $2x \leq 6$." An *and* inequality can be written more compactly by having one inequality on each side of the common part: "$2x \geq 1$ and $2x \leq 6$," can also be written as $1 \leq 2x \leq 6$.

In order for the compound inequality to be meaningful, the two parts of an *and* inequality must overlap; otherwise, no numbers satisfy the inequality. On the other hand, if the two parts of an *or* inequality overlap, then *all* numbers satisfy the inequality and as such the inequality is usually not meaningful.

Solving a compound inequality requires solving each part separately. For example, given the compound inequality "$x + 1 < 2$ or $x + 1 > 3$," the first inequality, $x + 1 < 2$, reduces to $x < 1$, and the second part, $x + 1 > 3$, reduces to $x > 2$, so the whole compound inequality can be written as "$x < 1$ or $x > 2$." Similarly, $1 \leq 2x \leq 6$ can be solved by dividing each term by 2, yielding $\frac{1}{2} \leq x \leq 3$.

Review Video: Compound Inequalities
Visit mometrix.com/academy and enter code: 786318

SOLVING INEQUALITIES INVOLVING ABSOLUTE VALUES

To solve an inequality involving an absolute value, first isolate the term with the absolute value. Then proceed to treat the two cases separately as with an absolute value equation, but flipping the inequality in the case where the expression in the absolute value is negative (since that essentially involves multiplying both sides by –1.) The two cases are then combined into a compound inequality; if the absolute value is on the greater side of the inequality, then it is an *or* compound inequality, if on the lesser side, then it's an *and*.

Consider the inequality $2 + |x - 1| \geq 3$. We can isolate the absolute value term by subtracting 2 from both sides: $|x - 1| \geq 1$. Now, we're left with the two cases $x - 1 \geq 1$ or $x - 1 \leq -1$: note that in the latter, negative case, the inequality is flipped. $x - 1 \geq 1$ reduces to $x \geq 2$, and $x - 1 \leq -1$ reduces to $x \leq 0$. Since in the inequality $|x - 1| \geq 1$ the absolute value is on the greater side, the two cases combine into an *or* compound inequality, so the final, solved inequality is "$x \leq 0$ or $x \geq 2$."

Review Video: Solving Absolute Value Inequalities
Visit mometrix.com/academy and enter code: 997008

SOLVING INEQUALITIES INVOLVING SQUARE ROOTS

Solving an inequality with a square root involves two parts. First, we solve the inequality as if it were an equation, isolating the square root and then squaring both sides of the equation. Second, we restrict the solution to the set of values of x for which the value inside the square root sign is non-negative.

For example, in the inequality, $\sqrt{x-2} + 1 < 5$, we can isolate the square root by subtracting 1 from both sides, yielding $\sqrt{x-2} < 4$. Squaring both sides of the inequality yields $x - 2 < 16$, so $x < 18$. Since we can't take the square root of a negative number, we also require the part inside the square root to be non-negative. In this case, that means $x - 2 \geq 0$. Adding 2 to both sides of the inequality yields $x \geq 2$. Our final answer is a compound inequality combining the two simple inequalities: $x \geq 2$ and $x < 18$, or $2 \leq x < 18$.

Note that we only get a compound inequality if the two simple inequalities are in opposite directions; otherwise, we take the one that is more restrictive.

The same technique can be used for other even roots, such as fourth roots. It is *not*, however, used for cube roots or other odd roots—negative numbers *do* have cube roots, so the condition that the quantity inside the root sign cannot be negative does not apply.

> **Review Video: <u>Solving Inequalities Involving Square Roots</u>**
> Visit mometrix.com/academy and enter code: 800288

SPECIAL CIRCUMSTANCES

Sometimes an inequality involving an absolute value or an even exponent is true for all values of x, and we don't need to do any further work to solve it. This is true if the inequality, once the absolute value or exponent term is isolated, says that term is greater than a negative number (or greater than or equal to zero). Since an absolute value or a number raised to an even exponent is *always* non-negative, this inequality is always true.

GRAPHICAL SOLUTIONS TO EQUATIONS AND INEQUALITIES

When equations are shown graphically, they are usually shown on a **Cartesian coordinate plane**. The Cartesian coordinate plane consists of two number lines placed perpendicular to each other and intersecting at the zero point, also known as the origin. The horizontal number line is known as the x-axis, with positive values to the right of the origin, and negative values to the left of the origin. The vertical number line is known as the y-axis, with positive values above the origin, and negative values below the origin. Any point on the plane can be identified by an ordered pair in the form (x, y), called coordinates. The x-value of the coordinate is called the abscissa, and the y-value of the coordinate is called the ordinate. The two number lines divide the plane into **four quadrants**: I, II, III, and IV.

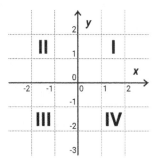

Note that in quadrant I $x > 0$ and $y > 0$, in quadrant II $x < 0$ and $y > 0$, in quadrant III $x < 0$ and $y < 0$, and in quadrant IV $x > 0$ and $y < 0$.

Recall that if the value of the slope of a line is positive, the line slopes upward from left to right. If the value of the slope is negative, the line slopes downward from left to right. If the y-coordinates are the same for two points on a line, the slope is 0 and the line is a **horizontal line**. If the x-

coordinates are the same for two points on a line, there is no slope and the line is a **vertical line**. Two or more lines that have equivalent slopes are **parallel lines**. **Perpendicular lines** have slopes that are negative reciprocals of each other, such as $\frac{a}{b}$ and $\frac{-b}{a}$.

> **Review Video: Cartesian Coordinate Plane and Graphing**
> Visit mometrix.com/academy and enter code: 115173

GRAPHING SIMPLE INEQUALITIES

To graph a simple inequality, we first mark on the number line the value that signifies the end point of the inequality. If the inequality is strict (involves a less than or greater than), we use a hollow circle; if it is not strict (less than or equal to or greater than or equal to), we use a solid circle. We then fill in the part of the number line that satisfies the inequality: to the left of the marked point for less than (or less than or equal to), to the right for greater than (or greater than or equal to).

For example, we would graph the inequality $x < 5$ by putting a hollow circle at 5 and filling in the part of the line to the left:

GRAPHING COMPOUND INEQUALITIES

To graph a compound inequality, we fill in both parts of the inequality for an *or* inequality, or the overlap between them for an *and* inequality. More specifically, we start by plotting the endpoints of each inequality on the number line. For an *or* inequality, we then fill in the appropriate side of the line for each inequality. Typically, the two component inequalities do not overlap, which means the shaded part is *outside* the two points. For an *and* inequality, we instead fill in the part of the line that meets both inequalities.

For the inequality "$x \leq -3$ or $x > 4$," we first put a solid circle at –3 and a hollow circle at 4. We then fill the parts of the line *outside* these circles:

GRAPHING INEQUALITIES INCLUDING ABSOLUTE VALUES

An inequality with an absolute value can be converted to a compound inequality. To graph the inequality, first convert it to a compound inequality, and then graph that normally. If the absolute value is on the greater side of the inequality, we end up with an *or* inequality; we plot the endpoints of the inequality on the number line and fill in the part of the line *outside* those points. If the absolute value is on the smaller side of the inequality, we end up with an *and* inequality; we plot the endpoints of the inequality on the number line and fill in the part of the line *between* those points.

For example, the inequality $|x + 1| \geq 4$ can be rewritten as $x \geq 3$ or $x \leq -5$. We place solid circles at the points 3 and –5 and fill in the part of the line *outside* them:

41

GRAPHING EQUATIONS IN TWO VARIABLES

One way of graphing an equation in two variables is to plot enough points to get an idea for its shape and then draw the appropriate curve through those points. A point can be plotted by substituting in a value for one variable and solving for the other. If the equation is linear, we only need two points and can then draw a straight line between them.

For example, consider the equation $y = 2x - 1$. This is a linear equation—both variables only appear raised to the first power—so we only need two points. When $x = 0$, $y = 2(0) - 1 = -1$. When $x = 2$, $y = 2(2) - 1 = 3$. We can therefore choose the points $(0, -1)$ and $(2, 3)$, and draw a line between them:

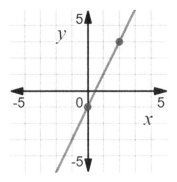

GRAPHING INEQUALITIES IN TWO VARIABLES

To graph an inequality in two variables, we first graph the border of the inequality. This means graphing the equation that we get if we replace the inequality sign with an equals sign. If the inequality is strict ($>$ or $<$), we graph the border with a dashed or dotted line; if it is not strict ($\geq$ or $\leq$), we use a solid line. We can then test any point not on the border to see if it satisfies the inequality. If it does, we shade in that side of the border; if not, we shade in the other side. As an example, consider $y > 2x + 2$. To graph this inequality, we first graph the border, $y = 2x + 2$. Since it is a strict inequality, we use a dashed line. Then, we choose a test point. This can be any point not on the border; in this case, we will choose the origin, $(0,0)$. (This makes the calculation easy and is generally a good choice unless the border passes through the origin.) Putting this into the original inequality, we get $0 > 2(0) + 2$, i.e., $0 > 2$. This is *not* true, so we shade in the side of the border that does *not* include the point $(0,0)$:

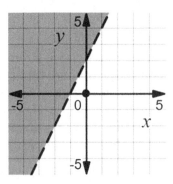

GRAPHING COMPOUND INEQUALITIES IN TWO VARIABLES

One way to graph a compound inequality in two variables is to first graph each of the component inequalities. For an *and* inequality, we then shade in only the parts where the two graphs overlap; for an *or* inequality, we shade in any region that pertains to either of the individual inequalities.

Consider the graph of "$y \geq x - 1$ and $y \leq -x$":

We first shade in the individual inequalities:

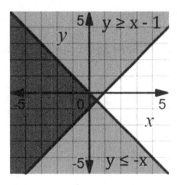

Now, since the compound inequality has an *and*, we only leave shaded the overlap—the part that pertains to *both* inequalities:

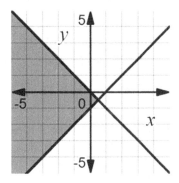

If instead the inequality had been "$y \geq x - 1$ or $y \leq -x$," our final graph would involve the *total* shaded area:

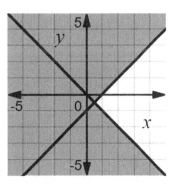

Review Video: Graphing Solutions to Inequalities
Visit mometrix.com/academy and enter code: 391281

Systems of Equations

SOLVING SYSTEMS OF EQUATIONS

A **system of equations** is a set of simultaneous equations that all use the same variables. A solution to a system of equations must be true for each equation in the system. **Consistent systems** are those with at least one solution. **Inconsistent systems** are systems of equations that have no solution.

Review Video: Solving Systems and Linear Equations
Visit mometrix.com/academy and enter code: 746745

SUBSTITUTION

To solve a system of linear equations by **substitution**, start with the easier equation and solve for one of the variables. Express this variable in terms of the other variable. Substitute this expression in the other equation and solve for the other variable. The solution should be expressed in the form (x, y). Substitute the values into both of the original equations to check your answer. Consider the following system of equations:

$$x + 6y = 15$$
$$3x - 12y = 18$$

Solving the first equation for x: $x = 15 - 6y$

Substitute this value in place of x in the second equation, and solve for y:

$$3(15 - 6y) - 12y = 18$$
$$45 - 18y - 12y = 18$$
$$30y = 27$$
$$y = \frac{27}{30} = \frac{9}{10} = 0.9$$

Plug this value for y back into the first equation to solve for x:

$$x = 15 - 6(0.9) = 15 - 5.4 = 9.6$$

Check both equations if you have time:

$$9.6 + 6(0.9) = 15 \qquad 3(9.6) - 12(0.9) = 18$$
$$9.6 + 5.4 = 15 \qquad 28.8 - 10.8 = 18$$
$$15 = 15 \qquad 18 = 18$$

Therefore, the solution is (9.6, 0.9).

Review Video: The Substitution Method
Visit mometrix.com/academy and enter code: 565151

ELIMINATION

To solve a system of equations using **elimination**, begin by rewriting both equations in standard form $Ax + By = C$. Check to see if the coefficients of one pair of like variables add to zero. If not, multiply one or both of the equations by a non-zero number to make one set of like variables add to zero. Add the two equations to solve for one of the variables. Substitute this value into one of the original equations to solve for the other variable. Check your work by substituting into the other equation. Now, let's look at solving the following system using the elimination method:

$$5x + 6y = 4$$
$$x + 2y = 4$$

If we multiply the second equation by -3, we can eliminate the y-terms:

$$5x + 6y = 4$$
$$-3x - 6y = -12$$

Add the equations together and solve for x:

$$2x = -8$$
$$x = \frac{-8}{2} = -4$$

Plug the value for x back in to either of the original equations and solve for y:

$$-4 + 2y = 4$$
$$y = \frac{4 + 4}{2} = 4$$

Check both equations if you have time:

$$5(-4) + 6(4) = 4 \qquad -4 + 2(4) = 4$$
$$-20 + 24 = 4 \qquad -4 + 8 = 4$$
$$4 = 4 \qquad 4 = 4$$

Therefore, the solution is $(-4,4)$.

> **Review Video: The Elimination Method**
> Visit mometrix.com/academy and enter code: 449121

GRAPHICALLY

To solve a system of linear equations **graphically**, plot both equations on the same graph. The solution of the equations is the point where both lines cross. If the lines do not cross (are parallel), then there is **no solution**.

For example, consider the following system of equations:

$$y = 2x + 7$$
$$y = -x + 1$$

Since these equations are given in slope-intercept form, they are easy to graph; the y-intercepts of the lines are $(0,7)$ and $(0,1)$. The respective slopes are 2 and -1, thus the graphs look like this:

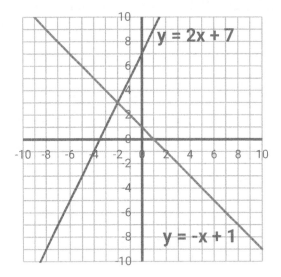

The two lines intersect at the point $(-2,3)$, thus this is the solution to the system of equations.

Solving a system graphically is generally only practical if both coordinates of the solution are integers; otherwise the intersection will lie between gridlines on the graph and the coordinates will be difficult or impossible to determine exactly. It also helps if, as in this example, the equations are in slope-intercept form or some other form that makes them easy to graph. Otherwise, another method of solution (by substitution or elimination) is likely to be more useful.

> **Review Video: Solving Systems by Graphing**
> Visit mometrix.com/academy and enter code: 634812

SOLVING SYSTEMS OF EQUATIONS USING THE TRACE FEATURE

Using the trace feature on a calculator requires that you rewrite each equation, isolating the y-variable on one side of the equal sign. Enter both equations in the graphing calculator and plot the graphs simultaneously. Use the trace cursor to find where the two lines cross. Use the zoom feature if necessary to obtain more accurate results. Always check your answer by substituting into the original equations. The trace method is likely to be less accurate than other methods due to the resolution of graphing calculators but is a useful tool to provide an approximate answer.

CALCULATIONS USING POINTS

Sometimes you need to perform calculations using only points on a graph as input data. Using points, you can determine what the **midpoint** and **distance** are. If you know the equation for a line, you can calculate the distance between the line and the point.

To find the **midpoint** of two points (x_1, y_1) and (x_2, y_2), average the x-coordinates to get the x-coordinate of the midpoint, and average the y-coordinates to get the y-coordinate of the midpoint. The formula is: $\left(\frac{x_1+x_2}{2}, \frac{y_1+y_2}{2}\right)$.

The **distance** between two points is the same as the length of the hypotenuse of a right triangle with the two given points as endpoints, and the two sides of the right triangle parallel to the x-axis and y-axis, respectively. The length of the segment parallel to the x-axis is the difference between the x-coordinates of the two points. The length of the segment parallel to the y-axis is the difference between the y-coordinates of the two points. Use the Pythagorean theorem $a^2 + b^2 = c^2$ or $c = \sqrt{a^2 + b^2}$ to find the distance. The formula is $d = \sqrt{(x_2 - x_1)^2 + (y_2 - y_1)^2}$.

When a line is in the format $Ax + By + C = 0$, where A, B, and C are coefficients, you can use a point (x_1, y_1) not on the line and apply the formula $d = \frac{|Ax_1 + By_1 + C|}{\sqrt{A^2 + B^2}}$ to find the distance between the line and the point (x_1, y_1).

> **Review Video: <u>Calculations Using Points on a Graph</u>**
> Visit mometrix.com/academy and enter code: 883228

Polynomial Algebra

MONOMIALS AND POLYNOMIALS

A **monomial** is a single constant, variable, or product of constants and variables, such as 7, x, $2x$, or x^3y. There will never be addition or subtraction symbols in a monomial. Like monomials have like variables, but they may have different coefficients. **Polynomials** are algebraic expressions that use addition and subtraction to combine two or more monomials. Two terms make a **binomial**, three terms make a **trinomial**, etc. The **degree of a monomial** is the sum of the exponents of the variables. The **degree of a polynomial** is the highest degree of any individual term.

> **Review Video: Polynomials**
> Visit mometrix.com/academy and enter code: 305005

SIMPLIFYING POLYNOMIALS

Simplifying polynomials requires combining like terms. The like terms in a polynomial expression are those that have the same variable raised to the same power. It is often helpful to connect the like terms with arrows or lines in order to separate them from the other monomials. Once you have determined the like terms, you can rearrange the polynomial by placing them together. Remember to include the sign that is in front of each term. Once the like terms are placed together, you can apply each operation and simplify. When adding and subtracting polynomials, only add and subtract the **coefficient**, or the number part; the variable and exponent stay the same.

> **Review Video: Adding and Subtracting Polynomials**
> Visit mometrix.com/academy and enter code: 124088

THE FOIL METHOD

In general, multiplying polynomials is done by multiplying each term in one polynomial by each term in the other and adding the results. In the specific case for multiplying binomials, there is a useful acronym, FOIL, that can help you make sure to cover each combination of terms. The **FOIL method** for $(Ax + By)(Cx + Dy)$ would be:

F	Multiply the *first* terms of each binomial	$(\overset{first}{\overbrace{Ax}} + By)(\overset{first}{\overbrace{Cx}} + Dy)$	ACx^2
O	Multiply the *outer* terms	$(\overset{outer}{\overbrace{Ax}} + By)(Cx + \overset{outer}{\overbrace{Dy}})$	$ADxy$
I	Multiply the *inner* terms	$(Ax + \overset{inner}{\overbrace{By}})(\overset{inner}{\overbrace{Cx}} + Dy)$	$BCxy$
L	Multiply the *last* terms of each binomial	$(Ax + \overset{last}{\overbrace{By}})(Cx + \overset{last}{\overbrace{Dy}})$	BDy^2

Then, add up the result of each and combine like terms: $ACx^2 + (AD + BC)xy + BDy^2$.

For example, using the FOIL method on binomials $(x + 2)$ and $(x - 3)$:

$$\text{First:} \quad (\boxed{x} + 2)(\boxed{x} + (-3)) \;\rightarrow\; (x)(x) = x^2$$
$$\text{Outer:} \quad (\boxed{x} + 2)\big(x + \boxed{(-3)}\big) \;\rightarrow\; (x)(-3) = -3x$$
$$\text{Inner:} \quad \big(x + \boxed{2}\big)(\boxed{x} + (-3)) \;\rightarrow\; (2)(x) = 2x$$
$$\text{Last:} \quad \big(x + \boxed{2}\big)\big(x + \boxed{(-3)}\big) \;\rightarrow\; (2)(-3) = -6$$

This results in: $(x^2) + (-3x) + (2x) + (-6)$

Combine like terms: $x^2 + (-3 + 2)x + (-6) = x^2 - x - 6$

Review Video: Multiplying Terms Using the FOIL Method
Visit mometrix.com/academy and enter code: 854792

DIVIDING POLYNOMIALS

Use long division to divide a polynomial by either a monomial or another polynomial of equal or lesser degree.

When **dividing by a monomial**, divide each term of the polynomial by the monomial.

When **dividing by a polynomial**, begin by arranging the terms of each polynomial in order of one variable. You may arrange in ascending or descending order, but be consistent with both polynomials. To get the first term of the quotient, divide the first term of the dividend by the first term of the divisor. Multiply the first term of the quotient by the entire divisor and subtract that product from the dividend. Repeat for the second and successive terms until you either get a remainder of zero or a remainder whose degree is less than the degree of the divisor. If the quotient has a remainder, write the answer as a mixed expression in the form:

$$\text{quotient} + \frac{\text{remainder}}{\text{divisor}}$$

For example, we can evaluate the following expression in the same way as long division:

$$\frac{x^3 - 3x^2 - 2x + 5}{x - 5}$$

$$
\begin{array}{r}
x^2 + 2x + 8 \\
x - 5 \overline{\smash{)}\ x^3 - 3x^2 - 2x + 5} \\
-(x^3 - 5x^2) \\
\hline
2x^2 - 2x \\
-(2x^2 - 10x) \\
\hline
8x + 5 \\
-(8x - 40) \\
\hline
45
\end{array}
$$

$$\frac{x^3 - 3x^2 - 2x + 5}{x - 5} = x^2 + 2x + 8 + \frac{45}{x - 5}$$

When **factoring** a polynomial, first check for a common monomial factor, that is, look to see if each coefficient has a common factor or if each term has an x in it. If the factor is a trinomial but not a perfect trinomial square, look for a factorable form, such as one of these:

$$x^2 + (a + b)x + ab = (x + a)(x + b)$$
$$(ac)x^2 + (ad + bc)x + bd = (ax + b)(cx + d)$$

For factors with four terms, look for groups to factor. Once you have found the factors, write the original polynomial as the product of all the factors. Make sure all of the polynomial factors are prime. Monomial factors may be *prime* or *composite*. Check your work by multiplying the factors to make sure you get the original polynomial.

Below are patterns of some special products to remember to help make factoring easier:

- Perfect trinomial squares: $x^2 + 2xy + y^2 = (x + y)^2$ or $x^2 - 2xy + y^2 = (x - y)^2$
- Difference between two squares: $x^2 - y^2 = (x + y)(x - y)$
- Sum of two cubes: $x^3 + y^3 = (x + y)(x^2 - xy + y^2)$
  - Note: the second factor is *not* the same as a perfect trinomial square, so do not try to factor it further.
- Difference between two cubes: $x^3 - y^3 = (x - y)(x^2 + xy + y^2)$
  - Again, the second factor is *not* the same as a perfect trinomial square.
- Perfect cubes: $x^3 + 3x^2y + 3xy^2 + y^3 = (x + y)^3$ and $x^3 - 3x^2y + 3xy^2 - y^3 = (x - y)^3$

RATIONAL EXPRESSIONS

Rational expressions are fractions with polynomials in both the numerator and the denominator; the value of the polynomial in the denominator cannot be equal to zero. Be sure to keep track of values that make the denominator of the original expression zero as the final result inherits the same restrictions. For example, a denominator of $x - 3$ indicates that the expression is not defined when $x = 3$ and, as such, regardless of any operations done to the expression, it remains undefined there.

To **add or subtract** rational expressions, first find the common denominator, then rewrite each fraction as an equivalent fraction with the common denominator. Finally, add or subtract the numerators to get the numerator of the answer, and keep the common denominator as the denominator of the answer.

When **multiplying** rational expressions, factor each polynomial and cancel like factors (a factor which appears in both the numerator and the denominator). Then, multiply all remaining factors in the numerator to get the numerator of the product, and multiply the remaining factors in the denominator to get the denominator of the product. Remember: cancel entire factors, not individual terms.

To **divide** rational expressions, take the reciprocal of the divisor (the rational expression you are dividing by) and multiply by the dividend.

> **Review Video: Rational Expressions**
> Visit mometrix.com/academy and enter code: 415183

SIMPLIFYING RATIONAL EXPRESSIONS

To simplify a rational expression, factor the numerator and denominator completely. Factors that are the same and appear in the numerator and denominator have a ratio of 1. For example, look at the following expression:

$$\frac{x - 1}{1 - x^2}$$

The denominator, $(1 - x^2)$, is a difference of squares. It can be factored as $(1 - x)(1 + x)$. The factor $1 - x$ and the numerator $x - 1$ are opposites and have a ratio of –1. Rewrite the numerator as $-1(1 - x)$. So, the rational expression can be simplified as follows:

$$\frac{x - 1}{1 - x^2} = \frac{-1(1 - x)}{(1 - x)(1 + x)} = \frac{-1}{1 + x}$$

Note that since the original expression is only defined for $x \neq \{-1, 1\}$, the simplified expression has the same restrictions.

> **Review Video: <u>Reducing Rational Expressions</u>**
> Visit mometrix.com/academy and enter code: 788868

Basic Functions

FUNCTION AND RELATION

When expressing functional relationships, the **variables** x and y are typically used. These values are often written as the **coordinates** (x, y). The x-value is the independent variable and the y-value is the dependent variable. A **relation** is a set of data in which there is not a unique y-value for each x-value in the dataset. This means that there can be two of the same x-values assigned to different y-values. A relation is simply a relationship between the x- and y-values in each coordinate but does not apply to the relationship between the values of x and y in the data set. A **function** is a relation where one quantity depends on the other. For example, the amount of money that you make depends on the number of hours that you work. In a function, each x-value in the data set has one unique y-value because the y-value depends on the x-value.

FUNCTIONS

A function has exactly one value of **output variable** (dependent variable) for each value of the **input variable** (independent variable). The set of all values for the input variable (here assumed to be x) is the domain of the function, and the set of all corresponding values of the output variable (here assumed to be y) is the range of the function. When looking at a graph of an equation, the easiest way to determine if the equation is a function or not is to conduct the vertical line test. If a vertical line drawn through any value of x crosses the graph in more than one place, the equation is not a function.

DETERMINING A FUNCTION

You can determine whether an equation is a **function** by substituting different values into the equation for x. You can display and organize these numbers in a data table. A **data table** contains the values for x and y, which you can also list as coordinates. In order for a function to exist, the table cannot contain any repeating x-values that correspond with different y-values. If each x-coordinate has a unique y-coordinate, the table contains a function. However, there can be repeating y-values that correspond with different x-values. An example of this is when the function contains an exponent. Example: if $x^2 = y$, $2^2 = 4$, and $(-2)^2 = 4$.

> **Review Video: Definition of a Function**
> Visit mometrix.com/academy and enter code: 784611

FINDING THE DOMAIN AND RANGE OF A FUNCTION

The **domain** of a function $f(x)$ is the set of all input values for which the function is defined. The **range** of a function $f(x)$ is the set of all possible output values of the function—that is, of every possible value of $f(x)$, for any value of x in the function's domain. For a function expressed in a table, every input-output pair is given explicitly. To find the domain, we just list all the x-values and to find the range, we just list all the values of $f(x)$. Consider the following example:

x	−1	4	2	1	0	3	8	6
$f(x)$	3	0	3	−1	−1	2	4	6

In this case, the domain would be $\{-1, 4, 2, 1, 0, 3, 8, 6\}$ or, putting them in ascending order, $\{-1, 0, 1, 2, 3, 4, 6, 8\}$. (Putting the values in ascending order isn't strictly necessary, but generally makes the set easier to read.) The range would be $\{3, 0, 3, -1, -1, 2, 4, 6\}$. Note that some of these values appear more than once. This is entirely permissible for a function; while each value of x must be matched to a unique value of $f(x)$, the converse is not true. We don't need to list each value more than once, so eliminating duplicates, the range is $\{3, 0, -1, 2, 4, 6\}$, or, putting them in ascending order, $\{-1, 0, 2, 3, 4, 6\}$.

Note that by definition of a function, no input value can be matched to more than one output value. It is good to double-check to make sure that the data given follows this and is therefore actually a function.

> **Review Video: <u>Domain and Range</u>**
> Visit mometrix.com/academy and enter code: 778133
>
> **Review Video: <u>Domain and Range of Quadratic Functions</u>**
> Visit mometrix.com/academy and enter code: 331768

WRITING A FUNCTION RULE USING A TABLE

If given a set of data, place the corresponding x- and y-values into a table and analyze the relationship between them. Consider what you can do to each x-value to obtain the corresponding y-value. Try adding or subtracting different numbers to and from x and then try multiplying or dividing different numbers to and from x. If none of these **operations** give you the y-value, try combining the operations. Once you find a rule that works for one pair, make sure to try it with each additional set of ordered pairs in the table. If the same operation or combination of operations satisfies each set of coordinates, then the table contains a function. The rule is then used to write the equation of the function in "$y =$" form.

DIRECT AND INVERSE VARIATIONS OF VARIABLES

Variables that vary directly are those that either both increase at the same rate or both decrease at the same rate. For example, in the functions $y = kx$ or $y = kx^n$, where k and n are positive, the value of y increases as the value of x increases and decreases as the value of x decreases.

Variables that vary inversely are those where one increases while the other decreases. For example, in the functions $y = \frac{k}{x}$ or $y = \frac{k}{x^n}$ where k and n are positive, the value of y increases as the value of x decreases and decreases as the value of x increases.

In both cases, k is the constant of variation.

PROPERTIES OF FUNCTIONS

There are many different ways to classify functions based on their structure or behavior. Important features of functions include:

- **End behavior**: the behavior of the function at extreme values ($f(x)$ as $x \to \pm\infty$)
- **y-intercept**: the value of the function at $f(0)$
- **Roots**: the values of x where the function equals zero ($f(x) = 0$)
- **Extrema**: minimum or maximum values of the function or where the function changes direction ($f(x) \geq k$ or $f(x) \leq k$)

CLASSIFICATION OF FUNCTIONS

An **invertible function** is defined as a function, $f(x)$, for which there is another function, $f^{-1}(x)$, such that $f^{-1}(f(x)) = x$. For example, if $f(x) = 3x - 2$ the inverse function, $f^{-1}(x)$, can be found:

$$x = 3(f^{-1}(x)) - 2$$
$$\frac{x + 2}{3} = f^{-1}(x)$$

$$f^{-1}(f(x)) = \frac{3x - 2 + 2}{3}$$
$$= \frac{3x}{3}$$
$$= x$$

Note that $f^{-1}(x)$ is a valid function over all values of x.

In a **one-to-one function**, each value of x has exactly one value for y on the coordinate plane (this is the definition of a function) and each value of y has exactly one value for x. While the vertical line test will determine if a graph is that of a function, the horizontal line test will determine if a function is a one-to-one function. If a horizontal line drawn at any value of y intersects the graph in more than one place, the graph is not that of a one-to-one function. Do not make the mistake of using the horizontal line test exclusively in determining if a graph is that of a one-to-one function. A one-to-one function must pass both the vertical line test and the horizontal line test. As such, one-to-one functions are invertible functions.

A **many-to-one function** is a function whereby the relation is a function, but the inverse of the function is not a function. In other words, each element in the domain is mapped to one and only one element in the range. However, one or more elements in the range may be mapped to the same element in the domain. A graph of a many-to-one function would pass the vertical line test, but not the horizontal line test. This is why many-to-one functions are not invertible.

A **monotone function** is a function whose graph either constantly increases or constantly decreases. Examples include the functions $f(x) = x$, $f(x) = -x$, or $f(x) = x^3$.

An **even function** has a graph that is symmetric with respect to the y-axis and satisfies the equation $f(x) = f(-x)$. Examples include the functions $f(x) = x^2$ and $f(x) = ax^n$, where a is any real number and n is a positive even integer.

An **odd function** has a graph that is symmetric with respect to the origin and satisfies the equation $f(x) = -f(-x)$. Examples include the functions $f(x) = x^3$ and $f(x) = ax^n$, where a is any real number and n is a positive odd integer.

> **Review Video: Even and Odd Functions**
> Visit mometrix.com/academy and enter code: 278985

Constant functions are given by the equation $f(x) = b$, where b is a real number. There is no independent variable present in the equation, so the function has a constant value for all x. The graph of a constant function is a horizontal line of slope 0 that is positioned b units from the x-axis. If b is positive, the line is above the x-axis; if b is negative, the line is below the x-axis.

Identity functions are identified by the equation $f(x) = x$, where every value of the function is equal to its corresponding value of x. The only zero is the point (0,0). The graph is a line with a slope of 1.

In **linear functions**, the value of the function changes in direct proportion to x. The rate of change, represented by the slope on its graph, is constant throughout. The standard form of a linear equation is $ax + cy = d$, where a, c, and d are real numbers. As a function, this equation is commonly in the form $y = mx + b$ or $f(x) = mx + b$ where $m = -\frac{a}{c}$ and $b = \frac{d}{c}$. This is known as the slope-intercept form, because the coefficients give the slope of the graphed function (m) and its y-intercept (b). Solve the equation $mx + b = 0$ for x to get $x = -\frac{b}{m}$, which is the only zero of the function. The domain and range are both the set of all real numbers.

> **Review Video: Linear Functions**
> Visit mometrix.com/academy and enter code: 699478

Algebraic functions are those that exclusively use polynomials and roots. These would include polynomial functions, rational functions, square root functions, and all combinations of these functions, such as polynomials as the radicand. These combinations may be joined by addition, subtraction, multiplication, or division, but may not include variables as exponents.

ABSOLUTE VALUE FUNCTIONS

An **absolute value function** is in the format $f(x) = |ax + b|$. Like other functions, the domain is the set of all real numbers. However, because absolute value indicates positive numbers, the range is limited to positive real numbers. To find the zero of an absolute value function, set the portion inside the absolute value sign equal to zero and solve for x. An absolute value function is also known as a piecewise function because it must be solved in pieces—one for if the value inside the absolute value sign is positive, and one for if the value is negative. The function can be expressed as

$$f(x) = \begin{cases} ax + b & \text{if } ax + b \geq 0 \\ -(ax + b) & \text{if } ax + b < 0 \end{cases}$$

This will allow for an accurate statement of the range. The graph of an example absolute value function, $f(x) = |2x - 1|$, is below:

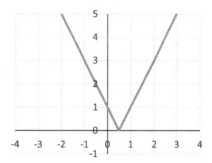

PIECEWISE FUNCTIONS

A **piecewise function** is a function that has different definitions on two or more different intervals. The following, for instance, is one example of a piecewise-defined function:

$$f(x) = \begin{cases} x^2, & x < 0 \\ x, & 0 \leq x \leq 2 \\ (x - 2)^2, & x > 2 \end{cases}$$

To graph this function, you would simply graph each part separately in the appropriate domain. The final graph would look like this:

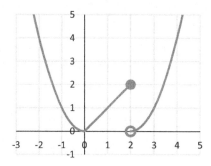

Note the filled and hollow dots at the discontinuity at $x = 2$. This is important to show which side of the graph that point corresponds to. Because $f(x) = x$ on the closed interval $0 \leq x \leq 2$, $f(2) = 2$. The point $(2, 2)$ is therefore marked with a filled circle, and the point $(2,0)$, which is the endpoint of the rightmost $(x - 2)^2$ part of the graph but *not actually part of the function*, is marked with a hollow dot to indicate this.

> **Review Video: Piecewise Functions**
> Visit mometrix.com/academy and enter code: 707921

QUADRATIC FUNCTIONS

A **quadratic function** is a function in the form $y = ax^2 + bx + c$, where a does not equal 0. While a linear function forms a line, a quadratic function forms a **parabola**, which is a u-shaped figure that either opens upward or downward. A parabola that opens upward is said to be a **positive quadratic function,** and a parabola that opens downward is said to be a **negative quadratic function**. The shape of a parabola can differ, depending on the values of a, b, and c. All parabolas contain a **vertex**, which is the highest possible point, the **maximum**, or the lowest possible point, the **minimum**. This is the point where the graph begins moving in the opposite direction. A quadratic function can have zero, one, or two solutions, and therefore zero, one, or two x-intercepts. Recall that the x-intercepts are referred to as the zeros, or roots, of a function. A quadratic function will have only one y-intercept. Understanding the basic components of a quadratic function can give you an idea of the shape of its graph.

Example graph of a positive quadratic function, $x^2 + 2x - 3$:

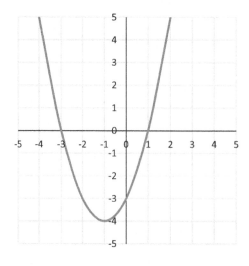

56

POLYNOMIAL FUNCTIONS

A **polynomial function** is a function with multiple terms and multiple powers of x, such as:

$$f(x) = a_n x^n + a_{n-1} x^{n-1} + a_{n-2} x^{n-2} + \cdots + a_1 x + a_0$$

where n is a non-negative integer that is the highest exponent in the polynomial and $a_n \neq 0$. The domain of a polynomial function is the set of all real numbers. If the greatest exponent in the polynomial is even, the polynomial is said to be of even degree and the range is the set of real numbers that satisfy the function. If the greatest exponent in the polynomial is odd, the polynomial is said to be odd and the range, like the domain, is the set of all real numbers.

RATIONAL FUNCTIONS

A **rational function** is a function that can be constructed as a ratio of two polynomial expressions: $f(x) = \frac{p(x)}{q(x)}$, where $p(x)$ and $q(x)$ are both polynomial expressions and $q(x) \neq 0$. The domain is the set of all real numbers, except any values for which $q(x) = 0$. The range is the set of real numbers that satisfies the function when the domain is applied. When you graph a rational function, you will have vertical asymptotes wherever $q(x) = 0$. If the polynomial in the numerator is of lesser degree than the polynomial in the denominator, the x-axis will also be a horizontal asymptote. If the numerator and denominator have equal degrees, there will be a horizontal asymptote not on the x-axis. If the degree of the numerator is exactly one greater than the degree of the denominator, the graph will have an oblique, or diagonal, asymptote. The asymptote will be along the line $y = \frac{p_n}{q_{n-1}} x + \frac{p_{n-1}}{q_{n-1}}$, where p_n and q_{n-1} are the coefficients of the highest degree terms in their respective polynomials.

SQUARE ROOT FUNCTIONS

A **square root function** is a function that contains a radical and is in the format $f(x) = \sqrt{ax + b}$. The domain is the set of all real numbers that yields a positive radicand or a radicand equal to zero. Because square root values are assumed to be positive unless otherwise identified, the range is all real numbers from zero to infinity. To find the zero of a square root function, set the radicand equal to zero and solve for x. The graph of a square root function is always to the right of the zero and always above the x-axis.

Example graph of a square root function, $f(x) = \sqrt{2x + 1}$:

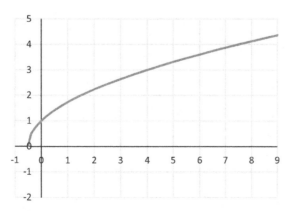

Lines and Planes

POINTS AND LINES

A **point** is a fixed location in space, has no size or dimensions, and is commonly represented by a dot. A **line** is a set of points that extends infinitely in two opposite directions. It has length, but no width or depth. A line can be defined by any two distinct points that it contains. A **line segment** is a portion of a line that has definite endpoints. A **ray** is a portion of a line that extends from a single point on that line in one direction along the line. It has a definite beginning, but no ending.

INTERACTIONS BETWEEN LINES

Intersecting lines are lines that have exactly one point in common. **Concurrent lines** are multiple lines that intersect at a single point. **Perpendicular lines** are lines that intersect at right angles. They are represented by the symbol ⊥. The shortest distance from a line to a point not on the line is a perpendicular segment from the point to the line. **Parallel lines** are lines in the same plane that have no points in common and never meet. It is possible for lines to be in different planes, have no points in common, and never meet, but they are not parallel because they are in different planes.

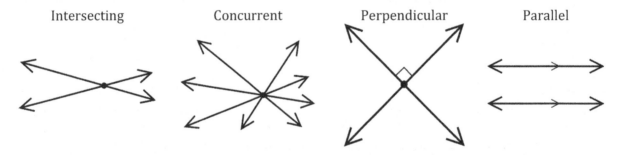

Review Video: **Parallel and Perpendicular Lines**
Visit mometrix.com/academy and enter code: 815923

A **transversal** is a line that intersects at least two other lines, which may or may not be parallel to one another. A transversal that intersects parallel lines is a common occurrence in geometry. A **bisector** is a line or line segment that divides another line segment into two equal lengths. A **perpendicular bisector** of a line segment is composed of points that are equidistant from the endpoints of the segment it is dividing.

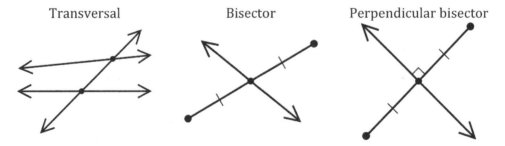

The **projection of a point on a line** is the point at which a perpendicular line drawn from the given point to the given line intersects the line. This is also the shortest distance from the given point to the line. The **projection of a segment on a line** is a segment whose endpoints are the points formed when perpendicular lines are drawn from the endpoints of the given segment to the given line. This is similar to the length a diagonal line appears to be when viewed from above.

Projection of a point on a line

Projection of a segment on a line

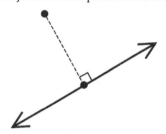
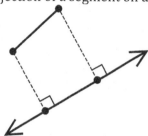

PLANES

A **plane** is a two-dimensional flat surface defined by three non-collinear points. A plane extends an infinite distance in all directions in those two dimensions. It contains an infinite number of points, parallel lines and segments, intersecting lines and segments, as well as parallel or intersecting rays. A plane will never contain a three-dimensional figure or skew lines, which are lines that don't intersect and are not parallel. Two given planes are either parallel or they intersect at a line. A plane may intersect a circular conic surface to form **conic sections**, such as a parabola, hyperbola, circle or ellipse.

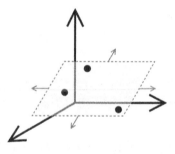

Review Video: Lines and Planes
Visit mometrix.com/academy and enter code: 554267

Angles

ANGLES AND VERTICES

An **angle** is formed when two lines or line segments meet at a common point. It may be a common starting point for a pair of segments or rays, or it may be the intersection of lines. Angles are represented by the symbol ∠.

The **vertex** is the point at which two segments or rays meet to form an angle. If the angle is formed by intersecting rays, lines, and/or line segments, the vertex is the point at which four angles are formed. The pairs of angles opposite one another are called vertical angles, and their measures are equal.

- An **acute** angle is an angle with a degree measure less than 90°.
- A **right** angle is an angle with a degree measure of exactly 90°.
- An **obtuse** angle is an angle with a degree measure greater than 90° but less than 180°.
- A **straight angle** is an angle with a degree measure of exactly 180°. This is also a semicircle.
- A **reflex angle** is an angle with a degree measure greater than 180° but less than 360°.

A **full angle** is an angle with a degree measure of exactly 360°. This is also a circle.

> **Review Video: <u>Angles</u>**
> Visit mometrix.com/academy and enter code: 264624

RELATIONSHIPS BETWEEN ANGLES

Two angles whose sum is exactly 90° are said to be **complementary**. The two angles may or may not be adjacent. In a right triangle, the two acute angles are complementary.

Two angles whose sum is exactly 180° are said to be **supplementary**. The two angles may or may not be adjacent. Two intersecting lines always form two pairs of supplementary angles. Adjacent supplementary angles will always form a straight line.

Two angles that have the same vertex and share a side are said to be **adjacent**. Vertical angles are not adjacent because they share a vertex but no common side.

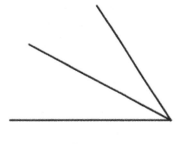

Adjacent
Share vertex and side

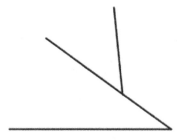

Not adjacent
Share part of a side, but not vertex

When two parallel lines are cut by a transversal, the angles that are between the two parallel lines are **interior angles**. In the diagram below, angles 3, 4, 5, and 6 are interior angles.

When two parallel lines are cut by a transversal, the angles that are outside the parallel lines are **exterior angles**. In the diagram below, angles 1, 2, 7, and 8 are exterior angles.

When two parallel lines are cut by a transversal, the angles that are in the same position relative to the transversal and a parallel line are **corresponding angles**. The diagram below has four pairs of corresponding angles: angles 1 and 5, angles 2 and 6, angles 3 and 7, and angles 4 and 8. Corresponding angles formed by parallel lines are congruent.

When two parallel lines are cut by a transversal, the two interior angles that are on opposite sides of the transversal are called **alternate interior angles**. In the diagram below, there are two pairs of alternate interior angles: angles 3 and 6, and angles 4 and 5. Alternate interior angles formed by parallel lines are congruent.

When two parallel lines are cut by a transversal, the two exterior angles that are on opposite sides of the transversal are called **alternate exterior angles**.

In the diagram below, there are two pairs of alternate exterior angles: angles 1 and 8, and angles 2 and 7. Alternate exterior angles formed by parallel lines are congruent.

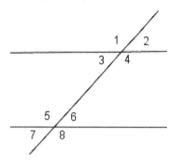

When two lines intersect, four angles are formed. The non-adjacent angles at this vertex are called vertical angles. Vertical angles are congruent. In the diagram, $\angle ABD \cong \angle CBE$ and $\angle ABC \cong \angle DBE$.

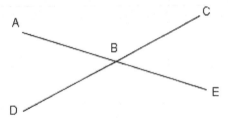

Two-Dimensional Shapes

POLYGONS

A **polygon** is a closed, two-dimensional figure with three or more straight line segments called **sides**. The point at which two sides of a polygon intersect is called the **vertex**. In a polygon, the number of sides is always equal to the number of vertices. A polygon with all sides congruent and all angles equal is called a **regular polygon**. Common polygons are:

Triangle = 3 sides
Quadrilateral = 4 sides
Pentagon = 5 sides
Hexagon = 6 sides
Heptagon = 7 sides
Octagon = 8 sides
Nonagon = 9 sides
Decagon = 10 sides
Dodecagon = 12 sides

More generally, an *n*-gon is a polygon that has *n* angles and *n* sides.

> **Review Video: Intro to Polygons**
> Visit mometrix.com/academy and enter code: 271869

The sum of the interior angles of an *n*-sided polygon is $(n - 2) \times 180°$. For example, in a triangle $n = 3$. So the sum of the interior angles is $(3 - 2) \times 180° = 180°$. In a quadrilateral, $n = 4$, and the sum of the angles is $(4 - 2) \times 180° = 360°$.

> **Review Video: Sum of Interior Angles**
> Visit mometrix.com/academy and enter code: 984991

APOTHEM AND RADIUS

A line segment from the center of a polygon that is perpendicular to a side of the polygon is called the **apothem**. A line segment from the center of a polygon to a vertex of the polygon is called a **radius**. In a regular polygon, the apothem can be used to find the area of the polygon using the formula $A = \frac{1}{2}ap$, where a is the apothem, and p is the perimeter.

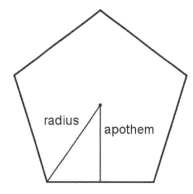

A **diagonal** is a line segment that joins two non-adjacent vertices of a polygon. The number of diagonals a polygon has can be found by using the formula:

$$\text{number of diagonals} = \frac{n(n-3)}{2}$$

Note that n is the number of sides in the polygon. This formula works for all polygons, not just regular polygons.

CONVEX AND CONCAVE POLYGONS

A **convex polygon** is a polygon whose diagonals all lie within the interior of the polygon. A **concave polygon** is a polygon with a least one diagonal that is outside the polygon. In the diagram below, quadrilateral $ABCD$ is concave because diagonal $\overline{AC}$ lies outside the polygon and quadrilateral $EFGH$ is convex because both diagonals lie inside the polygon.

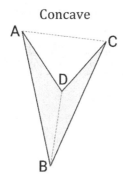
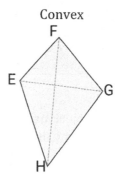

CONGRUENCE AND SIMILARITY

Congruent figures are geometric figures that have the same size and shape. All corresponding angles are equal, and all corresponding sides are equal. Congruence is indicated by the symbol $\cong$.

Congruent polygons

63

Similar figures are geometric figures that have the same shape, but do not necessarily have the same size. All corresponding angles are equal, and all corresponding sides are proportional, but they do not have to be equal. It is indicated by the symbol ~.

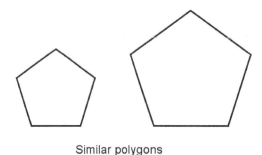

Similar polygons

Note that all congruent figures are also similar, but not all similar figures are congruent.

Review Video: What is a Congruent Shape?
Visit mometrix.com/academy and enter code: 492281

LINE OF SYMMETRY

A line that divides a figure or object into congruent parts is called a **line of symmetry**. An object may have no lines of symmetry, one line of symmetry, or multiple (i.e., more than one) lines of symmetry.

None   One   Multiple

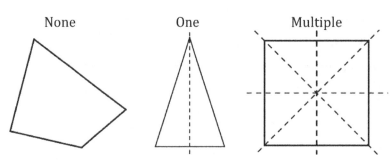

Review Video: Symmetry
Visit mometrix.com/academy and enter code: 528106

TRIANGLES

A triangle is a three-sided figure with the sum of its interior angles being 180°. The **perimeter of any triangle** is found by summing the three side lengths; $P = a + b + c$. For an equilateral triangle, this is the same as $P = 3a$, where a is any side length, since all three sides are the same length.

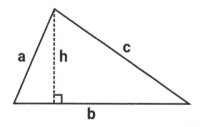

The **area of any triangle** can be found by taking half the product of one side length referred to as the base, often given the variable b and the perpendicular distance from that side to the opposite vertex called the altitude or height and given the variable h. In equation form that is $A = \frac{1}{2}bh$. Another formula that works for any triangle is $A = \sqrt{s(s-a)(s-b)(s-c)}$, where s is the semiperimeter: $\frac{a+b+c}{2}$, and a, b, and c are the lengths of the three sides. Special cases include isosceles triangles, $A = \frac{1}{2}b\sqrt{a^2 - \frac{b^2}{4}}$, where b is the unique side and a is the length of one of the two congruent sides, and equilateral triangles, $A = \frac{\sqrt{3}}{4}a^2$, where a is the length of a side.

PARTS OF A TRIANGLE

An **altitude** of a triangle is a line segment drawn from one vertex perpendicular to the opposite side. In the diagram that follows, $\overline{BE}$, $\overline{AD}$, and $\overline{CF}$ are altitudes. The length of an altitude is also called the height of the triangle. The three altitudes in a triangle are always concurrent. The point of concurrency of the altitudes of a triangle, O, is called the **orthocenter**. Note that in an obtuse triangle, the orthocenter will be outside the triangle, and in a right triangle, the orthocenter is the vertex of the right angle.

A **median** of a triangle is a line segment drawn from one vertex to the midpoint of the opposite side. In the diagram that follows, $\overline{BH}$, $\overline{AG}$, and $\overline{CI}$ are medians. This is not the same as the altitude, except the altitude to the base of an isosceles triangle and all three altitudes of an equilateral triangle. The point of concurrency of the medians of a triangle, T, is called the **centroid**. This is the same point as the orthocenter only in an equilateral triangle. Unlike the orthocenter, the centroid is always inside the triangle. The centroid can also be considered the exact center of the triangle. Any shape triangle can be perfectly balanced on a tip placed at the centroid. The centroid is also the point that is two-thirds the distance from the vertex to the opposite side.

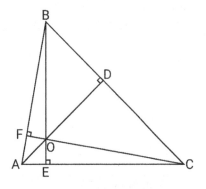 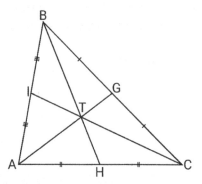

QUADRILATERALS

A **quadrilateral** is a closed two-dimensional geometric figure that has four straight sides. The sum of the interior angles of any quadrilateral is 360°.

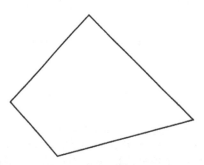

KITE

A **kite** is a quadrilateral with two pairs of adjacent sides that are congruent. A result of this is perpendicular diagonals. A kite can be concave or convex and has one line of symmetry.

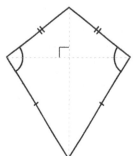 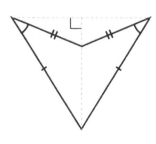

TRAPEZOID

Trapezoid: A trapezoid is defined as a quadrilateral that has at least one pair of parallel sides. There are no rules for the second pair of sides. So, there are no rules for the diagonals and no lines of symmetry for a trapezoid.

The **area of a trapezoid** is found by the formula $A = \frac{1}{2}h(b_1 + b_2)$, where h is the height (segment joining and perpendicular to the parallel bases), and b_1 and b_2 are the two parallel sides (bases). Do not use one of the other two sides as the height unless that side is also perpendicular to the parallel bases.

The **perimeter of a trapezoid** is found by the formula $P = a + b_1 + c + b_2$, where a, b_1, c, and b_2 are the four sides of the trapezoid.

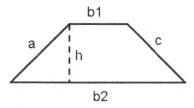

Review Video: <u>Area and Perimeter of a Trapezoid</u>
Visit mometrix.com/academy and enter code: 587523

Isosceles trapezoid: A trapezoid with equal base angles. This gives rise to other properties including: the two nonparallel sides have the same length, the two non-base angles are also equal, and there is one line of symmetry through the midpoints of the parallel sides.

PARALLELOGRAM

A **parallelogram** is a quadrilateral that has two pairs of opposite parallel sides. As such it is a special type of trapezoid. The sides that are parallel are also congruent. The opposite interior angles are always congruent, and the consecutive interior angles are supplementary. The diagonals of a parallelogram divide each other. Each diagonal divides the parallelogram into two congruent triangles. A parallelogram has no line of symmetry, but does have 180-degree rotational symmetry about the midpoint.

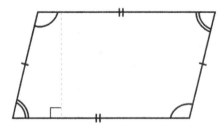

The **area of a parallelogram** is found by the formula $A = bh$, where b is the length of the base, and h is the height. Note that the base and height correspond to the length and width in a rectangle, so this formula would apply to rectangles as well. Do not confuse the height of a parallelogram with the length of the second side. The two are only the same measure in the case of a rectangle.

The **perimeter of a parallelogram** is found by the formula $P = 2a + 2b$ or $P = 2(a + b)$, where a and b are the lengths of the two sides.

> **Review Video: How to Find the Area and Perimeter of a Parallelogram**
> Visit mometrix.com/academy and enter code: 718313

RECTANGLE

A **rectangle** is a quadrilateral with four right angles. All rectangles are parallelograms and trapezoids, but not all parallelograms or trapezoids are rectangles. The diagonals of a rectangle are congruent. Rectangles have two lines of symmetry (through each pair of opposing midpoints) and 180-degree rotational symmetry about the midpoint.

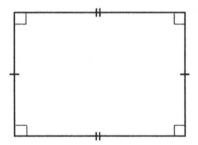

The **area of a rectangle** is found by the formula $A = lw$, where A is the area of the rectangle, l is the length (usually considered to be the longer side) and w is the width (usually considered to be the shorter side). The numbers for l and w are interchangeable.

The **perimeter of a rectangle** is found by the formula $P = 2l + 2w$ or $P = 2(l + w)$, where l is the length, and w is the width. It may be easier to add the length and width first and then double the result, as in the second formula.

RHOMBUS

A **rhombus** is a quadrilateral with four congruent sides. All rhombuses are parallelograms and kites; thus, they inherit all the properties of both types of quadrilaterals. The diagonals of a rhombus are perpendicular to each other. Rhombi have two lines of symmetry (along each of the diagonals) and 180° rotational symmetry. The **area of a rhombus** is half the product of the diagonals: $A = \frac{d_1 d_2}{2}$ and the perimeter of a rhombus is: $P = 2\sqrt{(d_1)^2 + (d_2)^2}$.

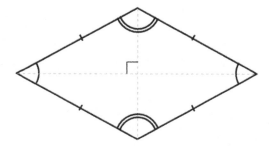

SQUARE

A **square** is a quadrilateral with four right angles and four congruent sides. Squares satisfy the criteria of all other types of quadrilaterals. The diagonals of a square are congruent and perpendicular to each other. Squares have four lines of symmetry (through each pair of opposing midpoints and along each of the diagonals) as well as 90° rotational symmetry about the midpoint.

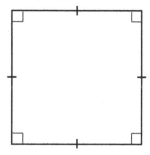

The **area of a square** is found by using the formula $A = s^2$, where s is the length of one side. The **perimeter of a square** is found by using the formula $P = 4s$, where s is the length of one side. Because all four sides are equal in a square, it is faster to multiply the length of one side by 4 than to add the same number four times. You could use the formulas for rectangles and get the same answer.

HIERARCHY OF QUADRILATERALS

The hierarchy of quadrilaterals is as follows:

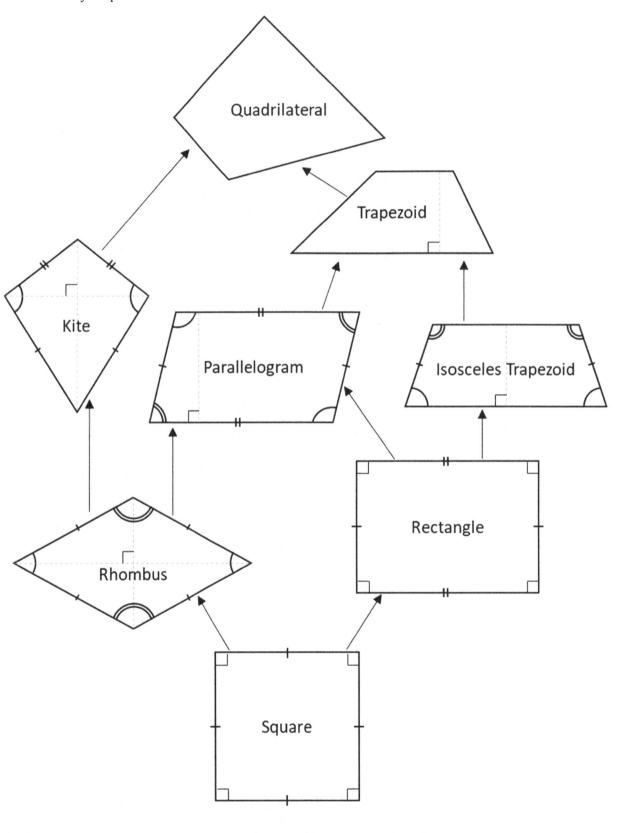

CIRCLES

The **center** of a circle is the single point from which every point on the circle is **equidistant**. The **radius** is a line segment that joins the center of the circle and any one point on the circle. All radii of a circle are equal. Circles that have the same center but not the same length of radii are **concentric**. The **diameter** is a line segment that passes through the center of the circle and has both endpoints on the circle. The length of the diameter is exactly twice the length of the radius. Point O in the diagram below is the center of the circle, segments $\overline{OX}$, $\overline{OY}$, and $\overline{OZ}$ are radii; and segment $\overline{XZ}$ is a diameter.

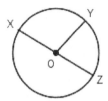

Review Video: Points of a Circle
Visit mometrix.com/academy and enter code: 420746

Review Video: The Diameter, Radius, and Circumference of Circles
Visit mometrix.com/academy and enter code: 448988

The **area of a circle** is found by the formula $A = \pi r^2$, where r is the length of the radius. If the diameter of the circle is given, remember to divide it in half to get the length of the radius before proceeding.

The **circumference** of a circle is found by the formula $C = 2\pi r$, where r is the radius. Again, remember to convert the diameter if you are given that measure rather than the radius.

Review Video: Area and Circumference of a Circle
Visit mometrix.com/academy and enter code: 243015

INSCRIBED AND CIRCUMSCRIBED FIGURES

These terms can both be used to describe a given arrangement of figures, depending on perspective. If each of the vertices of figure A lie on figure B, then it can be said that figure A is **inscribed** in figure B, but it can also be said that figure B is **circumscribed** about figure A. The following table and examples help to illustrate the concept. Note that the figures cannot both be circles, as they would be completely overlapping and neither would be inscribed or circumscribed.

Given	Description	Equivalent Description	Figures
Each of the sides of a pentagon is tangent to a circle	The circle is inscribed in the pentagon	The pentagon is circumscribed about the circle	
Each of the vertices of a pentagon lie on a circle	The pentagon is inscribed in the circle	The circle is circumscribed about the pentagon	

Three-Dimensional Shapes

SOLIDS

The **surface area of a solid object** is the area of all sides or exterior surfaces. For objects such as prisms and pyramids, a further distinction is made between base surface area (B) and lateral surface area (LA). For a prism, the total surface area (SA) is $SA = LA + 2B$. For a pyramid or cone, the total surface area is $SA = LA + B$.

The **surface area of a sphere** can be found by the formula $A = 4\pi r^2$, where r is the radius. The volume is given by the formula $V = \frac{4}{3}\pi r^3$, where r is the radius. Both quantities are generally given in terms of π.

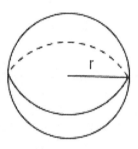

Review Video: Volume and Surface Area of a Sphere
Visit mometrix.com/academy and enter code: 786928

The **volume of any prism** is found by the formula $V = Bh$, where B is the area of the base, and h is the height (perpendicular distance between the bases). The surface area of any prism is the sum of the areas of both bases and all sides. It can be calculated as $SA = 2B + Ph$, where P is the perimeter of the base.

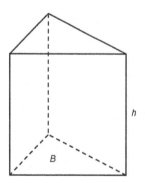

Review Video: Volume and Surface Area of a Prism
Visit mometrix.com/academy and enter code: 420158

For a **rectangular prism**, the volume can be found by the formula $V = lwh$, where V is the volume, l is the length, w is the width, and h is the height. The surface area can be calculated as $SA = 2lw + 2hl + 2wh$ or $SA = 2(lw + hl + wh)$.

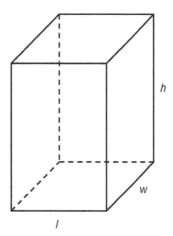

Review Video: <u>Volume and Surface Area of a Rectangular Prism</u>
Visit mometrix.com/academy and enter code: 282814

The **volume of a cube** can be found by the formula $V = s^3$, where s is the length of a side. The surface area of a cube is calculated as $SA = 6s^2$, where SA is the total surface area and s is the length of a side. These formulas are the same as the ones used for the volume and surface area of a rectangular prism, but simplified since all three quantities (length, width, and height) are the same.

Review Video: <u>Volume and Surface Area of a Cube</u>
Visit mometrix.com/academy and enter code: 664455

The **volume of a cylinder** can be calculated by the formula $V = \pi r^2 h$, where r is the radius, and h is the height. The surface area of a cylinder can be found by the formula $SA = 2\pi r^2 + 2\pi r h$. The

Formulas-
area of circle- $A = \pi r^2$
Circumference - $C = 2\pi r$
Surface area of sphere- $A = 4\pi r^2$
Volume of prism- $V = Bh$
Rectangular prism- $V = lwh$
Volume Cube- $V = S^3$
Volume Cylinder- $V = \pi r^2 h$

first term is the base area multiplied by two, and the second term is the perimeter of the base multiplied by the height.

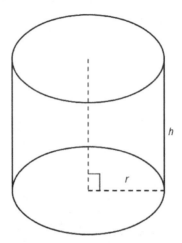

The **volume of a pyramid** is found by the formula $V = \frac{1}{3}Bh$, where B is the area of the base, and h is the height (perpendicular distance from the vertex to the base). Notice this formula is the same as $\frac{1}{3}$ times the volume of a prism. Like a prism, the base of a pyramid can be any shape.

Finding the **surface area of a pyramid** is not as simple as the other shapes we've looked at thus far. If the pyramid is a right pyramid, meaning the base is a regular polygon and the vertex is directly over the center of that polygon, the surface area can be calculated as $SA = B + \frac{1}{2}Ph_s$, where P is the perimeter of the base, and h_s is the slant height (distance from the vertex to the midpoint of one side of the base). If the pyramid is irregular, the area of each triangle side must be calculated individually and then summed, along with the base.

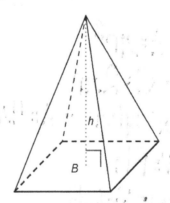

The **volume of a cone** is found by the formula $V = \frac{1}{3}\pi r^2 h$, where r is the radius, and h is the height. Notice this is the same as $\frac{1}{3}$ times the volume of a cylinder. The surface area can be calculated as $SA = \pi r^2 + \pi rs$, where s is the slant height. The slant height can be calculated using the Pythagorean theorem to be $\sqrt{r^2 + h^2}$, so the surface area formula can also be written as $SA = \pi r^2 + \pi r\sqrt{r^2 + h^2}$.

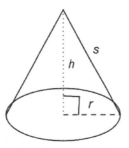

Review Video: <u>Volume and Surface Area of a Right Circular Cone</u>
Visit mometrix.com/academy and enter code: 573574

Probability

PROBABILITY

Probability is the likelihood of a certain outcome occurring for a given event. An **event** is any situation that produces a result. It could be something as simple as flipping a coin or as complex as launching a rocket. Determining the probability of an outcome for an event can be equally simple or complex. As such, there are specific terms used in the study of probability that need to be understood:

- **Compound event**—an event that involves two or more independent events (rolling a pair of dice and taking the sum)
- **Desired outcome** (or success)—an outcome that meets a particular set of criteria (a roll of 1 or 2 if we are looking for numbers less than 3)
- **Independent events**—two or more events whose outcomes do not affect one another (two coins tossed at the same time)
- **Dependent events**—two or more events whose outcomes affect one another (two cards drawn consecutively from the same deck)
- **Certain outcome**—probability of outcome is 100% or 1
- **Impossible outcome**—probability of outcome is 0% or 0
- **Mutually exclusive outcomes**—two or more outcomes whose criteria cannot all be satisfied in a single event (a coin coming up heads and tails on the same toss)
- **Random variable**—refers to all possible outcomes of a single event which may be discrete or continuous.

> **Review Video: Intro to Probability**
> Visit mometrix.com/academy and enter code: 212374

THEORETICAL AND EXPERIMENTAL PROBABILITY

Theoretical probability can usually be determined without actually performing the event. The likelihood of an outcome occurring, or the probability of an outcome occurring, is given by the formula:

$$P(A) = \frac{\text{Number of acceptable outcomes}}{\text{Number of possible outcomes}}$$

Note that $P(A)$ is the probability of an outcome A occurring, and each outcome is just as likely to occur as any other outcome. If each outcome has the same probability of occurring as every other possible outcome, the outcomes are said to be equally likely to occur. The total number of acceptable outcomes must be less than or equal to the total number of possible outcomes. If the two are equal, then the outcome is certain to occur and the probability is 1. If the number of acceptable outcomes is zero, then the outcome is impossible and the probability is 0. For example, if there are 20 marbles in a bag and 5 are red, then the theoretical probability of randomly selecting a red marble is 5 out of 20, $\left(\frac{5}{20} = \frac{1}{4}, 0.25, \text{ or } 25\%\right)$.

If the theoretical probability is unknown or too complicated to calculate, it can be estimated by an experimental probability. **Experimental probability**, also called empirical probability, is an estimate of the likelihood of a certain outcome based on repeated experiments or collected data. In other words, while theoretical probability is based on what *should* happen, experimental probability is based on what *has* happened. Experimental probability is calculated in the same way as theoretical probability, except that actual outcomes are used instead of possible outcomes. The more experiments performed or datapoints gathered, the better the estimate should be.

Theoretical and experimental probability do not always line up with one another. Theoretical probability says that out of 20 coin-tosses, 10 should be heads. However, if we were actually to toss 20 coins, we might record just 5 heads. This doesn't mean that our theoretical probability is incorrect; it just means that this particular experiment had results that were different from what was predicted. A practical application of empirical probability is the insurance industry. There are no set functions that define lifespan, health, or safety. Insurance companies look at factors from hundreds of thousands of individuals to find patterns that they then use to set the formulas for insurance premiums.

> **Review Video: Empirical Probability**
> Visit mometrix.com/academy and enter code: 513468

OBJECTIVE AND SUBJECTIVE PROBABILITY

Objective probability is based on mathematical formulas and documented evidence. Examples of objective probability include raffles or lottery drawings where there is a pre-determined number of possible outcomes and a predetermined number of outcomes that correspond to an event. Other cases of objective probability include probabilities of rolling dice, flipping coins, or drawing cards. Most gambling games are based on objective probability.

In contrast, **subjective probability** is based on personal or professional feelings and judgments. Often, there is a lot of guesswork following extensive research. Areas where subjective probability is applicable include sales trends and business expenses. Attractions set admission prices based on subjective probabilities of attendance based on varying admission rates in an effort to maximize their profit.

SAMPLE SPACE

The total set of all possible results of a test or experiment is called a **sample space**, or sometimes a universal sample space. The sample space, represented by one of the variables S, Ω, or U (for universal sample space) has individual elements called outcomes. Other terms for outcome that may be used interchangeably include elementary outcome, simple event, or sample point. The number of outcomes in a given sample space could be infinite or finite, and some tests may yield multiple unique sample sets. For example, tests conducted by drawing playing cards from a standard deck would have one sample space of the card values, another sample space of the card suits, and a third sample space of suit-denomination combinations. For most tests, the sample spaces considered will be finite.

An **event**, represented by the variable E, is a portion of a sample space. It may be one outcome or a group of outcomes from the same sample space. If an event occurs, then the test or experiment will generate an outcome that satisfies the requirement of that event. For example, given a standard deck of 52 playing cards as the sample space, and defining the event as the collection of face cards, then the event will occur if the card drawn is a J, Q, or K. If any other card is drawn, the event is said to have not occurred.

For every sample space, each possible outcome has a specific likelihood, or probability, that it will occur. The probability measure, also called the **distribution**, is a function that assigns a real number probability, from zero to one, to each outcome. For a probability measure to be accurate, every outcome must have a real number probability measure that is greater than or equal to zero and less than or equal to one. Also, the probability measure of the sample space must equal one, and the probability measure of the union of multiple outcomes must equal the sum of the individual probability measures.

Probabilities of events are expressed as real numbers from zero to one. They give a numerical value to the chance that a particular event will occur. The probability of an event occurring is the sum of the probabilities of the individual elements of that event. For example, in a standard deck of 52 playing cards as the sample space and the collection of face cards as the event, the probability of drawing a specific face card is $\frac{1}{52} = 0.019$, but the probability of drawing any one of the twelve face cards is $12(0.019) = 0.228$. Note that rounding of numbers can generate different results. If you multiplied 12 by the fraction $\frac{1}{52}$ before converting to a decimal, you would get the answer $\frac{12}{52} = 0.231$.

TREE DIAGRAM

For a simple sample space, possible outcomes may be determined by using a **tree diagram** or an organized chart. In either case, you can easily draw or list out the possible outcomes. For example, to determine all the possible ways three objects can be ordered, you can draw a tree diagram:

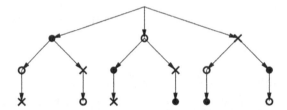

You can also make a chart to list all the possibilities:

First object	Second object	Third object
●	X	O
●	O	X
O	●	X
O	X	●
X	●	O
X	O	●

Either way, you can easily see there are six possible ways the three objects can be ordered.

If two events have no outcomes in common, they are said to be **mutually exclusive**. For example, in a standard deck of 52 playing cards, the event of all card suits is mutually exclusive to the event of all card values. If two events have no bearing on each other so that one event occurring has no influence on the probability of another event occurring, the two events are said to be independent. For example, rolling a standard six-sided die multiple times does not change that probability that a particular number will be rolled from one roll to the next. If the outcome of one event does affect the probability of the second event, the two events are said to be dependent. For example, if cards are drawn from a deck, the probability of drawing an ace after an ace has been drawn is different than the probability of drawing an ace if no ace (or no other card, for that matter) has been drawn.

In probability, the **odds in favor of an event** are the number of times the event will occur compared to the number of times the event will not occur. To calculate the odds in favor of an event, use the formula $\frac{P(A)}{1-P(A)}$, where $P(A)$ is the probability that the event will occur. Many times, odds in favor is given as a ratio in the form $\frac{a}{b}$ or $a:b$, where a is the probability of the event occurring and b is the complement of the event, the probability of the event not occurring. If the odds in favor are given as 2:5, that means that you can expect the event to occur two times for every 5 times that it does not occur. In other words, the probability that the event will occur is $\frac{2}{2+5} = \frac{2}{7}$.

In probability, the **odds against an event** are the number of times the event will not occur compared to the number of times the event will occur. To calculate the odds against an event, use the formula $\frac{1-P(A)}{P(A)}$, where $P(A)$ is the probability that the event will occur. Many times, odds against is given as a ratio in the form $\frac{b}{a}$ or $b:a$, where b is the probability the event will not occur (the complement of the event) and a is the probability the event will occur. If the odds against an event are given as 3:1, that means that you can expect the event to not occur 3 times for every one time it does occur. In other words, 3 out of every 4 trials will fail.

PERMUTATIONS AND COMBINATIONS

When trying to calculate the probability of an event using the $\frac{\text{desired outcomes}}{\text{total outcomes}}$ formula, you may frequently find that there are too many outcomes to individually count them. **Permutation** and **combination formulas** offer a shortcut to counting outcomes. A permutation is an arrangement of a specific number of a set of objects in a specific order. The number of **permutations** of r items given a set of n items can be calculated as $_nP_r = \frac{n!}{(n-r)!}$. Combinations are similar to permutations, except there are no restrictions regarding the order of the elements. While ABC is considered a different permutation than BCA, ABC and BCA are considered the same combination. The number of **combinations** of r items given a set of n items can be calculated as $_nC_r = \frac{n!}{r!(n-r)!}$ or $_nC_r = \frac{_nP_r}{r!}$.

Suppose you want to calculate how many different 5-card hands can be drawn from a deck of 52 cards. This is a combination since the order of the cards in a hand does not matter. There are 52 cards available, and 5 to be selected. Thus, the number of different hands is $_{52}C_5 = \frac{52!}{5! \times 47!} =$ 2,598,960.

> **Review Video: Probability - Permutation and Combination**
> Visit mometrix.com/academy and enter code: 907664

UNION AND INTERSECTION OF TWO SETS OF OUTCOMES

If A and B are each a set of elements or outcomes from an experiment, then the **union** (symbol ∪) of the two sets is the set of elements found in set A or set B. For example, if $A = \{2, 3, 4\}$ and $B = \{3, 4, 5\}$, $A \cup B = \{2, 3, 4, 5\}$. Note that the outcomes 3 and 4 appear only once in the union. For statistical events, the union is equivalent to "or"; $P(A \cup B)$ is the same thing as $P(A \text{ or } B)$. The **intersection** (symbol ∩) of two sets is the set of outcomes common to both sets. For the above sets

A and B, $A \cap B = \{3, 4\}$. For statistical events, the intersection is equivalent to "and"; $P(A \cap B)$ is the same thing as $P(A \text{ and } B)$. It is important to note that union and intersection operations commute. That is:

$$A \cup B = B \cup A \text{ and } A \cap B = B \cap A$$

COMPLEMENT OF AN EVENT

Sometimes it may be easier to calculate the possibility of something not happening, or the **complement of an event**. Represented by the symbol $\bar{A}$, the complement of A is the probability that event A does not happen. When you know the probability of event A occurring, you can use the formula $P(\bar{A}) = 1 - P(A)$, where $P(\bar{A})$ is the probability of event A not occurring, and $P(A)$ is the probability of event A occurring.

ADDITION RULE

The **addition rule** for probability is used for finding the probability of a compound event. Use the formula $P(A \text{ or } B) = P(A) + P(B) - P(A \text{ and } B)$, where $P(A \text{ and } B)$ is the probability of both events occurring to find the probability of a compound event. The probability of both events occurring at the same time must be subtracted to eliminate any overlap in the first two probabilities.

CONDITIONAL PROBABILITY

Given two events A and B, the **conditional probability** $P(A|B)$ is the probability that event A will occur, given that event B has occurred. The conditional probability cannot be calculated simply from $P(A)$ and $P(B)$; these probabilities alone do not give sufficient information to determine the conditional probability. It can, however, be determined if you are also given the probability of the intersection of events A and B, $P(A \cap B)$, the probability that events A and B both occur. Specifically, $P(A|B) = \frac{P(A \cap B)}{P(B)}$. For instance, suppose you have a jar containing two red marbles and two blue marbles, and you draw two marbles at random. Consider event A being the event that the first marble drawn is red, and event B being the event that the second marble drawn is blue. $P(A)$ is $\frac{1}{2}$, and $P(A \cap B)$ is $\frac{1}{3}$. (The latter may not be obvious, but may be determined by finding the product of $\frac{1}{2}$ and $\frac{2}{3}$). Therefore $P(A|B) = \frac{1/3}{1/2} = \frac{2}{3}$.

CONDITIONAL PROBABILITY IN EVERYDAY SITUATIONS

Conditional probability often arises in everyday situations in, for example, estimating the risk or benefit of certain activities. The conditional probability of having a heart attack given that you exercise daily may be smaller than the overall probability of having a heart attack. The conditional probability of having lung cancer given that you are a smoker is larger than the overall probability of having lung cancer. Note that changing the order of the conditional probability changes the meaning: the conditional probability of having lung cancer given that you are a smoker is a very different thing from the probability of being a smoker given that you have lung cancer. In an extreme case, suppose that a certain rare disease is caused only by eating a certain food, but even then, it is unlikely. Then the conditional probability of having that disease given that you eat the dangerous food is nonzero but low, but the conditional probability of having eaten that food given that you have the disease is 100%!

Review Video: Conditional Probability
Visit mometrix.com/academy and enter code: 397924

INDEPENDENCE

The conditional probability $P(A|B)$ is the probability that event A will occur given that event B occurs. If the two events are independent, we do not expect that whether or not event B occurs should have any effect on whether or not event A occurs. In other words, we expect $P(A|B) = P(A)$.

This can be proven using the usual equations for conditional probability and the joint probability of independent events. The conditional probability $P(A|B) = \frac{P(A \cap B)}{P(B)}$. If A and B are independent, then $P(A \cap B) = P(A)P(B)$. So $P(A|B) = \frac{P(A)P(B)}{P(B)} = P(A)$. By similar reasoning, if A and B are independent then $P(B|A) = P(B)$.

TWO-WAY FREQUENCY TABLES

If we have a two-way frequency table, it is generally a straightforward matter to read off the probabilities of any two events A and B, as well as the joint probability of both events occurring, $P(A \cap B)$. We can then find the conditional probability $P(A|B)$ by calculating $P(A|B) = \frac{P(A \cap B)}{P(B)}$. We could also check whether or not events are independent by verifying whether $P(A)P(B) = P(A \cap B)$.

For example, a certain store's recent T-shirt sales:

Size / Color	Small	Medium	Large	Total
Blue	25	40	35	100
White	27	25	22	74
Black	8	23	15	46
Total	60	88	72	220

Suppose we want to find the conditional probability that a customer buys a black shirt (event A), given that the shirt he buys is size small (event B). From the table, the probability $P(B)$ that a customer buys a small shirt is $\frac{60}{220} = \frac{3}{11}$. The probability $P(A \cap B)$ that he buys a small, black shirt is $\frac{8}{220} = \frac{2}{55}$. The conditional probability $P(A|B)$ that he buys a black shirt, given that he buys a small shirt, is therefore $P(A|B) = \frac{2/55}{3/11} = \frac{2}{15}$.

Similarly, if we want to check whether the event a customer buys a blue shirt, A, is independent of the event that a customer buys a medium shirt, B. From the table, $P(A) = \frac{100}{220} = \frac{5}{11}$ and $P(B) = \frac{88}{220} = \frac{4}{10}$. Also, $P(A \cap B) = \frac{40}{220} = \frac{2}{11}$. Since $\left(\frac{5}{11}\right)\left(\frac{4}{10}\right) = \frac{20}{220} = \frac{1}{11}$, $P(A)P(B) = P(A \cap B)$ and these two events are indeed independent.

MULTIPLICATION RULE

The **multiplication rule** can be used to find the probability of two independent events occurring using the formula $P(A \text{ and } B) = P(A) \times P(B)$, where $P(A \text{ and } B)$ is the probability of two independent events occurring, $P(A)$ is the probability of the first event occurring, and $P(B)$ is the probability of the second event occurring.

The multiplication rule can also be used to find the probability of two dependent events occurring using the formula $P(A \text{ and } B) = P(A) \times P(B|A)$, where $P(A \text{ and } B)$ is the probability of two dependent events occurring and $P(B|A)$ is the probability of the second event occurring after the first event has already occurred. Before using the multiplication rule, you MUST first determine whether the two events are *dependent* or *independent*.

Use a **combination of the multiplication** rule and the rule of complements to find the probability that at least one outcome of the element will occur. This is given by the general formula $P(\text{at least one event occurring}) = 1 - P(\text{no outcomes occurring})$. For example, to find the probability that at least one even number will show when a pair of dice is rolled, find the probability that two odd numbers will be rolled (no even numbers) and subtract from one. You can always use a tree diagram or make a chart to list the possible outcomes when the sample space is small, such as in the dice-rolling example, but in most cases it will be much faster to use the multiplication and complement formulas.

> **Review Video: Multiplication Rule**
> Visit mometrix.com/academy and enter code: 782598

EXPECTED VALUE

Expected value is a method of determining the expected outcome in a random situation. It is a sum of the weighted probabilities of the possible outcomes. Multiply the probability of an event occurring by the weight assigned to that probability (such as the amount of money won or lost). A practical application of the expected value is to determine whether a game of chance is really fair. If the sum of the weighted probabilities is equal to zero, the game is generally considered fair because the player has a fair chance to at least break even. If the expected value is less than zero, then players lose more than they win. For example, a lottery drawing might allow the player to choose any three-digit number, 000–999. The probability of choosing the winning number is 1:1000. If it costs \$1 to play, and a winning number receives \$500, the expected value is $\left(-\$1 \times \frac{999}{1,000}\right) + \left(\$499 \times \frac{1}{1,000}\right) = -\$0.50$. You can expect to lose on average 50 cents for every dollar you spend.

> **Review Video: Expected Value**
> Visit mometrix.com/academy and enter code: 643554

EXPECTED VALUE AND SIMULATORS

A die roll simulator will show the results of n rolls of a die. The result of each die roll may be recorded. For example, suppose a die is rolled 100 times. All results may be recorded. The numbers of 1s, 2s, 3s, 4s, 5s, and 6s, may be counted. The experimental probability of rolling each number will equal the ratio of the frequency of the rolled number to the total number of rolls. As the number of rolls increases, or approaches infinity, the experimental probability will approach the theoretical probability of $\frac{1}{6}$. Thus, the expected value for the roll of a die is shown to be $\left(1 \times \frac{1}{6}\right) + \left(2 \times \frac{1}{6}\right) + \left(3 \times \frac{1}{6}\right) + \left(4 \times \frac{1}{6}\right) + \left(5 \times \frac{1}{6}\right) + \left(6 \times \frac{1}{6}\right)$, or 3.5.

Statistical Analysis

MEASURES OF CENTRAL TENDENCY

A **measure of central tendency** is a statistical value that gives a reasonable estimate for the center of a group of data. There are several different ways of describing the measure of central tendency. Each one has a unique way it is calculated, and each one gives a slightly different perspective on the data set. Whenever you give a measure of central tendency, always make sure the units are the same. If the data has different units, such as hours, minutes, and seconds, convert all the data to the same unit, and use the same unit in the measure of central tendency. If no units are given in the data, do not give units for the measure of central tendency.

MEAN

The **statistical mean** of a group of data is the same as the arithmetic average of that group. To find the mean of a set of data, first convert each value to the same units, if necessary. Then find the sum of all the values, and count the total number of data values, making sure you take into consideration each individual value. If a value appears more than once, count it more than once. Divide the sum of the values by the total number of values and apply the units, if any. Note that the mean does not have to be one of the data values in the set, and may not divide evenly.

$$\text{mean} = \frac{\text{sum of the data values}}{\text{quantity of data values}}$$

For instance, the mean of the data set {88, 72, 61, 90, 97, 68, 88, 79, 86, 93, 97, 71, 80, 84, 89} would be the sum of the fifteen numbers divided by 15:

$$\frac{88 + 72 + 61 + 90 + 97 + 68 + 88 + 79 + 86 + 93 + 97 + 71 + 80 + 84 + 88}{15} = \frac{1242}{15}$$
$$= 82.8$$

While the mean is relatively easy to calculate and averages are understood by most people, the mean can be very misleading if it is used as the sole measure of central tendency. If the data set has outliers (data values that are unusually high or unusually low compared to the rest of the data values), the mean can be very distorted, especially if the data set has a small number of values. If unusually high values are countered with unusually low values, the mean is not affected as much. For example, if five of twenty students in a class get a 100 on a test, but the other 15 students have an average of 60 on the same test, the class average would appear as 70. Whenever the mean is skewed by outliers, it is always a good idea to include the median as an alternate measure of central tendency.

A **weighted mean**, or weighted average, is a mean that uses "weighted" values. The formula is weighted mean $= \frac{w_1 x_1 + w_2 x_2 + w_3 x_3 \ldots + w_n x_n}{w_1 + w_2 + w_3 + \cdots + w_n}$. Weighted values, such as $w_1, w_2, w_3, \ldots w_n$ are assigned to each member of the set $x_1, x_2, x_3, \ldots x_n$. When calculating the weighted mean, make sure a weight value for each member of the set is used.

> **Review Video: All About Averages**
> Visit mometrix.com/academy and enter code: 176521

MEDIAN

The **statistical median** is the value in the middle of the set of data. To find the median, list all data values in order from smallest to largest or from largest to smallest. Any value that is repeated in the set must be listed the number of times it appears. If there are an odd number of data values, the median is the value in the middle of the list. If there is an even number of data values, the median is the arithmetic mean of the two middle values.

For example, the median of the data set {88, 72, 61, 90, 97, 68, 88, 79, 86, 93, 97, 71, 80, 84, 88} is 86 since the ordered set is {61, 68, 71, 72, 79, 80, 84, **86**, 88, 88, 88, 90, 93, 97, 97}.

The big disadvantage of using the median as a measure of central tendency is that is relies solely on a value's relative size as compared to the other values in the set. When the individual values in a set of data are evenly dispersed, the median can be an accurate tool. However, if there is a group of rather large values or a group of rather small values that are not offset by a different group of values, the information that can be inferred from the median may not be accurate because the distribution of values is skewed.

MODE

The **statistical mode** is the data value that occurs the greatest number of times in the data set. It is possible to have exactly one mode, more than one mode, or no mode. To find the mode of a set of data, arrange the data like you do to find the median (all values in order, listing all multiples of data values). Count the number of times each value appears in the data set. If all values appear an equal number of times, there is no mode. If one value appears more than any other value, that value is the mode. If two or more values appear the same number of times, but there are other values that appear fewer times and no values that appear more times, all of those values are the modes.

For example, the mode of the data set {**88**, 72, 61, 90, 97, 68, **88**, 79, 86, 93, 97, 71, 80, 84, **88**} is 88.

The main disadvantage of the mode is that the values of the other data in the set have no bearing on the mode. The mode may be the largest value, the smallest value, or a value anywhere in between in the set. The mode only tells which value or values, if any, occurred the greatest number of times. It does not give any suggestions about the remaining values in the set.

> **Review Video: Mean, Median, and Mode**
> Visit mometrix.com/academy and enter code: 286207

DISPERSION

A **measure of dispersion** is a single value that helps to "interpret" the measure of central tendency by providing more information about how the data values in the set are distributed about the measure of central tendency. The measure of dispersion helps to eliminate or reduce the disadvantages of using the mean, median, or mode as a single measure of central tendency, and give a more accurate picture of the dataset as a whole. To have a measure of dispersion, you must know or calculate the range, standard deviation, or variance of the data set.

RANGE

The **range** of a set of data is the difference between the greatest and lowest values of the data in the set. To calculate the range, you must first make sure the units for all data values are the same, and then identify the greatest and lowest values. If there are multiple data values that are equal for the highest or lowest, just use one of the values in the formula. Write the answer with the same units as the data values you used to do the calculations.

> **Review Video: Statistical Range**
> Visit mometrix.com/academy and enter code: 778541

STANDARD DEVIATION

Standard deviation is a measure of dispersion that compares all the data values in the set to the mean of the set to give a more accurate picture. To find the standard deviation of a sample, use the formula

$$s = \sqrt{\frac{\sum_{i=1}^{n}(x_i - \bar{x})^2}{n-1}}$$

Note that s is the standard deviation of a sample, x represents the individual values in the data set, $\bar{x}$ is the mean of the data values in the set, and n is the number of data values in the set. The higher the value of the standard deviation is, the greater the variance of the data values from the mean. The units associated with the standard deviation are the same as the units of the data values.

> **Review Video: Standard Deviation**
> Visit mometrix.com/academy and enter code: 419469

VARIANCE

The **variance** of a sample, or just variance, is the square of the standard deviation of that sample. While the mean of a set of data gives the average of the set and gives information about where a specific data value lies in relation to the average, the variance of the sample gives information about the degree to which the data values are spread out and tells you how close an individual value is to the average compared to the other values. The units associated with variance are the same as the units of the data values squared.

PERCENTILE

Percentiles and quartiles are other methods of describing data within a set. **Percentiles** tell what percentage of the data in the set fall below a specific point. For example, achievement test scores are often given in percentiles. A score at the 80th percentile is one which is equal to or higher than 80 percent of the scores in the set. In other words, 80 percent of the scores were lower than that score.

Quartiles are percentile groups that make up quarter sections of the data set. The first quartile is the 25th percentile. The second quartile is the 50th percentile; this is also the median of the dataset. The third quartile is the 75th percentile.

SKEWNESS

Skewness is a way to describe the symmetry or asymmetry of the distribution of values in a dataset. If the distribution of values is symmetrical, there is no skew. In general the closer the mean of a data set is to the median of the data set, the less skew there is. Generally, if the mean is to the right of the median, the data set is *positively skewed*, or right-skewed, and if the mean is to the left of the median, the data set is *negatively skewed*, or left-skewed. However, this rule of thumb is not infallible. When the data values are graphed on a curve, a set with no skew will be a perfect bell curve.

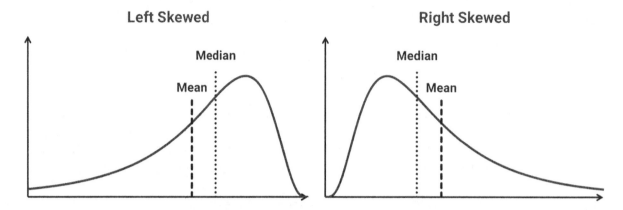

To estimate skew, use the formula:

$$\text{skew} = \frac{\sqrt{n(n-1)}}{n-2} \left(\frac{\frac{1}{n}\sum_{i=1}^{n}(x_i - \bar{x})^3}{\left(\frac{1}{n}\sum_{i=1}^{n}(x_i - \bar{x})^2\right)^{\frac{3}{2}}} \right)$$

Note that n is the datapoints in the set, x_i is the ith value in the set, and $\bar{x}$ is the mean of the set.

> **Review Video: Skew**
> Visit mometrix.com/academy and enter code: 661486

UNIMODAL VS. BIMODAL

If a distribution has a single peak, it would be considered **unimodal**. If it has two discernible peaks it would be considered **bimodal**. Bimodal distributions may be an indication that the set of data being considered is actually the combination of two sets of data with significant differences. A **uniform distribution** is a distribution in which there is *no distinct peak or variation* in the data. No values or ranges are particularly more common than any other values or ranges.

OUTLIER

An outlier is an extremely high or extremely low value in the data set. It may be the result of measurement error, in which case, the outlier is not a valid member of the data set. However, it may also be a valid member of the distribution. Unless a measurement error is identified, the experimenter cannot know for certain if an outlier is or is not a member of the distribution. There are arbitrary methods that can be employed to designate an extreme value as an outlier. One method designates an outlier (or possible outlier) to be any value less than $Q_1 - 1.5(IQR)$ or any value greater than $Q_3 + 1.5(IQR)$.

DATA ANALYSIS

SIMPLE REGRESSION

In statistics, **simple regression** is using an equation to represent a relation between independent and dependent variables. The independent variable is also referred to as the explanatory variable or the predictor and is generally represented by the variable x in the equation. The dependent variable, usually represented by the variable y, is also referred to as the response variable. The equation may be any type of function – linear, quadratic, exponential, etc. The best way to handle this task is to use the regression feature of your graphing calculator. This will easily give you the curve of best fit and provide you with the coefficients and other information you need to derive an equation.

LINE OF BEST FIT

In a scatter plot, the **line of best fit** is the line that best shows the trends of the data. The line of best fit is given by the equation $\hat{y} = ax + b$, where a and b are the regression coefficients. The regression coefficient a is also the slope of the line of best fit, and b is also the y-coordinate of the point at which the line of best fit crosses the y-axis. Not every point on the scatter plot will be on the line of best fit. The differences between the y-values of the points in the scatter plot and the corresponding y-values according to the equation of the line of best fit are the residuals. The line of best fit is also called the least-squares regression line because it is also the line that has the lowest sum of the squares of the residuals.

CORRELATION COEFFICIENT

The **correlation coefficient** is the numerical value that indicates how strong the relationship is between the two variables of a linear regression equation. A correlation coefficient of –1 is a perfect negative correlation. A correlation coefficient of +1 is a perfect positive correlation. Correlation coefficients close to –1 or +1 are very strong correlations. A correlation coefficient equal to zero indicates there is no correlation between the two variables. This test is a good indicator of whether or not the equation for the line of best fit is accurate. The formula for the correlation coefficient is

$$r = \frac{\sum_{i=1}^{n}(x_i - \bar{x})(y_i - \bar{y})}{\sqrt{\sum_{i=1}^{n}(x_i - \bar{x})^2} \sqrt{\sum_{i=1}^{n}(y_i - \bar{y})^2}}$$

where r is the correlation coefficient, n is the number of data values in the set, (x_i, y_i) is a point in the set, and $\bar{x}$ and $\bar{y}$ are the means.

Z-SCORE

A **z-score** is an indication of how many standard deviations a given value falls from the mean. To calculate a z-score, use the formula:

$$\frac{x - \mu}{\sigma}$$

x is the data value, μ is the mean of the data set, and σ is the standard deviation of the population. If the z-score is positive, the data value lies above the mean. If the z-score is negative, the data value falls below the mean. These scores are useful in interpreting data such as standardized test scores, where every piece of data in the set has been counted, rather than just a small random sample. In cases where standard deviations are calculated from a random sample of the set, the z-scores will not be as accurate.

CENTRAL LIMIT THEOREM

According to the **central limit theorem**, regardless of what the original distribution of a sample is, the distribution of the means tends to get closer and closer to a normal distribution as the sample size gets larger and larger (this is necessary because the sample is becoming more all-encompassing of the elements of the population). As the sample size gets larger, the distribution of the sample mean will approach a normal distribution with a mean of the population mean and a variance of the population variance divided by the sample size.

Displaying Information

FREQUENCY TABLES

Frequency tables show how frequently each unique value appears in a set. A **relative frequency table** is one that shows the proportions of each unique value compared to the entire set. Relative frequencies are given as percentages; however, the total percent for a relative frequency table will not necessarily equal 100 percent due to rounding. An example of a frequency table with relative frequencies is below.

Favorite Color	Frequency	Relative Frequency
Blue	4	13%
Red	7	22%
Green	3	9%
Purple	6	19%
Cyan	12	38%

> **Review Video: Data Interpretation of Graphs**
> Visit mometrix.com/academy and enter code: 200439

CIRCLE GRAPHS

Circle graphs, also known as *pie charts*, provide a visual depiction of the relationship of each type of data compared to the whole set of data. The circle graph is divided into sections by drawing radii to create central angles whose percentage of the circle is equal to the individual data's percentage of the whole set. Each 1% of data is equal to 3.6° in the circle graph. Therefore, data represented by a 90° section of the circle graph makes up 25% of the whole. When complete, a circle graph often looks like a pie cut into uneven wedges. The pie chart below shows the data from the frequency table referenced earlier where people were asked their favorite color.

Favorite Color

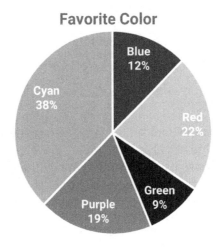

PICTOGRAPHS

A **pictograph** is a graph, generally in the horizontal orientation, that uses pictures or symbols to represent the data. Each pictograph must have a key that defines the picture or symbol and gives the quantity each picture or symbol represents. Pictures or symbols on a pictograph are not always shown as whole elements. In this case, the fraction of the picture or symbol shown represents the same fraction of the quantity a whole picture or symbol stands for. For example, a row with $3\frac{1}{2}$ ears of corn, where each ear of corn represents 100 stalks of corn in a field, would equal $3\frac{1}{2} \times 100 = 350$ stalks of corn in the field.

LINE GRAPHS

Line graphs have one or more lines of varying styles (solid or broken) to show the different values for a set of data. The individual data are represented as ordered pairs, much like on a Cartesian plane. In this case, the *x*- and *y*-axes are defined in terms of their units, such as dollars or time. The individual plotted points are joined by line segments to show whether the value of the data is increasing (line sloping upward), decreasing (line sloping downward), or staying the same (horizontal line). Multiple sets of data can be graphed on the same line graph to give an easy visual comparison. An example of this would be graphing achievement test scores for different groups of students over the same time period to see which group had the greatest increase or decrease in performance from year to year (as shown below).

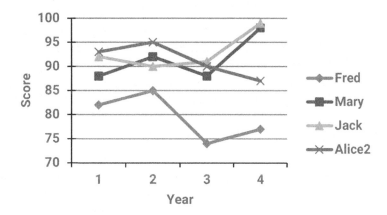

LINE PLOTS

A **line plot**, also known as a *dot plot*, has plotted points that are not connected by line segments. In this graph, the horizontal axis lists the different possible values for the data, and the vertical axis lists the number of times the individual value occurs. A single dot is graphed for each value to show the number of times it occurs. This graph is more closely related to a bar graph than a line graph. Do not connect the dots in a line plot or it will misrepresent the data.

STEM AND LEAF PLOTS

A **stem and leaf plot** is useful for depicting groups of data that fall into a range of values. Each piece of data is separated into two parts: the first, or left, part is called the stem; the second, or right, part is called the leaf. Each stem is listed in a column from smallest to largest. Each leaf that has the common stem is listed in that stem's row from smallest to largest. For example, in a set of two-digit numbers, the digit in the tens place is the stem, and the digit in the ones place is the leaf. With a stem and leaf plot, you can easily see which subset of numbers (10s, 20s, 30s, etc.) is the largest. This information is also readily available by looking at a histogram, but a stem and leaf plot also allows you to look closer and see exactly which values fall in that range. Using all of the test scores from above, we can assemble a stem and leaf plot like the one below.

Test Scores

7	4	8						
8	2	5	7	8	8			
9	0	0	1	2	2	3	5	8	9

> **Review Video: Stem and Leaf Plots**
> Visit mometrix.com/academy and enter code: 302339

BAR GRAPHS

A **bar graph** is one of the few graphs that can be drawn correctly in two different configurations – both horizontally and vertically. A bar graph is similar to a line plot in the way the data is organized on the graph. Both axes must have their categories defined for the graph to be useful. Rather than placing a single dot to mark the point of the data's value, a bar, or thick line, is drawn from zero to the exact value of the data, whether it is a number, percentage, or other numerical value. Longer bar lengths correspond to greater data values. To read a bar graph, read the labels for the axes to find the units being reported. Then, look where the bars end in relation to the scale given on the corresponding axis and determine the associated value.

The bar chart below represents the responses from our favorite-color survey.

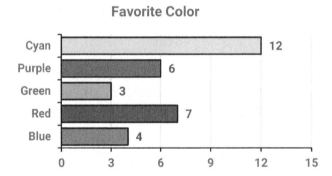

HISTOGRAMS

At first glance, a **histogram** looks like a vertical bar graph. The difference is that a bar graph has a separate bar for each piece of data and a histogram has one continuous bar for each *range* of data. For example, a histogram may have one bar for the range 0–9, one bar for 10–19, etc. While a bar graph has numerical values on one axis, a histogram has numerical values on both axes. Each range is of equal size, and they are ordered left to right from lowest to highest. The height of each column on a histogram represents the number of data values within that range. Like a stem and leaf plot, a histogram makes it easy to glance at the graph and quickly determine which range has the greatest quantity of values. A simple example of a histogram is below.

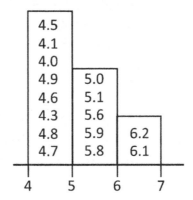

BIVARIATE DATA

Bivariate data is simply data from two different variables. (The prefix *bi-* means *two*.) In a *scatter plot*, each value in the set of data is plotted on a grid similar to a Cartesian plane, where each axis represents one of the two variables. By looking at the pattern formed by the points on the grid, you can often determine whether or not there is a relationship between the two variables, and what that relationship is, if it exists. The variables may be directly proportionate, inversely proportionate, or show no proportion at all. It may also be possible to determine if the data is linear, and if so, to find an equation to relate the two variables. The following scatter plot shows the relationship between preference for brand "A" and the age of the consumers surveyed.

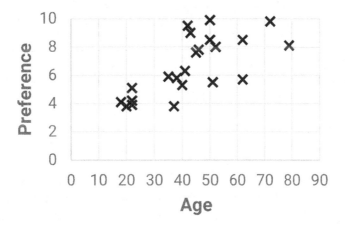

SCATTER PLOTS

Scatter plots are also useful in determining the type of function represented by the data and finding the simple regression. Linear scatter plots may be positive or negative. Nonlinear scatter plots are generally exponential or quadratic. Below are some common types of scatter plots:

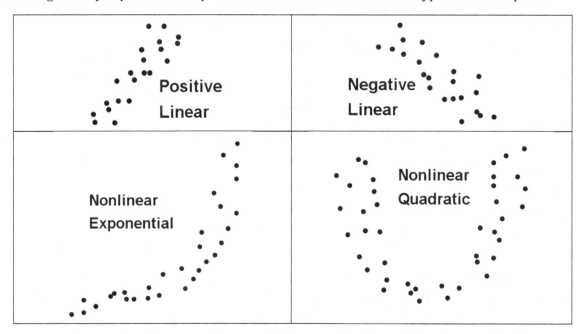

5-NUMBER SUMMARY

The **5-number summary** of a set of data gives a very informative picture of the set. The five numbers in the summary include the minimum value, maximum value, and the three quartiles. This information gives the reader the range and median of the set, as well as an indication of how the data is spread about the median.

BOX AND WHISKER PLOTS

A **box-and-whiskers plot** is a graphical representation of the 5-number summary. To draw a box-and-whiskers plot, plot the points of the 5-number summary on a number line. Draw a box whose ends are through the points for the first and third quartiles. Draw a vertical line in the box through the median to divide the box in half. Draw a line segment from the first quartile point to the minimum value, and from the third quartile point to the maximum value.

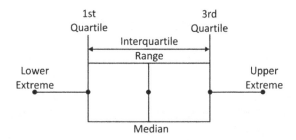

68-95-99.7 RULE

The **68–95–99.7 rule** describes how a normal distribution of data should appear when compared to the mean. This is also a description of a normal bell curve. According to this rule, 68 percent of the data values in a normally distributed set should fall within one standard deviation of the mean (34 percent above and 34 percent below the mean), 95 percent of the data values should fall within two standard deviations of the mean (47.5 percent above and 47.5 percent below the mean), and 99.7 percent of the data values should fall within three standard deviations of the mean, again, equally distributed on either side of the mean. This means that only 0.3 percent of all data values should fall more than three standard deviations from the mean. On the graph below, the normal curve is centered on the y-axis. The x-axis labels are how many standard deviations away from the center you are. Therefore, it is easy to see how the 68-95-99.7 rule can apply.

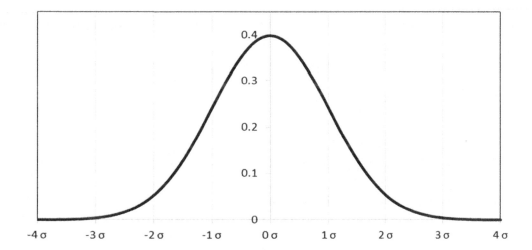

Reading

Informational Texts

TEXT FEATURES IN INFORMATIONAL TEXTS

The **title of a text** gives readers some idea of its content. The **table of contents** is a list near the beginning of a text, showing the book's sections and chapters and their coinciding page numbers. This gives readers an overview of the whole text and helps them find specific chapters easily. An **appendix**, at the back of the book or document, includes important information that is not present in the main text. Also at the back, an **index** lists the book's important topics alphabetically with their page numbers to help readers find them easily. **Glossaries**, usually found at the backs of books, list technical terms alphabetically with their definitions to aid vocabulary learning and comprehension. Boldface print is used to emphasize certain words, often identifying words included in the text's glossary where readers can look up their definitions. **Headings** separate sections of text and show the topic of each. **Subheadings** divide subject headings into smaller, more specific categories to help readers organize information. **Footnotes**, at the bottom of the page, give readers more information, such as citations or links. **Bullet points** list items separately, making facts and ideas easier to see and understand. A **sidebar** is a box of information to one side of the main text giving additional information, often on a more focused or in-depth example of a topic.

Illustrations and **photographs** are pictures that visually emphasize important points in text. The captions below the illustrations explain what those images show. Charts and tables are visual forms of information that make something easier to understand quickly. Diagrams are drawings that show relationships or explain a process. Graphs visually show the relationships among multiple sets of information plotted along vertical and horizontal axes. Maps show geographical information visually to help readers understand the relative locations of places covered in the text. Timelines are visual graphics that show historical events in chronological order to help readers see their sequence.

> **Review Video: Informative Text**
> Visit mometrix.com/academy and enter code: 924964

LANGUAGE USE
LITERAL AND FIGURATIVE LANGUAGE

As in fictional literature, informational text also uses both **literal language**, which means just what it says, and **figurative language**, which imparts more than literal meaning. For example, an informational text author might use a simile or direct comparison, such as writing that a racehorse "ran like the wind." Informational text authors also use metaphors or implied comparisons, such as "the cloud of the Great Depression." Imagery may also appear in informational texts to increase the reader's understanding of ideas and concepts discussed in the text.

EXPLICIT AND IMPLICIT INFORMATION

When informational text states something explicitly, the reader is told by the author exactly what is meant, which can include the author's interpretation or perspective of events. For example, a professor writes, "I have seen students go into an absolute panic just because they weren't able to complete the exam in the time they were allotted." This explicitly tells the reader that the students were afraid, and by using the words "just because," the writer indicates their fear was exaggerated out of proportion relative to what happened. However, another professor writes, "I have had

94

students come to me, their faces drained of all color, saying 'We weren't able to finish the exam.'" This is an example of implicit meaning: the second writer did not state explicitly that the students were panicked. Instead, he wrote a description of their faces being "drained of all color." From this description, the reader can infer that the students were so frightened that their faces paled.

> **Review Video: Explicit and Implicit Information**
> Visit mometrix.com/academy and enter code: 735771

TECHNICAL LANGUAGE

Technical language is more impersonal than literary and vernacular language. Passive voice makes the tone impersonal. For example, instead of writing, "We found this a central component of protein metabolism," scientists write, "This was found a central component of protein metabolism." While science professors have traditionally instructed students to avoid active voice because it leads to first-person ("I" and "we") usage, science editors today find passive voice dull and weak. Many journal articles combine both. Tone in technical science writing should be detached, concise, and professional. While one may normally write, "This chemical has to be available for proteins to be digested," professionals write technically, "The presence of this chemical is required for the enzyme to break the covalent bonds of proteins." The use of technical language appeals to both technical and non-technical audiences by displaying the author or speaker's understanding of the subject and suggesting their credibility regarding the message they are communicating.

TECHNICAL MATERIAL FOR NON-TECHNICAL READERS

Writing about **technical subjects** for **non-technical readers** differs from writing for colleagues because authors place more importance on delivering a critical message than on imparting the maximum technical content possible. Technical authors also must assume that non-technical audiences do not have the expertise to comprehend extremely scientific or technical messages, concepts, and terminology. They must resist the temptation to impress audiences with their scientific knowledge and expertise and remember that their primary purpose is to communicate a message that non-technical readers will understand, feel, and respond to. Non-technical and technical styles include similarities. Both should formally cite any references or other authors' work utilized in the text. Both must follow intellectual property and copyright regulations. This includes the author's protecting his or her own rights, or a public domain statement, as he or she chooses.

> **Review Video: Technical Passages**
> Visit mometrix.com/academy and enter code: 478923

NON-TECHNICAL AUDIENCES

Writers of technical or scientific material may need to write for many non-technical audiences. Some readers have no technical or scientific background, and those who do may not be in the same field as the authors. Government and corporate policymakers and budget managers need technical information they can understand for decision-making. Citizens affected by technology or science are a different audience. Non-governmental organizations can encompass many of the preceding groups. Elementary and secondary school programs also need non-technical language for presenting technical subject matter. Additionally, technical authors will need to use non-technical language when collecting consumer responses to surveys, presenting scientific or para-scientific material to the public, writing about the history of science, and writing about science and technology in developing countries.

95

USE OF EVERYDAY LANGUAGE

Authors of technical information sometimes must write using non-technical language that readers outside their disciplinary fields can comprehend. They should use not only non-technical terms, but also normal, everyday language to accommodate readers whose native language is different than the language the text is written in. For example, instead of writing that "eustatic changes like thermal expansion are causing hazardous conditions in the littoral zone," an author would do better to write that "a rising sea level is threatening the coast." When technical terms cannot be avoided, authors should also define or explain them using non-technical language. Although authors must cite references and acknowledge their use of others' work, they should avoid the kinds of references or citations that they would use in scientific journals—unless they reinforce author messages. They should not use endnotes, footnotes, or any other complicated referential techniques because non-technical journal publishers usually do not accept them. Including high-resolution illustrations, photos, maps, or satellite images and incorporating multimedia into digital publications will enhance non-technical writing about technical subjects. Technical authors may publish using non-technical language in e-journals, trade journals, specialty newsletters, and daily newspapers.

MAKING INFERENCES ABOUT INFORMATIONAL TEXT

With informational text, reader comprehension depends not only on recalling important statements and details, but also on reader inferences based on examples and details. Readers add information from the text to what they already know to draw inferences about the text. These inferences help the readers to fill in the information that the text does not explicitly state, enabling them to understand the text better. When reading a nonfictional autobiography or biography, for example, the most appropriate inferences might concern the events in the book, the actions of the subject of the autobiography or biography, and the message the author means to convey. When reading a nonfictional expository (informational) text, the reader would best draw inferences about problems and their solutions, and causes and their effects. When reading a nonfictional persuasive text, the reader will want to infer ideas supporting the author's message and intent.

STRUCTURES OR ORGANIZATIONAL PATTERNS IN INFORMATIONAL TEXTS

Informational text can be **descriptive**, appealing to the five senses and answering the questions what, who, when, where, and why. Another method of structuring informational text is sequence and order. **Chronological** texts relate events in the sequence that they occurred, from start to finish, while how-to texts organize information into a series of instructions in the sequence in which the steps should be followed. **Comparison-contrast** structures of informational text describe various ideas to their readers by pointing out how things or ideas are similar and how they are different. **Cause and effect** structures of informational text describe events that occurred and identify the causes or reasons that those events occurred. **Problem and solution** structures of informational texts introduce and describe problems and offer one or more solutions for each problem described.

DETERMINING AN INFORMATIONAL AUTHOR'S PURPOSE

Informational authors' purposes are why they write texts. Readers must determine authors' motivations and goals. Readers gain greater insight into a text by considering the author's motivation. This develops critical reading skills. Readers perceive writing as a person's voice, not simply printed words. Uncovering author motivations and purposes empowers readers to know what to expect from the text, read for relevant details, evaluate authors and their work critically, and respond effectively to the motivations and persuasions of the text. The main idea of a text is what the reader is supposed to understand from reading it; the purpose of the text is why the author has written it and what the author wants readers to do with its information. Authors state some purposes clearly, while other purposes may be unstated but equally significant. When stated purposes contradict other parts of a text, the author may have a hidden agenda. Readers can better evaluate a text's effectiveness, whether they agree or disagree with it, and why they agree or disagree through identifying unstated author purposes.

IDENTIFYING AUTHOR'S POINT OF VIEW OR PURPOSE

In some informational texts, readers find it easy to identify the author's point of view and purpose, such as when the author explicitly states his or her position and reason for writing. But other texts are more difficult, either because of the content or because the authors give neutral or balanced viewpoints. This is particularly true in scientific texts, in which authors may state the purpose of their research in the report, but never state their point of view except by interpreting evidence or data.

To analyze text and identify point of view or purpose, readers should ask themselves the following four questions:

1. With what main point or idea does this author want to persuade readers to agree?
2. How does this author's word choice affect the way that readers consider this subject?
3. How do this author's choices of examples and facts affect the way that readers consider this subject?
4. What is it that this author wants to accomplish by writing this text?

> **Review Video: Understanding the Author's Intent**
> Visit mometrix.com/academy and enter code: 511819

EVALUATING ARGUMENTS MADE BY INFORMATIONAL TEXT WRITERS

When evaluating an informational text, the first step is to identify the argument's conclusion. Then identify the author's premises that support the conclusion. Try to paraphrase premises for clarification and make the conclusion and premises fit. List all premises first, sequentially numbered, then finish with the conclusion. Identify any premises or assumptions not stated by the author but required for the stated premises to support the conclusion. Read word assumptions sympathetically, as the author might. Evaluate whether premises reasonably support the conclusion. For inductive reasoning, the reader should ask if the premises are true, if they support the conclusion, and if so, how strongly. For deductive reasoning, the reader should ask if the argument is valid or invalid. If all premises are true, then the argument is valid unless the conclusion can be false. If it can, then the argument is invalid. An invalid argument can be made valid through alterations such as the addition of needed premises.

USE OF RHETORIC IN INFORMATIONAL TEXTS

There are many ways authors can support their claims, arguments, beliefs, ideas, and reasons for writing in informational texts. For example, authors can appeal to readers' sense of **logic** by communicating their reasoning through a carefully sequenced series of logical steps to help "prove" the points made. Authors can appeal to readers' **emotions** by using descriptions and words that evoke feelings of sympathy, sadness, anger, righteous indignation, hope, happiness, or any other emotion to reinforce what they express and share with their audience. Authors may appeal to the **moral** or **ethical values** of readers by using words and descriptions that can convince readers that something is right or wrong. By relating personal anecdotes, authors can supply readers with more accessible, realistic examples of points they make, as well as appealing to their emotions. They can

provide supporting evidence by reporting case studies. They can also illustrate their points by making analogies to which readers can better relate.

Vocabulary and Word Relationships

SYNONYMS AND ANTONYMS

When you understand how words relate to each other, you will discover more in a passage. This is explained by understanding **synonyms** (e.g., words that mean the same thing) and **antonyms** (e.g., words that mean the opposite of one another). As an example, *dry* and *arid* are synonyms, and *dry* and *wet* are antonyms.

There are many pairs of words in English that can be considered synonyms, despite having slightly different definitions. For instance, the words *friendly* and *collegial* can both be used to describe a warm interpersonal relationship, and one would be correct to call them synonyms. However, *collegial* (kin to *colleague*) is often used in reference to professional or academic relationships, and *friendly* has no such connotation.

If the difference between the two words is too great, then they should not be called synonyms. *Hot* and *warm* are not synonyms because their meanings are too distinct. A good way to determine whether two words are synonyms is to substitute one word for the other word and verify that the meaning of the sentence has not changed. Substituting *warm* for *hot* in a sentence would convey a different meaning. Although warm and hot may seem close in meaning, warm generally means that the temperature is moderate, and hot generally means that the temperature is excessively high.

Antonyms are words with opposite meanings. *Light* and *dark*, *up* and *down*, *right* and *left*, *good* and *bad*: these are all sets of antonyms. Be careful to distinguish between antonyms and pairs of words that are simply different. *Black* and *gray*, for instance, are not antonyms because gray is not the opposite of black. *Black* and *white*, on the other hand, are antonyms.

Not every word has an antonym. For instance, many nouns do not. What would be the antonym of *chair*? During your exam, the questions related to antonyms are more likely to concern adjectives. You will recall that adjectives are words that describe a noun. Some common adjectives include *purple*, *fast*, *skinny*, and *sweet*. From those four adjectives, *purple* is the item that lacks a group of obvious antonyms.

> **Review Video: <u>What Are Synonyms and Antonyms?</u>**
> Visit mometrix.com/academy and enter code: 105612

AFFIXES

Affixes in the English language are morphemes that are added to words to create related but different words. Derivational affixes form new words based on and related to the original words. For example, the affix *–ness* added to the end of the adjective *happy* forms the noun *happiness*. Inflectional affixes form different grammatical versions of words. For example, the plural affix *–s* changes the singular noun *book* to the plural noun *books*, and the past tense affix *–ed* changes the present tense verb *look* to the past tense *looked*. Prefixes are affixes placed in front of words. For example, *heat* means to make hot; *preheat* means to heat in advance. Suffixes are affixes placed at the ends of words. The *happiness* example above contains the suffix *–ness*. Circumfixes add parts both before and after words, such as how *light* becomes *enlighten* with the prefix *en-* and the suffix *–en*. Interfixes create compound words via central affixes: *speed* and *meter* become *speedometer* via the interfix *–o–*.

> **Review Video: <u>Affixes</u>**
> Visit mometrix.com/academy and enter code: 782422

Word Roots, Prefixes, and Suffixes to Help Determine Meanings of Words

Many English words were formed from combining multiple sources. For example, the Latin *habēre* means "to have," and the prefixes *in-* and *im-* mean a lack or prevention of something, as in *insufficient* and *imperfect*. Latin combined *in-* with *habēre* to form *inhibēre,* whose past participle was *inhibitus*. This is the origin of the English word *inhibit,* meaning to prevent from having. Hence by knowing the meanings of both the prefix and the root, one can decipher the word meaning. In Greek, the root *enkephalo-* refers to the brain. Many medical terms are based on this root, such as encephalitis and hydrocephalus. Understanding the prefix and suffix meanings (*-itis* means inflammation; *hydro-* means water) allows a person to deduce that encephalitis refers to brain inflammation and hydrocephalus refers to water (or other fluid) in the brain.

> **Review Video: <u>Determining Word Meanings</u>**
> Visit mometrix.com/academy and enter code: 894894
>
> **Review Video: <u>Root Words in English</u>**
> Visit mometrix.com/academy and enter code: 896380

Prefixes

While knowing prefix meanings helps ESL and beginning readers learn new words, other readers take for granted the meanings of known words. However, prefix knowledge will also benefit them for determining meanings or definitions of unfamiliar words. For example, native English speakers and readers familiar with recipes know what *preheat* means. Knowing that *pre-* means in advance can also inform them that *presume* means to assume in advance, that *prejudice* means advance judgment, and that this understanding can be applied to many other words beginning with *pre-*. Knowing that the prefix *dis-* indicates opposition informs the meanings of words like *disbar, disagree, disestablish,* and many more. Knowing *dys-* means bad, impaired, abnormal, or difficult informs *dyslogistic, dysfunctional, dysphagia,* and *dysplasia.*

Suffixes

In English, certain suffixes generally indicate both that a word is a noun, and that the noun represents a state of being or quality. For example, *-ness* is commonly used to change an adjective into its noun form, as with *happy* and *happiness, nice* and *niceness,* and so on. The suffix *–tion* is commonly used to transform a verb into its noun form, as with *converse* and *conversation or move* and *motion.* Thus, if readers are unfamiliar with the second form of a word, knowing the meaning of the transforming suffix can help them determine meaning.

Prefixes for Numbers

Prefix	Definition	Examples
bi-	two	bisect, biennial
mono-	one, single	monogamy, monologue
poly-	many	polymorphous, polygamous
semi-	half, partly	semicircle, semicolon
uni-	one	uniform, unity

PREFIXES FOR TIME, DIRECTION, AND SPACE

Prefix	Definition	Examples
a-	in, on, of, up, to	abed, afoot
ab-	from, away, off	abdicate, abjure
ad-	to, toward	advance, adventure
ante-	before, previous	antecedent, antedate
anti-	against, opposing	antipathy, antidote
cata-	down, away, thoroughly	catastrophe, cataclysm
circum-	around	circumspect, circumference
com-	with, together, very	commotion, complicate
contra-	against, opposing	contradict, contravene
de-	from	depart
dia-	through, across, apart	diameter, diagnose
dis-	away, off, down, not	dissent, disappear
epi-	upon	epilogue
ex-	out	extract, excerpt
hypo-	under, beneath	hypodermic, hypothesis
inter-	among, between	intercede, interrupt
intra-	within	intramural, intrastate
ob-	against, opposing	objection
per-	through	perceive, permit
peri-	around	periscope, perimeter
post-	after, following	postpone, postscript
pre-	before, previous	prevent, preclude
pro-	forward, in place of	propel, pronoun
retro-	back, backward	retrospect, retrograde
sub-	under, beneath	subjugate, substitute
super-	above, extra	supersede, supernumerary
trans-	across, beyond, over	transact, transport
ultra-	beyond, excessively	ultramodern, ultrasonic

NEGATIVE PREFIXES

Prefix	Definition	Examples
a-	without, lacking	atheist, agnostic
in-	not, opposing	incapable, ineligible
non-	not	nonentity, nonsense
un-	not, reverse of	unhappy, unlock

EXTRA PREFIXES

Prefix	Definition	Examples
belli-	war, warlike	bellicose
bene-	well, good	benefit, benefactor
equi-	equal	equivalent, equilibrium
for-	away, off, from	forget, forswear
fore-	previous	foretell, forefathers
homo-	same, equal	homogenized, homonym
hyper-	excessive, over	hypercritical, hypertension
in-	in, into	intrude, invade
magn-	large	magnitude, magnify
mal-	bad, poorly, not	malfunction, malpractice
mis-	bad, poorly, not	misspell, misfire
mor-	death	mortality, mortuary
neo-	new	Neolithic, neoconservative
omni-	all, everywhere	omniscient, omnivore
ortho-	right, straight	orthogonal, orthodox
over-	above	overbearing, oversight
pan-	all, entire	panorama, pandemonium
para-	beside, beyond	parallel, paradox
phil-	love, like	philosophy, philanthropic
prim-	first, early	primitive, primary
re-	backward, again	revoke, recur
sym-	with, together	sympathy, symphony
vis-	to see	visage, visible

Below is a list of common suffixes and their meanings:

ADJECTIVE SUFFIXES

Suffix	Definition	Examples
-able (-ible)	capable of being	toler*able*, ed*ible*
-esque	in the style of, like	picturesque, grotesque
-ful	filled with, marked by	thankful, zestful
-ific	make, cause	terrific, beatific
-ish	suggesting, like	churlish, childish
-less	lacking, without	hopeless, countless
-ous	marked by, given to	religious, riotous

NOUN SUFFIXES

Suffix	Definition	Examples
-acy	state, condition	accuracy, privacy
-ance	act, condition, fact	acceptance, vigilance
-ard	one that does excessively	drunkard, sluggard
-ation	action, state, result	occupation, starvation
-dom	state, rank, condition	serfdom, wisdom
-er (-or)	office, action	teach*er*, elevat*or*, hon*or*
-ess	feminine	waitress, duchess
-hood	state, condition	manhood, statehood
-ion	action, result, state	union, fusion
-ism	act, manner, doctrine	barbarism, socialism
-ist	worker, follower	monopolist, socialist
-ity (-ty)	state, quality, condition	acid*ity*, civil*ity*, twen*ty*
-ment	result, action	Refreshment
-ness	quality, state	greatness, tallness
-ship	position	internship, statesmanship
-sion (-tion)	state, result	revi*sion*, expedi*tion*
-th	act, state, quality	warmth, width
-tude	quality, state, result	magnitude, fortitude

VERB SUFFIXES

Suffix	Definition	Examples
-ate	having, showing	separate, desolate
-en	cause to be, become	deepen, strengthen
-fy	make, cause to have	glorify, fortify
-ize	cause to be, treat with	sterilize, mechanize

DENOTATIVE VS. CONNOTATIVE MEANING

The **denotative** meaning of a word is the literal meaning. The **connotative** meaning goes beyond the denotative meaning to include the emotional reaction that a word may invoke. The connotative meaning often takes the denotative meaning a step further due to associations the reader makes with the denotative meaning. Readers can differentiate between the denotative and connotative meanings by first recognizing how authors use each meaning. Most non-fiction, for example, is fact-based and authors do not use flowery, figurative language. The reader can assume that the writer is using the denotative meaning of words. In fiction, the author may use the connotative meaning. Readers can determine whether the author is using the denotative or connotative meaning of a word by implementing context clues.

> **Review Video: Connotation and Denotation**
> Visit mometrix.com/academy and enter code: 310092

NUANCES OF WORD MEANING RELATIVE TO CONNOTATION, DENOTATION, DICTION, AND USAGE

A word's denotation is simply its objective dictionary definition. However, its connotation refers to the subjective associations, often emotional, that specific words evoke in listeners and readers. Two or more words can have the same dictionary meaning, but very different connotations. Writers use diction (word choice) to convey various nuances of thought and emotion by selecting synonyms for other words that best communicate the associations they want to trigger for readers. For example, a car engine is naturally greasy; in this sense, "greasy" is a neutral term. But when a person's smile, appearance, or clothing is described as "greasy," it has a negative connotation. Some words have even gained additional or different meanings over time. For example, *awful* used to be used to describe things that evoked a sense of awe. When *awful* is separated into its root word, awe, and suffix, -ful, it can be understood to mean "full of awe." However, the word is now commonly used to describe things that evoke repulsion, terror, or another intense, negative reaction.

> **Review Video: Word Usage**
> Visit mometrix.com/academy and enter code: 197863

CONTEXT CLUES

Readers of all levels will encounter words that they have either never seen or have encountered only on a limited basis. The best way to define a word in **context** is to look for nearby words that can assist in revealing the meaning of the word. For instance, unfamiliar nouns are often accompanied by examples that provide a definition. Consider the following sentence: *Dave arrived at the party in hilarious garb: a leopard-print shirt, buckskin trousers, and bright green sneakers.* If a reader was unfamiliar with the meaning of garb, he or she could read the examples (i.e., a leopard-print shirt, buckskin trousers, and high heels) and quickly determine that the word means *clothing*. Examples will not always be this obvious. Consider this sentence: *Parsley, lemon, and flowers were just a few of the items he used as garnishes.* Here, the word *garnishes* is exemplified by parsley, lemon, and flowers. Readers who have eaten in a variety of restaurants will probably be able to identify a garnish as something used to decorate a plate.

> **Review Video: Context Clues**
> Visit mometrix.com/academy and enter code: 613660

USING CONTRAST IN CONTEXT CLUES

In addition to looking at the context of a passage, readers can use contrast to define an unfamiliar word in context. In many sentences, the author will not describe the unfamiliar word directly; instead, he or she will describe the opposite of the unfamiliar word. Thus, you are provided with some information that will bring you closer to defining the word. Consider the following example: *Despite his intelligence, Hector's low brow and bad posture made him look obtuse.* The author writes that Hector's appearance does not convey intelligence. Therefore, *obtuse* must mean unintelligent. Here is another example: *Despite the horrible weather, we were beatific about our trip to Alaska.* The word *despite* indicates that the speaker's feelings were at odds with the weather. Since the weather is described as *horrible*, then *beatific* must mean something positive.

SUBSTITUTION TO FIND MEANING

In some cases, there will be very few contextual clues to help a reader define the meaning of an unfamiliar word. When this happens, one strategy that readers may employ is **substitution**. A good reader will brainstorm some possible synonyms for the given word, and he or she will substitute these words into the sentence. If the sentence and the surrounding passage continue to make sense, then the substitution has revealed at least some information about the unfamiliar word. Consider the sentence: *Frank's admonition rang in her ears as she climbed the mountain.* A reader unfamiliar with *admonition* might come up with some substitutions like *vow*, *promise*, *advice*, *complaint*, or *compliment*. All of these words make general sense of the sentence, though their meanings are diverse. However, this process has suggested that an admonition is some sort of message. The substitution strategy is rarely able to pinpoint a precise definition, but this process can be effective as a last resort.

Occasionally, you will be able to define an unfamiliar word by looking at the descriptive words in the context. Consider the following sentence: *Fred dragged the recalcitrant boy kicking and screaming up the stairs.* The words *dragged*, *kicking*, and *screaming* all suggest that the boy does not want to go up the stairs. The reader may assume that *recalcitrant* means something like unwilling or protesting. In this example, an unfamiliar adjective was identified.

Additionally, using description to define an unfamiliar noun is a common practice compared to unfamiliar adjectives, as in this sentence: *Don's wrinkled frown and constantly shaking fist identified him as a curmudgeon of the first order.* Don is described as having a *wrinkled frown and constantly shaking fist*, suggesting that a *curmudgeon* must be a grumpy person. Contrasts do not always provide detailed information about the unfamiliar word, but they at least give the reader some clues.

WORDS WITH MULTIPLE MEANINGS

When a word has more than one meaning, readers can have difficulty determining how the word is being used in a given sentence. For instance, the verb *cleave*, can mean either *join* or *separate*. When readers come upon this word, they will have to select the definition that makes the most sense. Consider the following sentence: *Hermione's knife cleaved the bread cleanly.* Since a knife cannot join bread together, the word must indicate separation. A slightly more difficult example would be the sentence: *The birds cleaved to one another as they flew from the oak tree.* Immediately, the presence of the words *to one another* should suggest that in this sentence *cleave* is being used to mean *join*. Discovering the intent of a word with multiple meanings requires the same tricks as defining an unknown word: look for contextual clues and evaluate the substituted words.

CONTEXT CLUES TO HELP DETERMINE MEANINGS OF WORDS

If readers simply bypass unknown words, they can reach unclear conclusions about what they read. However, looking for the definition of every unfamiliar word in the dictionary can slow their reading progress. Moreover, the dictionary may list multiple definitions for a word, so readers must search the word's context for meaning. Hence context is important to new vocabulary regardless of reader methods. Four types of context clues are examples, definitions, descriptive words, and opposites. Authors may use a certain word, and then follow it with several different examples of what it describes. Sometimes authors actually supply a definition of a word they use, which is especially true in informational and technical texts. Authors may use descriptive words that elaborate upon a vocabulary word they just used. Authors may also use opposites with negation that help define meaning.

EXAMPLES AND DEFINITIONS

An author may use a word and then give examples that illustrate its meaning. Consider this text: "Teachers who do not know how to use sign language can help students who are deaf or hard of hearing understand certain instructions by using gestures instead, like pointing their fingers to indicate which direction to look or go; holding up a hand, palm outward, to indicate stopping; holding the hands flat, palms up, curling a finger toward oneself in a beckoning motion to indicate 'come here'; or curling all fingers toward oneself repeatedly to indicate 'come on', 'more', or 'continue.'" The author of this text has used the word "gestures" and then followed it with examples, so a reader unfamiliar with the word could deduce from the examples that "gestures" means "hand motions." Readers can find examples by looking for signal words "for example," "for instance," "like," "such as," and "e.g."

While readers sometimes have to look for definitions of unfamiliar words in a dictionary or do some work to determine a word's meaning from its surrounding context, at other times an author may make it easier for readers by defining certain words. For example, an author may write, "The company did not have sufficient capital, that is, available money, to continue operations." The author defined "capital" as "available money," and heralded the definition with the phrase "that is." Another way that authors supply word definitions is with appositives. Rather than being introduced by a signal phrase like "that is," "namely," or "meaning," an appositive comes after the vocabulary word it defines and is enclosed within two commas. For example, an author may write, "The Indians introduced the Pilgrims to pemmican, cakes they made of lean meat dried and mixed with fat, which proved greatly beneficial to keep settlers from starving while trapping." In this example, the appositive phrase following "pemmican" and preceding "which" defines the word "pemmican."

DESCRIPTIONS

When readers encounter a word they do not recognize in a text, the author may expand on that word to illustrate it better. While the author may do this to make the prose more picturesque and vivid, the reader can also take advantage of this description to provide context clues to the meaning of the unfamiliar word. For example, an author may write, "The man sitting next to me on the airplane was obese. His shirt stretched across his vast expanse of flesh, strained almost to bursting." The descriptive second sentence elaborates on and helps to define the previous sentence's word "obese" to mean extremely fat. A reader unfamiliar with the word "repugnant" can decipher its meaning through an author's accompanying description: "The way the child grimaced and shuddered as he swallowed the medicine showed that its taste was particularly repugnant."

OPPOSITES

Text authors sometimes introduce a contrasting or opposing idea before or after a concept they present. They may do this to emphasize or heighten the idea they present by contrasting it with something that is the reverse. However, readers can also use these context clues to understand familiar words. For example, an author may write, "Our conversation was not cheery. We sat and talked very solemnly about his experience and a number of similar events." The reader who is not familiar with the word "solemnly" can deduce by the author's preceding use of "not cheery" that "solemn" means the opposite of cheery or happy, so it must mean serious or sad. Or if someone writes, "Don't condemn his entire project because you couldn't find anything good to say about it," readers unfamiliar with "condemn" can understand from the sentence structure that it means the opposite of saying anything good, so it must mean reject, dismiss, or disapprove. "Entire" adds another context clue, meaning total or complete rejection.

SYNTAX TO DETERMINE PART OF SPEECH AND MEANINGS OF WORDS

Syntax refers to sentence structure and word order. Suppose that a reader encounters an unfamiliar word when reading a text. To illustrate, consider an invented word like "splunch." If this word is used in a sentence like "Please splunch that ball to me," the reader can assume from syntactic context that "splunch" is a verb. We would not use a noun, adjective, adverb, or preposition with the object "that ball," and the prepositional phrase "to me" further indicates "splunch" represents an action. However, in the sentence, "Please hand that splunch to me," the reader can assume that "splunch" is a noun. Demonstrative adjectives like "that" modify nouns. Also, we hand someone some*thing*—a thing being a noun; we do not hand someone a verb, adjective, or adverb. Some sentences contain further clues. For example, from the sentence, "The princess wore the glittering splunch on her head," the reader can deduce that it is a crown, tiara, or something similar from the syntactic context, without knowing the word.

SYNTAX TO INDICATE DIFFERENT MEANINGS OF SIMILAR SENTENCES

The syntax, or structure, of a sentence affords grammatical cues that aid readers in comprehending the meanings of words, phrases, and sentences in the texts that they read. Seemingly minor differences in how the words or phrases in a sentence are ordered can make major differences in meaning. For example, two sentences can use exactly the same words but have different meanings based on the word order:

- "The man with a broken arm sat in a chair."
- "The man sat in a chair with a broken arm."

While both sentences indicate that a man sat in a chair, differing syntax indicates whether the man's or chair's arm was broken.

DETERMINING MEANING OF PHRASES AND PARAGRAPHS

Like unknown words, the meanings of phrases, paragraphs, and entire works can also be difficult to discern. Each of these can be better understood with added context. However, for larger groups of words, more context is needed. Unclear phrases are similar to unclear words, and the same methods can be used to understand their meaning. However, it is also important to consider how the individual words in the phrase work together. Paragraphs are a bit more complicated. Just as words must be compared to other words in a sentence, paragraphs must be compared to other paragraphs in a composition or a section.

DETERMINING MEANING IN VARIOUS TYPES OF COMPOSITIONS

To understand the meaning of an entire composition, the type of composition must be considered. **Expository writing** is generally organized so that each paragraph focuses on explaining one idea, or part of an idea, and its relevance. **Persuasive writing** uses paragraphs for different purposes to organize the parts of the argument. **Unclear paragraphs** must be read in the context of the paragraphs around them for their meaning to be fully understood. The meaning of full texts can also be unclear at times. The purpose of composition is also important for understanding the meaning of a text. To quickly understand the broad meaning of a text, look to the introductory and concluding paragraphs. Fictional texts are different. Some fictional works have implicit meanings, but some do not. The target audience must be considered for understanding texts that do have an implicit meaning, as most children's fiction will clearly state any lessons or morals. For other fiction, the application of literary theories and criticism may be helpful for understanding the text.

ADDITIONAL RESOURCES FOR DETERMINING WORD MEANING AND USAGE

While these strategies are useful for determining the meaning of unknown words and phrases, sometimes additional resources are needed to properly use the terms in different contexts. Some words have multiple definitions, and some words are inappropriate in particular contexts or modes of writing. The following tools are helpful for understanding all meanings and proper uses for words and phrases.

- **Dictionaries** provide the meaning of a multitude of words in a language. Many dictionaries include additional information about each word, such as its etymology, its synonyms, or variations of the word.
- **Glossaries** are similar to dictionaries, as they provide the meanings of a variety of terms. However, while dictionaries typically feature an extensive list of words and comprise an entire publication, glossaries are often included at the end of a text and only include terms and definitions that are relevant to the text they follow.

- **Spell Checkers** are used to detect spelling errors in typed text. Some spell checkers may also detect the misuse of plural or singular nouns, verb tenses, or capitalization. While spell checkers are a helpful tool, they are not always reliable or attuned to the author's intent, so it is important to review the spell checker's suggestions before accepting them.
- **Style Manuals** are guidelines on the preferred punctuation, format, and grammar usage according to different fields or organizations. For example, the Associated Press Stylebook is a style guide often used for media writing. The guidelines within a style guide are not always applicable across different contexts and usages, as the guidelines often cover grammatical or formatting situations that are not objectively correct or incorrect.

Figurative Language

LITERAL AND FIGURATIVE MEANING

When language is used **literally**, the words mean exactly what they say and nothing more. When language is used **figuratively**, the words mean something beyond their literal meaning. For example, "The weeping willow tree has long, trailing branches and leaves" is a literal description. But "The weeping willow tree looks as if it is bending over and crying" is a figurative description—specifically, a **simile** or stated comparison. Another figurative language form is **metaphor**, or an implied comparison. A good example is the metaphor of a city, state, or city-state as a ship, and its governance as sailing that ship. Ancient Greek lyrical poet Alcaeus is credited with first using this metaphor, and ancient Greek tragedian Aeschylus then used it in *Seven Against Thebes,* and then Plato used it in the *Republic.*

FIGURES OF SPEECH

A **figure of speech** is a verbal expression whose meaning is figurative rather than literal. For example, the phrase "butterflies in the stomach" does not refer to actual butterflies in a person's stomach. It is a metaphor representing the fluttery feelings experienced when a person is nervous or excited—or when one "falls in love," which does not mean physically falling. "Hitting a sales target" does not mean physically hitting a target with arrows as in archery; it is a metaphor for meeting a sales quota. "Climbing the ladder of success" metaphorically likens advancing in one's career to ascending ladder rungs. Similes, such as "light as a feather" (meaning very light, not a feather's actual weight), and hyperbole, like "I'm starving/freezing/roasting," are also figures of speech. Figures of speech are often used and crafted for emphasis, freshness of expression, or clarity.

> **Review Video: Figures of Speech**
> Visit mometrix.com/academy and enter code: 111295

FIGURATIVE LANGUAGE

Figurative language extends past the literal meanings of words. It offers readers new insight into the people, things, events, and subjects covered in a work of literature. Figurative language also enables readers to feel they are sharing the authors' experiences. It can stimulate the reader's senses, make comparisons that readers find intriguing or even startling, and enable readers to view the world in different ways. When looking for figurative language, it is important to consider the context of the sentence or situation. Phrases that appear out of place or make little sense when read literally are likely instances of figurative language. Once figurative language has been recognized, context is also important to determining the type of figurative language being used and its function. For example, when a comparison is being made, a metaphor or simile is likely being used. This means the comparison may emphasize or create irony through the things being compared. Seven specific types of figurative language include: alliteration, onomatopoeia, personification, imagery, similes, metaphors, and hyperbole.

> **Review Video: Figurative Language**
> Visit mometrix.com/academy and enter code: 584902

ALLITERATION AND ONOMATOPOEIA

Alliteration describes a series of words beginning with the same sounds. **Onomatopoeia** uses words imitating the sounds of things they name or describe. For example, in his poem "Come Down, O Maid," Alfred Tennyson writes of "The moan of doves in immemorial elms, / And murmuring of innumerable bees." The word "moan" sounds like some sounds doves make, "murmuring" represents the sounds of bees buzzing. Onomatopoeia also includes words that are simply meant to represent sounds, such as "meow," "kaboom," and "whoosh."

PERSONIFICATION

Another type of figurative language is **personification**. This is describing a non-human thing, like an animal or an object, as if it were human. The general intent of personification is to describe things in a manner that will be comprehensible to readers. When an author states that a tree *groans* in the wind, he or she does not mean that the tree is emitting a low, pained sound from a mouth. Instead, the author means that the tree is making a noise similar to a human groan. Of course, this personification establishes a tone of sadness or suffering. A different tone would be established if the author said that the tree was *swaying* or *dancing*. Alfred Tennyson's poem "The Eagle" uses all of these types of figurative language: "He clasps the crag with crooked hands." Tennyson used alliteration, repeating /k/ and /kr/ sounds. These hard-sounding consonants reinforce the imagery, giving visual and tactile impressions of the eagle.

SIMILES AND METAPHORS

Similes are stated comparisons using "like" or "as." Similes can be used to stimulate readers' imaginations and appeal to their senses. Because a simile includes *like* or *as,* the device creates more space between the description and the thing being described than a metaphor does. If an author says that *a house was like a shoebox*, then the tone is different than the author saying that the house *was* a shoebox. Authors will choose between a metaphor and a simile depending on their intended tone.

Similes also help compare fictional characters to well-known objects or experiences, so the reader can better relate to them. William Wordsworth's poem about "Daffodils" begins, "I wandered lonely as a cloud." This simile compares his loneliness to that of a cloud. It is also personification, giving a cloud the human quality loneliness. In his novel *Lord Jim* (1900), Joseph Conrad writes in Chapter 33, "I would have given anything for the power to soothe her frail soul, tormenting itself in its invincible ignorance like a small bird beating about the cruel wires of a cage." Conrad uses the word "like" to compare the girl's soul to a small bird. His description of the bird beating at the cage shows the similar helplessness of the girl's soul to gain freedom.

A **metaphor** is a type of figurative language in which the writer equates something with another thing that is not particularly similar, instead of using *like* or *as*. For instance, *the bird was an arrow arcing through the sky*. In this sentence, the arrow is serving as a metaphor for the bird. The point of a metaphor is to encourage the reader to consider the item being described in a *different way*. Let's continue with this metaphor for a flying bird. You are asked to envision the bird's flight as being similar to the arc of an arrow. So, you imagine the flight to be swift and bending. Metaphors are a way for the author to describe an item *without being direct and obvious*. This literary device is a lyrical and suggestive way of providing information. Note that the reference for a metaphor will not always be mentioned explicitly by the author. Consider the following description of a forest in winter: *Swaying skeletons reached for the sky and groaned as the wind blew through them.* In this example, the author is using *skeletons* as a metaphor for leafless trees. This metaphor creates a spooky tone while inspiring the reader's imagination.

LITERARY EXAMPLES OF METAPHOR

A **metaphor** is an implied comparison, i.e., it compares something to something else without using "like", "as", or other comparative words. For example, in "The Tyger" (1794), William Blake writes, "Tyger Tyger, burning bright, / In the forests of the night." Blake compares the tiger to a flame not by saying it is like a fire, but by simply describing it as "burning." Henry Wadsworth Longfellow's poem "O Ship of State" (1850) uses an extended metaphor by referring consistently throughout the entire poem to the state, union, or republic as a seagoing vessel, referring to its keel, mast, sail, rope, anchors, and to its braving waves, rocks, gale, tempest, and "false lights on the shore." Within the extended metaphor, Wordsworth uses a specific metaphor: "the anchors of thy hope!"

TED HUGHES' ANIMAL METAPHORS

Ted Hughes frequently used animal metaphors in his poetry. In "The Thought Fox," a model of concise, structured beauty, Hughes characterizes the poet's creative process with succinct, striking imagery of an idea entering his head like a wild fox. Repeating "loneliness" in the first two stanzas emphasizes the poet's lonely work: "Something else is alive / Beside the clock's loneliness." He treats an idea's arrival as separate from himself. Three stanzas detail in vivid images a fox's approach from the outside winter forest at starless midnight—its nose, "Cold, delicately" touching twigs and leaves; "neat" paw prints in snow; "bold" body; brilliant green eyes; and self-contained, focused progress—"Till, with a sudden sharp hot stink of fox," he metaphorically depicts poetic inspiration as the fox's physical entry into "the dark hole of the head." Hughes ends by summarizing his vision of a poet as an interior, passive idea recipient, with the outside world unchanged: "The window is starless still; the clock ticks, / The page is printed."

> **Review Video: Metaphors in Writing**
> Visit mometrix.com/academy and enter code: 133295

HYPERBOLE

Hyperbole is excessive exaggeration used for humor or emphasis rather than for literal meaning. For example, in *To Kill a Mockingbird*, Harper Lee wrote, "People moved slowly then. There was no hurry, for there was nowhere to go, nothing to buy and no money to buy it with, nothing to see outside the boundaries of Maycomb County." This was not literally true; Lee exaggerates the scarcity of these things for emphasis. In "Old Times on the Mississippi," Mark Twain wrote, "I… could have hung my hat on my eyes, they stuck out so far." This is not literal, but makes his description vivid and funny. In his poem "As I Walked Out One Evening", W. H. Auden wrote, "I'll love you, dear, I'll love you / Till China and Africa meet, / And the river jumps over the mountain / And the salmon sing in the street." He used things not literally possible to emphasize the duration of his love.

> **Review Video: Hyperbole and Understatement**
> Visit mometrix.com/academy and enter code: 308470

LITERARY IRONY

In literature, irony demonstrates the opposite of what is said or done. The three types of irony are **verbal irony**, **situational irony**, and **dramatic irony**. Verbal irony uses words opposite to the meaning. Sarcasm may use verbal irony. One common example is describing something that is confusing as "clear as mud." For example, in his 1986 movie *Hannah and Her Sisters,* author, director, and actor Woody Allen says to his character's date, "I had a great evening; it was like the Nuremburg Trials." Notice these employ similes. In situational irony, what happens contrasts with what was expected. O. Henry's short story *The Gift of the Magi* uses situational irony: a husband and wife each sacrifice their most prized possession to buy each other a Christmas present. The irony is that she sells her long hair to buy him a watch fob, while he sells his heirloom pocket-watch to buy her the jeweled combs for her hair she had long wanted; in the end, neither of them can use their gifts. In dramatic irony, narrative informs audiences of more than its characters know. For example, in *Romeo and Juliet,* the audience is made aware that Juliet is only asleep, while Romeo believes her to be dead, which then leads to Romeo's death.

> **Review Video: <u>What is the Definition of Irony?</u>**
> Visit mometrix.com/academy and enter code: 374204

IDIOMS

Idioms create comparisons, and often take the form of similes or metaphors. Idioms are always phrases and are understood to have a meaning that is different from its individual words' literal meaning. For example, "break a leg" is a common idiom that is used to wish someone luck or tell them to perform well. Literally, the phrase "break a leg" means to injure a person's leg, but the phrase takes on a different meaning when used as an idiom. Another example is "call it a day," which means to temporarily stop working on a task, or find a stopping point, rather than literally referring to something as "a day." Many idioms are associated with a region or group. For example, an idiom commonly used in the American South is "'til the cows come home." This phrase is often used to indicate that something will take or may last for a very long time, but not that it will literally last until the cows return to where they reside.

Reading Comprehension

UNDERSTANDING A PASSAGE

One of the most important skills in reading comprehension is the identification of **topics** and **main ideas**. There is a subtle difference between these two features. The topic is the subject of a text (i.e., what the text is all about). The main idea, on the other hand, is the most important point being made by the author. The topic is usually expressed in a few words at the most while the main idea often needs a full sentence to be completely defined. As an example, a short passage might be written on the topic of penguins, and the main idea could be written as *Penguins are different from other birds in many ways*. In most nonfiction writing, the topic and the main idea will be **stated directly** and often appear in a sentence at the very beginning or end of the text. When being tested on an understanding of the author's topic, you may be able to skim the passage for the general idea by reading only the first sentence of each paragraph. A body paragraph's first sentence is often— but not always—the main **topic sentence** which gives you a summary of the content in the paragraph.

However, there are cases in which the reader must figure out an **unstated** topic or main idea. In these instances, you must read every sentence of the text and try to come up with an overarching idea that is supported by each of those sentences.

Note: The main idea should not be confused with the thesis statement. While the main idea gives a brief, general summary of a text, the thesis statement provides a **specific perspective** on an issue that the author supports with evidence.

> **Review Video: Topics and Main Ideas**
> Visit mometrix.com/academy and enter code: 407801

Supporting details are smaller pieces of evidence that provide backing for the main point. In order to show that a main idea is correct or valid, an author must add details that prove their point. All texts contain details, but they are only classified as supporting details when they serve to reinforce some larger point. Supporting details are most commonly found in informative and persuasive texts. In some cases, they will be clearly indicated with terms like *for example* or *for instance*, or they will be enumerated with terms like *first*, *second*, and *last*. However, you need to be prepared for texts that do not contain those indicators. As a reader, you should consider whether the author's supporting details really back up his or her main point. Details can be factual and correct, yet they may not be **relevant** to the author's point. Conversely, details can be relevant, but be ineffective because they are based on opinion or assertions that cannot be proven.

> **Review Video: Supporting Details**
> Visit mometrix.com/academy and enter code: 396297

An example of a main idea is: *Giraffes live in the Serengeti of Africa*. A supporting detail about giraffes could be: *A giraffe in this region benefits from a long neck by reaching twigs and leaves on tall trees*. The main idea gives the general idea that the text is about giraffes. The supporting detail gives a specific fact about how the giraffes eat.

ORGANIZATION OF THE TEXT

The way a text is organized can help readers understand the author's intent and his or her conclusions. There are various ways to organize a text, and each one has a purpose and use. Usually, authors will organize information logically in a passage so the reader can follow and locate the

information within the text. However, since not all passages are written with the same logical structure, you need to be familiar with several different types of passage structure.

> **Review Video: <u>Organizational Methods to Structure Text</u>**
> Visit mometrix.com/academy and enter code: 606263
>
> **Review Video: <u>Sequence of Events in a Story</u>**
> Visit mometrix.com/academy and enter code: 807512

CHRONOLOGICAL

When using **chronological** order, the author presents information in the order that it happened. For example, biographies are typically written in chronological order. The subject's birth and childhood are presented first, followed by their adult life, and lastly the events leading up to the person's death.

CAUSE AND EFFECT

One of the most common text structures is **cause and effect**. A **cause** is an act or event that makes something happen, and an **effect** is the thing that happens as a result of the cause. A cause-and-effect relationship is not always explicit, but there are some terms in English that signal causes, such as *since*, *because*, and *due to*. Furthermore, terms that signal effects include *consequently, therefore, this leads to*. As an example, consider the sentence *Because the sky was clear, Ron did not bring an umbrella*. The cause is the clear sky, and the effect is that Ron did not bring an umbrella. However, readers may find that sometimes the cause-and-effect relationship will not be clearly noted. For instance, the sentence *He was late and missed the meeting* does not contain any signaling words, but the sentence still contains a cause (he was late) and an effect (he missed the meeting).

> **Review Video: <u>Cause and Effect</u>**
> Visit mometrix.com/academy and enter code: 868099

MULTIPLE EFFECTS

Be aware of the possibility for a single cause to have **multiple effects.** (e.g., *Single cause*: Because you left your homework on the table, your dog engulfed the assignment. *Multiple effects*: As a result, you receive a failing grade, your parents do not allow you to go out with your friends, you miss out on the new movie, and one of your classmates spoils it for you before you have another chance to watch it).

MULTIPLE CAUSES

Also, there is the possibility for a single effect to have **multiple causes.** (e.g., *Single effect*: Alan has a fever. *Multiple causes*: An unexpected cold front came through the area, and Alan forgot to take his multi-vitamin to avoid getting sick.) Additionally, an effect can in turn be the cause of another effect, in what is known as a cause-and-effect chain. (e.g., As a result of her disdain for procrastination, Lynn prepared for her exam. This led to her passing her test with high marks. Hence, her resume was accepted and her application was approved.)

CAUSE AND EFFECT IN PERSUASIVE ESSAYS

Persuasive essays, in which an author tries to make a convincing argument and change the minds of readers, usually include cause-and-effect relationships. However, these relationships should not always be taken at face value. Frequently, an author will assume a cause or take an effect for granted. To read a persuasive essay effectively, readers need to judge the cause-and-effect relationships that the author is presenting. For instance, imagine an author wrote the following: *The*

114

parking deck has been unprofitable because people would prefer to ride their bikes. The relationship is clear: the cause is that people prefer to ride their bikes, and the effect is that the parking deck has been unprofitable. However, readers should consider whether this argument is conclusive. Perhaps there are other reasons for the failure of the parking deck: a down economy, excessive fees, etc. Too often, authors present causal relationships as if they are fact rather than opinion. Readers should be on the alert for these dubious claims.

PROBLEM-SOLUTION

Some nonfiction texts are organized to **present a problem** followed by a solution. For this type of text, the problem is often explained before the solution is offered. In some cases, as when the problem is well known, the solution may be introduced briefly at the beginning. Other passages may focus on the solution, and the problem will be referenced only occasionally. Some texts will outline multiple solutions to a problem, leaving readers to choose among them. If the author has an interest or an allegiance to one solution, he or she may fail to mention or describe accurately some of the other solutions. Readers should be careful of the author's agenda when reading a problem-solution text. Only by understanding the author's perspective and interests can one develop a proper judgment of the proposed solution.

COMPARE AND CONTRAST

Many texts follow the **compare-and-contrast** model in which the similarities and differences between two ideas or things are explored. Analysis of the similarities between ideas is called **comparison**. In an ideal comparison, the author places ideas or things in an equivalent structure, i.e., the author presents the ideas in the same way. If an author wants to show the similarities between cricket and baseball, then he or she may do so by summarizing the equipment and rules for each game. Be mindful of the similarities as they appear in the passage and take note of any differences that are mentioned. Often, these small differences will only reinforce the more general similarity.

> **Review Video: Compare and Contrast Essays**
> Visit mometrix.com/academy and enter code: 798319

Thinking critically about ideas and conclusions can seem like a daunting task. One way to ease this task is to understand the basic elements of ideas and writing techniques. Looking at the ways different ideas relate to each other can be a good way for readers to begin their analysis. For instance, sometimes authors will write about two ideas that are in opposition to each other. Or, one author will provide his or her ideas on a topic, and another author may respond in opposition. The analysis of these opposing ideas is known as **contrast**. Contrast is often marred by the author's obvious partiality to one of the ideas. A discerning reader will be put off by an author who does not engage in a fair fight. In an analysis of opposing ideas, both ideas should be presented in clear and reasonable terms. If the author does prefer a side, you need to read carefully to determine the areas where the author shows or avoids this preference. In an analysis of opposing ideas, you should proceed through the passage by marking the major differences point by point with an eye that is looking for an explanation of each side's view. For instance, in an analysis of capitalism and communism, there is an importance in outlining each side's view on labor, markets, prices, personal responsibility, etc. Additionally, as you read through the passages, you should note whether the opposing views present each side in a similar manner.

SEQUENCE

Readers must be able to identify a text's **sequence**, or the order in which things happen. Often, when the sequence is very important to the author, the text is indicated with signal words like *first,* *then*, *next*, and *last*. However, a sequence can be merely implied and must be noted by the reader. Consider the sentence *He walked through the garden and gave water and fertilizer to the plants*. Clearly, the man did not walk through the garden before he collected water and fertilizer for the plants. So, the implied sequence is that he first collected water, then he collected fertilizer, next he walked through the garden, and last he gave water or fertilizer as necessary to the plants. Texts do not always proceed in an orderly sequence from first to last. Sometimes they begin at the end and start over at the beginning. As a reader, you can enhance your understanding of the passage by taking brief notes to clarify the sequence.

MAKING CONNECTIONS TO ENHANCE COMPREHENSION

Reading involves thinking. For good comprehension, readers make **text-to-self**, **text-to-text**, and **text-to-world connections**. Making connections helps readers understand text better and predict what might occur next based on what they already know, such as how characters in the story feel or what happened in another text. Text-to-self connections with the reader's life and experiences make literature more personally relevant and meaningful to readers. Readers can make connections before, during, and after reading—including whenever the text reminds them of something similar they have encountered in life or other texts. The genre, setting, characters, plot elements, literary structure and devices, and themes an author uses allow a reader to make connections to other works of literature or to people and events in their own lives. Venn diagrams and other graphic organizers help visualize connections. Readers can also make double-entry notes: key content, ideas, events, words, and quotations on one side, and the connections with these on the other.

SUMMARIZING LITERATURE TO SUPPORT COMPREHENSION

When reading literature, especially demanding works, **summarizing** helps readers identify important information and organize it in their minds. They can also identify themes, problems, and solutions, and can sequence the story. Readers can summarize before, during, and after they read. They should use their own words, as they do when describing a personal event or giving directions. Previewing a text's organization before reading by examining the book cover, table of contents, and illustrations also aids summarizing. Making notes of key words and ideas in a graphic organizer while reading can benefit readers in the same way. Graphic organizers are another useful method; readers skim the text to determine main ideas and then narrow the list with the aid of the organizer. Unimportant details should be omitted in summaries. Summaries can be organized using description, problem-solution, comparison-contrast, sequence, main ideas, or cause-and-effect.

> **Review Video: Summarizing Text**
> Visit mometrix.com/academy and enter code: 172903

PARAPHRASING

Paraphrasing is another method that the reader can use to aid in comprehension. When paraphrasing, one puts what they have read into their own words by rephrasing what the author has written, or one "translates" all of what the author shared into their own words by including as many details as they can.

Making Predictions and Inferences

MAKING PREDICTIONS

When we read literature, **making predictions** about what will happen in the writing reinforces our purpose for reading and prepares us mentally. A **prediction** is a guess about what will happen next. Readers constantly make predictions based on what they have read and what they already know. We can make predictions before we begin reading and during our reading. Consider the following sentence: *Staring at the computer screen in shock, Kim blindly reached over for the brimming glass of water on the shelf to her side.* The sentence suggests that Kim is distracted, and that she is not looking at the glass that she is going to pick up. So, a reader might predict that Kim is going to knock over the glass. Of course, not every prediction will be accurate: perhaps Kim will pick the glass up cleanly. Nevertheless, the author has certainly created the expectation that the water might be spilled.

As we read on, we can test the accuracy of our predictions, revise them in light of additional reading, and confirm or refute our predictions. Predictions are always subject to revision as the reader acquires more information. A reader can make predictions by observing the title and illustrations; noting the structure, characters, and subject; drawing on existing knowledge relative to the subject; and asking "why" and "who" questions. Connecting reading to what we already know enables us to learn new information and construct meaning. For example, before third-graders read a book about Johnny Appleseed, they may start a KWL chart—a list of what they *Know*, what they *Want* to know or learn, and what they have *Learned* after reading. Activating existing background knowledge and thinking about the text before reading improves comprehension.

> **Review Video: Predictive Reading**
> Visit mometrix.com/academy and enter code: 437248

Test-taking tip: To respond to questions requiring future predictions, your answers should be based on evidence of past or present behavior and events.

EVALUATING PREDICTIONS

When making predictions, readers should be able to explain how they developed their prediction. One way readers can defend their thought process is by citing textual evidence. Textual evidence to evaluate reader predictions about literature includes specific synopses of the work, paraphrases of the work or parts of it, and direct quotations from the work. These references to the text must support the prediction by indicating, clearly or unclearly, what will happen later in the story. A text may provide these indications through literary devices such as foreshadowing. Foreshadowing is anything in a text that gives the reader a hint about what is to come by emphasizing the likelihood of an event or development. Foreshadowing can occur through descriptions, exposition, and dialogue. Foreshadowing in dialogue usually occurs when a character gives a warning or expresses a strong feeling that a certain event will occur. Foreshadowing can also occur through irony. However, unlike other forms of foreshadowing, the events that seem the most likely are the opposite of what actually happens. Instances of foreshadowing and irony can be summarized, paraphrased, or quoted to defend a reader's prediction.

> **Review Video: Textual Evidence for Predictions**
> Visit mometrix.com/academy and enter code: 261070

DRAWING CONCLUSIONS FROM INFERENCES

Inferences about literary text are logical conclusions that readers make based on their observations and previous knowledge. An inference is based on both what is found in a passage or a story and what is known from personal experience. For instance, a story may say that a character is frightened and can hear howling in the distance. Based on both what is in the text and personal knowledge, it is a logical conclusion that the character is frightened because he hears the sound of wolves. A good inference is supported by the information in a passage.

IMPLICIT AND EXPLICIT INFORMATION

By inferring, readers construct meanings from text that are personally relevant. By combining their own schemas or concepts and their background information pertinent to the text with what they read, readers interpret it according to both what the author has conveyed and their own unique perspectives. Inferences are different from **explicit information**, which is clearly stated in a passage. Authors do not always explicitly spell out every meaning in what they write; many meanings are implicit. Through inference, readers can comprehend implied meanings in the text, and also derive personal significance from it, making the text meaningful and memorable to them. Inference is a natural process in everyday life. When readers infer, they can draw conclusions about what the author is saying, predict what may reasonably follow, amend these predictions as they continue to read, interpret the import of themes, and analyze the characters' feelings and motivations through their actions.

EXAMPLE OF DRAWING CONCLUSIONS FROM INFERENCES

Read the excerpt and decide why Jana finally relaxed.

> Jana loved her job, but the work was very demanding. She had trouble relaxing. She called a friend, but she still thought about work. She ordered a pizza, but eating it did not help. Then, her kitten jumped on her lap and began to purr. Jana leaned back and began to hum a little tune. She felt better.

You can draw the conclusion that Jana relaxed because her kitten jumped on her lap. The kitten purred, and Jana leaned back and hummed a tune. Then she felt better. The excerpt does not explicitly say that this is the reason why she was able to relax. The text leaves the matter unclear, but the reader can infer or make a "best guess" that this is the reason she is relaxing. This is a logical conclusion based on the information in the passage. It is the best conclusion a reader can make based on the information he or she has read. Inferences are based on the information in a passage, but they are not directly stated in the passage.

Test-taking tip: While being tested on your ability to make correct inferences, you must look for **contextual clues**. An answer can be true, but not the best or most correct answer. The contextual clues will help you find the answer that is the **best answer** out of the given choices. Be careful in your reading to understand the context in which a phrase is stated. When asked for the implied meaning of a statement made in the passage, you should immediately locate the statement and read the **context** in which the statement was made. Also, look for an answer choice that has a similar phrase to the statement in question.

> **Review Video: Inference**
> Visit mometrix.com/academy and enter code: 379203
>
> **Review Video: How to Support a Conclusion**
> Visit mometrix.com/academy and enter code: 281653

Interactions with Texts

PURPOSES FOR WRITING

In order to be an effective reader, one must pay attention to the author's **position** and **purpose**. Even those texts that seem objective and impartial, like textbooks, have a position and bias. Readers need to take these positions into account when considering the author's message. When an author uses emotional language or clearly favors one side of an argument, his or her position is clear. However, the author's position may be evident not only in what he or she writes, but also in what he or she doesn't write. In a normal setting, a reader would want to review some other texts on the same topic in order to develop a view of the author's position. If this was not possible, then you would want to at least acquire some background about the author. However, since you are in the middle of an exam and the only source of information is the text, you should look for language and argumentation that seems to indicate a particular stance on the subject.

> **Review Video: Author's Position**
> Visit mometrix.com/academy and enter code: 827954

Usually, identifying the author's **purpose** is easier than identifying his or her position. In most cases, the author has no interest in hiding his or her purpose. A text that is meant to entertain, for instance, should be written to please the reader. Most narratives, or stories, are written to entertain, though they may also inform or persuade. Informative texts are easy to identify, while the most difficult purpose of a text to identify is persuasion because the author has an interest in making this purpose hard to detect. When a reader discovers that the author is trying to persuade, he or she should be skeptical of the argument. For this reason, persuasive texts often try to establish an entertaining tone and hope to amuse the reader into agreement. On the other hand, an informative tone may be implemented to create an appearance of authority and objectivity.

An author's purpose is evident often in the organization of the text (e.g., section headings in bold font points to an informative text). However, you may not have such organization available to you in your exam. Instead, if the author makes his or her main idea clear from the beginning, then the likely purpose of the text is to inform. If the author begins by making a claim and provides various arguments to support that claim, then the purpose is probably to persuade. If the author tells a story or wants to gain the reader's attention more than to push a particular point or deliver information, then his or her purpose is most likely to entertain. As a reader, you must judge authors on how well they accomplish their purpose. In other words, you need to consider the type of passage (e.g., technical, persuasive, etc.) that the author has written and if the author has followed the requirements of the passage type.

MAKING LOGICAL CONCLUSIONS ABOUT A PASSAGE

A reader should always be drawing conclusions from the text. Sometimes conclusions are **implied** from written information, and other times the information is **stated directly** within the passage. One should always aim to draw conclusions from information stated within a passage, rather than to draw them from mere implications. At times an author may provide some information and then describe a counterargument. Readers should be alert for direct statements that are subsequently rejected or weakened by the author. Furthermore, you should always read through the entire passage before drawing conclusions. Many readers are trained to expect the author's conclusions at either the beginning or the end of the passage, but many texts do not adhere to this format.

Drawing conclusions from information implied within a passage requires confidence on the part of the reader. **Implications** are things that the author does not state directly, but readers can assume

119

based on what the author does say. Consider the following passage: *I stepped outside and opened my umbrella. By the time I got to work, the cuffs of my pants were soaked.* The author never states that it is raining, but this fact is clearly implied. Conclusions based on implication must be well supported by the text. In order to draw a solid conclusion, readers should have **multiple pieces of evidence**. If readers have only one piece, they must be assured that there is no other possible explanation than their conclusion. A good reader will be able to draw many conclusions from information implied by the text, which will be a great help on the exam.

DRAWING CONCLUSIONS

A common type of inference that a reader has to make is **drawing a conclusion**. The reader makes this conclusion based on the information provided within a text. Certain facts are included to help a reader come to a specific conclusion. For example, a story may open with a man trudging through the snow on a cold winter day, dragging a sled behind him. The reader can logically **infer** from the setting of the story that the man is wearing heavy winter clothes in order to stay warm. Information is implied based on the setting of a story, which is why **setting** is an important element of the text. If the same man in the example was trudging down a beach on a hot summer day, dragging a surf board behind him, the reader would assume that the man is not wearing heavy clothes. The reader makes inferences based on their own experiences and the information presented to them in the story.

Test-taking tip: When asked to identify a conclusion that may be drawn, look for critical "hedge" phrases, such as *likely*, *may*, *can*, and *will often*, among many others. When you are being tested on this knowledge, remember the question that writers insert into these hedge phrases to cover every possibility. Often an answer will be wrong simply because there is no room for exception. Extreme positive or negative answers (such as always or never) are usually not correct. When answering these questions, the reader **should not** use any outside knowledge that is not gathered directly or reasonably inferred from the passage. Correct answers can be derived straight from the passage.

EXAMPLE

Read the following sentence from *Little Women* by Louisa May Alcott and draw a conclusion based upon the information presented:

> *You know the reason Mother proposed not having any presents this Christmas was because it is going to be a hard winter for everyone; and she thinks we ought not to spend money for pleasure, when our men are suffering so in the army.*

Based on the information in the sentence, the reader can conclude, or **infer**, that the men are away at war while the women are still at home. The pronoun *our* gives a clue to the reader that the character is speaking about men she knows. In addition, the reader can assume that the character is speaking to a brother or sister, since the term "Mother" is used by the character while speaking to another person. The reader can also come to the conclusion that the characters celebrate Christmas, since it is mentioned in the **context** of the sentence. In the sentence, the mother is presented as an unselfish character who is opinionated and thinks about the wellbeing of other people.

COMPARING TWO STORIES

When presented with two different stories, there will be **similarities** and **differences** between the two. A reader needs to make a list, or other graphic organizer, of the points presented in each story. Once the reader has written down the main point and supporting points for each story, the two sets of ideas can be compared. The reader can then present each idea and show how it is the same or different in the other story. This is called **comparing and contrasting ideas**.

The reader can compare ideas by stating, for example: "In Story 1, the author believes that humankind will one day land on Mars, whereas in Story 2, the author believes that Mars is too far away for humans to ever step foot on." Note that the two viewpoints are different in each story that the reader is comparing. A reader may state that: "Both stories discussed the likelihood of humankind landing on Mars." This statement shows how the viewpoint presented in both stories is based on the same topic, rather than how each viewpoint is different. The reader will complete a comparison of two stories with a conclusion.

> **Review Video: Comparing Two Stories**
> Visit mometrix.com/academy and enter code: 833765

OUTLINING A PASSAGE

As an aid to drawing conclusions, **outlining** the information contained in the passage should be a familiar skill to readers. An effective outline will reveal the structure of the passage and will lead to solid conclusions. An effective outline will have a title that refers to the basic subject of the text, though the title does not need to restate the main idea. In most outlines, the main idea will be the first major section. Each major idea in the passage will be established as the head of a category. For instance, the most common outline format calls for the main ideas of the passage to be indicated with Roman numerals. In an effective outline of this kind, each of the main ideas will be represented by a Roman numeral and none of the Roman numerals will designate minor details or secondary ideas. Moreover, all supporting ideas and details should be placed in the appropriate place on the outline. An outline does not need to include every detail listed in the text, but it should feature all of those that are central to the argument or message. Each of these details should be listed under the corresponding main idea.

> **Review Video: Outlining**
> Visit mometrix.com/academy and enter code: 584445

USING GRAPHIC ORGANIZERS

Ideas from a text can also be organized using **graphic organizers**. A graphic organizer is a way to simplify information and take key points from the text. A graphic organizer such as a timeline may have an event listed for a corresponding date on the timeline, while an outline may have an event listed under a key point that occurs in the text. Each reader needs to create the type of graphic organizer that works the best for him or her in terms of being able to recall information from a story. Examples include a spider-map, which takes a main idea from the story and places it in a bubble with supporting points branching off the main idea. An outline is useful for diagramming the main and supporting points of the entire story, and a Venn diagram compares and contrasts characteristics of two or more ideas.

> **Review Video: Graphic Organizers**
> Visit mometrix.com/academy and enter code: 665513

121

SUMMARIZING

A helpful tool is the ability to **summarize** the information that you have read in a paragraph or passage format. This process is similar to creating an effective outline. First, a summary should accurately define the main idea of the passage, though the summary does not need to explain this main idea in exhaustive detail. The summary should continue by laying out the most important supporting details or arguments from the passage. All of the significant supporting details should be included, and none of the details included should be irrelevant or insignificant. Also, the summary should accurately report all of these details. Too often, the desire for brevity in a summary leads to the sacrifice of clarity or accuracy. Summaries are often difficult to read because they omit all of the graceful language, digressions, and asides that distinguish great writing. However, an effective summary should communicate the same overall message as the original text.

EVALUATING A PASSAGE

It is important to understand the logical conclusion of the ideas presented in an informational text. **Identifying a logical conclusion** can help you determine whether you agree with the writer or not. Coming to this conclusion is much like making an inference: the approach requires you to combine the information given by the text with what you already know and make a logical conclusion. If the author intended for the reader to draw a certain conclusion, then you can expect the author's argumentation and detail to be leading in that direction.

One way to approach the task of drawing conclusions is to make brief **notes** of all the points made by the author. When the notes are arranged on paper, they may clarify the logical conclusion. Another way to approach conclusions is to consider whether the reasoning of the author raises any pertinent questions. Sometimes you will be able to draw several conclusions from a passage. On occasion these will be conclusions that were never imagined by the author. Therefore, be aware that these conclusions must be **supported directly by the text**.

EVALUATION OF SUMMARIES

A summary of a literary passage is a condensation in the reader's own words of the passage's main points. Several guidelines can be used in evaluating a summary. The summary should be complete yet concise. It should be accurate, balanced, fair, neutral, and objective, excluding the reader's own opinions or reactions. It should reflect in similar proportion how much each point summarized was covered in the original passage. Summary writers should include tags of attribution, like "Macaulay argues that" to reference the original author whose ideas are represented in the summary. Summary writers should not overuse quotations; they should only quote central concepts or phrases they cannot precisely convey in words other than those of the original author. Another aspect of evaluating a summary is considering whether it can stand alone as a coherent, unified composition. In addition, evaluation of a summary should include whether its writer has cited the original source of the passage they have summarized so that readers can find it.

Language

Parts of Speech

THE EIGHT PARTS OF SPEECH
NOUNS

When you talk about a person, place, thing, or idea, you are talking about a **noun**. The two main types of nouns are **common** and **proper** nouns. Also, nouns can be abstract (i.e., general) or concrete (i.e., specific).

COMMON NOUNS

Common nouns are generic names for people, places, and things. Common nouns are not usually capitalized.

Examples of common nouns:

> *People*: boy, girl, worker, manager

> *Places*: school, bank, library, home

> *Things*: dog, cat, truck, car

PROPER NOUNS

Proper nouns name specific people, places, or things. All proper nouns are capitalized.

Examples of proper nouns:

> *People*: Abraham Lincoln, George Washington, Martin Luther King, Jr.

> *Places*: Los Angeles, California; New York; Asia

> *Things*: Statue of Liberty, Earth, Lincoln Memorial

Note: When referring to the planet that we live on, capitalize *Earth*. When referring to the dirt, rocks, or land, lowercase *earth*.

GENERAL AND SPECIFIC NOUNS

General nouns are the names of conditions or ideas. **Specific nouns** name people, places, and things that are understood by using your senses.

General nouns:

> *Condition*: beauty, strength

> *Idea*: truth, peace

Specific nouns:

People: baby, friend, father

Places: town, park, city hall

Things: rainbow, cough, apple, silk, gasoline

COLLECTIVE NOUNS

Collective nouns are the names for a group of people, places, or things that may act as a whole. The following are examples of collective nouns: *class, company, dozen, group, herd, team,* and *public.* Collective nouns usually require an article, which denotes the noun as being a single unit. For instance, a choir is a group of singers. Even though there are many singers in a choir, the word choir is grammatically treated as a single unit. If we refer to the members of the group, and not the group itself, it is no longer a collective noun.

Incorrect: The *choir are* going to compete nationally this year.

Correct: The *choir is* going to compete nationally this year.

Incorrect: The *members* of the choir *is* competing nationally this year.

Correct: The *members* of the choir *are* competing nationally this year.

PRONOUNS

Pronouns are words that are used to stand in for nouns. A pronoun may be classified as personal, intensive, relative, interrogative, demonstrative, indefinite, and reciprocal.

Personal: *Nominative* is the case for nouns and pronouns that are the subject of a sentence. *Objective* is the case for nouns and pronouns that are an object in a sentence. *Possessive* is the case for nouns and pronouns that show possession or ownership.

Singular

	Nominative	Objective	Possessive
First Person	I	me	my, mine
Second Person	you	you	your, yours
Third Person	he, she, it	him, her, it	his, her, hers, its

Plural

	Nominative	Objective	Possessive
First Person	we	us	our, ours
Second Person	you	you	your, yours
Third Person	they	them	their, theirs

Intensive: I myself, you yourself, he himself, she herself, the (thing) itself, we ourselves, you yourselves, they themselves

Relative: which, who, whom, whose

Interrogative: what, which, who, whom, whose

Demonstrative: this, that, these, those

Indefinite: all, any, each, everyone, either/neither, one, some, several

Reciprocal: each other, one another

> **Review Video: Nouns and Pronouns**
> Visit mometrix.com/academy and enter code: 312073

VERBS

If you want to write a sentence, then you need a verb. Without a verb, you have no sentence. The verb of a sentence indicates action or being. In other words, the verb shows something's action or state of being or the action that has been done to something.

TRANSITIVE AND INTRANSITIVE VERBS

A **transitive verb** is a verb whose action (e.g., drive, run, jump) indicates a receiver (e.g., car, dog, kangaroo). **Intransitive verbs** do not indicate a receiver of an action. In other words, the action of the verb does not point to a subject or object.

> **Transitive**: He plays the piano. | The piano was played by him.

> **Intransitive**: He plays. | John plays well.

A dictionary will tell you whether a verb is transitive or intransitive. Some verbs can be transitive and intransitive.

ACTION VERBS AND LINKING VERBS

Action verbs show what the subject is doing. In other words, an action verb shows action. Unlike most types of words, a single action verb, in the right context, can be an entire sentence. **Linking verbs** link the subject of a sentence to a noun or pronoun, or they link a subject with an adjective. You always need a verb if you want a complete sentence. However, linking verbs on their own cannot be a complete sentence.

Common linking verbs include *appear, be, become, feel, grow, look, seem, smell, sound,* and *taste*. However, any verb that shows a condition and connects to a noun, pronoun, or adjective that describes the subject of a sentence is a linking verb.

Action: He sings. | Run! | Go! | I talk with him every day. | She reads.

Linking:

> Incorrect: I am.

> Correct: I am John. | The roses smell lovely. | I feel tired.

Note: Some verbs are followed by words that look like prepositions, but they are a part of the verb and a part of the verb's meaning. These are known as phrasal verbs, and examples include *call off, look up,* and *drop off*.

> **Review Video: Action Verbs and Linking Verbs**
> Visit mometrix.com/academy and enter code: 743142

VOICE

Transitive verbs come in active or passive **voice**. If something does an action or is acted upon, then you will know whether a verb is active or passive. When the subject of the sentence is doing the action, the verb is in **active voice**. When the subject is acted upon, the verb is in **passive voice**.

Active: Jon drew the picture. (The subject *Jon* is doing the action of *drawing a picture*.)

Passive: The picture is drawn by Jon. (The subject *picture* is receiving the action from Jon.)

VERB TENSES

A verb **tense** shows the different form of a verb to point to the time of an action. The present and past tense are indicated by the verb's form. An action in the present, *I talk*, can change form for the past: *I talked*. However, for the other tenses, an auxiliary (i.e., helping) verb is needed to show the change in form. These helping verbs include *am, are, is | have, has, had | was, were, will* (or *shall*).

Present: I talk	Present perfect: I have talked
Past: I talked	Past perfect: I had talked
Future: I will talk	Future perfect: I will have talked

Present: The action happens at the current time.

Example: He *walks* to the store every morning.

To show that something is happening right now, use the progressive present tense: I *am walking*.

Past: The action happened in the past.

Example: He *walked* to the store an hour ago.

Future: The action is going to happen later.

Example: I *will walk* to the store tomorrow.

Present perfect: The action started in the past and continues into the present or took place previously at an unspecified time

Example: I *have walked* to the store three times today.

Past perfect: The second action happened in the past. The first action came before the second.

Example: Before I walked to the store (Action 2), I *had walked* to the library (Action 1).

Future perfect: An action that uses the past and the future. In other words, the action is complete before a future moment.

Example: When she comes for the supplies (future moment), I *will have walked* to the store (action completed before the future moment).

> **Review Video: Present Perfect, Past Perfect, and Future Perfect Verb Tenses**
> Visit mometrix.com/academy and enter code: 269472

CONJUGATING VERBS

When you need to change the form of a verb, you are **conjugating** a verb. The key forms of a verb are singular, present tense (dream); singular, past tense (dreamed); and the past participle (have dreamed). Note: the past participle needs a helping verb to make a verb tense. For example, I *have dreamed* of this day. The following tables demonstrate some of the different ways to conjugate a verb:

Singular

Tense	First Person	Second Person	Third Person
Present	I dream	You dream	He, she, it dreams
Past	I dreamed	You dreamed	He, she, it dreamed
Past Participle	I have dreamed	You have dreamed	He, she, it has dreamed

Plural

Tense	First Person	Second Person	Third Person
Present	We dream	You dream	They dream
Past	We dreamed	You dreamed	They dreamed
Past Participle	We have dreamed	You have dreamed	They have dreamed

MOOD

There are three **moods** in English: the indicative, the imperative, and the subjunctive.

The **indicative mood** is used for facts, opinions, and questions.

Fact: You can do this.

Opinion: I think that you can do this.

Question: Do you know that you can do this?

The **imperative** is used for orders or requests.

Order: You are going to do this!

Request: Will you do this for me?

The **subjunctive mood** is for wishes and statements that go against fact.

Wish: I wish that I were famous.

Statement against fact: If I were you, I would do this. (This goes against fact because I am not you. You have the chance to do this, and I do not have the chance.)

ADJECTIVES

An **adjective** is a word that is used to modify a noun or pronoun. An adjective answers a question: *Which one? What kind?* or *How many?* Usually, adjectives come before the words that they modify, but they may also come after a linking verb.

Which one? The *third* suit is my favorite.

What kind? This suit is *navy blue.*

How many? I am going to buy *four* pairs of socks to match the suit.

> **Review Video: Descriptive Text**
> Visit mometrix.com/academy and enter code: 174903

ARTICLES

Articles are adjectives that are used to distinguish nouns as definite or indefinite. **Definite** nouns are preceded by the article *the* and indicate a specific person, place, thing, or idea. **Indefinite** nouns are preceded by *a* or *an* and do not indicate a specific person, place, thing, or idea. *A, an,* and *the* are the only articles. Note: *An* comes before words that start with a vowel sound. For example, "Are you going to get an **u**mbrella?"

Definite: I lost *the* bottle that belongs to me.

Indefinite: Does anyone have *a* bottle to share?

> **Review Video: Function of Articles**
> Visit mometrix.com/academy and enter code: 449383

COMPARISON WITH ADJECTIVES

Some adjectives are relative and other adjectives are absolute. Adjectives that are **relative** can show the comparison between things. **Absolute** adjectives can also show comparison, but they do so in a different way. Let's say that you are reading two books. You think that one book is perfect, and the other book is not exactly perfect. It is not possible for one book to be more perfect than the other. Either you think that the book is perfect, or you think that the book is imperfect. In this case, perfect and imperfect are absolute adjectives.

Relative adjectives will show the different **degrees** of something or someone to something else or someone else. The three degrees of adjectives include positive, comparative, and superlative.

The **positive** degree is the normal form of an adjective.

Example: This work is *difficult.* | She is *smart.*

The **comparative** degree compares one person or thing to another person or thing.

Example: This work is *more difficult* than your work. | She is *smarter* than me.

128

The **superlative** degree compares more than two people or things.

Example: This is the *most difficult* work of my life. | She is the *smartest* lady in school.

ADVERBS

An **adverb** is a word that is used to **modify** a verb, adjective, or another adverb. Usually, adverbs answer one of these questions: *When? Where? How?* and *Why?* The negatives *not* and *never* are considered adverbs. Adverbs that modify adjectives or other adverbs **strengthen** or **weaken** the words that they modify.

Examples:

He walks *quickly* through the crowd.

The water flows *smoothly* on the rocks.

Note: Adverbs are usually indicated by the morpheme *-ly*, which has been added to the root word. For instance, *quick* can be made into an adverb by adding *-ly* to construct *quickly*. Some words that end in *-ly* do not follow this rule and can behave as other parts of speech. Examples of adjectives ending in *-ly* include: *early, friendly, holy, lonely, silly*, and *ugly*. To know if a word that ends in *-ly* is an adjective or adverb, check your dictionary. Also, while many adverbs end in *-ly*, you need to remember that not all adverbs end in *-ly*.

Examples:

He is *never* angry.

You walked *across* the bridge.

COMPARISON WITH ADVERBS

The rules for comparing adverbs are the same as the rules for adjectives.

The **positive** degree is the standard form of an adverb.

Example: He arrives *soon*. | She speaks *softly* to her friends.

The **comparative** degree compares one person or thing to another person or thing.

Example: He arrives *sooner* than Sarah. | She speaks *more softly* than him.

The **superlative** degree compares more than two people or things.

Example: He arrives *soonest* of the group. | She speaks the *most softly* of any of her friends.

PREPOSITIONS

A **preposition** is a word placed before a noun or pronoun that shows the relationship between an object and another word in the sentence.

Common prepositions:

about	before	during	on	under
after	beneath	for	over	until
against	between	from	past	up
among	beyond	in	through	with
around	by	of	to	within
at	down	off	toward	without

Examples:

The napkin is *in* the drawer.

The Earth rotates *around* the Sun.

The needle is *beneath* the haystack.

Can you find "me" *among* the words?

Review Video: <u>Prepositions</u>
Visit mometrix.com/academy and enter code: 946763

CONJUNCTIONS

Conjunctions join words, phrases, or clauses and they show the connection between the joined pieces. **Coordinating conjunctions** connect equal parts of sentences. **Correlative conjunctions** show the connection between pairs. **Subordinating conjunctions** join subordinate (i.e., dependent) clauses with independent clauses.

COORDINATING CONJUNCTIONS

The **coordinating conjunctions** include: *and, but, yet, or, nor, for,* and *so*

Examples:

The rock was small, *but* it was heavy.

She drove in the night, *and* he drove in the day.

CORRELATIVE CONJUNCTIONS

The **correlative conjunctions** are: *either...or | neither...nor | not only...but also*

Examples:

> *Either* you are coming *or* you are staying.

> He *not only* ran three miles *but also* swam 200 yards.

> **Review Video: Coordinating and Correlative Conjunctions**
> Visit mometrix.com/academy and enter code: 390329
>
> **Review Video: Adverb Equal Comparisons**
> Visit mometrix.com/academy and enter code: 231291

SUBORDINATING CONJUNCTIONS

Common **subordinating conjunctions** include:

after	since	whenever
although	so that	where
because	unless	wherever
before	until	whether
in order that	when	while

Examples:

> I am hungry *because* I did not eat breakfast.

> He went home *when* everyone left.

> **Review Video: Subordinating Conjunctions**
> Visit mometrix.com/academy and enter code: 958913

INTERJECTIONS

Interjections are words of exclamation (i.e., audible expression of great feeling) that are used alone or as a part of a sentence. Often, they are used at the beginning of a sentence for an introduction. Sometimes, they can be used in the middle of a sentence to show a change in thought or attitude.

> Common Interjections: Hey! | Oh, | Ouch! | Please! | Wow!

131

Agreement and Sentence Structure

SUBJECTS AND PREDICATES

SUBJECTS

The **subject** of a sentence names who or what the sentence is about. The subject may be directly stated in a sentence, or the subject may be the implied *you*. The **complete subject** includes the simple subject and all of its modifiers. To find the complete subject, ask *Who* or *What* and insert the verb to complete the question. The answer, including any modifiers (adjectives, prepositional phrases, etc.), is the complete subject. To find the **simple subject**, remove all of the modifiers in the complete subject. Being able to locate the subject of a sentence helps with many problems, such as those involving sentence fragments and subject-verb agreement.

Examples:

The small, red car is the one that he wants for Christmas.

(simple subject: car; complete subject: The small, red car)

The young artist is coming over for dinner.

(simple subject: artist; complete subject: The young artist)

> **Review Video: Subjects in English**
> Visit mometrix.com/academy and enter code: 444771

In **imperative** sentences, the verb's subject is understood (e.g., [You] Run to the store), but is not actually present in the sentence. Normally, the subject comes before the verb. However, the subject comes after the verb in sentences that begin with *There are* or *There was*.

Direct:

John knows the way to the park.	Who knows the way to the park?	John
The cookies need ten more minutes.	What needs ten minutes?	The cookies
By five o'clock, Bill will need to leave.	Who needs to leave?	Bill
There are five letters on the table for him.	What is on the table?	Five letters
There were coffee and doughnuts in the house.	What was in the house?	Coffee and doughnuts

Implied:

Go to the post office for me.	Who is going to the post office?	You
Come and sit with me, please?	Who needs to come and sit?	You

PREDICATES

In a sentence, you always have a predicate and a subject. The subject tells what the sentence is about, and the **predicate** explains or describes the subject.

Think about the sentence *He sings*. In this sentence, we have a subject (He) and a predicate (sings). This is all that is needed for a sentence to be complete. Most sentences contain more information, but if this is all the information that you are given, then you have a complete sentence.

Now, let's look at another sentence: *John and Jane sing on Tuesday nights at the dance hall.*

subject   predicate

John and Jane   sing on Tuesday nights at the dance hall.

SUBJECT-VERB AGREEMENT

Verbs **agree** with their subjects in number. In other words, singular subjects need singular verbs. Plural subjects need plural verbs. **Singular** is for **one** person, place, or thing. **Plural** is for **more than one** person, place, or thing. Subjects and verbs must also share the same point of view, as in first, second, or third person. The present tense ending *-s* is used on a verb if its subject is third person singular; otherwise, the verb's ending is not modified.

> **Review Video: Subject-Verb Agreement**
> Visit mometrix.com/academy and enter code: 479190

NUMBER AGREEMENT EXAMPLES:

singular   singular
subject   verb

Single Subject and Verb: Dan   calls   home.

Dan is one person. So, the singular verb *calls* is needed.

plural   plural
subject   verb

Plural Subject and Verb: Dan and Bob   call   home.

More than one person needs the plural verb *call*.

PERSON AGREEMENT EXAMPLES:

First Person: I *am* walking.

Second Person: You *are* walking.

Third Person: He *is* walking.

COMPLICATIONS WITH SUBJECT-VERB AGREEMENT
WORDS BETWEEN SUBJECT AND VERB

Words that come between the simple subject and the verb have no bearing on subject-verb agreement.

Examples:

singular   singular
subject   verb

The joy of my life returns home tonight.

The phrase *of my life* does not influence the verb *returns*.

133

singular
subject

singular
verb

The question that still remains unanswered is "Who are you?"

Don't let the phrase "*that still remains…*" trouble you. The subject *question* goes with *is*.

COMPOUND SUBJECTS

A compound subject is formed when two or more nouns joined by *and*, *or*, or *nor* jointly act as the subject of the sentence.

JOINED BY AND

When a compound subject is joined by *and*, it is treated as a plural subject and requires a plural verb.

Examples:

plural
subject   plural
verb

You and Jon are invited to come to my house.

plural
subject   plural
verb

The pencil and paper belong to me.

JOINED BY OR/NOR

For a compound subject joined by *or* or *nor*, the verb must agree in number with the part of the subject that is closest to the verb (italicized in the examples below).

Examples:

subject   verb

Today or tomorrow is the day.

subject   verb

Stan or Phil wants to read the book.

subject   verb

Neither the pen nor the book is on the desk.

subject   verb

Either the blanket or pillows arrive this afternoon.

INDEFINITE PRONOUNS AS SUBJECT

An indefinite pronoun is a pronoun that does not refer to a specific noun. Different indefinite pronouns may only function as a singular noun, only function as a plural noun, or change depending on how they are used.

ALWAYS SINGULAR

Pronouns such as *each*, *either*, *everybody*, *anybody*, *somebody*, and *nobody* are always singular.

Examples:

singular
subject

singular
verb

Each of the runners has a different bib number.

singular
verb

singular
subject

Is either of you ready for the game?

Note: The words *each* and *either* can also be used as adjectives (e.g., *each* person is unique). When one of these adjectives modifies the subject of a sentence, it is always a singular subject.

singular
subject

singular
verb

Everybody grows a day older every day.

singular
subject

singular
verb

Anybody is welcome to bring a tent.

ALWAYS PLURAL

Pronouns such as *both*, *several*, and *many* are always plural.

Examples:

plural
subject

plural
verb

Both of the siblings were too tired to argue.

plural
subject

plural
verb

Many have tried, but none have succeeded.

DEPEND ON CONTEXT

Pronouns such as *some*, *any*, *all*, *none*, *more*, and *most* can be either singular or plural depending on what they are representing in the context of the sentence.

Examples:

singular
subject

singular
verb

All of my dog's food was still there in his bowl.

plural
subject

plural
verb

By the end of the night, all of my guests were already excited about coming to my next party.

OTHER CASES INVOLVING PLURAL OR IRREGULAR FORM

Some nouns are **singular in meaning but plural in form**: news, mathematics, physics, and economics.

> The *news is* coming on now.

> *Mathematics is* my favorite class.

Some nouns are plural in form and meaning, and have **no singular equivalent**: scissors and pants.

> Do these *pants come* with a shirt?

> The *scissors are* for my project.

Mathematical operations are **irregular** in their construction, but are normally considered to be **singular in meaning**.

> *One plus one is* two.

> *Three times three is* nine.

Note: Look to your **dictionary** for help when you aren't sure whether a noun with a plural form has a singular or plural meaning.

COMPLEMENTS

A complement is a noun, pronoun, or adjective that is used to give more information about the subject or verb in the sentence.

DIRECT OBJECTS

A direct object is a noun or pronoun that takes or receives the **action** of a verb. (Remember: a complete sentence does not need a direct object, so not all sentences will have them. A sentence needs only a subject and a verb.) When you are looking for a direct object, find the verb and ask *who* or *what*.

Examples:

> I took *the blanket*.

> Jane read *books*.

INDIRECT OBJECTS

An indirect object is a word or group of words that show how an action had an **influence** on someone or something. If there is an indirect object in a sentence, then you always have a direct object in the sentence. When you are looking for the indirect object, find the verb and ask *to/for whom or what*.

Examples:

indirect direct
object object
We taught the old dog a new trick.

indirect direct
object object
I gave them a math lesson.

> **Review Video: Direct and Indirect Objects**
> Visit mometrix.com/academy and enter code: 817385

PREDICATE NOMINATIVES AND PREDICATE ADJECTIVES

As we looked at previously, verbs may be classified as either action verbs or linking verbs. A linking verb is so named because it links the subject to words in the predicate that describe or define the subject. These words are called predicate nominatives (if nouns or pronouns) or predicate adjectives (if adjectives).

Examples:

subject predicate
nominative
My father is a lawyer.

subject predicate
adjective
Your mother is patient.

PRONOUN USAGE

The **antecedent** is the noun that has been replaced by a pronoun. A pronoun and its antecedent **agree** when they have the same number (singular or plural) and gender (male, female, or neutral).

Examples:

antecedent pronoun
Singular agreement: John came into town, and he played for us.

antecedent pronoun
Plural agreement: John and Rick came into town, and they played for us.

To determine which is the correct pronoun to use in a compound subject or object, try each pronoun **alone** in place of the compound in the sentence. Your knowledge of pronouns will tell you which one is correct.

Example:

Bob and (I, me) will be going.

Test: (1) *I will be going* or (2) *Me will be going*. The second choice cannot be correct because *me* cannot be used as the subject of a sentence. Instead, *me* is used as an object.

Answer: Bob and I will be going.

When a pronoun is used with a noun immediately following (as in "we boys"), try the sentence **without the added noun**.

Example:

(We/Us) boys played football last year.

Test: (1) *We played football last ye*ar or (2) *Us played football last year*. Again, the second choice cannot be correct because *us* cannot be used as a subject of a sentence. Instead, *us* is used as an object.

Answer: We boys played football last year.

Review Video: Pronoun Usage
Visit mometrix.com/academy and enter code: 666500

Review Video: What is Pronoun-Antecedent Agreement?
Visit mometrix.com/academy and enter code: 919704

A pronoun should point clearly to the **antecedent**. Here is how a pronoun reference can be unhelpful if it is puzzling or not directly stated.

antecedent   pronoun
Unhelpful: Ron and Jim went to the store, and he bought soda.

Who bought soda? Ron or Jim?

antecedent   pronoun
Helpful: Jim went to the store, and he bought soda.

The sentence is clear. Jim bought the soda.

Some pronouns change their form by their placement in a sentence. A pronoun that is a **subject** in a sentence comes in the **subjective case**. Pronouns that serve as **objects** appear in the **objective case**. Finally, the pronouns that are used as **possessives** appear in the **possessive case**.

Examples:

Subjective case: *He* is coming to the show.

The pronoun *He* is the subject of the sentence.

Objective case: Josh drove *him* to the airport.

The pronoun *him* is the object of the sentence.

Possessive case: The flowers are *mine*.

The pronoun *mine* shows ownership of the flowers.

The word *who* is a subjective-case pronoun that can be used as a **subject**. The word *whom* is an objective-case pronoun that can be used as an **object**. The words *who* and *whom* are common in subordinate clauses or in questions.

Examples:

$$\overset{\text{subject}}{\text{who}} \ \overset{\text{verb}}{\text{wants}}$$

He knows who wants to come.

$$\overset{\text{object}}{\text{whom}} \ \overset{\text{verb}}{\text{want}}$$

He knows the man whom we want at the party.

CLAUSES

A clause is a group of words that contains both a subject and a predicate (verb). There are two types of clauses: independent and dependent. An **independent clause** contains a complete thought, while a **dependent (or subordinate) clause** does not. A dependent clause includes a subject and a verb, and may also contain objects or complements, but it cannot stand as a complete thought without being joined to an independent clause. Dependent clauses function within sentences as adjectives, adverbs, or nouns.

Example:

$$\underbrace{\text{I am running}}_{\substack{\text{independent} \\ \text{clause}}} \ \underbrace{\text{because I want to stay in shape.}}_{\substack{\text{dependent} \\ \text{clause}}}$$

The clause *I am running* is an independent clause: it has a subject and a verb, and it gives a complete thought. The clause *because I want to stay in shape* is a dependent clause: it has a subject and a verb, but it does not express a complete thought. It adds detail to the independent clause to which it is attached.

Review Video: What is a Clause?
Visit mometrix.com/academy and enter code: 940170

Review Video: Independent and Dependent Clauses
Visit mometrix.com/academy and enter code: 556903

TYPES OF DEPENDENT CLAUSES

ADJECTIVE CLAUSES

An **adjective clause** is a dependent clause that modifies a noun or a pronoun. Adjective clauses begin with a relative pronoun (*who, whose, whom, which,* and *that*) or a relative adverb (*where, when,* and *why*).

Also, adjective clauses come after the noun that the clause needs to explain or rename. This is done to have a clear connection to the independent clause.

Examples:

$$\underbrace{\text{I learned the reason}}_{\substack{\text{independent} \\ \text{clause}}} \ \underbrace{\text{why I won the award.}}_{\substack{\text{adjective} \\ \text{clause}}}$$

$$\underbrace{\text{This is the place}}_{\substack{\text{independent} \\ \text{clause}}} \ \underbrace{\text{where I started my first job.}}_{\substack{\text{adjective} \\ \text{clause}}}$$

An adjective clause can be an essential or nonessential clause. An essential clause is very important to the sentence. **Essential clauses** explain or define a person or thing. **Nonessential clauses** give

139

more information about a person or thing but are not necessary to define them. Nonessential clauses are set off with commas while essential clauses are not.

Examples:

essential
clause

A person who works hard at first can often rest later in life.

nonessential
clause

Neil Armstrong, who walked on the moon, is my hero.

ADVERB CLAUSES

An **adverb clause** is a dependent clause that modifies a verb, adjective, or adverb. In sentences with multiple dependent clauses, adverb clauses are usually placed immediately before or after the independent clause. An adverb clause is introduced with words such as *after, although, as, before, because, if, since, so, unless, when, where,* and *while.*

Examples:

adverb
clause

When you walked outside, I called the manager.

adverb
clause

I will go with you unless you want to stay.

NOUN CLAUSES

A **noun clause** is a dependent clause that can be used as a subject, object, or complement. Noun clauses begin with words such as *how, that, what, whether, which, who,* and *why.* These words can also come with an adjective clause. Unless the noun clause is being used as the subject of the sentence, it should come after the verb of the independent clause.

Examples:

noun
clause

The real mystery is how you avoided serious injury.

noun
clause

What you learn from each other depends on your honesty with others.

SUBORDINATION

When two related ideas are not of equal importance, the ideal way to combine them is to make the more important idea an independent clause and the less important idea a dependent or subordinate clause. This is called **subordination**.

Example:

> **Separate ideas**: The team had a perfect regular season. The team lost the championship.

> **Subordinated**: Despite having a perfect regular season, *the team lost the championship.*

PHRASES

A phrase is a group of words that functions as a single part of speech, usually a noun, adjective, or adverb. A **phrase** is not a complete thought, but it adds detail or explanation to a sentence, or renames something within the sentence.

PREPOSITIONAL PHRASES

One of the most common types of phrases is the prepositional phrase. A **prepositional phrase** begins with a preposition and ends with a noun or pronoun that is the object of the preposition. Normally, the prepositional phrase functions as an **adjective** or an **adverb** within the sentence.

Examples:

prepositional
phrase

The picnic is on the blanket.

prepositional
phrase

I am sick with a fever today.

prepositional
phrase

Among the many flowers, John found a four-leaf clover.

VERBAL PHRASES

A **verbal** is a word or phrase that is formed from a verb but does not function as a verb. Depending on its particular form, it may be used as a noun, adjective, or adverb. A verbal does **not** replace a verb in a sentence.

Examples:

verb

Correct: Walk a mile daily.

This is a complete sentence with the implied subject *you.*

verbal

Incorrect: To walk a mile.

This is not a sentence since there is no functional verb.

There are three types of verbal: **participles**, **gerunds**, and **infinitives**. Each type of verbal has a corresponding **phrase** that consists of the verbal itself along with any complements or modifiers.

PARTICIPLES

A **participle** is a type of verbal that always functions as an adjective. The present participle always ends with -*ing*. Past participles end with -*d, -ed, -n,* or -*t*.

Examples: verb: dance | present participle: dancing | past participle: danced

Participial phrases most often come right before or right after the noun or pronoun that they modify.

Examples:

participial phrase
Shipwrecked on an island, the boys started to fish for food.

participial phrase
Having been seated for five hours, we got out of the car to stretch our legs.

participial phrase
Praised for their work, the group accepted the first-place trophy.

GERUNDS

A **gerund** is a type of verbal that always functions as a **noun**. Like present participles, gerunds always end with -*ing*, but they can be easily distinguished from one another by the part of speech they represent (participles always function as adjectives). Since a gerund or gerund phrase always functions as a noun, it can be used as the subject of a sentence, the predicate nominative, or the object of a verb or preposition.

Examples:

gerund
We want to be known for teaching the poor.
object of preposition

gerund
Coaching this team is the best job of my life.
subject

gerund
We like practicing our songs in the basement.
object of verb

INFINITIVES

An **infinitive** is a type of verbal that can function as a noun, an adjective, or an adverb. An infinitive is made of the word *to* and the basic form of the verb. As with all other types of verbal phrases, an infinitive phrase includes the verbal itself and all of its complements or modifiers.

Examples:

infinitive
To join the team is my goal in life.
noun

infinitive
The animals have enough food to eat for the night.
adjective

infinitive
People lift weights to exercise their muscles.
adverb

> **Review Video: Gerunds, Infinitives, and Participles**
> Visit mometrix.com/academy and enter code: 634263

APPOSITIVE PHRASES

An **appositive** is a word or phrase that is used to explain or rename nouns or pronouns. Noun phrases, gerund phrases, and infinitive phrases can all be used as appositives.

Examples:

appositive
Terriers, hunters at heart, have been dressed up to look like lap dogs.

The noun phrase *hunters at heart* renames the noun *terriers*.

appositive
His plan, to save and invest his money, was proven as a safe approach.

The infinitive phrase explains what the plan is.

Appositive phrases can be **essential** or **nonessential**. An appositive phrase is essential if the person, place, or thing being described or renamed is too general for its meaning to be understood without the appositive.

Examples:

essential
Two of America's Founding Fathers, George Washington and Thomas Jefferson, served as presidents.

nonessential
George Washington and Thomas Jefferson, two Founding Fathers, served as presidents.

ABSOLUTE PHRASES

An absolute phrase is a phrase that consists of **a noun followed by a participle**. An absolute phrase provides **context** to what is being described in the sentence, but it does not modify or explain any particular word; it is essentially independent.

143

Examples:

noun participle
The alarm **ringing**, he pushed the snooze button.
absolute phrase

noun participle
The music **paused**, she continued to dance through the crowd.
absolute phrase

PARALLELISM

When multiple items or ideas are presented in a sentence in series, such as in a list, the items or ideas must be stated in grammatically equivalent ways. In other words, if one idea is stated in gerund form, the second cannot be stated in infinitive form. For example, to write, *I enjoy reading and to study* would be incorrect. An infinitive and a gerund are not equivalent. Instead, you should write *I enjoy reading and studying*. In lists of more than two, all items must be parallel.

Example:

Incorrect: He stopped at the office, grocery store, and the pharmacy before heading home.

The first and third items in the list of places include the article *the*, so the second item needs it as well.

Correct: He stopped at the office, *the* grocery store, and the pharmacy before heading home.

Example:

Incorrect: While vacationing in Europe, she went biking, skiing, and climbed mountains.

The first and second items in the list are gerunds, so the third item must be as well.

Correct: While vacationing in Europe, she went biking, skiing, and *mountain climbing*.

> **Review Video: Parallel Construction**
> Visit mometrix.com/academy and enter code: 831988

SENTENCE PURPOSE

There are four types of sentences: declarative, imperative, interrogative, and exclamatory.

A **declarative** sentence states a fact and ends with a period.

The football game starts at seven o'clock.

An **imperative** sentence tells someone to do something and generally ends with a period. An urgent command might end with an exclamation point instead.

Don't forget to buy your ticket.

An **interrogative** sentence asks a question and ends with a question mark.

Are you going to the game on Friday?

An **exclamatory** sentence shows strong emotion and ends with an exclamation point.

I can't believe we won the game!

SENTENCE STRUCTURE

Sentences are classified by structure based on the type and number of clauses present. The four classifications of sentence structure are the following:

Simple: A simple sentence has one independent clause with no dependent clauses. A simple sentence may have **compound elements** (i.e., compound subject or verb).

Examples:

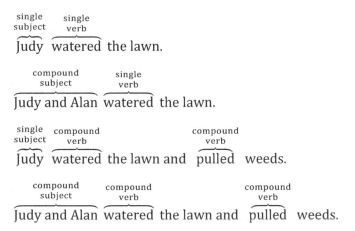

Compound: A compound sentence has two or more independent clauses with no dependent clauses. Usually, the independent clauses are joined with a comma and a coordinating conjunction or with a semicolon.

Examples:

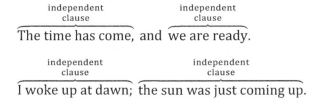

Complex: A complex sentence has one independent clause and at least one dependent clause.

Examples:

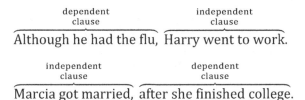

Compound-Complex: A compound-complex sentence has at least two independent clauses and at least one dependent clause.

Examples:

independent   dependent   independent
clause   clause   clause

John is my friend who went to India, and he brought back souvenirs.

independent   independent   dependent
clause   clause   clause

You may not realize this, but we heard the music that you played last night.

> **Review Video: Sentence Structure**
> Visit mometrix.com/academy and enter code: 700478

Sentence variety is important to consider when writing an essay or speech. A variety of sentence lengths and types creates rhythm, makes a passage more engaging, and gives writers an opportunity to demonstrate their writing style. Writing that uses the same length or type of sentence without variation can be boring or difficult to read. To evaluate a passage for effective sentence variety, it is helpful to note whether the passage contains diverse sentence structures and lengths. It is also important to pay attention to the way each sentence starts and avoid beginning with the same words or phrases.

SENTENCE FRAGMENTS

Recall that a group of words must contain at least one **independent clause** in order to be considered a sentence. If it doesn't contain even one independent clause, it is called a **sentence fragment**.

The appropriate process for **repairing** a sentence fragment depends on what type of fragment it is. If the fragment is a dependent clause, it can sometimes be as simple as removing a subordinating word (e.g., when, because, if) from the beginning of the fragment. Alternatively, a dependent clause can be incorporated into a closely related neighboring sentence. If the fragment is missing some required part, like a subject or a verb, the fix might be as simple as adding the missing part.

Examples:

> **Fragment**: Because he wanted to sail the Mediterranean.
>
> **Removed subordinating word**: He wanted to sail the Mediterranean.
>
> **Combined with another sentence**: Because he wanted to sail the Mediterranean, he booked a Greek island cruise.

RUN-ON SENTENCES

Run-on sentences consist of multiple independent clauses that have not been joined together properly. Run-on sentences can be corrected in several different ways:

Join clauses properly: This can be done with a comma and coordinating conjunction, with a semicolon, or with a colon or dash if the second clause is explaining something in the first.

Example:

>**Incorrect**: I went on the trip, we visited lots of castles.

>**Corrected**: I went on the trip, and we visited lots of castles.

Split into separate sentences: This correction is most effective when the independent clauses are very long or when they are not closely related.

Example:

>**Incorrect**: The drive to New York takes ten hours, my uncle lives in Boston.

>**Corrected**: The drive to New York takes ten hours. My uncle lives in Boston.

Make one clause dependent: This is the easiest way to make the sentence correct and more interesting at the same time. It's often as simple as adding a subordinating word between the two clauses or before the first clause.

Example:

>**Incorrect**: I finally made it to the store and I bought some eggs.

>**Corrected**: When I finally made it to the store, I bought some eggs.

Reduce to one clause with a compound verb: If both clauses have the same subject, remove the subject from the second clause, and you now have just one clause with a compound verb.

Example:

>**Incorrect**: The drive to New York takes ten hours, it makes me very tired.

>**Corrected**: The drive to New York takes ten hours and makes me very tired.

Note: While these are the simplest ways to correct a run-on sentence, often the best way is to completely reorganize the thoughts in the sentence and rewrite it.

> **Review Video: <u>Fragments and Run-on Sentences</u>**
> Visit mometrix.com/academy and enter code: 541989

DANGLING AND MISPLACED MODIFIERS
DANGLING MODIFIERS

A dangling modifier is a dependent clause or verbal phrase that does not have a clear logical connection to a word in the sentence.

Example:

Incorrect: Reading each magazine article, the stories caught my attention.

The word *stories* cannot be modified by *Reading each magazine article*. People can read, but stories cannot read. Therefore, the subject of the sentence must be a person.

Corrected: Reading each magazine article, I was entertained by the stories.

Example:

Incorrect: Ever since childhood, my grandparents have visited me for Christmas.

The speaker in this sentence can't have been visited by her grandparents when *they* were children, since she wouldn't have been born yet. Either the modifier should be clarified or the sentence should be rearranged to specify whose childhood is being referenced.

Clarified: Ever since I was a child, my grandparents have visited for Christmas.

Rearranged: I have enjoyed my grandparents visiting for Christmas, ever since childhood.

MISPLACED MODIFIERS

Because modifiers are grammatically versatile, they can be put in many different places within the structure of a sentence. The danger of this versatility is that a modifier can accidentally be placed where it is modifying the wrong word or where it is not clear which word it is modifying.

Example:

Incorrect: She read the book to a crowd that was filled with beautiful pictures.

The book was filled with beautiful pictures, not the crowd.

Corrected: She read the book that was filled with beautiful pictures to a crowd.

Example:

$$\text{modifier}$$

Ambiguous: Derek saw a bus nearly hit a man <u>on his way to work</u>.

Was Derek on his way to work or was the other man?

Derek: <u>On his way to work,</u> Derek saw a bus nearly hit a man.

The other man: Derek saw a bus nearly hit a man <u>who was on his way to work</u>.

SPLIT INFINITIVES

A split infinitive occurs when a modifying word comes between the word *to* and the verb that pairs with *to*.

Example: To *clearly* explain vs. *To explain* clearly | To *softly* sing vs. *To sing* softly

Though considered improper by some, split infinitives may provide better clarity and simplicity in some cases than the alternatives. As such, avoiding them should not be considered a universal rule.

DOUBLE NEGATIVES

Standard English allows **two negatives** only when a **positive** meaning is intended. For example, *The team was not displeased with their performance*. Double negatives to emphasize negation are not used in standard English.

Negative modifiers (e.g., never, no, and not) should not be paired with other negative modifiers or negative words (e.g., none, nobody, nothing, or neither). The modifiers *hardly, barely*, and *scarcely* are also considered negatives in standard English, so they should not be used with other negatives.

Punctuation

END PUNCTUATION

PERIODS

Use a period to end all sentences except direct questions and exclamations. Periods are also used for abbreviations.

Examples: 3 p.m. | 2 a.m. | Mr. Jones | Mrs. Stevens | Dr. Smith | Bill, Jr. | Pennsylvania Ave.

Note: An abbreviation is a shortened form of a word or phrase.

QUESTION MARKS

Question marks should be used following a **direct question**. A polite request can be followed by a period instead of a question mark.

Direct Question: What is for lunch today? | How are you? | Why is that the answer?

Polite Requests: Can you please send me the item tomorrow. | Will you please walk with me on the track.

> **Review Video: Question Marks**
> Visit mometrix.com/academy and enter code: 118471

EXCLAMATION MARKS

Exclamation marks are used after a word group or sentence that shows much feeling or has special importance. Exclamation marks should not be overused. They are saved for proper **exclamatory interjections**.

Example: We're going to the finals! | You have a beautiful car! | "That's crazy!" she yelled.

> **Review Video: Exclamation Points**
> Visit mometrix.com/academy and enter code: 199367

COMMAS

The comma is a punctuation mark that can help you understand connections in a sentence. Not every sentence needs a comma. However, if a sentence needs a comma, you need to put it in the right place. A comma in the wrong place (or an absent comma) will make a sentence's meaning unclear. These are some of the rules for commas:

Use Case	Example
Before a **coordinating conjunction** joining independent clauses	Bob caught three fish, and I caught two fish.
After an **introductory phrase**	After the final out, we went to a restaurant to celebrate.
After an **adverbial clause**	Studying the stars, I was awed by the beauty of the sky.
Between **items in a series**	I will bring the turkey, the pie, and the coffee.
For **interjections**	Wow, you know how to play this game.
After *yes* and *no* responses	No, I cannot come tomorrow.
Separate **nonessential modifiers**	John Frank, who coaches the team, was promoted today.
Separate **nonessential appositives**	Thomas Edison, an American inventor, was born in Ohio.
Separate **nouns of direct address**	You, John, are my only hope in this moment.
Separate **interrogative tags**	This is the last time, correct?
Separate **contrasts**	You are my friend, not my enemy.
Writing **dates**	July 4, 1776, is an important date to remember.
Writing **addresses**	He is meeting me at 456 Delaware Avenue, Washington, D.C., tomorrow morning.
Writing **geographical names**	Paris, France, is my favorite city.
Writing **titles**	John Smith, PhD, will be visiting your class today.
Separate **expressions like *he said***	"You can start," she said, "with an apology."

Also, you can use a comma **between coordinate adjectives** not joined with *and*. However, not all adjectives are coordinate (i.e., equal or parallel).

Incorrect: The kind, brown dog followed me home.

Correct: The kind, loyal dog followed me home.

There are two simple ways to know if your adjectives are coordinate. One, you can join the adjectives with *and*: *The kind and loyal dog.* Two, you can change the order of the adjectives: *The loyal, kind dog.*

> **Review Video: When to Use a Comma**
> Visit mometrix.com/academy and enter code: 786797

SEMICOLONS

The semicolon is used to connect major sentence pieces of equal value. Some rules for semicolons include:

Use Case	Example
Between closely connected independent clauses **not connected with a coordinating conjunction**	You are right; we should go with your plan.
Between independent clauses **linked with a transitional word**	I think that we can agree on this; however, I am not sure about my friends.
Between items in a **series that has internal punctuation**	I have visited New York, New York; Augusta, Maine; and Baltimore, Maryland.

> **Review Video: How to Use Semicolons**
> Visit mometrix.com/academy and enter code: 370605

151

COLONS

The colon is used to call attention to the words that follow it. A colon must come after a **complete independent clause**. The rules for colons are as follows:

Use Case	Example
After an independent clause to **make a list**	I want to learn many languages: Spanish, German, and Italian.
For **explanations**	There is one thing that stands out on your resume: responsibility.
To give a **quote**	He started with an idea: "We are able to do more than we imagine."
After the **greeting in a formal letter**	To Whom It May Concern:
Show **hours and minutes**	It is 3:14 p.m.
Separate a **title and subtitle**	The essay is titled "America: A Short Introduction to a Modern Country."

Review Video: Colons
Visit mometrix.com/academy and enter code: 868673

PARENTHESES

Parentheses are used for additional information. Also, they can be used to put labels for letters or numbers in a series. Parentheses should be not be used very often. If they are overused, parentheses can be a distraction instead of a help.

Examples:

Extra Information: The rattlesnake (see Image 2) is a dangerous snake of North and South America.

Series: Include in the email (1) your name, (2) your address, and (3) your question for the author.

Review Video: Parentheses
Visit mometrix.com/academy and enter code: 947743

QUOTATION MARKS

Use quotation marks to close off **direct quotations** of a person's spoken or written words. Do not use quotation marks around indirect quotations. An indirect quotation gives someone's message without using the person's exact words. Use **single quotation marks** to close off a quotation inside a quotation.

Direct Quote: Nancy said, "I am waiting for Henry to arrive."

Indirect Quote: Henry said that he is going to be late to the meeting.

Quote inside a Quote: The teacher asked, "Has everyone read 'The Gift of the Magi'?"

Quotation marks should be used around the titles of **short works**: newspaper and magazine articles, poems, short stories, songs, television episodes, radio programs, and subdivisions of books or websites.

Examples:

"Rip Van Winkle" (short story by Washington Irving)

"O Captain! My Captain!" (poem by Walt Whitman)

Although it is not standard usage, quotation marks are sometimes used to highlight **irony** or the use of words to mean something other than their dictionary definition. This type of usage should be employed sparingly, if at all.

Examples:

The boss warned Frank that he was walking on "thin ice."	Frank is not walking on real ice. Instead, he is being warned to avoid mistakes.
The teacher thanked the young man for his "honesty."	The quotation marks around *honesty* show that the teacher does not believe the young man's explanation.

> **Review Video: <u>Quotation Marks</u>**
> Visit mometrix.com/academy and enter code: 884918

Periods and commas are put **inside** quotation marks. Colons and semicolons are put **outside** the quotation marks. Question marks and exclamation points are placed inside quotation marks when they are part of a quote. When the question or exclamation mark goes with the whole sentence, the mark is left outside of the quotation marks.

Examples:

Period and comma	We read "The Gift of the Magi," "The Skylight Room," and "The Cactus."
Semicolon	They watched "The Nutcracker"; then, they went home.
Exclamation mark that is a part of a quote	The crowd cheered, "Victory!"
Question mark that goes with the whole sentence	Is your favorite short story "The Tell-Tale Heart"?

APOSTROPHES

An apostrophe is used to show **possession** or the **deletion of letters in contractions**. An apostrophe is not needed with the possessive pronouns *his, hers, its, ours, theirs, whose*, and *yours*.

Singular Nouns: David's car | a book's theme | my brother's board game

Plural Nouns that end with -*s*: the scissors' handle | boys' basketball

Plural Nouns that end without -*s*: Men's department | the people's adventure

> **Review Video: <u>When to Use an Apostrophe</u>**
> Visit mometrix.com/academy and enter code: 213068
>
> **Review Video: <u>Punctuation Errors in Possessive Pronouns</u>**
> Visit mometrix.com/academy and enter code: 221438

HYPHENS

Hyphens are used to **separate compound words**. Use hyphens in the following cases:

Use Case	Example
Compound numbers from 21 to 99 when written out in words	This team needs twenty-five points to win the game.
Written-out fractions that are used as adjectives	The recipe says that we need a three-fourths cup of butter.
Compound adjectives that come before a noun	The well-fed dog took a nap.
Unusual compound words that would be hard to read or easily confused with other words	This is the best anti-itch cream on the market.

Note: This is not a complete set of the rules for hyphens. A dictionary is the best tool for knowing if a compound word needs a hyphen.

> **Review Video: Hyphens**
> Visit mometrix.com/academy and enter code: 981632

DASHES

Dashes are used to show a **break** or a **change in thought** in a sentence or to act as parentheses in a sentence. When typing, use two hyphens to make a dash. Do not put a space before or after the dash. The following are the functions of dashes:

Use Case	Example
Set off parenthetical statements or an **appositive with internal punctuation**	The three trees—oak, pine, and magnolia—are coming on a truck tomorrow.
Show a **break or change in tone or thought**	The first question—how silly of me—does not have a correct answer.

ELLIPSIS MARKS

The ellipsis mark has **three** periods (...) to show when **words have been removed** from a quotation. If a **full sentence or more** is removed from a quoted passage, you need to use **four** periods to show the removed text and the end punctuation mark. The ellipsis mark should not be used at the beginning of a quotation. The ellipsis mark should also not be used at the end of a quotation unless some words have been deleted from the end of the final sentence.

Example:

"Then he picked up the groceries...paid for them...later he went home."

BRACKETS

There are two main reasons to use brackets:

Use Case	Example
Placing **parentheses inside of parentheses**	The hero of this story, Paul Revere (a silversmith and industrialist [see Ch. 4]), rode through towns of Massachusetts to warn of advancing British troops.
Adding **clarification or detail to a quotation** that is not part of the quotation	The father explained, "My children are planning to attend my alma mater [State University]."

Review Video: Brackets
Visit mometrix.com/academy and enter code: 727546

Common Usage Mistakes

WORD CONFUSION
WHICH, THAT, AND WHO

The words *which*, *that*, and *who* can act as **relative pronouns** to help clarify or describe a noun.

Which is used for things only.

> Example: Andrew's car, *which is old and rusty,* broke down last week.

That is used for people or things. *That* is usually informal when used to describe people.

> Example: Is this the only book *that Louis L'Amour wrote?*

> Example: Is Louis L'Amour the author *that wrote Western novels?*

Who is used for people or for animals that have an identity or personality.

> Example: Mozart was the composer *who wrote those operas.*

> Example: John's dog, *who is called Max,* is large and fierce.

HOMOPHONES

Homophones are words that sound alike (or similar) but have different **spellings** and **definitions**. A homophone is a type of **homonym**, which is a pair or group of words that are pronounced or spelled the same, but do not mean the same thing.

TO, TOO, AND TWO

To can be an adverb or a preposition for showing direction, purpose, and relationship. See your dictionary for the many other ways to use *to* in a sentence.

> Examples: I went to the store. | I want to go with you.

Too is an adverb that means *also, as well, very,* or *in excess.*

> Examples: I can walk a mile too. | You have eaten too much.

Two is a number.

> Example: You have two minutes left.

THERE, THEIR, AND THEY'RE

There can be an adjective, adverb, or pronoun. Often, *there* is used to show a place or to start a sentence.

> Examples: I went there yesterday. | There is something in his pocket.

Their is a pronoun that is used to show ownership.

> Examples: He is their father. | This is their fourth apology this week.

They're is a contraction of *they are.*

> Example: Did you know that they're in town?

KNEW AND NEW

Knew is the past tense of *know*.

> Example: I knew the answer.

New is an adjective that means something is current, has not been used, or is modern.

> Example: This is my new phone.

THEN AND THAN

Then is an adverb that indicates sequence or order:

> Example: I'm going to run to the library and then come home.

Than is special-purpose word used only for comparisons:

> Example: Susie likes chips more than candy.

ITS AND IT'S

Its is a pronoun that shows ownership.

> Example: The guitar is in its case.

It's is a contraction of *it is*.

> Example: It's an honor and a privilege to meet you.

Note: The *h* in honor is silent, so *honor* starts with the vowel sound *o*, which must have the article *an*.

YOUR AND YOU'RE

Your is a pronoun that shows ownership.

> Example: This is your moment to shine.

You're is a contraction of *you are*.

> Example: Yes, you're correct.

SAW AND SEEN

Saw is the past-tense form of *see*.

> Example: I saw a turtle on my walk this morning.

Seen is the past participle of *see*.

> Example: I have seen this movie before.

AFFECT AND EFFECT

There are two main reasons that *affect* and *effect* are so often confused: 1) both words can be used as either a noun or a verb, and 2) unlike most homophones, their usage and meanings are closely related to each other. Here is a quick rundown of the four usage options:

Affect (n): feeling, emotion, or mood that is displayed

Example: The patient had a flat *affect*. (i.e., his face showed little or no emotion)

Affect (v): to alter, to change, to influence

Example: The sunshine *affects* the plant's growth.

Effect (n): a result, a consequence

Example: What *effect* will this weather have on our schedule?

Effect (v): to bring about, to cause to be

Example: These new rules will *effect* order in the office.

The noun form of *affect* is rarely used outside of technical medical descriptions, so if a noun form is needed on the test, you can safely select *effect*. The verb form of *effect* is not as rare as the noun form of *affect*, but it's still not all that likely to show up on your test. If you need a verb and you can't decide which to use based on the definitions, choosing *affect* is your best bet.

HOMOGRAPHS

Homographs are words that share the same spelling, but have different meanings and sometimes different pronunciations. To figure out which meaning is being used, you should be looking for context clues. The context clues give hints to the meaning of the word. For example, the word *spot* has many meanings. It can mean "a place" or "a stain or blot." In the sentence "After my lunch, I saw a spot on my shirt," the word *spot* means "a stain or blot." The context clues of "After my lunch" and "on my shirt" guide you to this decision. A homograph is another type of homonym.

BANK

(noun): an establishment where money is held for savings or lending

(verb): to collect or pile up

CONTENT

(noun): the topics that will be addressed within a book

(adjective): pleased or satisfied

(verb): to make someone pleased or satisfied

FINE

(noun): an amount of money that acts a penalty for an offense

(adjective): very small or thin

(adverb): in an acceptable way

(verb): to make someone pay money as a punishment

INCENSE

(noun): a material that is burned in religious settings and makes a pleasant aroma

(verb): to frustrate or anger

LEAD

(noun): the first or highest position

(noun): a heavy metallic element

(verb): to direct a person or group of followers

(adjective): containing lead

OBJECT

(noun): a lifeless item that can be held and observed

(verb): to disagree

PRODUCE

(noun): fruits and vegetables

(verb): to make or create something

REFUSE

(noun): garbage or debris that has been thrown away

(verb): to not allow

SUBJECT

(noun): an area of study

(verb): to force or subdue

TEAR

(noun): a fluid secreted by the eyes

(verb): to separate or pull apart

The Writing Process

BRAINSTORMING

Brainstorming is a technique that is used to find a creative approach to a subject. This can be accomplished by simple **free-association** with a topic. For example, with paper and pen, write every thought that you have about the topic in a word or phrase. This is done without critical thinking. You should put everything that comes to your mind about the topic on your scratch paper. Then, you need to read the list over a few times. Next, look for patterns, repetitions, and clusters of ideas. This allows a variety of fresh ideas to come as you think about the topic.

FREE WRITING

Free writing is a more structured form of brainstorming. The method involves taking a limited amount of time (e.g., 2 to 3 minutes) to write everything that comes to mind about the topic in complete sentences. When time expires, review everything that has been written down. Many of your sentences may make little or no sense, but the insights and observations that can come from free writing make this method a valuable approach. Usually, free writing results in a fuller expression of ideas than brainstorming because thoughts and associations are written in complete sentences. However, both techniques can be used to complement each other.

PLANNING

Planning is the process of organizing a piece of writing before composing a draft. Planning can include creating an outline or a graphic organizer, such as a Venn diagram, a spider-map, or a flowchart. These methods should help the writer identify their topic, main ideas, and the general organization of the composition. Preliminary research can also take place during this stage. Planning helps writers organize all of their ideas and decide if they have enough material to begin their first draft. However, writers should remember that the decisions they make during this step will likely change later in the process, so their plan does not have to be perfect.

DRAFTING

Writers may then use their plan, outline, or graphic organizer to compose their first draft. They may write subsequent drafts to improve their writing. Writing multiple drafts can help writers consider different ways to communicate their ideas and address errors that may be difficult to correct without rewriting a section or the whole composition. Most writers will vary in how many drafts they choose to write, as there is no "right" number of drafts. Writing drafts also takes away the pressure to write perfectly on the first try, as writers can improve with each draft they write.

REVISING, EDITING, AND PROOFREADING

Once a writer completes a draft, they can move on to the revising, editing, and proofreading steps to improve their draft. These steps begin with making broad changes that may apply to large sections of a composition and then making small, specific corrections. **Revising** is the first and broadest of these steps. Revising involves ensuring that the composition addresses an appropriate audience, includes all necessary material, maintains focus throughout, and is organized logically. Revising may occur after the first draft to ensure that the following drafts improve upon errors from the first draft. Some revision should occur between each draft to avoid repeating these errors. The **editing** phase of writing is narrower than the revising phase. Editing a composition should include steps such as improving transitions between paragraphs, ensuring each paragraph is on topic, and improving the flow of the text. The editing phase may also include correcting grammatical errors that cannot be fixed without significantly altering the text. **Proofreading** involves fixing misspelled words, typos, other grammatical errors, and any remaining surface-level flaws in the composition.

RECURSIVE WRITING PROCESS

However you approach writing, you may find comfort in knowing that the revision process can occur in any order. The **recursive writing process** is not as difficult as the phrase may make it seem. Simply put, the recursive writing process means that you may need to revisit steps after completing other steps. It also implies that the steps are not required to take place in any certain order. Indeed, you may find that planning, drafting, and revising can all take place at about the same time. The writing process involves moving back and forth between planning, drafting, and revising, followed by more planning, more drafting, and more revising until the writing is satisfactory.

> **Review Video: <u>Recursive Writing Process</u>**
> Visit mometrix.com/academy and enter code: 951611

TECHNOLOGY IN THE WRITING PROCESS

Modern technology has yielded several tools that can be used to make the writing process more convenient and organized. Word processors and online tools, such as databases and plagiarism detectors, allow much of the writing process to be completed in one place, using one device.

TECHNOLOGY FOR PLANNING AND DRAFTING

For the planning and drafting stages of the writing process, word processors are a helpful tool. These programs also feature formatting tools, allowing users to create their own planning tools or create digital outlines that can be easily converted into sentences, paragraphs, or an entire essay draft. Online databases and references also complement the planning process by providing convenient access to information and sources for research. Word processors also allow users to keep up with their work and update it more easily than if they wrote their work by hand. Online word processors often allow users to collaborate, making group assignments more convenient. These programs also allow users to include illustrations or other supplemental media in their compositions.

TECHNOLOGY FOR REVISING, EDITING, AND PROOFREADING

Word processors also benefit the revising, editing, and proofreading stages of the writing process. Most of these programs indicate errors in spelling and grammar, allowing users to catch minor errors and correct them quickly. There are also websites designed to help writers by analyzing text for deeper errors, such as poor sentence structure, inappropriate complexity, lack of sentence variety, and style issues. These websites can help users fix errors they may not know to look for or may have simply missed. As writers finish these steps, they may benefit from checking their work for any plagiarism. There are several websites and programs that compare text to other documents and publications across the internet and detect any similarities within the text. These websites show the source of the similar information, so users know whether or not they referenced the source and unintentionally plagiarized its contents.

TECHNOLOGY FOR PUBLISHING

Technology also makes managing written work more convenient. Digitally storing documents keeps everything in one place and is easy to reference. Digital storage also makes sharing work easier, as documents can be attached to an email or stored online. This also allows writers to publish their work easily, as they can electronically submit it to other publications or freely post it to a personal blog, profile, or website.

Outlining and Organizing Ideas

MAIN IDEAS, SUPPORTING DETAILS, AND OUTLINING A TOPIC

A writer often begins the first paragraph of a paper by stating the **main idea** or point, also known as the **topic sentence**. The rest of the paragraph supplies particular details that develop and support the main point. One way to visualize the relationship between the main point and supporting information is by considering a table: the tabletop is the main point, and each of the table's legs is a supporting detail or group of details. Both professional authors and students can benefit from planning their writing by first making an outline of the topic. Outlines facilitate quick identification of the main point and supporting details without having to wade through the additional language that will exist in the fully developed essay, article, or paper. Outlining can also help readers to analyze a piece of existing writing for the same reason. The outline first summarizes the main idea in one sentence. Then, below that, it summarizes the supporting details in a numbered list. Writing the paper then consists of filling in the outline with detail, writing a paragraph for each supporting point, and adding an introduction and conclusion.

INTRODUCTION

The purpose of the introduction is to capture the reader's attention and announce the essay's main idea. Normally, the introduction contains 50-80 words, or 3-5 sentences. An introduction can begin with an interesting quote, a question, or a strong opinion—something that will **engage** the reader's interest and prompt them to keep reading. If you are writing your essay to a specific prompt, your introduction should include a **restatement or summarization** of the prompt so that the reader will have some context for your essay. Finally, your introduction should briefly state your **thesis or main idea**: the primary thing you hope to communicate to the reader through your essay. Don't try to include all of the details and nuances of your thesis, or all of your reasons for it, in the introduction. That's what the rest of the essay is for!

> **Review Video: Introduction**
> Visit mometrix.com/academy and enter code: 961328

THESIS STATEMENT

The thesis is the main idea of the essay. A temporary thesis, or working thesis, should be established early in the writing process because it will serve to keep the writer focused as ideas develop. This temporary thesis is subject to change as you continue to write.

The temporary thesis has two parts: a **topic** (i.e., the focus of your essay based on the prompt) and a **comment**. The comment makes an important point about the topic. A temporary thesis should be interesting and specific. Also, you need to limit the topic to a manageable scope. These three questions are useful tools to measure the effectiveness of any temporary thesis:

- Does the focus of my essay have enough interest to hold an audience?
- Is the focus of my essay specific enough to generate interest?
- Is the focus of my essay manageable for the time limit? Too broad? Too narrow?

The thesis should be a generalization rather than a fact because the thesis prepares readers for facts and details that support the thesis. The process of bringing the thesis into sharp focus may help in outlining major sections of the work. Once the thesis and introduction are complete, you can address the body of the work.

> **Review Video: Thesis Statements**
> Visit mometrix.com/academy and enter code: 691033

SUPPORTING THE THESIS

Throughout your essay, the thesis should be **explained clearly and supported** adequately by additional arguments. The thesis sentence needs to contain a clear statement of the purpose of your essay and a comment about the thesis. With the thesis statement, you have an opportunity to state what is noteworthy of this particular treatment of the prompt. Each sentence and paragraph should build on and support the thesis.

When you respond to the prompt, use parts of the passage to support your argument or defend your position. Using supporting evidence from the passage strengths your argument because readers can see your attention to the entire passage and your response to the details and facts within the passage. You can use facts, details, statistics, and direct quotations from the passage to uphold your position. Be sure to point out which information comes from the original passage and base your argument around that evidence.

BODY

In an essay's introduction, the writer establishes the thesis and may indicate how the rest of the piece will be structured. In the body of the piece, the writer **elaborates** upon, **illustrates**, and **explains** the **thesis statement**. How writers arrange supporting details and their choices of paragraph types are development techniques. Writers may give examples of the concept introduced in the thesis statement. If the subject includes a cause-and-effect relationship, the author may explain its causality. A writer will explain or analyze the main idea of the piece throughout the body, often by presenting arguments for the veracity or credibility of the thesis statement. Writers may use development to define or clarify ambiguous terms. Paragraphs within the body may be organized using natural sequences, like space and time. Writers may employ **inductive reasoning**, using multiple details to establish a generalization or causal relationship, or **deductive reasoning**, proving a generalized hypothesis or proposition through a specific example or case.

> **Review Video: Drafting Body Paragraphs**
> Visit mometrix.com/academy and enter code: 724590

PARAGRAPHS

After the introduction of a passage, a series of body paragraphs will carry a message through to the conclusion. Each paragraph should be **unified around a main point**. Normally, a good topic sentence summarizes the paragraph's main point. A topic sentence is a general sentence that gives an introduction to the paragraph.

The sentences that follow support the topic sentence. However, though it is usually the first sentence, the topic sentence can come as the final sentence to the paragraph if the earlier sentences give a clear explanation of the paragraph's topic. This allows the topic sentence to function as a concluding sentence. Overall, the paragraphs need to stay true to the main point. This means that any unnecessary sentences that do not advance the main point should be removed.

The main point of a paragraph requires adequate development (i.e., a substantial paragraph that covers the main point). A paragraph of two or three sentences does not cover a main point. This is especially true when the main point of the paragraph gives strong support to the argument of the thesis. An occasional short paragraph is fine as a transitional device. However, a well-developed argument will have paragraphs with more than a few sentences.

METHODS OF DEVELOPING PARAGRAPHS

Common methods of adding substance to paragraphs include examples, illustrations, analogies, and cause and effect.

- **Examples** are supporting details to the main idea of a paragraph or a passage. When authors write about something that their audience may not understand, they can provide an example to show their point. When authors write about something that is not easily accepted, they can give examples to prove their point.
- **Illustrations** are extended examples that require several sentences. Well-selected illustrations can be a great way for authors to develop a point that may not be familiar to their audience.
- **Analogies** make comparisons between items that appear to have nothing in common. Analogies are employed by writers to provoke fresh thoughts about a subject. These comparisons may be used to explain the unfamiliar, to clarify an abstract point, or to argue a point. Although analogies are effective literary devices, they should be used carefully in arguments. Two things may be alike in some respects but completely different in others.
- **Cause and effect** is an excellent device to explain the connection between an action or situation and a particular result. One way that authors can use cause and effect is to state the effect in the topic sentence of a paragraph and add the causes in the body of the paragraph. This method can give an author's paragraphs structure, which always strengthens writing.

TYPES OF PARAGRAPHS

A **paragraph of narration** tells a story or a part of a story. Normally, the sentences are arranged in chronological order (i.e., the order that the events happened). However, flashbacks (i.e., an anecdote from an earlier time) can be included.

A **descriptive paragraph** makes a verbal portrait of a person, place, or thing. When specific details are used that appeal to one or more of the senses (i.e., sight, sound, smell, taste, and touch), authors give readers a sense of being present in the moment.

A **process paragraph** is related to time order (i.e., First, you open the bottle. Second, you pour the liquid, etc.). Usually, this describes a process or teaches readers how to perform a process.

Comparing two things draws attention to their similarities and indicates a number of differences. When authors contrast, they focus only on differences. Both comparing and contrasting may be done point-by-point, noting both the similarities and differences of each point, or in sequential paragraphs, where you discuss all the similarities and then all the differences, or vice versa.

BREAKING TEXT INTO PARAGRAPHS

For most forms of writing, you will need to use multiple paragraphs. As such, determining when to start a new paragraph is very important. Reasons for starting a new paragraph include:

- To mark off the introduction and concluding paragraphs
- To signal a shift to a new idea or topic
- To indicate an important shift in time or place
- To explain a point in additional detail
- To highlight a comparison, contrast, or cause and effect relationship

PARAGRAPH LENGTH

Most readers find that their comfort level for a paragraph is between 100 and 200 words. Shorter paragraphs cause too much starting and stopping and give a choppy effect. Paragraphs that are too long often test the attention span of readers. Two notable exceptions to this rule exist. In scientific or scholarly papers, longer paragraphs suggest seriousness and depth. In journalistic writing, constraints are placed on paragraph size by the narrow columns in a newspaper format.

The first and last paragraphs of a text will usually be the introduction and conclusion. These special-purpose paragraphs are likely to be shorter than paragraphs in the body of the work. Paragraphs in the body of the essay follow the subject's outline (e.g., one paragraph per point in short essays and a group of paragraphs per point in longer works). Some ideas require more development than others, so it is good for a writer to remain flexible. A paragraph of excessive length may be divided, and shorter ones may be combined.

COHERENT PARAGRAPHS

A smooth flow of sentences and paragraphs without gaps, shifts, or bumps will lead to paragraph **coherence**. Ties between old and new information can be smoothed using several methods:

- **Linking ideas clearly**, from the topic sentence to the body of the paragraph, is essential for a smooth transition. The topic sentence states the main point, and this should be followed by specific details, examples, and illustrations that support the topic sentence. The support may be direct or indirect. In **indirect support**, the illustrations and examples may support a sentence that in turn supports the topic directly.
- The **repetition of key words** adds coherence to a paragraph. To avoid dull language, variations of the key words may be used.
- **Parallel structures** are often used within sentences to emphasize the similarity of ideas and connect sentences giving similar information.
- Maintaining a **consistent verb tense** throughout the paragraph helps. Shifting tenses affects the smooth flow of words and can disrupt the coherence of the paragraph.

> **Review Video: How to Write a Good Paragraph**
> Visit mometrix.com/academy and enter code: 682127

SEQUENCE WORDS AND PHRASES

When a paragraph opens with the topic sentence, the second sentence may begin with a phrase like *first of all*, introducing the first supporting detail or example. The writer may introduce the second supporting item with words or phrases like *also*, *in addition*, and *besides*. The writer might introduce succeeding pieces of support with wording like, *another thing*, *moreover*, *furthermore*, or *not only that, but*. The writer may introduce the last piece of support with *lastly*, *finally*, or *last but not least*. Writers get off the point by presenting off-target items not supporting the main point. For example, a main point *my dog is not smart* is supported by the statement, *he's six years old and still doesn't answer to his name*. But *he cries when I leave for school* is not supportive, as it does not indicate lack of intelligence. Writers stay on point by presenting only supportive statements that are directly relevant to and illustrative of their main point.

TRANSITIONS

Transitions between sentences and paragraphs guide readers from idea to idea and indicate relationships between sentences and paragraphs. Writers should be judicious in their use of transitions, inserting them sparingly. They should also be selected to fit the author's purpose—transitions can indicate time, comparison, and conclusion, among other purposes. Tone is also important to consider when using transitional phrases, varying the tone for different audiences. For example, in a scholarly essay, *in summary* would be preferable to the more informal *in short*.

When working with transitional words and phrases, writers usually find a natural flow that indicates when a transition is needed. In reading a draft of the text, it should become apparent where the flow is disrupted. At this point, the writer can add transitional elements during the revision process. Revising can also afford an opportunity to delete transitional devices that seem heavy handed or unnecessary.

TYPES OF TRANSITIONAL WORDS

Time	Afterward, immediately, earlier, meanwhile, recently, lately, now, since, soon, when, then, until, before, etc.
Sequence	too, first, second, further, moreover, also, again, and, next, still, besides, finally
Comparison	similarly, in the same way, likewise, also, again, once more
Contrasting	but, although, despite, however, instead, nevertheless, on the one hand... on the other hand, regardless, yet, in contrast.
Cause and Effect	because, consequently, thus, therefore, then, to this end, since, so, as a result, if... then, accordingly
Examples	for example, for instance, such as, to illustrate, indeed, in fact, specifically
Place	near, far, here, there, to the left/right, next to, above, below, beyond, opposite, beside
Concession	granted that, naturally, of course, it may appear, although it is true that
Repetition, Summary, or Conclusion	as mentioned earlier, as noted, in other words, in short, on the whole, to summarize, therefore, as a result, to conclude, in conclusion
Addition	and, also, furthermore, moreover
Generalization	in broad terms, broadly speaking, in general

> **Review Video: Transitional Words and Phrases**
> Visit mometrix.com/academy and enter code: 197796
>
> **Review Video: Transitions**
> Visit mometrix.com/academy and enter code: 707563
>
> **Review Video: How to Effectively Connect Sentences**
> Visit mometrix.com/academy and enter code: 948325

CONCLUSION

Two important principles to consider when writing a conclusion are strength and closure. A strong conclusion gives the reader a sense that the author's main points are meaningful and important, and that the supporting facts and arguments are convincing, solid, and well developed. When a conclusion achieves closure, it gives the impression that the writer has stated all necessary information and points and completed the work, rather than simply stopping after a specified length. Some things to avoid when writing concluding paragraphs include:

- Introducing a completely new idea
- Beginning with obvious or unoriginal phrases like "In conclusion" or "To summarize"
- Apologizing for one's opinions or writing
- Repeating the thesis word for word rather than rephrasing it
- Believing that the conclusion must always summarize the piece

> **Review Video: Drafting Conclusions**
> Visit mometrix.com/academy and enter code: 209408

Writing Style and Form

WRITING STYLE AND LINGUISTIC FORM

Linguistic form encodes the literal meanings of words and sentences. It comes from the phonological, morphological, syntactic, and semantic parts of a language. **Writing style** consists of different ways of encoding the meaning and indicating figurative and stylistic meanings. An author's writing style can also be referred to as his or her **voice**.

Writers' stylistic choices accomplish three basic effects on their audiences:

- They **communicate meanings** beyond linguistically dictated meanings,
- They communicate the **author's attitude**, such as persuasive or argumentative effects accomplished through style, and
- They communicate or **express feelings**.

Within style, component areas include:

- Narrative structure
- Viewpoint
- Focus
- Sound patterns
- Meter and rhythm
- Lexical and syntactic repetition and parallelism
- Writing genre
- Representational, realistic, and mimetic effects
- Representation of thought and speech
- Meta-representation (representing representation)
- Irony
- Metaphor and other indirect meanings
- Representation and use of historical and dialectal variations
- Gender-specific and other group-specific speech styles, both real and fictitious
- Analysis of the processes for inferring meaning from writing

LEVEL OF FORMALITY

The relationship between writer and reader is important in choosing a **level of formality** as most writing requires some degree of formality. **Formal writing** is for addressing a superior in a school or work environment. Business letters, textbooks, and newspapers use a moderate to high level of formality. **Informal writing** is appropriate for private letters, personal emails, and business correspondence between close associates.

For your exam, you will want to be aware of informal and formal writing. One way that this can be accomplished is to watch for shifts in point of view in the essay. For example, unless writers are using a personal example, they will rarely refer to themselves (e.g., *I* think that *my* point is very clear.") to avoid being informal when they need to be formal.

Also, be mindful of an author who addresses his or her audience **directly** in their writing (e.g., "Readers, *like you*, will understand this argument.") as this can be a sign of informal writing. Good writers understand the need to be consistent with their level of formality. Shifts in levels of formality or point of view can confuse readers and cause them to discount the message.

CLICHÉS

Clichés are phrases that have been **overused** to the point that the phrase has no importance or has lost the original meaning. These phrases have no originality and add very little to a passage. Therefore, most writers will avoid the use of clichés. Another option is to make changes to a cliché so that it is not predictable and empty of meaning.

Examples:

When life gives you lemons, make lemonade.

Every cloud has a silver lining.

JARGON

Jargon is **specialized vocabulary** that is used among members of a certain trade or profession. Since jargon is understood by only a small audience, writers will use jargon in passages that will only be read by a specialized audience. For example, medical jargon should be used in a medical journal but not in a New York Times article. Jargon includes exaggerated language that tries to impress rather than inform. Sentences filled with jargon are not precise and are difficult to understand.

Examples:

"He is going to *toenail* these frames for us." (Toenail is construction jargon for nailing at an angle.)

"They brought in a *kip* of material today." (Kip refers to 1000 pounds in architecture and engineering.)

SLANG

Slang is an **informal** and sometimes private language that is understood by some individuals. Slang terms have some usefulness, but they can have a small audience. So, most formal writing will not include this kind of language.

Examples:

"Yes, the event was a blast!" (In this sentence, *blast* means that the event was a great experience.)

"That attempt was an epic fail." (By *epic fail*, the speaker means that his or her attempt was not a success.)

COLLOQUIALISM

A colloquialism is a word or phrase that is found in informal writing. Unlike slang, **colloquial language** will be familiar to a greater range of people. However, colloquialisms are still considered inappropriate for formal writing. Colloquial language can include some slang, but these are limited to contractions for the most part.

Examples:

"Can *y'all* come back another time?" (Y'all is a contraction of "you all.")

"Will you stop him from building this *castle in the air*?" (A "castle in the air" is an improbable or unlikely event.)

ACADEMIC LANGUAGE

In educational settings, students are often expected to use academic language in their schoolwork. Academic language is also commonly found in dissertations and theses, texts published by academic journals, and other forms of academic research. Academic language conventions may vary between fields, but general academic language is free of slang, regional terminology, and noticeable grammatical errors. Specific terms may also be used in academic language, and it is important to understand their proper usage. A writer's command of academic language impacts their ability to communicate in an academic or professional context. While it is acceptable to use colloquialisms, slang, improper grammar, or other forms of informal speech in social settings or at home, it is inappropriate to practice non-academic language in academic contexts.

TONE

Tone may be defined as the writer's **attitude** toward the topic, and to the audience. This attitude is reflected in the language used in the writing. The tone of a work should be **appropriate to the topic** and to the intended audience. While it may be fine to use slang or jargon in some pieces, other texts should not contain such terms. Tone can range from humorous to serious and any level in between. It may be more or less formal, depending on the purpose of the writing and its intended audience. All these nuances in tone can flavor the entire writing and should be kept in mind as the work evolves.

WORD SELECTION

A writer's choice of words is a signature of their style. Careful thought about the use of words can improve a piece of writing. A passage can be an exciting piece to read when attention is given to the use of vivid or specific nouns rather than general ones.

Example:

> General: His kindness will never be forgotten.

> Specific: His thoughtful gifts and bear hugs will never be forgotten.

Attention should also be given to the kind of verbs that are used in sentences. Active verbs (e.g., run, swim) are about an action. Whenever possible, an **active verb should replace a linking verb** to provide clear examples for arguments and to strengthen a passage overall. When using an active verb, one should be sure that the verb is used in the active voice instead of the passive voice. Verbs are in the active voice when the subject is the one doing the action. A verb is in the passive voice when the subject is the recipient of an action.

Example:

> Passive: The winners were called to the stage by the judges.

> Active: The judges called the winners to the stage.

CONCISENESS

Conciseness is writing that communicates a message in the fewest words possible. Writing concisely is valuable because short, uncluttered messages allow the reader to understand the author's message more easily and efficiently. Planning is important in writing concise messages. If

170

you have in mind what you need to write beforehand, it will be easier to make a message short and to the point. Do not state the obvious.

Revising is also important. After the message is written, make sure you have effective, pithy sentences that efficiently get your point across. When reviewing the information, imagine a conversation taking place, and concise writing will likely result.

APPROPRIATE KINDS OF WRITING FOR DIFFERENT TASKS, PURPOSES, AND AUDIENCES

When preparing to write a composition, consider the audience and purpose to choose the best type of writing. Three common types of writing are persuasive, expository, and narrative. **Persuasive**, or argumentative writing, is used to convince the audience to take action or agree with the author's claims. **Expository** writing is meant to inform the audience of the author's observations or research on a topic. **Narrative** writing is used to tell the audience a story and often allows more room for creativity. While task, purpose, and audience inform a writer's mode of writing, these factors also impact elements such as tone, vocabulary, and formality.

For example, students who are writing to persuade their parents to grant them some additional privilege, such as permission for a more independent activity, should use more sophisticated vocabulary and diction that sounds more mature and serious to appeal to the parental audience. However, students who are writing for younger children should use simpler vocabulary and sentence structure, as well as choose words that are more vivid and entertaining. They should treat their topics more lightly, and include humor when appropriate. Students who are writing for their classmates may use language that is more informal, as well as age-appropriate.

> **Review Video: <u>Writing Purpose and Audience</u>**
> Visit mometrix.com/academy and enter code: 146627

CHSPE Practice Test #1

Mathematics

1. $\frac{1}{3} + \frac{1}{4} =$
   - a. 2/7
   - b. 1/7
   - c. 7/12
   - d. 7/8

2. A hotel charges $48.00 per day for a room. In addition, there is a 7% tax. What is the total cost for the room for one night?
   - a. $48.00
   - b. $51.36
   - c. $55.00
   - d. $81.60

3. A box of cereal is priced at *x* cents per box. A customer has a coupon for 25 cents off. If the store doubles the value of each coupon, how much does the customer pay for the box of cereal?
   - a. $x - 25$
   - b. $x - 50$
   - c. $x + 25$
   - d. $x + 50$

4. If 12 is added to the product of 13 and 7, the result is
   - a. 32
   - b. 79
   - c. 103
   - d. 240

5. What is the perimeter of the triangle *ABC*?

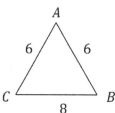

   - a. 14s
   - b. 18
   - c. 20
   - d. 48

172

6. Which of the following is a multiple of 3, 4, and 5?

    a. 120
    b. 150
    c. 170
    d. 190

7. What is the mode of the following numbers: 14, 17, 14, 12, 13, 15, 22, 11?

    a. 13.5
    b. 14
    c. 14.75
    d. 16.5

8. What is 65 increased by 33%?

    a. 21.45
    b. 33.25
    c. 75.65
    d. 86.45

9. What is 2.34×10^6 written in standard notation?

    a. 0.000234
    b. 23,400
    c. 234,000
    d. 2,340,000

10. What is the value of $-9 - (-8)$?

    a. -1
    b. -17
    c. 1
    d. 17

11. $2(7 + 8)^2 - 12(6 \times 2) =$

    a. 119
    b. 225
    c. 306
    d. 604

12. $\frac{3}{16} \times \frac{4}{33} =$

    a. 1/44
    b. 3/8
    c. 3/32
    d. 5/12

13. Convert the decimal 0.1650 into a fraction.

    a. 33/40
    b. 2/5
    c. 33/200
    d. 165/200

14. Simplify $\sqrt{48}$.

   a. $5\sqrt{2}$
   b. $4\sqrt{2}$
   c. $4\sqrt{3}$
   d. $4\sqrt{5}$

15. Alabama's birthrate increased from 66,000 births per year to 70,100 births per year. What is the percent of increase?

   a. 4.7%
   b. 5.8%
   c. 6.21%
   d. 7.33%

16. The dimensions of a pool are 30 feet by 20 feet by 6 feet. What volume of water is needed to fill the pool, in cubic feet?

   a. $300\ ft^3$
   b. $600\ ft^3$
   c. $3,000\ ft^3$
   d. $3,600\ ft^3$

17. The ratio of blue food coloring to yellow food coloring used in making green cake frosting is 3 to 2. If 18 drops of blue food coloring are used, how many drops of yellow food coloring are needed?

   a. 2
   b. 6
   c. 8
   d. 12

18. What is the difference between 3.8 and .571?

   a. .73
   b. 2.567
   c. 3.229
   d. 4.26

19. 5 more than 6 times a number is 77. What is the number?

   a. 12
   b. 17
   c. 72
   d. 82

20. Karen received scores of 74, 63, 61, 42, 90, and 78 on her math tests. What was Karen's average score for these six tests?

   a. 64
   b. 66
   c. 68
   d. 70

21. Tom works 25 hours a week and earns $7.75 per hour. He received a raise that increases his weekly pay to $206.25. What is the increase in Tom's weekly pay?

    a. $12.50
    b. $13.25
    c. $13.75
    d. $14.50

206.25 − 193.57

22. Jamie eats 4 bagels a day. If a bagel weighs 8 ounces, how many pounds of bagels does Jamie eat per week?

    a. 2 pounds
    b. 12 pounds, 8 ounces
    c. 14 pounds
    d. 17 pounds, 9 ounces

32 ounces × 7   224 ounces

23. Barbara is throwing a six-sided die. If she throws a 4 on her first throw, what is the probability that her next throw will not be a four?

    a. 1/6
    b. 1/2
    c. 2/3
    d. 5/6

24. If the radius of a circle is 8, then the area of the circle is

    a. 4
    b. 8
    c. 64π
    d. $64 + \pi$

25. What is the perimeter of triangle *ABC*?

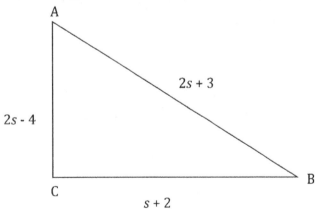

    a. $3s + 5$
    b. $5s + 1$
    c. $5s + 9$
    d. $6s + 3$

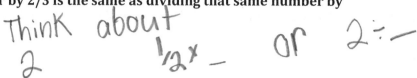

26. Multiplying a number by 2/3 is the same as dividing that same number by

a. ~~2/3~~
b. ~~3/4~~
c. ~~1~~
d. 3/2

Think about 2  *½x or 2 ÷ —*

27. On his last math test, Sam got 2 questions correct for every 3 questions he missed. If the test had a total of 60 questions, how many questions did Sam answer correctly?

a. 12
b. 24
c. 36
d. 60

2:3 ratio

28. Solve for *m*:

$$5m + 8 = 48$$

a. $m = 5$
b. $m = 8$
c. $m = 10$
d. $m = 18$

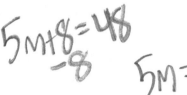

29. Solve $(3x + 1)(7x + 10)$

a. $12x^2 + 17x + 10$
b. $21x^2 + 37x + 10$
c. $21x^2 + 23x + 10$
d. $21x^2 + 37x + 9$

30. Joseph purchased 12 pounds of peaches at 80 cents per pound. He calculated the total amount as $12 \times \$0.80 = \$9.60$. Another method Joseph could have used to calculate the total cost of the peaches is:

a. $(10 \times \$0.80) + (2 \times \$0.80)$
b. $(12 \times \$0.40) + (2 \times \$0.80)$
c. $(12 \times \$0.20) + (12 \times \$0.20)$
d. $(2 \times \$0.80) + (10 \times \$0.40)$

31. What is the value of the expression $-3 \times 5^2 + 2(4 - 18) + 33$?

a. -130
b. -70
c. -20
d. 74

32. $10x - 36 + 4x - 6 + x = 3$. What is the value of x?

a. 3
b. 4
c. 6
d. 10

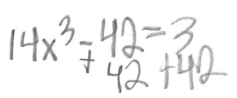

$14x^3 \div 42 = 3$
$\div 42 + 42$

$= 3$
$14x^3 = 45$
$x^3 = 3.21$

33. Hunter planted a combination of tomatoes, broccoli, and bell peppers in a ratio of 3:2:1 in his garden. If the garden had a total of 72 plants, how many tomatoes are in his garden?
    a. 12
    b. 24
    c. 32
    d. 36

34. What is the area of triangle *RST*?

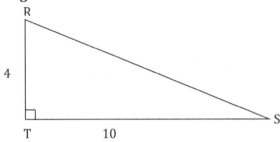

    a. 7
    b. 14
    c. 20
    d. 40

35. Dividing a number by 2 is the same as multiplying that number by
    a. 2
    b. 1
    c. ¼
    d. ½

36. How many seconds are there in 36 hours?
    a. 2,160
    b. 51,840
    c. 129,600
    d. 132,200

36 hours | 60 minutes | 60 sec
1 hour | 1 Min

37. If $6x + 12 = 18$, what is the value of $9x$?
    a. 0
    b. 1
    c. 6
    d. 9

$9x + 12 = 18$
$-12 \quad 12$
$9x = 6$

38. A box in the form of a rectangular solid has a square base of 5 feet in length, a width of 5 feet, and a height of *h* feet. If the volume of the rectangular solid is 200 cubic feet, which of the following equations may be used to find *h*?
    a. $5h = 200$
    b. $5h^2 = 200$
    c. $25h = 200$
    d. $h = 200 \div 5$

39. 3/4 = 9/x. What is the value of x?
    a. 4
    b. 9
    c. 12
    d. 36

40. If the area of a square is 64, the side of the square equals
    a. 4
    b. 8
    c. 32
    d. 64

41. −17 is greater than which of the following numbers?
    a. −10
    b. −24
    c. 0
    d. 17

42. If $7\sqrt{x} + 16 = 79$, what is the value of x?
    a. 6
    b. 9
    c. 27
    d. 81

$$7\sqrt{x} + 16 = 79 \qquad 7\sqrt{x} = 63$$
$$-16 \quad -16$$

43. If $6a = 18$ and $3b = 9$, what is the value of a/b?
    a. 2/3
    b. 1/2
    c. 1
    d. 3/2

44. What is the product of 39 and 62?
    a. 23
    b. 101
    c. 2,418
    d. 3,516

45. Rhonda is putting carpet in her living room. She chose carpet that costs $12 a square yard. What is the total cost of carpeting her living room?

```
|--------- 21 ft. ---------|
|                          |
|                          | 12 ft.
|                          |
|--------------------------|
```

    a. $3,024
    b. $1,008
    c. $336
    d. $224

46. What is the mode of the following numbers: 21, 32, 21, 19, 23, 26, 22, and 18?

    a. 21
    b. 21.5
    c. 22.75
    d. 32

47. The solution $x = -5$ makes which of the following equations true?

    a. $14 - x = 9$
    b. $x + 3 = 8$
    c. $30/x = 6$
    d. $12x = -60$

48. On a road map, 1/4 inch represents 8 miles of actual road distance. The towns of Dinuba and Clovis are represented by points 2 1/8 inches apart on the map. What in the actual distance, in miles, between the two towns?

    a. 32
    b. 40
    c. 60
    d. 68

49. A doctor performs 24 surgeries in a week. If she performed four surgeries on Monday, how many surgeries were performed each day, on average, to finish by Friday?

    a. 3
    b. 4
    c. 5
    d. 6

50. Robert is planning to drive 1,800 miles on a cross-country trip. If his car gets 30 miles to the gallon, and his tank holds 12 gallons of gas, how many tanks of gas will he need to complete the trip?

    a. 3 tanks of gas
    b. 5 tanks of gas
    c. 30 tanks of gas
    d. 60 tanks of gas

Language

Refer to the following for questions 1 - 18:

These questions present a sentence, all or part of which is underlined. Beneath each sentence you will find four ways of phrasing the underlined part. The first of these repeats the original; the other three are different. If you think the original is best, choose the first answer; otherwise, choose one of the other answers.

1. If he stops to consider the ramifications of this decision, it is probable that he will rethink his original decision a while longer.

    a. it is probable that he will rethink his original decision.
    b. he will rethink his original decision over again.
    c. he probably will rethink his original decision.
    d. he will most likely rethink his original decision for a bit.

2. "When you get older," she said "you will no doubt understand what I mean."

    a. older," she said "you will no doubt
    b. older" she said "you will no doubt
    c. older," she said, "you will no doubt
    d. older," she said "you will not

3. Dr. Anderson strolled past the nurses, examining a bottle of pills.

    a. Dr. Anderson strolled past the nurses, examining a bottle of pills.
    b. Dr. Anderson strolled past the nurses examining a bottle of pills.
    c. Dr. Anderson strolled past, the nurses examining a bottle of pills.
    d. Examining a bottle of pills, Dr. Anderson strolled past the nurses.

4. Karl and Henry raced to the reservoir, climbed the ladder, and then they dove into the cool water.

    a. raced to the reservoir, climbed the ladder, and then they dove into
    b. first raced to the reservoir, climbed the ladder, and then they dove into
    c. raced to the reservoir, they climbed the ladder, and then they dove into
    d. raced to the reservoir, climbed the ladder, and dove into

5. Did either Tracy or Vanessa realize that her decision would be so momentous?

    a. Tracy or Vanessa realize that her decision would be.
    b. Tracy or Vanessa realize that each of their decision was.
    c. Tracy or Vanessa realize that her or her decision would be.
    d. Tracy or Vanessa realize that their decision would be.

6. Despite their lucky escape, Jason and his brother could not hardly enjoy themselves.

    a. Jason and his brother could not hardly enjoy themselves.
    b. Jason and his brother could not enjoy themselves.
    c. Jason and Jason's brother could not hardly enjoy themselves.
    d. Jason and his brother could not enjoy them.

7. Stew recipes call <u>for rosemary, parsley, thyme, and these sort of herbs</u>.

    a. for rosemary, parsley, thyme, and these sort of herbs.
    b. for: rosemary; parsley; thyme; and these sort of herbs.
    c. for rosemary, parsley, thyme, and these sorts of herbs.
    d. for rosemary, parsley, thyme, and this sorts of herbs.

8. Mr. King, <u>an individual of considerable influence, created a personal fortune and gave back</u> to the community.

    a. an individual of considerable influence, created a personal fortune and gave back.
    b. an individual of considerable influence, he created a personal fortune and gave back.
    c. an individual of considerable influence created a personal fortune and gave back.
    d. an individual of considerable influence, created a personal fortune and gave it back.

9. <u>She is the person whose opinion matters the most</u>.

    a. She is the person whose opinion matters the most.
    b. She is the person to whom opinion matters the most.
    c. She is the person who matters the most, in my opinion.
    d. She is the person for whom opinion matters the most.

10. Which sentence is written correctly?

    a. Due to his disheveled appearance, she thought he hadn't slept.
    b. Due to his disheveled appearance she thought he hadn't slept.
    c. Due to his disheveled appearance – she thought he hadn't slept.
    d. Due to his disheveled appearance; she thought he hadn't slept.

11. Which sentence is the clearest?

    a. Drawn by her daughter, there is a picture on her office wall.
    b. There is a picture drawn by her daughter on her office wall.
    c. Drawn, there is a picture on her office wall by her daughter.
    d. By her daughter, a picture is drawn on her office wall.

12. Each received _____ trophy to take home.

    a. it's
    b. her
    c. their
    d. our

13. Eli _____ insisted that it wasn't his fault.

    a. tearfully
    b. tearilly
    c. with tears
    d. teary

14. Margaret _____ the committee into thinking the project was all her work.

    a. missled
    b. misled
    c. mislead
    d. mislled

15. Tomorrow, Atticus will _____ cupcakes to school.

  a. brought
  b. had brought
  c. bring
  d. broughten

16. Each participant in the course on being a good father received _____ signed copy of the teacher's book.

  a. their
  b. our
  c. his
  d. ones

17. Several of the runners _____ not to complete the race; they met the rest of us by the finish line.

  a. decide
  b. decided
  c. decides
  d. were deciding

18. Stephanie writes _____.

  a. good
  b. well
  c. clear
  d. more

Refer to the following for questions 19 - 22:

Identify the misspelled word in the sentences below.

19. Judy's neighbor was friends with her neice and invited her on the holiday sleigh ride.

  a. neighbor
  b. friends
  c. neice
  d. sleigh

20. Oscar was truely sad to be enforcing the hateful judgement.

  a. truely
  b. enforcing
  c. hateful
  d. judgement

21. When they hurried the magnificent conveyance along, they were sure that they would be victoryous.

  a. hurried
  b. magnificent
  c. conveyance
  d. victoryous

22. Professor Rinkie told the story but preferred omitting the forgettable occurence with the horses.

- a. preferred
- b. omitting
- c. forgettable
- d. occurence

Refer to the following for questions 23 - 30:

The following sentences test your ability to recognize grammar and usage errors. Each sentence contains either a single error or no error at all. No sentence contains more than one error. The error, if there is one, is lettered. If the sentence contains an error, select the one lettered part that must be changed to make the sentence correct. If the sentence is correct, select Choice D.

23. The information that <u>he was given</u> by the two doctors <u>make him realize</u> how much his <u>grandfather's health</u> had declined.

- a. he was given
- b. make him realize
- c. grandfather's health
- d. No error

24. Quincy and his son Zane, <u>neither </u>of <u>whom</u> enjoy sporting events, <u>is going</u> to see a movie instead.

- a. neither
- b. whom
- c. is going
- d. No error

25. The entire audience (a) <u>are</u> rapt for the (b) <u>duration</u> of the performance and applaud (c) <u>loudly</u> when the curtain falls.

- a. are
- b. duration of the performance and applaud (c)
- c. loudly
- d. No error

26. (a) <u>When asked about</u> her major job responsibilities, (b) <u>Jodi answered that</u> she responded to client questions, conducted interviews, wrote reports, and (c) <u>giving presentations</u>.

- a. When asked about
- b. Jodi answered that
- c. giving presentations
- d. No error

183

27. In the time of the dinosaurs, other <u>flora and fauna</u> on earth <u>are</u> very different from what we're <u>used to</u> today.

    a. flora and fauna
    b. are
    c. used to
    d. No error

28. Our <u>dogs don't</u> behave well at home with us, <u>but may</u> be <u>a good achiever</u> in obedience school.

    a. dogs don't
    b. but may
    c. a good achiever
    d. No error

29. Everyone <u>in the firm</u> <u>participated in</u> the gift exchange and brought <u>their present</u> to the reception desk for distribution.

    a. in the firm
    b. participated in
    c. their present
    d. No error

30. My <u>aunt was</u> very surprised when my mom <u>told her</u> that <u>Henry was</u> better at Spanish than my sister.

    a. aunt was
    b. told her
    c. Henry was
    d. No error

Refer to the following for questions 31 - 36:

(1) One of the pioneer sculptors of the nineteenth century was Honore Daumier (1810-1879). (2) He is well-known particularly for caricature heads that were created between 1830 and 1832. (3) His later works anticipate the work of Rodin, what with their highly cut-out surfaces offset by studied, flowing poses.

(4) Although Daumier was one of the first modern sculptors, his work did not serve as an influence to later artists. (5) This is because nearly all of the other artists of the time hardly ever got to see any of it. (6) This is also true of the sculpture of Degas, who was known as a painter rather than a sculptor, and whose sculpture also was not widely exhibited at the time. (7) And yet, Degas was clearly the greatest sculptor of the era. (8) His bronze casts of dancers and horses retain the layered feeling of the wax models that were their first versions. (9) His more complex scenes seem like crosses between sculpture and painting. (10) When looked at more closely, they display a feeling of mass that the painted canvas cannot by itself convey. (11) It is the interplay between the separate masses in these scenes that involves the viewer and gives them their sense of intrigue.

31. Which is the best version of the underlined part of sentence 2 (reproduced below)?

He is well-known particularly for caricature heads that were created between 1830 and 1832.

    a. (As it is now)
    b. He is well known, particularly
    c. He is particularly well known
    d. He is well known particularly

32. Which is the best version of the underlined part of sentence 3 (reproduced below)?

His later works anticipate the work of Rodin, what with their highly cut-out surfaces offset by studied, flowing poses.

    a. (As it is now)
    b. of Rodin; what with highly cut out surfaces
    c. of Rodin, with highly cut-out surfaces
    d. of Rodin, with cut-out surfaces

33. In context, which is the best revision of sentence 5 (reproduced below)?

This is because nearly all of the other artists of the time hardly ever got to see any of it.

    a. (As it is now)
    b. This is because it was almost never exhibited at the time.
    c. His work was hardly ever exhibited.
    d. This is because they hardly ever saw any of it.

34. In context, which is the best way to revise sentence 6 (reproduced below)?

This is also true of the sculpture of Degas, who was known as a painter rather than a sculptor, and whose sculpture also was not widely exhibited at the time.

    a. Add "In addition," to the beginning of the sentence.
    b. Delete the words ", and whose sculpture was also not widely exhibited at the time."
    c. Change the words "sculpture of Degas" to read "work of Degas".
    d. Change "This is also true" to "This was also true".

35. Which sentence is best inserted after sentence 7?

    a. A large body of his sculpted works can be found in museums today.
    b. His paintings were famous even before the time of his death.
    c. He made sculptures out of bronze, stone, and even wood.
    d. You can see pictures of his work in many books.

36. Which is best added to the beginning of sentence 10?

    a. Increasingly,
    b. And yet,
    c. Beneath this,
    d. However,

Refer to the following for questions 37 - 43:

Madame President

A

(1) Before they had the right to vote, women have attempted to gain the nations highest executive office. (2) Victoria Woodhull ran as a third party candidate in 1872. (3) Although she did not win, she became the first woman who owned an investment firm on wall street. (4) In 1884 and 1888, the lawyer Belva Lockwood also ran as a third party candidate. (5) Margaret Chase Smith (who served in both houses of Congress) was the first woman nominated by a major party: the Republicans.

B

(6) Nine other women have sought for the presidency since the 1970s. (7) Five of them were Democrats and one was a Republican and three represented third parties. (8) I think it's about time this country had a woman as president. (9) Only two women have been nominated as vice president: Democrat Geraldine Ferraro in 1984 and Republican Sarah Palin in 2008. (10) Many people believe that soon the United States will join countries such as Britain, India, Germany, Chile, and Liberia, that have women heads of state.

37. Sentence (1): *"Before they had the right to vote, women have attempted to gain the nations highest executive office."*

What correction should be made to this sentence?

    a. capitalize <u>executive office</u>
    b. change <u>nations</u> to <u>nation's</u>
    c. put *finally* between <u>to</u> and <u>gain</u>
    d. no correction is needed

38. Sentence (3): *"Although she did not win, she became the first woman who owned an investment firm on wall street."*

What correction should be made to this sentence?

    a. change <u>became</u> to <u>become</u>
    b. capitalize <u>wall street</u>
    c. change <u>Although</u> to <u>Though</u>
    d. capitalize <u>investment firm</u>

39. Sentence (5): *"Margaret Chase Smith (who served in both houses of Congress) was the first woman nominated by a major part: the Republicans."*

What correction should be made to this sentence?

    a. change the parentheses to commas
    b. do not capitalize <u>Republicans</u>
    c. change <u>woman</u> to <u>women</u>
    d. no correction is necessary

40. Sentence (6): *"Nine other <u>women have seeked for</u> the presidency since the 1970s."*

Which of the following is the best way to write the underlined portion of this sentence? If you think the original is the best way to write the sentence, choose answer A.

    a. women have seeked for
    b. woman have seeked for
    c. women have seek for
    d. women have sought

41. Sentence (7): *"Five of them were Democrats and one was a Republican, and three represented third parties."*

What correction should be made to this sentence?

    a. add a comma after <u>Democrats</u> and delete the <u>and</u> after <u>Democrats</u>
    b. change <u>them</u> to <u>those</u>
    c. change <u>were</u> to <u>was</u>
    d. no correction is necessary

42. Which revision would improve the overall organization of this article?

    a. switch paragraphs A and B
    b. place the final sentence at the beginning of paragraph B
    c. delete sentence (8)
    d. place sentence (2) at the end of paragraph A

43. Sentence (10): *"Many people believe that the United States will soon join countries such as Britain, India, Germany, Chile, and Liberia, that have women heads of state."*

What correction should be made to this sentence?

    a. remove the comma after <u>Liberia</u>
    b. remove the unnecessary commas
    c. change the spelling of <u>believe</u> to <u>beleive</u>
    d. no correction is necessary

Refer to the following for questions 44 - 48:

The upcoming sentences are given to measure your ability to correctly and efficiently convey meaning. When you are choosing your answer, remember that the sentences should utilize conventional written English, including grammar, word selection, conventional sentence structure, and punctuation.

There will be either a section or a complete sentence underlined. Beneath the sentence there are different choices. The first choice (A) will be the same as the underlined section. The remaining choices give different substitutions that could replace the underlined section.

Choose the letter that corresponds with the choice that best conveys the meaning of the original sentence. If the original wording is the best, select answer choice A. If not, choose one of the other choices. The correct answer is the one that keeps the original meaning and makes the sentence the most effective. Make sure your choice makes the sentence understandable without being cumbersome or unclear.

44. Minerals are nutritionally significant elements <u>that assist to make your body</u> work properly.

    a. that assist to make your body
    b. that help your body
    c. that making your body
    d. that work to make your body

45. Of the two, <u>the oldest brother</u> had a much more difficult time in school.

    a. the oldest brother
    b. the older brother
    c. the earliest brother
    d. the best brother

46. The duck waddled toward the pond, <u>her five ducklings following just behind her</u>.

    a. her five ducklings following just behind her
    b. and then there were five ducklings following in back of her
    c. therefore the ducklings were following behind
    d. and so her five ducklings were following just behind her

47. <u>Fair teachers understand that he or she</u> cannot treat any student with favoritism.

    a. Fair teachers understand that he or she
    b. Fair teachers understand that he
    c. Fair teachers understand that she
    d. Fair teachers understand that they

48. We will begin with painting <u>first, and then secondly</u> we will start the decoupage process.

    a. first, and then secondly
    b. firstly, and then secondly
    c. first, and then second
    d. first, then second

Reading

Refer to the following for questions 1 - 12:

Cultivation of Tomato Plants

Tomato plants should be started in window boxes or greenhouses in late March so that they will be ready for the garden after the last frost. Use a soil of equal parts of sand, peat moss, and manure, and plant the seeds about a quarter of an inch deep. After covering, water them through a cloth to protect the soil and cover the box with a pane of glass. Keep the box in a warm place for a few days, then place it in a sunny window. After the second leaf makes its appearance on the seedling, transplant the plant to another box, placing the seedlings two inches apart. Another alternative is to put the sprouted seedlings in four-inch pots, setting them deeper in the soil than they stood in the seedbed. To make the stem stronger, pinch out the top bud when the seedlings are four or five inches in height.

Finally, place the plants in their permanent positions after they have grown to be twelve or fifteen inches high. When transplanting, parts of some of the longest leaves should be removed. Large plants may be set five or six inches deep.

The soil should be fertilized the previous season. Fresh, stable manure, used as fertilizer, would delay the time of fruiting. To improve the condition of the soil, work in a spade full of old manure to a depth of at least a foot. Nitrate of soda, applied at about two hundred pounds per acre, may be used to give the plant a good start.

Plants grown on supports may be set two feet apart in the row, with the rows three or four feet apart depending upon the variety. Plants not supported by stakes or other methods should be set four feet apart.

Unsupported vines give a lighter yield, and much of the fruit is likely to rot during the wet seasons. Use well-sharpened stakes about two inches in diameter and five feet long. Drive the stakes into the ground at least six inches from the plants so that the roots will not be injured. Tie the tomato vines to the stakes with strings made out of strips of cloth, as twine is likely to cut them. Care must be taken not to wrap the limbs so tightly as to interfere with their growth. The training should start before the plants begin to trail on the ground.

1. What is the overall purpose of this passage?
   a. To describe how soil should be treated in order to plant tomatoes
   b. To give an overview of how tomato plants are cultured
   c. To teach the reader how to operate a farm
   d. To describe a method of supporting tomato vines

2. According to the passage, why is late March the best time to germinate tomato seeds?
   a. The last frost has already passed by this time.
   b. It is warm enough by then to germinate them in window boxes.
   c. By the time the last frost passes, they will be ready to transplant outdoors.
   d. The seeds might not be fertile if one were to wait longer.

3. What does the passage imply as the reason that the seeds should not be planted outdoors immediately?

    a. A late freeze might kill the seedlings.
    b. The soil outdoors is too heavy for new seedlings.
    c. A heavy rain might wash away the seedlings.
    d. New seedlings need to be close to one another and then be moved apart later.

4. Generally speaking, the culturing method consists of what?

    a. Tying the germinated seedlings to stakes.
    b. Watering the new plants regularly.
    c. Sheltering the plants from wind and frost.
    d. Moving the strongest plants progressively to larger pots and then outdoors.

5. What would happen if the bud weren't pinched out of the seedlings when they are in individual pots?

    a. The plants would be weaker.
    b. The plants would freeze.
    c. The plants would need more water.
    d. The plants would not survive as long.

6. Why are the plants set further apart each time they are replanted?

    a. The soil is being depleted each time they are planted.
    b. The plants are larger and need more soil for nourishment.
    c. More room is required in order to plant the stakes for support.
    d. More room is required so that nitrate of soda can be added.

7. Why are the newly planted seeds watered through a cloth?

    a. They are unsightly.
    b. The cloth keeps them warm.
    c. The heavy stream of water may disrupt the soil.
    d. The water needs to be filtered.

8. What fertilizers mentioned in the text are used optionally to nourish the plants?

    a. Glass pane
    b. Sand
    c. Peat moss
    d. Nitrate of soda

9. Why is old manure preferred to fresh manure?

    a. Fresh manure delays the plant's production of tomatoes.
    b. Fresh manure smells worse.
    c. Old manure is less expensive.
    d. Old manure mixes more readily with nitrate of soda.

10. Why do you suppose supported plants are set farther apart than unsupported ones?

    a. The stakes take up a lot of room.
    b. More room is required to water them.
    c. Unsupported plants grow taller.
    d. The support system lets the vines spread out over a larger area.

11. What is the purpose of the last paragraph?
    a. To explain why unsupported plants give rotten fruit
    b. To explain why cloth is used rather than wire
    c. To describe in detail how tomato plants are cultured
    d. To instruct the reader in the method of supporting tomato vines for culture

12. When are the plants tied to stakes?
    a. As soon as the plants are transplanted outdoors.
    b. When the plants begin to bear fruit.
    c. Before the plants drag on the ground.
    d. After the last frost once the roots have set.

Refer to the following for questions 13 - 24:

The Coins of Ancient Greece

We don't usually think of coins as works of art, and most of them really do not invite us to do so. The study of coins, their development, and their history is termed *numismatics*. Numismatics is a topic of great interest to archaeologists and anthropologists, but not usually from the perspective of visual delectation. The coin is intended, after all, to be a utilitarian object, not an artistic one. Many early Greek coins are aesthetically pleasing as well as utilitarian, however, and not simply because they are the earliest examples of coin design. Rather, Greek civic individualism provides the reason. Every Greek political entity expressed its identity through its coinage.

The idea of stamping metal pellets of a standard weight with an identifying design had its origin on the Ionian Peninsula around 600 BC. Each of the Greek city-states produced its own coinage adorned with its particular symbols. The designs were changed frequently to commemorate battles, treaties, and other significant occasions. In addition to their primary use as a pragmatic means of facilitating commerce, Greek coins were clearly an expression of civic pride. The popularity of early coinage led to a constant demand for new designs, such that there arose a class of highly skilled artisans who took great pride in their work, so much so that they sometimes even signed it. As a result, Greek coins provide us not only with an invaluable source of historical knowledge but also with a genuine expression of the evolving Greek sense of form. These minuscule works reflect the development of Greek sculpture from the sixth to the second century BC as dependably as do larger works made of marble. And since they are stamped with the place and date of their production, they provide a historical record of artistic development that is remarkably dependable and complete.

13. What is the purpose of this passage?
    a. To attract new adherents to numismatics as a pastime
    b. To show how ancient Greeks used coins in commerce
    c. To teach the reader that money was invented in Greece
    d. To describe ancient Greek coinage as an art form

14. What is meant by the phrase "most of them really do not invite us to do so," as used in the first sentence?

   a. Money is not usually included when sending an invitation.
   b. Most coins are not particularly attractive.
   c. Invitations are not generally engraved onto coins.
   d. Coins do not speak.

15. What is a synonym for *delectation*, as used in the third sentence?

   a. Savoring
   b. Choosing
   c. Deciding
   d. Refusing

16. What is meant by the term *numismatics*?

   a. The study of numbers
   b. Egyptian history
   c. Greek history
   d. The study of coins

17. According to the text, how do ancient Greek coins differ from most other coinage?

   a. They are different simply because they were the first coins.
   b. Each political entity made its own coins.
   c. They were made of precious metals.
   d. They were designed with extraordinary care.

18. How often were new coins designed in ancient Greece?

   a. Monthly
   b. Not very often
   c. Whenever there was a significant occasion to commemorate
   d. When the old ones wore out

19. What is indicated by the fact that the artisans who designed the coins sometimes signed them?

   a. They took pride in their work
   b. They were being held accountable for their work
   c. The signature certified the value of the coin
   d. The Greeks had developed writing

20. What is meant by the term *pragmatic*, as used in the fourth sentence of the second paragraph?

   a. Valuable
   b. Monetary
   c. Useful
   d. Practical

21. According to the passage, how are Greek coins similar to Greek sculpture?

a. Some sculptures were made of metal.
b. The coins were smaller.
c. Shapes were stamped into the coins.
d. Coin designs evolved along with the Greek sense of form.

22. Why is it significant that new coin designs were required frequently?

a. This indicates that there was a lot of commercial activity going on.
b. This gave the designers a lot of practice.
c. There were a lot of things to commemorate.
d. The Greeks needed to find new sources of precious metals.

23. Why is it significant that the coins were dated, according to the passage?

a. The dates contributed to the designs
b. The age of the designers could be determined.
c. It allows historians to track the evolution of Greek artistic styles.
d. It allows historians to know when battles and treaties took place.

24. What was the primary purpose of the Greek coin?

a. To commemorate treaties and battles.
b. To provide minuscule works of art.
c. They were used as adornments.
d. To facilitate commerce.

Refer to the following for questions 25 - 36:

Garth

The next morning, she realized that she had slept. This surprised her—so long had sleep been denied her! She opened her eyes and saw the sun at the window. And then, beside it in the window, the deformed visage of Garth. Quickly, she shut her eyes again, feigning sleep. But he was not fooled. Presently, she heard his voice, soft and kind: "Don't be afraid. I'm your friend. I came to watch you sleep, is all. There now, I am behind the wall. You can open your eyes."

The voice seemed pained and plaintive. The Hungarian opened her eyes, and saw the window empty. Steeling herself, she arose, went to it, and looked out. She saw the man below, cowering by the wall, looking grief-stricken and resigned. Making an effort to overcome her revulsion, she spoke to him as kindly as she could.

"Come," she said, but Garth, seeing her lips move, thought she was sending him away. He rose and began to lumber off, his eyes lowered and filled with despair.

"Come!" she cried again, but he continued to move off. Then, she swept from the cell, ran to him, and took his arm. Feeling her touch, Garth trembled uncontrollably. Feeling that she drew him toward her, he lifted his supplicating eye, and his whole face lit up with joy.

She drew him into the garden, where she sat upon a wall, and for a while, they sat and contemplated one another. The more the Hungarian looked at Garth, the more deformities she discovered. The twisted spine, the lone eye, the huge torso

193

over the tiny legs. She couldn't comprehend how a creature so awkwardly constructed could exist. And yet, from the air of sadness and gentleness that pervaded his figure, she began to reconcile herself to it.

"Did you call me back?" asked he.

"Yes," she replied, nodding. He recognized the gesture.

"Ah," he exclaimed. "Do you know that I am deaf?"

"Poor fellow," exclaimed the Hungarian, with an expression of pity.

"You'd think nothing more could be wrong with me," Garth put in, somewhat bitterly. But he was happier than he could remember having been.

25. Why was the girl surprised that she had slept?
a. She usually tried to avoid sleeping.
b. It had been a long time since she had had the chance to sleep.
c. She hadn't intended to go to sleep.
d. Garth looked so frightening that she thought he would keep her awake.

26. Why did she shut her eyes again when she saw Garth in the window?
a. She wanted to sleep some more.
b. The sun was so bright that it hurt her eyes.
c. She didn't want to look at Garth.
d. She wanted Garth to think she was still sleeping.

27. What two characteristics are contrasted in Garth?
a. Ugliness and gentleness
b. Fear and merriment
c. Happiness and sadness
d. Anger and fearfulness

28. During this passage, how do the girl's emotions toward Garth change?
a. They go from fear to loathing.
b. They go from anger to fear.
c. They go from fear to disdain.
d. They go from revulsion to pity.

29. Why does the girl have to steel herself to approach the window and look out at Garth?
a. She has not eaten for a long time.
b. She is repelled by his appearance.
c. She is blinded by the sun behind him.
d. The window is open and it is cold.

30. How does Garth feel toward the girl when he first moves away from the window?
a. He is curious about her.
b. He is sad because she appears to reject him.
c. He is angry at her for pretending to sleep.
d. He expects her to scold him.

31. Why does Garth withdraw from the girl when she first speaks to him?

a. He expects her to hurt him.
b. He misunderstands her because he cannot hear.
c. People are always mean to him.
d. He doesn't want her to feel revulsion because of his appearance.

32. What is a synonym for the word supplicating?

a. Castigating
b. Menacing
c. Repeating
d. Begging

33. Why is it surprising that the girl takes Garth's arm?

a. She is engaged to someone else.
b. She has to reach through the window.
c. He is deaf.
d. She was very frightened of him initially.

34. Which of the following adjectives might you use to describe the girl's personality?

a. Determined
b. Robust
c. Contemplative
d. Sympathetic

35. Which of the following adjectives would you use to describe Garth's feelings toward himself?

a. Contemplative
b. Destitute
c. Unhappy
d. Deflated

36. Why is Garth so happy in the last sentence?

a. Because he can understand the girl.
b. He has learned to read lips.
c. Because the girl figured out that he is deaf.
d. Because the girl seems to accept him.

Refer to the following for questions 37 - 42:

New Zealand Inhabitants

The islands of New Zealand are among the most remote of all the Pacific islands. New Zealand is an archipelago, with two large islands and a number of smaller ones. Its climate is far cooler than the rest of Polynesia. According to Māori legends, it was colonized in the early 15th century by a wave of Polynesian voyagers who traveled southward in their canoes and settled on North Island. At this time, New Zealand was already known to the Polynesians, who had probably first landed there some 400 years earlier.

The Polynesian southward migration was limited by the availability of food. Traditional Polynesian tropical crops such as taro and yams will grow on North Island, but the climate of South Island is too cold for them. Coconuts will not grow on either island. The first settlers were forced to rely on hunting and gathering, and, of course, fishing. Especially on South Island, most settlements remained close to the sea. At the time of the Polynesian influx, enormous flocks of moa birds had their rookeries on the island shores. These flightless birds were easy prey for the settlers, and, within a few centuries, had been hunted to extinction. Fish, shellfish, and the roots of ferns were other important sources of food, but even these began to diminish in quantity as the human population increased. The Māori had few other sources of meat: dogs, smaller birds, and rats. Archaeological evidence shows that human flesh was also eaten and that tribal warfare increased markedly after the moa disappeared.

By far, the most important farmed crop in prehistoric New Zealand was the sweet potato. This tuber is hearty enough to grow throughout the islands and could be stored to provide food during the winter months, when other food-gathering activities were difficult. The availability of the sweet potato made possible a significant increase in the human population. Māori tribes often lived in encampments called *pā*, which were fortified with earthen embankments and usually located near the best sweet potato farmlands.

37. A definition for the word *archipelago* is:

a. A country
b. A place in the Southern Hemisphere
c. A group of islands
d. A roosting place for birds

38. This article is primarily about what?

a. The geology of New Zealand
b. New Zealand's early history
c. The culture of New Zealand's first colonists
d. Food sources used by New Zealand's first colonists

39. According to the passage, when was New Zealand first explored?

a. In the 15th century
b. Around the 11th century
c. Thousands of years ago
d. By flightless birds

40. Why did early settlements remain close to the sea?

a. The people liked to swim.
b. The people didn't want to get far from the boats they had come in.
c. Taro and yams grow only close to the beaches.
d. They were dependent upon sea creatures for their food.

41. Why do you suppose tribal warfare increased after the moa disappeared?

a. Increased competition for food led the people to fight.
b. Some groups blamed others for the moa's extinction.
c. They had more time on their hands since they couldn't hunt the moa, so they fought.
d. One group was trying to consolidate political control over the entire country.

42. How did the colder weather of New Zealand make it difficult for the Polynesians to live there?

a. The Polynesians weren't used to making warm clothes.
b. Cold water fish are harder to catch.
c. Some of them froze.
d. Some of their traditional crops would not grow there.

Refer to the following for questions 43 - 54:

Passage 5

The phylum Annelida, named for the Latin word anellus, meaning "ring", includes earthworms, leeches, and other similar organisms. In their typical form, these animals exhibit bilateral symmetry, a cylindrical cross section, and an elongate body divided externally into segments (metameres) by a series of rings (annuli). They are segmented internally as well, with most of the internal organs repeated in series in each segment. This organization is termed metamerism. Metameric segmentation is the distinguishing feature of this phylum, and provides it with a degree of evolutionary plasticity in that certain segments can be modified and specialized to perform specific functions. For example, in some species certain of the locomotor parapodia, or feet, may be modified for grasping, and some portions of the gut may evolve digestive specializations.

The gut is a straight, muscular tube that functions independently of the muscular activity in the body wall. The Annelida resemble the nematodes, another worm phylum, in possessing a fluid-filled internal cavity separating the gut from the body wall. In both phyla, this cavity is involved in locomotion. However, in the annelids, this space is formed at a much later time during the development of the embryo, and presumably evolved much later as well. This fluid-filled internal space is called a true coelum.

The annelid excretory and circulatory systems are well developed, and some members of the phylum have evolved respiratory organs. The nervous system offers a particular example of metameric specialization. It is concentrated anteriorly into enlarged cerebral ganglia connected to a ventral nerve cord that extends posteriorly and is organized into repeating segmental ganglia.

This phylum includes members bearing adaptations required for aquatic (marine or freshwater) or terrestrial habitats. They may be free-living entities or exist as parasites. Among the best known are the earthworm Lumbricus, the water leech Hirudo, and the marine worm Nereis.

43. What is the purpose of this passage?

a. To describe the annelid nervous system.
b. To describe the annelid digestive system.
c. To introduce distinctive features of annelid anatomy.
d. To define metamerism.

44. What is meant by the term *metamerism*?

    a. Segmentation of the anatomy
    b. A series of rings
    c. Bilateral symmetry
    d. Evolutionary plasticity

45. What is meant by the term *parapodia*?

    a. Specialization
    b. Grasping appendages
    c. Locomotion
    d. Feet

46. Which of the following is one evolutionary advantage of segmentation?

    a. segmented animals have many feet.
    b. segmented animals have a fluid-filled coelom.
    c. parts of some segments can become specialized to perform certain functions.
    d. segments can evolve.

47. A group of worms other than the Annelida are called:

    a. Lumbricus
    b. Nematodes
    c. Leeches
    d. Parapodia

48. Some annelid feet may be specialized in order to:

    a. be used for locomotion.
    b. be segmented.
    c. be fluid-filled.
    d. grasp things.

49. A difference between the annelid coelum and the fluid-filled cavity of other worms is that:

    a. the annelid coelum is involved in locomotion.
    b. the annelid coelum is formed later.
    c. the annelid coelum is formed during embryology.
    d. the annelid coelum is cylindrical in cross section.

50. An example of metameric specialization in the nervous system is:

    a. segmental ganglia
    b. the ventral nerve cord
    c. respiratory organs
    d. cerebral ganglia

51. The main difference between the Annelida and all other animal phyla is that:

    a. the Annelida are worms.
    b. the Annelida include the leeches.
    c. the Annelida are metameric.
    d. the Annelida are aquatic.

52. The purpose of the last paragraph in the passage is to:

   a. give familiar examples of members of the annelid phylum.

   b. show that annelids may be parasites.

   c. tell the reader that annelids may be adapted to aquatic environments.

   d. show that there are many annelids in nature and that they are adapted to a wide variety of habitats.

53. The fluid-filled cavity in the nematodes is used for:

   a. defense

   b. reproduction

   c. feeding

   d. movement

54. Members of the Annelida are:

   a. free-living animals.

   b. parasites.

   c. aquatic.

   d. all the above

Essay

54. *Instructions: Read the following prompt. Do you agree or disagree with the statement? Use examples from current events, history, or your own experience to support your point of view. Take a few moments to plan a response. Then, write your response in essay form.*

Fast food restaurants should be held legally responsible for the current rise in obesity in children.

Answer Key and Explanations

Mathematics

1. C: To add fractions with different denominators, find the Least Common Multiple of the denominators, convert the fractions, and then add:

$$\frac{1}{3} + \frac{1}{4} = \frac{4}{12} + \frac{3}{12} = \frac{7}{12}$$

2. B: Multiply the cost of the room by the tax:

$$\$48.00 \times .07 = \$3.36$$

Add the total tax to the cost of the room:

$$\$48.00 + \$3.36 = \$51.36$$

3. B: Because the coupon has double value, the reduction is $2(.25) = 50$ cents. The cost of the cereal is $x - 50$ cents.

4. C: The product is the result of multiplying two numbers.

The product of $13 \times 7 = 91$. Add 12 to get 103.

5. C: The perimeter of a triangle is the sum of the lengths of its sides. Add the three sides of triangle *ABC* to find the perimeter:

$$6 + 6 + 8 = 20$$

6. A: The number must be evenly divisible by 3, 4, and 5 to be a multiple of all three numbers.

7. B: The mode is the value of the term that occurs most. Of these terms, the number 14 occurs twice

8. D: To increase a number by a given percent, take the percent of the original number and add it to the original number

$$65 \times .33 = 21.45$$

Add the result to the original number:

$$21.45 + 65 = 86.45$$

9. D: To change this number from scientific notation to standard notation, move the decimal point to the right six places:

$$2.34 \times 10^6 = 2,340,000$$

10. A: To subtract these two integers, change the subtraction sign to addition, then change the sign of the number being subtracted to its opposite:

$$-9 - (-8) = -9 + 8 = -1$$

201

11. C: Remember the order of operations when solving this equation. First, simplify all operations inside parentheses. Second, simplify any exponential expressions. Third, perform all multiplications and divisions as they occur in the problem from left to right. Fourth, perform all additions and subtractions as they occur in the problem from left to right:

$$2(7 + 8)^2 - 12(6 \times 2)$$
$$= 2(15)^2 - 12(12)$$
$$= 2(225) - 12(12)$$
$$= 450 - 144$$
$$= 306$$

12. A: To multiply fractions, first simplify the fractions by canceling like factors from the numerators and denominators:

$$\frac{3}{16} \times \frac{4}{33} = \frac{1}{4} \times \frac{1}{11}$$

Then multiply the numerators and multiply the denominators:

$$\frac{1}{4} \times \frac{1}{11} = \frac{1}{44}$$

13. C: Because the last decimal place is the ten thousandths place, the fraction is as well:

$$0.1650 = 1,650/10,000$$
$$= 165/1,000$$
$$= 33/200$$

14. C: First, factor out the perfect square factor from under the radical:

$$\sqrt{48} = \sqrt{16 \times 3}$$

Simplify and reduce the radicals:

$$\sqrt{16} \times \sqrt{3} = \sqrt{3}$$

15. C: First, find the difference in the number of births per year:

$$70,100 - 66,000 = 4,100$$

Then, set up an equation to determine the percent increase:

$$\frac{4,100}{66,000} \times 100 = 6.21\%$$

16. D: The volume of a rectangular prism is a x b x c. The volume of the pool is the product of the three numbers: $30 \times 20 \times 6 = 3,600 \text{ ft}^3$

17. D: Set up and solve a proportion. To solve the proportion, cross-multiply:

$$\frac{3 = 2}{18x}$$

$$3x = 36$$
$$x = 12$$

18. C: The word "difference" signifies a subtraction problem. When subtracting decimals, align the decimals vertically:

$$3.8$$
$$-.571$$
$$= 3.229$$

19. A: Put this into an algebraic equation:

$$5 + 6x = 77$$

Subtract 5 from both sides:

$$6x = 72$$

Divide both sides by 6 to get $x = 12$

20. C: To find the average, divide the sum of the terms by the number of terms:

$$408 \div 6 = 68$$

21. A: First, calculate Tom's current weekly pay. Multiply the number of hours worked by his hourly wage:

$$25 \times \$7.75 = \$193.75$$

The increase in pay is the new total wage minus the previous total wage:

$$\$206.25 - \$193.75 = \$12.50$$

22. C: First, calculate the total number of ounces of bagels Jamie eats per day:
4 bagels × 8 ounces = 32 ounces of bagels a day
Convert ounces to pounds. There are 16 ounces to 1 pound:
32 ounces ÷ 16 ounces = 2 pounds. Jamie eats 2 pound of bagels a day.
This question is asking for the total number of pounds eaten each week:
2 pounds × 7 days = 14 pounds per week

23. D: Throws of a die are independent events—one outcome will not have an effect on the next outcome. Therefore, the results of any previous throw is irrelevant to the problem. The probability that the next throw will not result in a 4 leaves 5 possible outcomes:

1, 2, 3, 5, and 6

There is a total of 6 possible outcomes, so the probability is $\frac{5}{6}$

24. C: The formula for the area of a circle is πr². Square the radius and multiply by π:

$$8^2\pi = 64\pi$$

25. B: The perimeter of a triangle is the sum of the lengths of the sides:

$$(s + 2) + (2s + 3) + (2s - 4) = 5s + 1$$

26. D: Division is the opposite, or the reciprocal, of multiplication.

The reciprocal of 2/3 is 3/2

27. B: The ratio of correct to incorrect answers is 2:3, giving a whole of 5. It takes 12 sets of 5 questions to total 60 questions. To determine how many correct answers Sam gave, multiply 2 by 12, for a total of 24

28. B: Get all of the variables on one side of the equation and solve. First subtract 8 from each side:

$$5m + 8 = 48$$
$$= 5m = 40$$

Then divide both sides by 5:

$$m = 8$$

29. B: Use the FOIL method (First, Outer, Inner, Last) to solve this equation:

$$(3x + 1)(7x + 10)$$
$$= (3x)(7x) + (3x)(10) + (1)(7x) + (1)(10)$$
$$= 21x^2 + 30x + 7x + 10$$

Combine like terms to get the answer:

$$21x^2 + 37x + 10$$

30. A: The answer is expanded to simplify the calculations. The total of Choice A is \$8.00 + \$1.60, which is the same as the total calculated in the problem.

31. B: Use the order of operations to find the value for this expression: parentheses, exponents, multiplication and division, addition and subtraction.

$$-3 \times 5^2 + 2(4 - 18) + 33$$
$$-3 \times 5^2 + 2(-14) + 33$$
$$-3 \times 25 + 2(-14) + 33$$
$$-75 + (-28) + 33$$
$$-70$$

32. A: Simplify the equation:

$$10x - 36 + 4x - 6 + x = 3$$
$$15x - 42 = 3$$
$$15x = 45$$
$$x = 3$$

33. D: A ratio of 3:2:1 gives a whole of 6. It takes 12 sets of 6 plants to total 72 plants. To determine how many tomatoes Hunter planted, multiply 3 by 12, for a total of 36

34. C: Area of a triangle is one-half base times height.

$$\frac{1}{2}(10)(4) = 20$$

35. D: Division is the opposite, or the reciprocal, of multiplication. If you divide a number by 2, you have to multiply it by ½ to get the same result.

36. C: Convert the units from hours to seconds:

$$36 \text{ hours} \times 60 \text{ minutes/hour} \times 60 \text{ seconds/minute} = 129,600$$

37. D: Get all of the variables on one side of the equation and solve. First subtract 12 from each side:

$$6x + 12 = 18$$
$$6x = 6$$

Divide by 6:

$$x = 1$$

Insert the value of x:

$$9(1) = 9$$

38. C: Use the formula Volume = length x width x height:

$$200 = 5 \times 5 \times h$$
$$25h = 200$$

39. C: Cross multiply:

$$3x = 36$$

Divide by 3:

$$x = 12$$

40. B: A square is a rectangle with four equal sides. The formula for the area of a square is (side)². To find the side of the square, take the square root of the area:

$$\sqrt{64} = 8$$

41. B: If the points are plotted on a number line, only -24 is to the left of -17 on the number line. For negative numbers, the number closest to the zero on the number line is the greater number.

42. D: Get all of the variables on one side of the equation and solve.

$$7\sqrt{x} + 16 = 79 \quad \text{Subtract 16 from both sides of the equation}$$
$$7\sqrt{x} = 63 \quad \text{Divide both sides by 7}$$
$$\sqrt{x} = 9 \quad \text{Square both sides}$$
$$x = 81$$

43. C: Solve for a and b:

$$6a = 18$$

205

Divide by 6:

$$a = 3$$
$$3b = 9$$

Divide by 3:

$$b = 3$$

Plug a and b into the equation:

$$\frac{a}{b} = \frac{3}{3} = 1$$

44. C: The product is the outcome of a multiplication problem:

$$39 \times 62 = 2{,}418$$

45. C: Find the area of the living room using the formula $A = l \times w$:

$$21 \times 12 = 252\text{ft}^2$$

There are 9 square feet in one square yard. Convert square feet to square yards:

$$252 \div 9 = 28 \text{ yd}^2$$

Multiply to find the cost of the carpet:

$$28 \ yd^2 \times \frac{12}{yd^2} = \$336$$

46. A: The mode is the number that occurs most often. Only 21 occurs more than once in this data set

47. D: Try -5 for x in each equation. Only Choice D is true when -5 is substituted for x.

48. D: If 1/4 inch represents 8 miles, then 1 inch represents $4 \times 8 = 32$ miles. Two inches represents $2 \times 32 = 64$ inches. An 1/8 of an inch represents $8 \div 2 = 4$ miles. Then 2 ×1/8 inches represents $64 + 4 = 68$ miles

49. C: First, subtract the surgeries the doctor performed on Monday:

$$24 - 4 = 20$$

There are four days left to perform surgeries. Divide the number of surgeries left by the number of days:

$$20 \div 4 = 5 \text{ surgeries per day}$$

50. B: First, determine how many miles can be driven on one tank of gas by multiplying the numbers of gallons in a tank by the miles per gallon:

12 gallon/tank x 30 miles/gallon = 360 miles
Next, divide the total miles for the trip by the number of miles driven per tank of gas to determine how many total tanks of gas Robert will need:

1,800 miles ÷ 360 miles/tank = 5 tanks

Language

1. C: The original sentence is redundant and wordy.

2. C: The syntax of the original sentence is fine, but a comma after *said* but before the open-quotation mark is required.

3. D: In the original sentence, the modifier is placed too far away from the word it modifies.

4. D: The verb structure should be consistent in a sentence with parallel structures.

5. A: The singular pronoun *her* is appropriate since the antecedents are joined by *or*. Also, the subjunctive verb form is required to indicate something indefinite.

6. B: The combination of *hardly* and *not* constitutes a double negative.

7. C: The plural demonstrative adjective *these* should be used with the plural noun *sorts*.

8. A: This sentence contains a number of parallel structures that must be treated consistently.

9. A: In this sentence, *whose* is the appropriate possessive pronoun to modify *opinion*.

10. A: When a dependent clause precedes an independent clause, a comma should separate the two.

11. B: There are misplaced modifiers.

12. B: The possessive for "each" is singular. The only singular possessive choice is B: her.

13. A: The word needed here is an adverb. Tearfully is the best choice.

14. B: Choice B: gives the correct spelling.

15. C: The correct choice must complete the future perfect form. Bring is the correct choice.

16. C: Each requires a singular possessive. The only singular possessive form is "his".

17. B: The verb tense of this sentence needs to be in the past.

18. B: The correct choice must be an adverb; well is the correct choice.

19. C: The correct spelling is niece.

20. A: The correct spelling is truly.

21. D: The correct spelling is victorious.

22. D: The correct spelling is occurrence.

23. B: The verb tense is incorrect. It should be "made" rather than "make."

24. C: The verb "is" is singular, and does not agree with the plural subject "Quincy and his son Zane." The verb should be "are" instead.

25. A: A collective noun, "the audience" is singular, and takes singular verbs. Therefore, "are" is incorrect, and should be "is."

26. D: The verb "giving" is in the wrong form. It should be "gave."

27. B: In the time of the dinosaurs refers to the past. Therefore, the present "are" is incorrect. It should be "were."

28. C: "Dogs" is plural. The sentence should read "good achievers" rather than "a good achiever."

29. C: Everyone is a singular pronoun so the "their" later in the sentence is an incorrect replacement.

30. D: There are no errors in this sentence.

31. C: The adverb "particularly" clearly modifies the adjectival phrase "well known" and no hyphen is needed. Choice B subtly changes the meaning. Choice D corrects the spelling of the original, but is a more awkward phrasing.

32. C: This eliminates the slang expression "what with". Choice D subtly changes the meaning.

33. B: Choice A reads poorly and fails to fully connect why the artists did not see his work. Choice C fails to make the connection with the preceding sentence, establishing itself as the explanation for Daumier's lack of influence, and choice D fails to explain why other artists did not see Daumier's work.

34. B: Since the sentence begins with "This is also true," the phrase in choice B is redundant with the preceding sentence. None of the other choices address this.

35. A: This expands upon the previous sentence by explaining why he is considered the greatest sculptor of the era.

36. D: The word "however" shows that the sentence will provide a contrast to the preceding sentence. Choice B does this as well, but repeats the same expression used two sentences before.

37. B: The apostrophe is needed in *nations* to show possession of the *highest executive office*. Choice A is not correct because executive office is not a proper noun that needs capitalization. Choice C is wrong because you do not want to separate an infinitive. Also, choice D is wrong because there is an error in the sentence.

38. B: *Wall Street* is the name of a street in New York. So, it needs capitalization. Choice A is wrong because this would make an error in verb tense. Choice C is incorrect because the words *although* and *though* are nearly synonyms. So, choosing *although* is not an error. Choice D is incorrect as well because *investment firm* is a common noun. It is not the name of a certain investment firm. So, no capitalization is needed.

39. A: The information in the parentheses is not necessary information. However, the information is closely connected to the sentence. So, commas should be used instead of parentheses. Choice B is wrong because *Republicans* is the name of a certain political party and needs capitalization. Choice C is incorrect because the sentence needs a singular noun for *Margaret Chase Smith*. Choice D is not correct because there is a mistake in the sentence.

40. D: The question tests on irregular verb forms. The sentence needs the past participle of *seek* which is *sought*. So, choice A is incorrect. Choice B is also wrong because the singular subject causes a problem with subject-verb agreement. Choice C is incorrect because the problem is not with the verb tense.

41. A: This is a run-on sentence that can be corrected with a comma between the short independent clauses. Choice B is not correct because the pronoun *them* is correct. Choice C is incorrect. If you made the change, then you would have an error in subject-verb agreement. Choice D is wrong because there is an error in the sentence.

42. C: Sentence (8) is a personal opinion that does not help this passage. Choice A is incorrect. Changing the order of the paragraphs only hurts the chronological order of the passage. Choices B and D are incorrect. The reason is that moving these sentences upsets the unity and coherence of the piece.

43. A: The sentence places a comma after each country correctly because they are items in a series. However, a comma is not needed after Liberia because it is the last item in the series. Choice B is incorrect because the commas are necessary for the items in the series. The exception is the comma after Liberia. Choice D is incorrect because believe is spelled correctly and there is an error in the sentence.

44. B: Answer choice B is precise and clear. Answer choice A keeps the meaning, but is awkward and wordy. Answer choice C uses the wrong verb tense. Answer choice D would put the word *work* into the sentence twice. It is not completely incorrect, but it is not the best choice.

45. B: When comparing two people or things, the correct comparative word would be *older* rather than *oldest*. If there were more than two, you would use the comparative word *oldest*. The other choices change the intended original meaning of the sentence.

46. A: The sentence is precise and clear in its original form. This type of sentence is an absolute construction, including a noun and a modifier. Absolute constructions squeeze two sentences into one. In this case the modifier is a participle phrase.

47. D: The plural subject *teachers* agrees with the pronoun *they*. Pronouns have to agree with gender, number and person. If the subject had been singular, such as *teacher*, then the pronoun would have needed to also be singular. In that case the correct sentence might have been: A fair teacher understands that he or she cannot treat any student with favoritism.

48. C: When putting things or people in order, the words must agree in the series. You can use *first, second, third,* and so forth, or you may use *firstly, secondly, thirdly*, and so forth. In this sentence, answer choice C is the best choice because the two words *first* and *second* agree in the series, and in this case it sounds better. *Firstly* and *secondly* sound awkward. Also, it is correct to use *and then* in the sentence rather than answer choice D which uses only the word *then*.

Reading

1. B: The passage gives general instructions for tomato plant culture from seeding to providing support for the vines. Answers A and D are too specific, focusing on details of the text. Answer C is too general: the passage does not fully describe how to operate a farm.

2. C: The passage states that seeds germinated in late March will be ready for the garden after the last frost.

3. A: The passage states that seeds germinated in late March will be ready for the garden after the last frost, implying that exposure to freezing temperatures would harm them.

4. D: The text describes a sequence of window boxes followed by pots and finally outdoor planting.

5. A: The text states that pinching the bud is done to make the plants stronger.

6. B: Larger plants have longer roots and require more soil and water for nourishment.

7. C: The text states that the cloth is used to protect the soil. We can infer that this is because a stream of water may disrupt it and uproot the seedlings.

8. D: Nitrate of soda is suggested as an additive to the garden soil to give the plants "a good start".

9. A: The text states that use of fresh manure will delay fruiting.

10. D: The text indicates that unsupported plants flop on the ground. The support system spreads the vines, giving the fruit more room. Thus, the plants require more space and must be planted further apart.

11. D: Although all the other answers mention information contained in the paragraph, the overall purpose of this paragraph is, as stated, to describe the support procedure.

12. C: The last sentence tells us that training of the plants, or supporting them, should begin before they trail on the ground.

13. D: The passage describes the artistry of ancient Greek coins and gives the reasons why so much effort went into designing them.

14. B: The first sentence indicates that coins are utilitarian objects, and few are designed well enough to be worth considering them as anything more.

15. A: *Delectation* means to savor or to enjoy the flavor or beauty of something, in this case the design of the coins.

16. D: The word is defined in the second sentence of the passage.

17. D: The passage describes the coins as artistic objects, not simply because they were the first coins, but also because of the historical situation which is described, and which led to their being designed with great care and pride.

18. C: The text states that new coins were developed frequently, to commemorate battles, treaties, etc.

19. A: The text tells us that the designers were highly skilled and that they were so proud of their work that they signed it.

20. D: The sentence contrasts the artistic content of the coins with their use as a practical means of commercial exchange.

21. D: The text tells us that coin designs changed along with larger sculptures to reflect changing Greek artistic tastes.

22. B: The frequent need for new designs meant that the artisans who did the work had ample opportunity to perfect their skills.

23. C: The text tells us that the dated coins provide a dependable record of Greek artistic development.

24. D: Coins were developed as a means of commercial exchange, and the text tells us that this was their main use.

25. B: In the first sentence the phrase "so long had sleep been denied her" tells us she had been prevented from sleeping for some time.

26. D: The text tells us she was feigning, which means to pretend, to be asleep.

27. A: Despite his ugliness and deformity, Garth is a gentle soul who wants to be accepted as a friend by the girl.

28. D: At first repelled by the sight of Garth in the window, the girl eventually expresses pity when she learns that he is deaf, too.

29. B: Garth's deformities are repugnant to her at first, and she must overcome this emotion.

30. B: He calls back to her that he is hidden from sight, and his voice is described as plaintive and pained.

31. B: The text tells us that he sees her lips move and assumes she is sending him away, because he cannot hear that she is calling to him.

32. D: Supplicating means to ask or beg for something earnestly or humbly.

33. D: At first, she was amazed at the extent of Garth's deformities, but she has quickly become more sympathetic and has come to pity him.

34. D: The girl quickly understands Garth's sadness about his own condition and sympathizes with him.

35. C: Garth is sad that he is so deformed that other people are frequently repelled and try to avoid contact with him.

36. D: The girl has shown that she sympathizes with him by taking his arm, and Garth feels that he is being accepted despite his deformities.

37. C: An archipelago is a large group or chain of islands.

38. D: The article deals primarily with the ways the colonists fed themselves: their crops and the foods they hunted. While the history and agriculture discussed are part of the Māori culture, that is not the focus of the passage.

39. B: The article states that the islands were colonized by Polynesians in the 15th century but that the first visitors had arrived some 400 years earlier than that.

40. D: The passage states that the first settlers were forced to rely on fishing for their food.

41. A: When an increased population had driven a major food source to extinction, they began to fight for control over the remaining food supply.

42. D: The article tells us that coconuts did not grow in New Zealand, and that some of the other crops would grow only on North Island.

43. C: The passage describes several distinctive features of annelid anatomy and tells how some of them differ from other worms.

44. A: The term is defined in the text as an organization of the anatomy into segments.

45. D: The term is defined in the text between commas.

46. C: The text gives the example of feet specializing into grasping organs to illustrate this evolutionary advantage of segmental plasticity.

47. B: *Nematodes* differ from the annelids in the structure of the coelum. *Lumbricus* and leeches are both members of the Annelida.

48. D: The text gives the example of parapodia modified for grasping to illustrate evolutionary plasticity among metameres.

49. B: The text states that the annelid coelum is formed later during embryology and probably evolved at a later time, as well.

50. D: The text indicates that the cerebral ganglia are enlarged, whereas the remaining ganglia in the nerve cord are merely repeating (unspecialized) units.

51. C: The text defines metemeres as segments, and discusses segmentation as the distinguishing feature of the phylum.

52. D: The paragraph tells us that annelids can live in salt or fresh water and on land, and then gives examples.

53. D: The text indicates that both nematodes and annelids possess a fluid-filled cavity which is involved in locomotion, or movement.

54. D: The last paragraph indicates that annelids occupy all the habitats listed and gives examples.

CHSPE Practice Test #2

Mathematics

1. In the figure below, ΔJKL is dilated to the image $\Delta J' K' L'$.

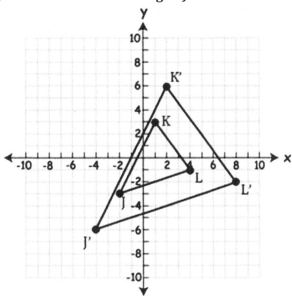

What is the scale factor of the dilation?

    a. $\frac{1}{3}$

    b. $\frac{1}{2}$

    c. 2

    d. 3

2. For which of the following data sets would the mean be an appropriate measure of center to use?

    a. 7, 7, 9, 10, 10, 11, 13, 14, 46, 50

    b. 6, 8, 11, 15, 17, 17, 21, 22, 25, 25

    c. 4, 9, 36, 41, 43, 44, 48, 48, 49, 50

    d. 2, 91, 92, 96, 96, 98, 100, 102, 104, 105

3. Which of these does NOT simulate randomly selecting a student from a group of 8 students?

    a. Creating an octagonal spinner, assigning each side to a different person, and spinning it

    b. Assigning each student a unique coin flip value of HHH, HHT, HTH, THH, TTH, THT, HTT, or TTT and flipping a coin three times

    c. Assigning each student a unique musical note A–G and blindly hitting a white key on a piano

    d. Assigning each student a unique number 1-8 and randomly drawing from 8 numbered index cards

4. Eli borrows $12 from his brother to buy a video game. Before Eli pays his brother back, another game he wants goes on sale, so he borrows an additional $20 from his brother to buy the game. How much money does Eli owe his brother?

    a. −$32
    b. −$8
    c. $8
    d. $32

5. Which of these is a net of a triangular pyramid?

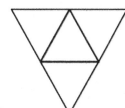

a.

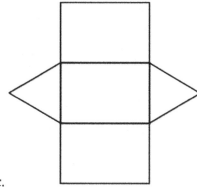

c.

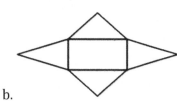

b.

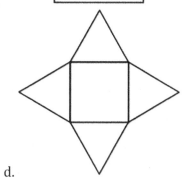

d.

6. Evaluate $x^2 - (2y - 3)$ if $x = 4$ and $y = 3$.

    a. 12
    b. 13
    c. 10
    d. 8

7. An ice-cream shop offers sundaes that include a choice of an ice cream flavor, a topping, and a sauce (either hot fudge or caramel). The different ice cream flavors are chocolate, vanilla, and strawberry. The choices of toppings are sprinkles and cherries. Which of the following tree diagrams correctly shows the total number of ice-cream sundaes that could be created using one flavor of ice cream, one topping, and either hot fudge or caramel?

a.

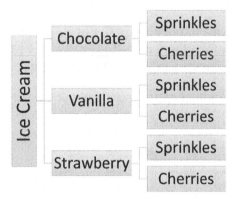

c.

b.

d.

8. Three teachers from a county are chosen at random to attend a conference for high school science educators. What is the approximate probability that two women from the same department will be chosen?

	Biology	Chemistry	Physics
Women	26	31	20
Men	16	11	25

a. 8.6%
b. 10.7%
c. 11.9%
d. 13.8%

9. **What is the probability of spinning a D on the spinner below?**

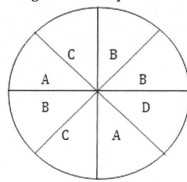

    a. $\frac{1}{8}$

    b. $\frac{1}{7}$

    c. $\frac{3}{8}$

    d. $\frac{6}{7}$

10. $\left(y^2 + 9y - 2\right) + \left(4y^2 - y - 5\right) =$

    a. $5y^2 + 8y - 7$
    b. $5y^2 + 8y + 10$
    c. $5y^2 + 10y - 7$
    d. $5y^2 + 10y + 10$

11. **Joshua has to earn more than 92 points on the state test in order to qualify for an academic scholarship. Each question is worth 4 points, and the test has a total of 30 questions. Let x represent the number of test questions.**

Which of the following graphs best represents the number of questions Joshua must answer correctly?

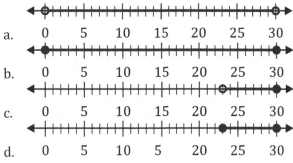

Refer to the following for question 12:

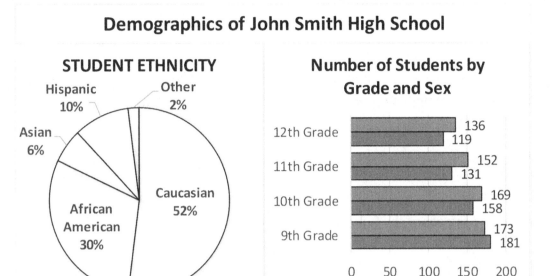

12. Which of these is the greatest quantity?

a. The average number of male students in the 11th and 12th grades
b. The number of Hispanic students at the school
c. The difference in the number of male and female students at the school
d. The difference in the number of 9th and 12th grade students at the school

Refer to the following for question 13:

This data shows the number of students at a high school who are enrolled in various electives.

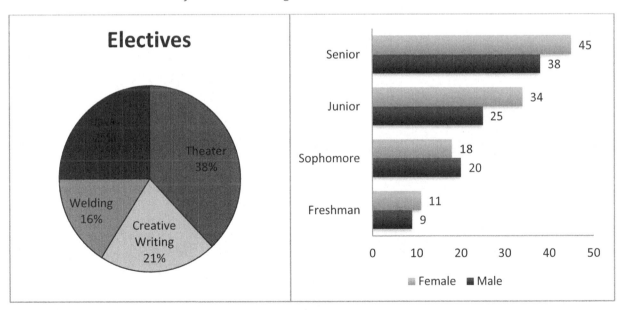

13. A sophomore is randomly selected to be interviewed for the school paper. What is the approximate probability that the student is male?

    a. 0.53
    b. 0.47
    c. 0.19
    d. 0.10

14. Two angles of a triangle measure 15° and 70°, respectively. What is the size of the third angle?

    a. 90 degrees
    b. 80 degrees
    c. 75 degrees
    d. 95 degrees

15. What are the factors of the following polynomial: $x^2 - x - 56$?

    a. $(x - 7)(x + 8)$
    b. $(x + 7)(x - 8)$
    c. $(x - 7)(x - 8)$
    d. $(x + 7)(x + 8)$

16. If $x^2 + 5x = 6$, then what does x equal?

    a. −6 or −1
    b. −6 or 1
    c. −1 or 6
    d. 1 or 6

17. Which of the following figures show parallelogram $WXYZ$ being carried onto its image $W'X'Y'Z'$ by a reflection across the x-axis?

a.

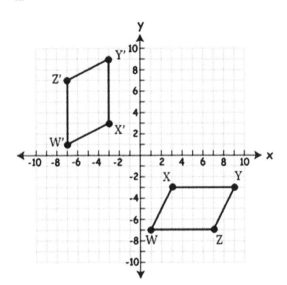

c.

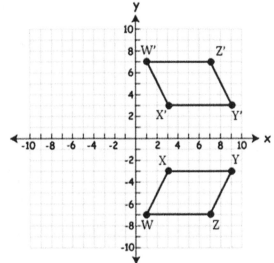

b.

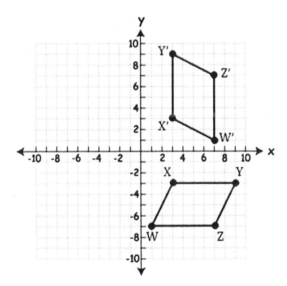

d.

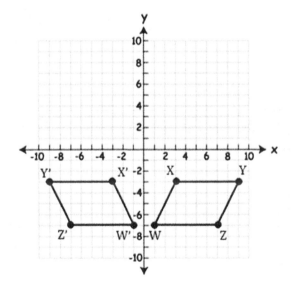

219

18. The figure shows an irregular quadrilateral and the lengths of its sides. Which of the following equations best shows the perimeter of the quadrilateral?

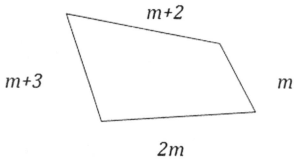

a. $m^4 + 5$
b. $2m^4 + 5$
c. $4m + 5$
d. $5m + 5$

19. One method for calculating the area of a circle is to dissect it into a number of wedges. The circle below has a radius r and has been evenly dissected into 16 wedges.

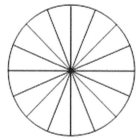

If the wedges are rearranged alternately to create a shape resembling a rectangle, as shown below, what is the approximate length of the rectangle?

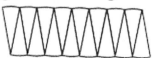

a. π
b. πr
c. r
d. πr^2

20. What are the factors of the following polynomial: $2x^2 + 7x - 15$?
a. $(2x + 5)(x - 3)$
b. $(x + 5)(2x - 3)$
c. $(2x - 5)(x + 3)$
d. $(x - 5)(2x + 3)$

21. Simplify the following expression: $3\frac{1}{6} - 1\frac{5}{6}$.

    a. $2\frac{1}{3}$

    b. $1\frac{1}{3}$

    c. $2\frac{1}{9}$

    d. $\frac{5}{6}$

22. 75 students are surveyed. 36 of the students like only pepperoni pizza. 22 of the students like only supreme pizza. 12 of the students like neither kind of pizza. How many students like pepperoni *and* supreme pizza?

    a.   2

    b.   3

    c.   4

    d.   5

23. In order to analyze the real estate market for two different zip codes within the city, a realtor examines the most recent 100 home sales in each zip code. She considered a house which sold within the first month of its listing to have a market time of one month; likewise, she considered a house to have a market time of two months if it sold after having been on the market for one month but by the end of the second month. Using this definition of market time, she determined the frequency of sales by the number of months on the market. The results are displayed below.

Which of the following is a true statement for these data?

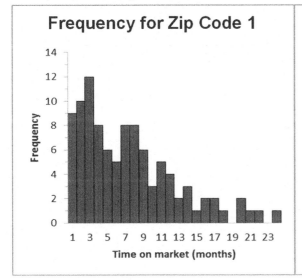 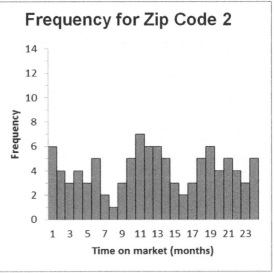

    a.   The median time a house spends on the market in Zip Code 1 is five months less than Zip Code 2

    b.   On average, a house spent seven months longer on the market in Zip Code 2 than in Zip Code 1.

    c.   The mode time on the market is higher for Zip Code 1 than for Zip Code 2.

    d.   The median time on the market is less than the mean time on the market for Zip Code 1.

24. Given the equation $2^x = 64$, what is the value of x?

    a. 4
    b. 5
    c. 6
    d. 7

25. A crane raises one end of a 3300 lb steel beam. The other end rests upon the ground. If the crane supports 30% of the beam's weight, how many pounds does it support?

    a. 330 lbs
    b. 990 lbs
    c. 700 lbs
    d. 1100 lbs

26. Determine the volume of a rectangular box with a length of 5 inches, a height of 7 inches, and a width of 9 inches.

    a. 445.095 in^3
    b. 315 in^3
    c. 45 in^3
    d. 35 in^3

27. What is the value of x, shown in the diagram below?

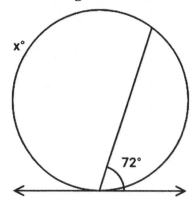

    a. 36
    b. 72
    c. 144
    d. 216

28. A random sample of 250 students at a high school were asked these three questions:

Do you drink coffee?
Do you drink tea?
Do you drink hot chocolate?

The results of the survey are shown below. If these data are representative of the population of students at the school, which of these is most probable?

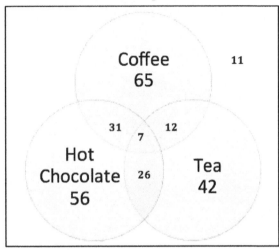

a. A student chosen at random drinks tea.
b. If a student chosen at random drinks hot chocolate, he also drinks at least one other beverage.
c. If a student chosen at random drinks coffee and hot chocolate, he also drinks tea.
d. A student chosen at random does not drink coffee, tea, or hot chocolate.

29. Solve the following for x:

$$x^2 + 8x + 16 = 0$$

a. $x = -4, 4$
b. $x = 4$
c. $x = -4$
d. $x = -2, 2$

30. A target is made of concentric circles as shown below. The width of each band is a and the center is a circle with radius a. Which of the following gives the area A of the shaded region as a function of a?

    a. $A = 12\pi a^2$
    b. $A = 15\pi a^2$
    c. $A = 18\pi a^2$
    d. $A = 25\pi a^2$

31. In an election in Kimball County, Candidate A gained 36,800 votes. His opponent, Candidate B, had 32,100 votes. 2,100 votes went to write-in candidates. What percentage of the vote went to Candidate A?

    a. 51.8%
    b. 53.4%
    c. 45.2%
    d. 46.8%

32. A blouse normally sells for $138, but is on sale for 25% off. What is the cost of the blouse?

    a. $67
    b. $103.50
    c. $34.50
    d. $113

33. A dress is marked down by 20% and placed on a clearance rack, on which is posted a sign reading, "Take an extra 25% off already reduced merchandise." What fraction of the original price is the final sale price of the dress?

    a. $\dfrac{9}{20}$
    b. $\dfrac{11}{20}$
    c. $\dfrac{2}{5}$
    d. $\dfrac{3}{5}$

34. Eloisa's monthly car payment is $400. She is trading her car in for a newer model with a monthly payment of $525. What is the percent increase in her monthly payment?

    a. 25%
    b. 31.25%
    c. 35%
    d. 42.75%

35. Which graph represents the linear equation $2x + 4y = 8$?

a.

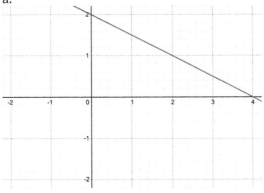

c.

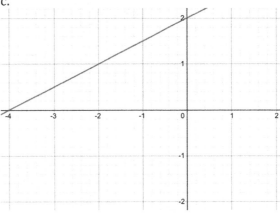

b.

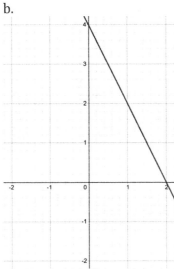

d.

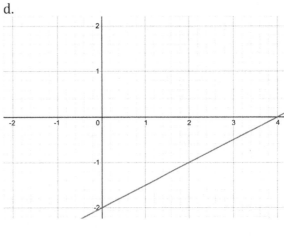

36. What is the simplest form of the following polynomial?

$$4x^3 + 5x - x^3 + 2x^2 + 17 - 3x^3 + 5x - 2x^2 + 3$$

   a. $10x + 20$
   b. $x + 2$
   c. $x^3 + 4x^2$
   d. $x^3 + 2$

37. The right circular cylinder shown in the figure below has a height of 10 units and a radius of 1 unit. Points O and P are the centers of the top and bottom surfaces, respectively. A slice is cut from the cylinder as shown, so that the angle at the top, O, is 60 degrees, and the angle at the bottom, P, is 60 degrees. What is the volume of the slice?

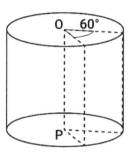

    a.   31.4 units^3
    b.   5.23 units^3
    c.   10.47 units^3
    d.   7.85 units^3

38. There are n musicians in a marching band. All play either a drum or a brass instrument. If p represents the fraction of musicians playing drums, how many play a brass instrument?

    a. $pn - 1$
    b. $p(n - 1)$
    c. $(p - 1)n$
    d. $(1 - p)n$

39. A six-sided die is thrown one time. What is the probability of the throw yielding an odd number?

    a.   60%
    b.   50%
    c.   25%
    d.   10%

40. Solve for x in the following equation: $4(2x - 6) = 10x - 6$.

    a. $x = 5$
    b. $x = -7$
    c. $x = -9$
    d. $x = 10$

41. Given that the two horizontal lines in the diagram below are parallel, which pair of angles is congruent?

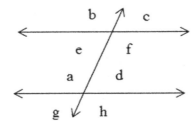

a. e and b
b. d and h
c. g and c
d. d and f

42. Sean and Hillary are baking cookies for a bake sale. Sean baked 48 chocolate chip cookies, and Hillary baked 36 sugar cookies. If 50 cookies were sold altogether, how many were left over at the end of the bake sale?

a. 43 cookies
b. 33 cookies
c. 34 cookies
d. 44 cookies

43. The equation $w - 57 = -279$ is given. Solve for w.

a. $w = -336$
b. $w = -222$
c. $w = 222$
d. $w = 336$

44. The two shortest sides of a right triangle are 6 and 8 units long, respectively. What is the length of the perimeter?

a. 10 units
b. 18 units
c. 24 units
d. 14 units

45. Find the difference: $(-8x^2 + 5xy - 4y - 10) - (-8x^2 + 12y^2 + 5x - 6y - 10)$.

a. $5xy + 12y^2 + 5x - 10y - 20$
b. $5xy - 12y^2 - 5x + 2y - 20$
c. $5xy - 12y^2 - 5x + 2y$
d. $-16x^2 + 5xy - 12y^2 - 5x + 2y$

46. Which of the following statements is true?

a. A number is divisible by 3 if the sum of the digits is divisible by 3.
b. A number is divisible by 4 if the last digit is divisible by 2.
c. A number is divisible by 7 if the sum of the digits is divisible by 7.
d. A number is divisible by 6 if the sum of the last two digits is divisible by 6.

47. **What is the probability of spinning a 2 on the first try on the spinner below?**

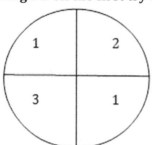

a. $\frac{1}{2}$

b. $\frac{1}{3}$

c. $\frac{1}{4}$

d. $\frac{2}{4}$

48. **Find the area of the rectangle.**

a. 10 ft^2

b. 12 ft^2

c. 20 ft^2

d. 24 ft^2

49. Marissa goes for a jog with her dog every morning. The distance jogged can be modeled by the equation $d = \frac{1}{10}m$, where d is the distance jogged in miles, and m is the number of minutes jogged. Which graph best represents the relationship between minutes and distance?

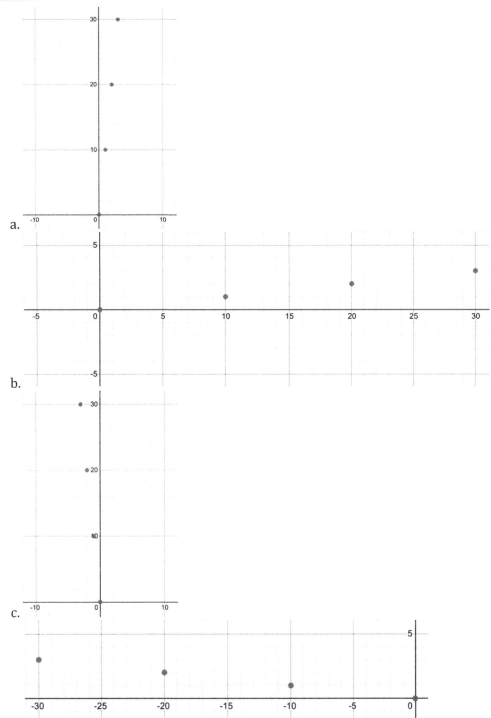

a.

b.

c.

d.

50. Marcus is putting chicken wire around his rectangular garden. He decides to add cantaloupes to his garden so he needs to expand the size of the garden. He finds that by moving the boundary line back x feet on each of the four sides, he fences a rectangular space 34 yd² larger than the original plan and spends an extra $36 on fencing, which costs $1.50 per linear foot. How much does he spend?

   a. $145.50
   b. $171
   c. $352
   d. $223.50

Language

1. Which of the following sentences is correct?

    a. Sonja works very hard, she is tired all the time.
    b. Sonja works very hard she is tired all the time.
    c. Sonja works very hard, however, she is tired all the time.
    d. Sonja works very hard; she is tired all the time.

2. Choose the word that correctly fills the blank the following sentence:

    Mrs. Simmons asked her students to get their books, read the first chapter, and _____ the questions at the end.

    a. answer
    b. to answer
    c. answering
    d. will answer

3. Choose the correct spelling of the word that fills the blank in the following sentence:

    Plastic trash that ends up in the ocean can have a _____, or harmful, effect on marine life.

    a. diliterious
    b. deleterious
    c. delaterious
    d. dilaterious

4. Which of the following choices best defines the underlined word?

    The impoverished shepherds stumbled upon the <u>stele</u> while desperately searching for some lost sheep; they were surprised and puzzled by the bizarre lines and squiggles that covered its face.

    a. An item that has been looted from a tomb
    b. A sign that indicates direction
    c. The side of a cliff
    d. A large, inscribed stone

5. The following sentence is which of the following sentence types?

    The questions in this test can give you an idea of what kinds of questions you might find on the actual test; however, they are not duplicates of the actual test questions, which cover the same subject material but may differ in form and content.

    a. Simple
    b. Complex
    c. Compound
    d. Compound-complex

6. Which of the following choices best completes the selection below?

    The letter _____ explained all his hopes and dreams for my success; _____ outpouring of his love for me.

    a. my grandfather, it contained an
    b. from my grandfather, which containing
    c. grandfather, since it contained
    d. from my grandfather, it contained an

7. Which of the following choices is correct?

    a. Whether the unexamined life is worth living or not; there is little doubt that people who do not carefully consider their actions often fall into difficulties.

    b. There are basically two ways to live: with your conscience or moral code, which can be a difficult and painful road; or against your conscience, which may seem easy and attractive until you discover how much pain and suffering you've caused others.

    c. Folding the paper over carefully so the contents were in full view; Caroline, fearful of what was coming next in the article, leaned closer to the printed page in order to more fully absorb the awful truths contained there.

    d. It is unnecessary to become a philosopher to take a careful look at your existence to understand the nature of it; its application; its fundamental principles, and its future.

8. The statements below exhibit which of the following grammatical errors?

Many literary scholars also point to the traditions of the Welsh story collection known as the *Mabinogion* for the origins. And even the name of the legendary King Arthur.

    a. Incorrectly placed comma

    b. Incorrect use of capitalization

    c. Incomplete sentence

    d. There is no error

9. What is the meaning of the underlined word?

The girls sat at the table, comforting each other and sobbing through <u>lachrymose</u> stories about their own struggles with bad haircuts.

    a. Consolatory

    b. Blithe

    c. Mournful

    d. Lethargic

10. Which of the following choices best completes the sentence?

_____, there's no way you can be a part of the swimming relay competition.

    a. Unless you find a new partner

    b. You have a new partner

    c. This is your partner

    d. As you can find a partner

11. Which of the following choices shows the best way to punctuate the sentence?

    a. I packed a picnic to take to the park with my friends; I made sure that I brought all of the plates and cups, too.

    b. I packed a picnic to take to the park with my friends, I made sure that I brought all of the plates and cups, too.

    c. I packed a picnic to take to the park with my friends I made sure that I brought all of the plates and cups, too.

    d. I packed a picnic to take to the park with my friends: I made sure that I brought all of the plates and cups, too.

12. A student who is a non-native speaker of English hands in a composition that includes the following sentences:

Yesterday I go to the park. I have a good time swimming on the pool.

Which kinds of errors did the student make?

   a. subject/verb agreement and word order
   b. verb tense and preposition use
   c. misplaced modifier and sentence fragment
   d. pronoun error and dangling modifier

13. Which of the following best approximates the meaning of the underlined word?

The discussion over the new park had begun well, but it soon descended into an <u>acrimonious</u> debate over misuse of tax revenues.

   a. Shocking
   b. Childish
   c. Rancorous
   d. Revealing

14. Of the following, which sentence is correctly punctuated?

   a. "I told you that it would be ready next week; it will be ready next week."
   b. "I told you, that it would be ready next week it will be ready next week."
   c. "I told you that it would be ready next week, it will be ready next week."
   d. "I told you that it would be ready next week it will be ready next week."

15. Which of the following choices best completes the sentence?

Natalie reviewed the notes carefully, with one eye on the judge's _____ and another eye on the _____ of the decision. There was certainly more than one way to _____ the case.

   a. interpretation, evolve, interpret
   b. interpretation, evolution, interpret
   c. interpret, evolution, interpretation
   d. interpretation, evolution, interpretation

16. Based on how it is used in this sentence, what does the word *omniscient* mean?

The floor supervisor seemed to be omniscient, always intervening just in time to prevent a problem.

   a. Cautious
   b. All-knowing
   c. Micromanaging
   d. Eager

17. Read the following introduction from an essay about Mary Shelley.

Mary Shelley conceived of Dr. Frankenstein and the hideous monster he created, which helped the English novelist to make an immeasurable impact on literature and popular culture.

Which of the following statements most effectively revises this introduction?

a. English novelist Mary Shelley had an immeasurable impact on literature and popular culture when she conceived of Dr. Frankenstein and the hideous monster he created.
b. Dr. Frankenstein created a hideous monster, and they were conceived by English novelist Mary Shelley, who had an immeasurable impact on literature and popular culture.
c. English novelist Mary Shelley conceived of Dr. Frankenstein and the hideous monster he created and had an immeasurable impact on literature and popular culture.
d. Novelist Mary Shelley from England had an immeasurable impact on literature and popular culture when she conceived of Dr. Frankenstein and the hideous monster he created.

18. Which of the following sentences is correct?

a. Jason loves candy including: lollipops, chocolate bars, and gumdrops.
b. Jason loves candy except: lollipops, chocolate bars, and gumdrops.
c. Jason loves candy, for example: lollipops, chocolate bars, and gumdrops.
d. Jason loves candy: lollipops, chocolate bars, and gumdrops.

19. Choose the word that best fills the blank in the following sentence:

The selection of the winning lottery numbers is entirely _____, with numbers being drawn at random out of a large ball.

a. diverse
b. arbitrary
c. deliberate
d. ubiquitous

20. Which of the following sentences is correct?

a. I am going to buy a new car it is a blue sedan.
b. I am going to buy a new car, it is a blue sedan.
c. I am going to buy a new car; it is a blue sedan.
d. I am going to buy a new car, therefore, it is a blue sedan.

21. Which of the following shows the correct punctuation for this quote from Richard Feynman?

a. If you thought that science was certain—well, that is just an error on your part.
b. If you thought that science was certain, well that is just an error on your part.
c. If you thought that, science was certain, well, that is just an error—on your part.
d. If you thought—that science was certain—well, that is just an error on your part.

22. Which of the following revisions would most improve the word choice in this sentence?

Employees are forced to check in at the main entrance if they arrive at the facility without their ID badge.

a. Change *forced* to *required*
b. Change *main* to *primary*
c. Change *if* to *whenever*
d. Change *facility* to *building*

23. Which of the following sentences uses correct capitalization?

a. "This bill was signed into law by the President."
b. "Some of our cousins lived in Washington, D.C."
c. "He wrote that he plans to come South to visit."
d. "My classes include English, Science, and Math."

24. Which of the following is essential in the concluding statement of an argument?

a. The introduction of new points that might lead to future arguments.
b. A summary of the argument that clearly reinforces its main points.
c. A contradiction of the argument's main points to provide fresh perspectives.
d. An unrelated detail that might lighten the audience's mood after a heated debate.

25. Read the sentences, and then answer the question that follows.

I often have heard arguments claiming that complete freedom of speech could lead to dangerous situations. Without complete freedom of speech, we are hardly living in a free society.

Which word would best link these sentences?

a. However
b. Therefore
c. So
d. Supposedly

26. Which of the following statements would best conclude an essay about playwright William Shakespeare?

a. William Shakespeare died of unknown causes on April 23, 1616.
b. William Shakespeare wrote the most important plays ever written, and I think his best one is definitely *Romeo and Juliet.*
c. William Shakespeare's plays have been staged in theaters throughout the world, yet he will always be most closely associated with the Globe Theater in London.
d. Although William Shakespeare died in 1616, the artistry and eternal relevance of his work destined it to thrive for hundreds of years into the future.

27. Read the sentences, and then answer the question that follows.

In the past, television has been criticized as a medium without the complexity and artfulness of cinema. Contemporary programs, such as Mad Men, *are widely celebrated for their intricately structured narratives and beautifully realized design.*

Which of the following statements best links these sentences?

a. Today's television shows prove that the medium has not changed much.
b. *Mad Men* is a television show about the advertising business of the 1960s.
c. This attitude has changed drastically over time.
d. Television now offers a wide range of comedies, dramas, and reality shows.

Refer to the following for questions 28 - 37:

Are You SAD?

A

(1) For many healthy people, the coming of winter gets them down. (2) Some hibernation tendencies are common. (3) If you notice true depression a sense of hopelessness less energy, or anxiety, you may be suffering from seasonal affective disorder or SAD. (4) Some people experience SAD during spring and summer for most people, however, winter is the season to be SAD.

B

(5) Researchers are not certainly what causes SAD. (6) One suggestion is that having our regular body rhythms disrupted when less sunlight is available is the culprit. (7) Another study blames increased production of melatonin: a hormone related to sleep. (8) During the dark winter months, the body makes more melatonin. (9) At the same time, it makes less serotonin: the brain chemical that effects our moods. (10) Fewer sunlight means less serotonin. (11) So far, risk factors has not been identified.

C

(12) Most people with SAD just tough it out and waiting for spring. (14) If you have symptoms that last more than two weeks, it is time to see a doctor. (15) People with mild cases of SAD need to spend time outside, exercise regularly, and go to social events or travel. (16) The good news is that spring always comes?

28. Sentence (1): *"For many healthy people, the coming of winter gets them down."*

What correction should be made to this sentence?

    a.   delete the comma
    b.   change <u>gets</u> to plural form
    c.   change <u>healthy</u> to <u>healthly</u>
    d.   no correction is needed

29. Sentence (3): *"If you notice true depression a sense of hopelessness less energy, or anxiety, you may be suffering from seasonal affective disorder or SAD."*

What correction should be made to this sentence?

    a.   remove the comma after <u>disorder</u>
    b.   place a comma after <u>hopelessness</u>
    c.   capitalize <u>seasonal affective disorder</u>
    d.   no correction is needed

30. Sentence (4): *"Some people experience SAD during spring <u>and summer for most</u> people, however, winter is the season to be SAD."*

Which of the following is the best way to write the underlined portion of the sentence? If you think the original is the best way to write the sentence, choose answer A.

- a. and summer for most
- b. and summer, for most
- c. and summer: for most
- d. and summer. For most

31. Sentence (5): *"Researchers are not certainly what causes SAD."*

What correction should be made to this sentence?

- a. change <u>certainly</u> to <u>certain</u>
- b. do not use capital letters for <u>SAD</u>
- c. end the sentence with a question mark
- d. no correction is necessary

32. Sentence (8): *"During the dark winter months, the body makes more melatonin."*

What correction should be made to this sentence?

- a. put a comma between <u>dark</u> and <u>winter</u>
- b. change <u>more</u> to <u>much</u>
- c. capitalize <u>melatonin</u>
- d. no correction is needed

33. Sentence (9): *"At the same time, it makes less serotonin: the brain chemical that effects our moods."*

What correction should be made to this sentence?

- a. change <u>effects</u> to <u>affects</u>
- b. move the first phrase to after <u>serotonin</u>
- c. change <u>less</u> to <u>fewer</u>
- d. no correction is needed

34. Sentence (10): *"Fewer sunlight means less serotonin."*

What correction should be made to this sentence?

- a. change <u>means</u> to <u>mean</u>
- b. capitalize <u>serotonin</u>
- c. change <u>less</u> to <u>fewer</u>
- d. change <u>Fewer</u> to <u>Less</u>

35. Sentence (11): *"<u>So far, risk factors has not</u> been identified."*

What is the best way to write the underlined portion of the sentence? If you think the original is the best way to write the sentence, choose answer A.

- a. So far, risk factors has not
- b. so far, risk factors has not
- c. So far, risk factor have not
- d. So far, risk factors have not

36. Sentence (12): *"Most people with SAD just tough it out and waiting for spring."*

What correction should be made to this sentence?

a. write <u>SAD</u> as <u>sad</u>
b. change <u>tough</u> to <u>toughing</u>
c. change <u>waiting</u> to <u>wait</u>
d. no correction is necessary

37. Sentence (16): *"The good news is that spring always comes?"*

What correction should be made to this sentence?

a. change <u>good</u> to <u>well</u>
b. change the question mark to a period
c. capitalize <u>spring</u>
d. no correction is necessary

Refer to the following for questions 38 - 44:

Only Temporary

A

(1) Many businesses in the United States regularly hire "temps" or temporary workers. (2) Now known as the staffing industry, temp work employs nearly 3 million people and generating more than $40 billion annually. (3) Because jobs are no longer secure, many people find that moving from job to job is a good way to improve they're skills. (4) They sometimes find the perfect job and are hired as a full-time employee. (5) Businesses love temps, they save the company money because temps do not receive benefits.

B

(6) Would temp work be a good move for you? (7) If you are the kind of worker who bores quickly and needs new challenges, temping may be the way to go. (8) Temp work may offer a more flexible schedule and it gives a changing work environment. (9) On the down side, you will not get benefits like paid vacations or health insurance. (10) You may not always be treated very well because temp workers come and go.

C

(11) If you're looking for a job, temp work can add valuable experience to your résumé. (12) It also allows you time to look for and interviewing for a new and permanent job. (13) In addition, temp work is a great way to explore different careers. (14) Many temp jobs are temp-to-hire because the company needs to fill a position and is looking among temp workers for a permanant hire. (15) You may be just the employee they are seeking!

38. Sentence (1): *"Many businesses in the United States regularly hire "temps" or temporary workers."*

What correction should be made to this sentence?

   a. remove the quotation marks from <u>temps</u>
   b. remove <u>or temporary workers</u> from the sentence
   c. change the spelling of <u>temporary</u> to <u>temparary</u>
   d. place a comma after <u>temps</u>

39. Sentence (2): *"Now known as the staffing industry, temp work employs nearly 3 million people and generating more than $40 billion annually."*

What correction should be made to this sentence?

   a. change <u>industry</u> to <u>industries</u>
   b. change <u>work</u> to <u>works</u>
   c. change <u>employs</u> to <u>employing</u>
   d. change <u>generating</u> to <u>generates</u>

40. Sentence (3): *"Because jobs are no longer secure, many people find that moving from job to job is a good way to improve they're skills."*

What correction should be made to this sentence?

   a. change <u>Because</u> to <u>Since</u>
   b. remove the comma after <u>secure</u>
   c. change <u>skills</u> to <u>skill</u>
   d. change <u>they're</u> to <u>their</u>

41. Sentence (4): *"They sometimes find the perfect job and <u>are hired as a full-time employee</u>."*

Which of the following is the best way to write the underlined portion of this sentence? If you think the original is the best way to write the sentence, choose answer A.

   a. are hired as a full-time employee.
   b. are hired as full-time employees.
   c. is hired as a full-time employee.
   d. is hired as a fulltime employee.

42. Sentence (5): *"<u>Businesses love temps, they save</u> the company money, because temps do not receive benefits."*

Which of the following is the best way to write the underlined portion of this sentence? If you think the original is the best way to write the sentence, choose answer A.

   a. Businesses love temps, they save
   b. Businesses love temps, it saves
   c. Businesses love temps; they save
   d. Businesses love temps, they saves

43. Sentence (8): *"Temp work may offer a more <u>flexible schedule and it gives</u> a changing work environment."*

Which of the following is the best way to write the underlined portion of this sentence? If you think the original is the best way to write the sentence, choose answer A.

   a. flexible schedule and it gives
   b. flexible schedule and it give
   c. flexible schedules and it gives
   d. flexible schedule, and it gives

44. Sentence (11): *"If you're looking for a job, temp work can add valueable experience to your résumé."*

What correction should be made to this sentence?

   a. put a hyphen between <u>temp</u> and <u>work</u>
   b. change <u>you're</u> to <u>your</u>
   c. change <u>valueable</u> to <u>valuable</u>
   d. no correction is necessary

Refer to the following for questions 45 - 48:

Picking the Perfect Pet

A

(1) Today's choices for pets go beyond the question of whether to get a cat or a dog? (2) Gerbils, rabbits, and amphibians is all popular options. (3) Before heading to an animal shelter, you need to know what pet makes sense for your home or classroom. (4) An obvious question to answer if you rent is if pets are permitted. (5) Some apartment complex places weight and size limits on pets or charge fees. (6) After gaining permission from the manager, your pet needs to be considered for other issues.

B

(7) If allergies effect someone in your home, be sure to select a pet that will not aggravate the condition. (8) Some dog breeds like the schnauzer and the poodle are acceptable pets for those who are sensitive to fur and dander.

C

(9) Irregardless of the pet you choose, think about other costs such as veterinary care and vaccinations, food costs, licensing, and equipment. (10) Does the pet need a special kind of home? (11) Who will be responsible for feeding and cleaning up after

the animal? (12) Taking time to do a little research can save you a lot of heartache and expense later.

45. Sentence (1): *"Today's choices for pets go beyond the question of whether to get a cat or a dog?"*

What correction should be made to this sentence?

a. change the question mark to a period
b. change Today's to Todays
c. change question to questions
d. no correction is necessary

46. Sentence 2: "Gerbils, rabbits, and amphibians is all popular options."

What correction should be made to this sentence?

a. remove the comma after Gerbils
b. change amphibians to amfibians
c. change is to are
d. change Gerbils to Hamsters

47. Sentence 5: "Some apartment complex places weight and size limits on pets or charge fees."

Which of the following is the best way to write the underlined portion of this sentence? If you think the original is the best way to write the sentence, choose option 1.

a. Some apartment complex places weight
b. Some apartment complex places wait
c. Some apartment complexes places weight
d. Some apartment complexes place weight

48. Sentence (6): *"After gaining permission from the manager, your pet needs to be considered for other issues."*

What correction should be made to this sentence?

a. delete the comma
b. change permission to permision
c. rewrite the independent clause
d. No correction is needed

Reading

Refer to the following for questions 1 - 6:

George Washington Carver was always interested in plants. When he was a child, he was known as the "plant doctor." He had a secret garden where he grew all kinds of plants. People would ask him for advice when they had sick plants. Sometimes he'd take their plants to his garden and nurse them back to health.

Later, when he was teaching at Tuskegee Institute, he put his plant skills to good use. Many people in the South had been growing only cotton on their land. Cotton plants use most of the nutrients in the soil. (Nutrients provide nourishment to plants.) So the soil becomes "worn out" after a few years. Eventually, cotton will no longer grow on this land.

This was especially bad for poor African American farmers, who relied on selling cotton to support themselves. Carver was dedicated to helping those farmers, so he came up with a plan.

Carver knew that certain plants put nutrients back into the soil. One of those plants is the peanut! Peanuts are also a source of protein.

Carver thought that if those farmers planted peanuts, the plants would help restore their soil, provide food for their animals, and provide protein for their families--quite a plant! In 1896 peanuts were not even recognized as a crop in the United States, but Carver would help change that.

Carver told farmers to rotate their crops: plant cotton one year, then the next year plant peanuts and other soil-restoring plants, like peas and sweet potatoes. It worked! The peanut plants grew and produced lots of peanuts. The plants added enough nutrients to the soil so cotton grew the next year.

1. Why was George Washington Carver known as the "plant doctor"?
   a. He grew peanuts on sick soil.
   b. He was a plant pathologist.
   c. He could nurse sick plants back to health.
   d. He knew plants could put nutrients back into the soil.

2. How is this passage structured?
   a. cause and effect
   b. problem and solution
   c. chronological order
   d. proposition and support

3. According to the passage, what problem were cotton farmers facing?
   a. They needed food for their animals.
   b. Peanuts were not recognized as a crop in the United States.
   c. They were growing too much cotton.
   d. The cotton had stripped the land of its nutrients.

4. How did Carver resolve the farmers' problem?

  a. He told the farmers to rotate their crops.
  b. He came up with a plan.
  c. He invented the peanut.
  d. He gave advice to farmers with sick plants.

5. This passage is mainly about

  a. how George Washington Carver became a teacher at the Tuskegee Institute.
  b. how George Washington Carver helped farmers improve their crop production.
  c. why George Washington Carver studied plants.
  d. how George Washington Carver made peanuts a recognized crop in the United States.

6. According to this passage, "crop rotation" can be described as

  a. planting a soil depleting crop like cotton one year, and then planting a soil restoring plant like peanuts, the next year.
  b. growing only one crop on the land year after year.
  c. nursing sick plants back to health
  d. studying plants at an institute.

Refer to the following for questions 7 - 10:

"His pride," said Miss Lucas, "does not offend me so much as pride often does, because there is an excuse for it. One cannot wonder that so very fine a young man, with family, fortune, everything in his favour, should think highly of himself. If I may so express it, he has a right to be proud."

"That is very true," replied Elizabeth, "and I could easily forgive his pride, if he had not mortified mine."

"Pride," observed Mary, who piqued herself upon the solidity of her reflections, "is a very common failing I believe. By all that I have ever read, I am convinced that it is very common indeed, that human nature is particularly prone to it, and that there are very few of us who do not cherish a feeling of self-complacency on the score of some quality or other, real or imaginary. Vanity and pride are different things, though the words are often used synonymously. A person may be proud without being vain. Pride relates more to our opinion of ourselves, vanity to what we would have others think of us."

7. Why doesn't the gentleman's pride offend Miss Lucas?

  a. She admires his vanity.
  b. It is human nature to be proud.
  c. He is poor and homeless.
  d. He is handsome and rich.

8. What are Elizabeth's feelings towards the gentleman?

  a. She is offended by him.
  b. She is proud of him.
  c. She wants to get to know him better.
  d. She is glad he is rich.

9. Which sentence best states the theme of this passage?

   a. Pride and vanity are offensive.
   b. Fame and fortune can make a person proud.
   c. Every person is proud in one way or another.
   d. If you have a fortune, you deserve to be proud.

10. According to the passage, what is the difference between pride and vanity?

   a. Pride relates to a person's abilities; vanity relates to a person's looks.
   b. Men are proud; women are vain.
   c. Pride is what you think of yourself; vanity is what you want others to think of you.
   d. Pride is part of human nature; vanity is not.

Refer to the following for questions 11 - 15:

JOB HAZARDS ANALYSIS

1.0 PURPOSE AND SCOPE

This procedure describes the Job Hazard Analysis (JHA) process for identifying, evaluating, controlling, and communicating potential hazards and environmental impacts associated with operations or work by the Tank Operations Contractor (TOC). It applies to all TOC work activities, including the performance of field work involving general plant maintenance, operations, and environmental remediation. This procedure applies to subcontractors who do not have an approved job hazard analysis process. Everyone is required to work safely and to maintain a safe work environment. Training procedures have been reviewed to ensure that workers are trained to the general hazards associated with work at the tank farms. Visitors should be briefed on the general safety hazards they may be exposed to and controls expected of them as part of their orientation.

2.0 IMPLEMENTATION

This procedure is effective on the date shown in the header.

3.0 RESPONSIBILITIES

Responsibilities are contained within Section 4.0.

4.0 Methods for Implementation of Controls

In order to effectively implement necessary controls to mitigate or eliminate hazards to the workers, the following guidelines should be used:

4.1. The following hierarchy of methods to eliminate or mitigate hazards shall be used in descending order, when feasible and appropriate:

   1. Eliminate the hazard or substitution (e.g., different chemical cleaning agent)
   2. Utilize engineering controls (e.g., ventilation)
   3. Administrative controls (e.g., dose monitoring)
   4. Personal protective equipment (PPE) (e.g., self-contained breathing apparatus)

4.2. Controls within the qualification or training of the worker that are often used do not need to be discussed in the work instructions. Examples: Use of leather gloves, safety glasses of the proper type that the worker normally uses.

4.3. Controls within the qualification or training of the worker that are seldom used, and are applicable to the entire work activity, should be placed in the precautions as a reminder that the hazard exists and the workers are expected to take the appropriate actions. Examples: Use of hearing protection due to a noisy environment at the job site, or observation of overhead lines when they are present at the job site.

4.4. Controls within the qualification and training of the workers, but for hazards that are introduced at specific steps or by specific actions during the job, should have a warning or caution statement immediately prior to the step but require no detailed mitigation instructions in the work instructions. Example: a warning for the release of pressure when breaching a system that may have residual pressure.

4.5. Controls not within the qualification and training of the workers for hazards should have detailed instructions for how the workers are to mitigate the hazard and should be in the work instructions or procedure in a way that is prominent and prevents or mitigates the hazard. Example: the steps required to successfully release the pressure on a system in an operation which is not normally performed.

11. This document is

    a. a government request for proposals
    b. a process for making rules for working safely
    c. a portion of a contract
    d. a set of rules for working efficiently

12. According to the procedure, if a worker is exposed to a hazardous chemical, which of the following is the last thing that should be tried to prevent injury or illness?

    a. Use a different chemical.
    b. Install fans to keep fumes away from the worker.
    c. Measure the amount of exposure of each affected worker.
    d. Give the worker protective clothing.

13. Welders must always use goggles and are taught to use them as part of their basic training. According to the text, the use of goggles during specific welding operations should

    a. be prominently displayed at the beginning of the work instruction.
    b. be displayed as a caution prior to the welding step described in the work instruction.
    c. be described in detail in the work instruction.
    d. not be discussed in the work instruction.

14. This passage would normally need to be read and understood by

    a. managers at the site.
    b. laborers at the site.
    c. visitors to the site.
    d. workers making deliveries to the site.

15. Which of the following requires the most comprehensive description within the work instructions?

   a. Controls that are part of the worker's training and are used routinely
   b. Controls that are part of the worker's training but that are seldom used
   c. Controls that are part of the worker's training and that are required for specific steps in the work procedure
   d. Controls that are not part of the worker's training

Refer to the following for questions 16 - 20:

Stories have been a part of the world since the beginning of recorded time. For centuries before the invention of the printing press, stories of the world were passed down to generations through oral tradition. With the invention of the printing press, which made written material available to wide ranges of audiences, books were mass-produced and introduced into greater society.

For the last several centuries, books have been at the forefront of education and entertainment. With the invention of the internet, reliance on books for information quickly changed. Soon, almost everything that anyone needed to know could be accessed through the internet. Large, printed volumes of encyclopedias became unnecessary as all of the information was easily available online.

Despite the progression of the internet, printed media was still very popular in the forms of both fiction and non-fiction books. While waiting for an appointment, enduring a several-hour flight, or relaxing before sleep, books have been a reliable and convenient source of entertainment, and one that society has not been willing to give up.

With the extreme convenience of technology, printed books are likely going to become a thing of the past. Inventions such as the iPad from Macintosh and the Kindle have made the need for any kind of printed media unnecessary. With a rechargeable battery, a large screen, and the ability to have several books saved on file, electronic options will soon take over and society will no longer utilize printed books.

Although some people may say that the act of reading is not complete without turning a page, sliding a finger across the screen (or pressing a button) is just as satisfying to the reader. The iPad and Kindle are devices that have qualities similar to a computer and can be used for so much more than just reading. Therefore, these devices are better than books because they have multiple uses.

Storytelling is a longstanding societal tradition, and will always be an important way to communicate ideas and provide information as well as entertainment. Centuries ago, stories could only be remembered and retold through speech. Printed media changed the way the world communicated and was connected, and now, as we move forward with technology, it is only a matter of time before we must say goodbye to the printed past by welcoming in the digital and electronic future.

16. What is the main argument of this essay?

   a. iPad and Kindles are easier to read than books.
   b. The printing press was a great invention.
   c. The Internet is how people receive information.
   d. Technology will soon replace printed material.

17. What is the main purpose of paragraph 1?

a. To define oral tradition
b. To stress the importance of the printing press
c. To explain the progression of storytelling within society
d. To introduce the essay

18. According to the essay, what was the first way that stories were communicated and passed down?

a. Oral tradition
b. Printed books
c. Technology
d. Hand-written copies

19. Which of the following statements is an opinion?

a. Despite the progression of the Internet, printed media was still very popular in the forms of both fiction and non-fiction books.
b. Although some people may say that the act of reading is not complete without turning a page, sliding a finger across the screen (or pressing a button) to read more onto the next page is just as satisfying to the reader.
c. With the invention of the internet, reliance on books for information quickly changed.
d. Stories have been a part of the world since the beginning of recorded time.

20. Which of the following reflects a secondary argument made by the author?

a. Devices such as the iPad or Kindle are better than books because they have multiple uses.
b. Books are still important to have while waiting for an appointment or taking a flight.
c. Printed encyclopedias are still used and more convenient that using the internet.
d. With technology, there will soon be no need for stories.

Refer to the following for questions 21 - 27:

Zakov arrived at the prison shortly before noon, having dropped Ludmilla off at the train station beforehand. He was relieved to find that Gorkhi had gone, for he found the chief to be a bit bombastic, and was disposed to conduct the interrogation without him if he could. He was fortunate in that one of Gorkhi's men recognized him and let him in to see the prisoner.

He found the student sitting on the floor of a damp cell. The only illumination came from a small window set high in the concrete wall. Nasadev raised red-rimmed eyes when the door opened, amid a clatter of keys and bolts, and Zakov found himself again amazed at the lad's homeliness, rendered even more pathetic by features wet and swollen from weeping. Somewhat discomfited by his own reaction, he forced a smile.

The young man attempted to rise, but was hindered by the shackles about his ankles.

"Please, remain seated," offered Zakov quickly, and joined him on the earthen floor. "Ludmilla delivered your note. Just what kind of trouble are you in?"

"They are saying that I killed Olga," the youth replied, his face contorted in a grimace. "As if I could! I adored her," he cried. "But things look rather bleak for me, the way they found my knife. Only you can help me, sir. I know your reputation. Please help me, sir! Not for myself, but for my family. This will destroy them..." His tears welled up again, and he sniffled and dabbed vainly at his cheeks with his dirty sleeve.

Zakov looked at him sympathetically. Ludmilla had told him the student was pathetic, and she was right: the ordinary face, the weak chin, now damp with tears and perspiration, made him seem a most unlikely suitor. He must have been deeply hurt by Olga's rejection. And she, delicate, spirited and appealing, must have found his attentions tedious and annoying, the more so since he had neither fortune nor prospects. Had she derided him, mocked him, gone too far setting trial to his devotion until he killed her?

"What made the police suspect you?" he asked.

"They talked to some of the other students, and my name came up." Nasadev was almost whining. "One of them found a letter I had written, but never sent. He told the others. It made me angry, but I guess it was foolish of me to think that such a girl could ever like someone like me. But she was nice to me, nonetheless. She told me about the play she was writing, and how she hoped to go to Moscow."

Zakov found that his heart went out to the poor, infatuated youth. But pity was not enough to resolve the charges the student faced.

"So the other students mentioned your name," he continued. "That explains why the police spoke to you, but it's not enough for them to bring charges. What else happened?"

Nasadev replied plaintively, fixing Zakov with an imploring look. "We had a quarrel. In the park. The day before they found her. Someone must have heard us and they told the police. They came and searched my room in the dormitory, found my diary, some other letters I had written."

"What was the quarrel about?"

Nasadev hesitated, would not meet Zakov's eye. "I had asked her to marry me. I know it was crazy...how could I support her? But I was afraid she would stop seeing me, that someone else would come along and I would lose her."

"And what did she say?" Zakov knew the answer already, but he had to ask.

"She turned me down. She didn't laugh at me, but she turned me down. And that was in my diary, too." Nasadev was practically inaudible.

Zakov stayed a while longer, asked a few more questions. A deep sadness seemed to fill his heart as he regarded the small cell and its single miserable occupant. Finally, with a shiver, he called for Gorkhi's man to open the door and he left.

21. Zakov thought that Gorkhi, the police chief, was
   a. pretentious
   b. enthusiastic
   c. moderate
   d. uncooperative

22. **The passage suggests that Nasadev's cell**

    a. was modern
    b. had only a bed in it
    c. was spacious
    d. was unfurnished

23. **Nasadev's frame of mind during the interview can best be described as**

    a. courageous
    b. determined
    c. desperate
    d. calculating

24. **Zakov's attitude toward Nasadev appears to be one of**

    a. disgust
    b. magnanimity
    c. sympathy
    d. malice

25. **Nasadev's look, when he replies to Zakov's question (Lines 69–70) implies that he is**

    a. begging for help
    b. looking for words
    c. exhausted
    d. unable to think clearly

26. **When the student tells Zakov that Olga's rejection of his proposal was in the diary found by the police (Line 76), his voice**

    a. whines
    b. is hard to hear
    c. contains a signal
    d. breaks

27. **By the time Zakov leaves, he**

    a. has proved Nasadev's guilt
    b. is angry at Gorkhi
    c. has found a possible motive for Nasadev to have committed the murder
    d. has proved Nasadev's innocence

Refer to the following for questions 28 - 32:

Global warming and the depletion of natural resources are constant threats to the future of our planet. All people have a responsibility to be proactive participants in the fight to save Earth by working now to conserve resources for later. Participation begins with our everyday choices. From what you buy to what you do to how much you use, your decisions affect the planet and everyone around you. Now is the time to take action.

When choosing what to buy, look for sustainable products made from renewable or recycled resources. The packaging of the products you buy is just as important as the products themselves. Is the item minimally packaged in a recycled container? How did the product reach the store? Locally grown food and other products manufactured within your community are the best choices. The fewer miles a product traveled to reach you, the fewer resources it required.

You can continue to make a difference for the planet in how you use what you bought and the resources you have available. Remember the locally grown food you purchased? Don't pile it on your plate at dinner. Food that remains on your plate is a wasted resource, and you can always go back for seconds. You should try to be aware of your consumption of water and energy. Turn off the water when you brush your teeth, and limit your showers to five minutes. Turn off the lights, and don't leave appliances or chargers plugged in when not in use.

Together, we can use less, waste less, recycle more, and make the right choices. It may be the only chance we have.

28. What is the author's tone?

a. The author's tone is optimistic.
b. The author's tone is pessimistic.
c. The author's tone is matter-of-fact.
d. The author's tone is angry.

29. Why does the author say it is important to buy locally grown food?

a. Buying locally grown food supports people in your community.
b. Locally grown food travels the least distance to reach you and therefore uses fewer resources.
c. Locally grown food uses less packaging.
d. Locally grown food is healthier for you because it has been exposed to fewer pesticides.

30. What does the author imply will happen if people do not follow his suggestions?

a. The author implies we will run out of resources in the next 10 years.
b. The author implies water and energy prices will rise sharply in the near future.
c. The author implies global warming and the depletion of natural resources will continue.
d. The author implies local farmers will lose their farms.

31. What is the best definition of the underlined word in the selection below, taken from the third paragraph of the passage?

You should try to be aware of your <u>consumption</u> of water and energy.

a. Using the greatest amount
b. Illness of the lungs
c. Using the least amount
d. Depletion of goods

32. Which of the following is one way the author specifies that a person can try to be aware of their consumption of water and energy?

a. Food that remains on your plate is a wasted resource, and you can always go back for a second helping.
b. Locally grown food and other products manufactured within your community are the best choices.
c. Don't leave appliances or chargers plugged in when not in use.
d. Participation begins with our everyday choices.

Refer to the following for questions 33 - 40:

Excerpt of a judicial review summary written by Bernard Schwartz

Judicial review, the power of courts to determine the legality of governmental acts, usually refers to the authority of judges to decide a law's constitutionality. Although state courts exercised judicial review prior to the ratification of the Constitution, the doctrine is most often traced to the landmark U.S. Supreme Court decision Marbury v. Madison (1803), which struck down an act of Congress as unconstitutional. In a now classic opinion, Chief Justice John Marshall found the power of judicial review implied in the Constitution's status as "the supreme Law of the Land" prevailing over ordinary laws.

Both federal and state courts have exercised judicial review. Federal courts review federal and state acts to ensure their conformity to the Constitution and the supremacy of federal over state law; state courts review laws to ensure their conformity to the U.S. Constitution and their own state constitutions. The power of judicial review can be exercised by any court in which a constitutional issue arises.

Judicial review gained added importance in the late nineteenth and early twentieth centuries, as courts passed judgement on laws regulating corporate behavior and working conditions. In these years, the Supreme Court repeatedly struck down laws regulating wages, hours of labor, and safety standards. This is often called the Lochner Era, after Lochner v. New York, a 1905 decision ruling a New York maximum-hours law unconstitutional on the grounds that it violated the Fourteenth Amendment. During this period, the Supreme Court invalidated no fewer than 228 state laws.

Justice Oliver Wendell Holmes Jr., dissenting from many of these decisions, urged judges to defer to legislatures. In the later 1930's, the Supreme Court adopted the Holmes approach-partly in response to the threat of President Franklin Delano Roosevelt's "court packing" plan of 1937. Deferring to legislative judgement, the Supreme Court thereafter upheld virtually all laws regulating business and property rights, including laws similar to those invalidated during the Lochner Era.

Under the chief justiceship of Earl Warren (1953-1969) and beyond, however, the Court moved toward striking down law restricting personal rights and liberties guaranteed by the Bill of Rights, particularly measures limiting freedom of expression, freedom or religion, the right of criminal defendants, equal treatment of the sexes, and the rights of minorities to equal protection of the law. In another extension of judicial review, the Court read new rights into the Constitution, notably the right of privacy (including abortion rights) and invalidated laws restricting those rights. Many other countries including Germany, Italy, France, and Japan, adopted the principle of judicial review after World War II, making constitutional law one the more important recent American exports.

33. Which of the following statements about judicial review does the passage best support?
a. States should defer to the Federal Government when interpreting the Constitution.
b. Judicial Review was started due to the Lochner Era.
c. The Constitution overrides state law in some cases.
d. Judicial Review was founded by Earl Warren Chief Justice of the Supreme Court.

34. From the passage, it can be inferred ordinary laws created by lawmakers must be within the framework of the Constitution. Which of the following sentences supports this claim the best?

    a. Although state courts exercised...
    b. Both federal and state courts...
    c. Judicial review gained added importance...
    d. During this period, the Supreme...

35. Which of the following words best characterizes the content of the passage?

    a. historical
    b. transcription
    c. prospective
    d. demonstrative

36. The word *ratification* as used in this passage refers to

    a. endorsement
    b. disapprove
    c. limiting
    d. embargo

37. The word *dissenting* as used in this passage refers to

    a. headstrong
    b. compatible
    c. obliging
    d. contradictory

38. The explanation of judicial review is based on

    a. Constitutional arguments
    b. Chief Justice Warren
    c. Marbury v Madison
    d. Lochner v New York

39. What was Franklin Delano Roosevelt's contribution to the process of Judicial Review according to the summary?

    a. The appointment of Earl Warren to the Court
    b. Adopted the Holmes approach according to the author
    c. Threatened the Court according to the author
    d. Upheld laws regulating business

40. Which of the following was done during the Lochner Era according to the summary?

    a. State laws were struck down repeatedly
    b. Justice Holmes retired
    c. The courts were unable to pass judgement on corporate behavior
    d. The courts upheld laws regulating wages

Refer to the following for questions 41 - 45:

> Chang-rae Lee's debut and award-winning novel *Native Speaker* is about Henry Park, a Korean American individual who struggles to find his place as an immigrant in a suburb of New York City. This novel addresses the notion that, as the people

who know us best, our family, peers, and lovers are the individuals who direct our lives and end up defining us. Henry Park is confronted with this reality at the very start of the novel, which begins:

The day my wife left she gave me a list of who I was.

Upon separating from his wife, Park struggles with racial and ethnic identity issues due to his loneliness. Through Park's work as an undercover operative for a private intelligence agency, the author presents the theme of espionage as a metaphor for the internal divide that Park experiences as an immigrant. This dual reality creates two worlds for Park and increases his sense of uncertainty with regard to his place in society. While he constantly feels like an outsider looking in, he also feels like he belongs to neither world.

Chang-rae Lee is also a first-generation Korean American immigrant. He immigrated to America at the early age of three. Themes of identity, race, and cultural alienation pervade his works. His interest in these themes no doubt stems from his firsthand experience as a kid growing up in a Korean household while going to an American school. Lee is also the author of *A Gesture Life* and *Aloft*. The protagonists of these novels are similar in that they deal with labels placed on them based on race, color, and language. Consequently, all of these characters struggle to belong in America.

Lee's novels address differences within a nation's mix of race, religion, and history, and the necessity of assimilation between cultures. In his works and through his characters, Lee shows us both the difficulties and the subtleties of the immigrant experience in America. He urges us to consider the role of borders and to think about why the idea of opening up one's borders is so frightening. In an ever-changing world in which cultures are becoming more intermingled, the meaning of identity must be constantly redefined, especially when the security of belonging to a place is becoming increasingly elusive. As our world grows smaller with increasing technological advances, these themes in Lee's novels become even more pertinent.

41. Which of the following best describes the purpose of this passage?
   a. To criticize
   b. To analyze
   c. To entertain
   d. To inform

42. Why does the author of the passage quote the first line of the novel *Native Speaker*?
   a. To illustrate one of the themes in the novel
   b. To show how the book is semi-autobiographical
   c. It is the main idea of the novel
   d. To create interest in the novel

43. According to the passage, which of the following is NOT a main theme of Lee's novels?
   a. Identity
   b. Culture
   c. Immigration
   d. Espionage

44. According to the passage, why do Lee's novels focus on race and cultural identity?

   a. Because Lee was born in Korea

   b. Because Lee's ancestors are Korean

   c. Because Lee immigrated to America at a young age

   d. Because Lee feels racial and cultural issues are the biggest problem facing America

45. How does the author of the passage feel about the ideas presented in Lee's novels?

   a. Concerned about the disappearance of cultures in a rapidly expanding and mixed world

   b. Excited that immigrants are easily able to redefine and establish themselves in new cultures

   c. Certain that all borders will eventually be eliminated so world cultures will commingle and fully assimilate

   d. Critical regarding the role technology has played in society and how it destroys the immigrant experience

Refer to the following for questions 46 - 48:

New Zealand Inhabitants

The islands of New Zealand are among the most remote of all the Pacific islands. New Zealand is an archipelago, with two large islands and a number of smaller ones. Its climate is far cooler than the rest of Polynesia. According to Māori legends, it was colonized in the early 15th century by a wave of Polynesian voyagers who traveled southward in their canoes and settled on North Island. At this time, New Zealand was already known to the Polynesians, who had probably first landed there some 400 years earlier.

The Polynesian southward migration was limited by the availability of food. Traditional Polynesian tropical crops such as taro and yams will grow on North Island, but the climate of South Island is too cold for them. Coconuts will not grow on either island. The first settlers were forced to rely on hunting and gathering, and, of course, fishing. Especially on South Island, most settlements remained close to the sea. At the time of the Polynesian influx, enormous flocks of moa birds had their rookeries on the island shores. These flightless birds were easy prey for the settlers, and, within a few centuries, had been hunted to extinction. Fish, shellfish, and the roots of ferns were other important sources of food, but even these began to diminish in quantity as the human population increased. The Māori had few other sources of meat: dogs, smaller birds, and rats. Archaeological evidence shows that human flesh was also eaten and that tribal warfare increased markedly after the moa disappeared.

By far, the most important farmed crop in prehistoric New Zealand was the sweet potato. This tuber is hearty enough to grow throughout the islands and could be stored to provide food during the winter months, when other food-gathering activities were difficult. The availability of the sweet potato made possible a significant increase in the human population. Māori tribes often lived in encampments called *pā*, which were fortified with earthen embankments and usually located near the best sweet potato farmlands.

254

46. What was a significant difference between the sweet potato and other crops known to the Polynesians?
   a. The sweet potato provided more protein.
   b. The sweet potato would grow on North Island.
   c. The sweet potato could be stored during the winter.
   d. The sweet potato could be cultured near their encampments.

47. Why was it important that sweet potatoes could be stored?
   a. They could be eaten in winter, when other foods were scarce.
   b. They could be traded for fish and other goods.
   c. They could be taken along by groups of warriors going to war.
   d. They tasted better after a few weeks of storage.

48. What was it about the moa that made them easy for the Māori to catch?
   a. They were fat.
   b. They roosted by the shore.
   c. They were not very smart.
   d. They were unable to fly.

Refer to the following for questions 49 - 52:

There Will Come Soft Rains

By Sara Teasdale

There will come soft rains and the smell of the ground,

And swallows circling with their shimmering sound;

And frogs in the pools singing at night,

5 And wild plum trees in tremulous white;

Robins will wear their feathery fire

Whistling their whims on a low fence-wire;

10 And not one will know of the war, not one

Will care at last when it is done.

Not one would mind, neither bird nor tree

15 If mankind perished utterly;

And Spring herself, when she woke at dawn,

Would scarcely know that we were gone

49. Which line uses personification?

a. Line 2
b. Line 4
c. Line 7
d. Line 11

50. The "we" used in line 12 refers to

a. all of mankind.
b. the victors of the war.
c. Americans.
d. the poet and the reader.

51. This poem is an example of a(n)

a. sonnet.
b. rhymed verse.
c. free verse.
d. lyric.

52. Which of these statements offers the best summary of the poem?

a. Nature does not care about the affairs of mankind.
b. It is the government's responsibility to fight a war.
c. War has a devastating impact on nature.
d. Wars should not be fought in the spring.

Refer to the following for questions 53 - 54:

The Bermuda Triangle

The area known as the Bermuda Triangle has become such a part of popular culture that it can be difficult to separate fact from fiction. The interest first began when five Navy planes vanished in 1945, officially resulting from "causes or reasons unknown." The explanations about other accidents in the Triangle range from the scientific to the supernatural. Researchers have never been able to find anything truly mysterious about what happens in the Bermuda Triangle, if there even is a Bermuda Triangle. What is more, one of the biggest challenges in considering the phenomenon is deciding how much area actually represents the Bermuda Triangle. Most consider the Triangle to stretch from Miami out to Puerto Rico and to include the island of Bermuda. Others expand the area to include all of the Caribbean islands and to extend eastward as far as the Azores, which are closer to Europe than they are to North America.

The problem with having a larger Bermuda Triangle is that it increases the odds of accidents. There is near-constant travel, by ship and by plane, across the Atlantic, and accidents are expected to occur. In fact, the Bermuda Triangle happens to fall within one of the busiest navigational regions in the world, and the reality of greater activity creates the possibility for more to go wrong. Shipping records suggest that there is not a greater than average loss of vessels within the Bermuda Triangle, and many researchers have argued that the reputation of the Triangle makes any accident seem out of the ordinary. In fact, most accidents fall within the expected margin of error. The increase in ships from East Asia no doubt contributes to an increase in accidents. And as for the story of the Navy planes that

256

disappeared within the Triangle, many researchers now conclude that it was the result of mistakes on the part of the pilots who were flying into storm clouds and simply got lost.

53. Which of the following describes this type of writing?

    a. Narrative
    b. Persuasive
    c. Expository
    d. Technical

54. Which of the following sentences is most representative of a summary sentence for this passage?

    a. The problem with having a larger Bermuda Triangle is that it increases the odds of accidents.
    b. The area that is called the Bermuda Triangle happens to fall within one of the busiest navigational regions in the world, and the reality of greater activity creates the possibility for more to go wrong.
    c. One of the biggest challenges in considering the phenomenon is deciding how much area actually represents the Bermuda Triangle.
    d. Researchers have never been able to find anything truly mysterious about what happens in the Bermuda Triangle, if there even is a Bermuda Triangle.

Essay Question

1. Merit pay for teachers is the practice of giving increased pay based upon the improvement in student performance. It is a controversial idea among educators and policy makers. Those who support this idea say that, with it, school districts are able to select and retain the best teachers and to improve student performance. Others argue that merit pay systems lead to teacher competition for the best students and to test-driven teaching practices that are detrimental to the overall quality of education.

In your essay, select either of these points of view, or suggest an alternative approach, and make a case for it. Use specific reasons and appropriate examples **to support your position and to show how it is superior to the others.**

Answer Key and Explanations

Mathematics

1. C: To determine the scale factor of the dilation, compare the coordinates of $\Delta J'K'L'$ to the coordinates of ΔJKL. J is at $(-2\ -3)$ and J' is at $(-4, -6)$, which means that the coordinates of J were multiplied by a scale factor of 2 to get the coordinates of J'. K is at $(1, 3)$ and K' is at $(2, 6)$. L is at $(4, -1)$ and L' is at $(8, -2)$. As can be seen, the coordinates of K and L were also multiplied by a scale factor of 2 to get to the coordinates of K' and L'. Answer B is the scale factor going from $\Delta J'K'L'$ to ΔJKL. Answer D results if 3 was incorrectly added or subtracted from the y-coordinates in points K and L to get K' and L'. Answer A is the reciprocal of answer D.

2. B: Data sets A and C are asymmetrical: data set A is skewed toward lower values, and data set C is skewed toward higher values. This makes the mean a poor measure of center. Data set D is mostly symmetrical, but has a small outlier. The mean is very sensitive to outliers, and is not an appropriate measure of center for data sets that include them. Data set B is roughly symmetrical and has no outliers; the mean would be an appropriate measure of center here.

3. C: There are seven musical notes A–G, so this would not work for eight students.

4. D: Since the question asks how much money Eli owes his brother, the expression that would represent this scenario is $12 + 20$ because he borrowed \$12 and then borrowed an additional \$20. When adding two numbers with the same sign, we find the sum of the two numbers and the answer gets the sign of both numbers. Therefore, $12 + 20 = 32$. The amount of money Eli owes his brother is \$32.

5. A: A triangular pyramid has four triangular faces. The arrangement of these faces in a two-dimensional figure is a net of a triangular pyramid if the figure can be folded to form a triangular pyramid. Choice B represents a rectangular pyramid, choice C is a triangular prism, and choice D is a square pyramid.

6. B: Substitute each of the given values for x and y into the equation, and simplify using the order of operations.

$$(4)^2 - (2(3) - 3) = 16 - (6 - 3) = 16 - 3 = 13$$

7. A: A tree diagram shows the different combinations possible by listing each option as a sort of hierarchy. To start, we list all possibilities for the first category. Here, our first category is ice cream flavor, so we need three branches to represent the three different flavors. Next, we must decide between three different toppings. Because each topping can be paired with any flavor, we need three branches coming from each flavor, to show all the flavor/topping combinations. Finally, we must decide on hot fudge or caramel. Again, each choice can be added to any of our already existing combinations, so we'll need two more branches coming from each topping choice. When finished, we can follow the branches from top to bottom to see every possible combination of ice cream sundae that can be created. Because choice A shows every possible branch, it has to be our answer. Choice B leaves out the toppings, choice C forgets the ice cream flavors as options, and choice D does not take into account the final choice of hot fudge or caramel sauce.

8. C: There are three ways in which two women from the same department can be selected: two women can be selected from Biology, two women can be selected from Chemistry, or two women

259

can be selected from Physics. Since the events of choosing one woman and then another are both independent events, multiply the two probabilities together to get the probability of choosing two women from the same department.

Biology	Chemistry	Physics
$\dfrac{26}{129} \times \dfrac{25}{128} = \dfrac{650}{16{,}512}$	$\dfrac{31}{129} \times \dfrac{30}{128} = \dfrac{930}{16{,}512}$	$\dfrac{20}{129} \times \dfrac{19}{128} = \dfrac{380}{16{,}512}$

Since any of these is a distinct possible outcome, the probability that two women will be selected from the same department is the sum of these outcomes.

$$\frac{650}{16{,}512} + \frac{930}{16{,}512} + \frac{380}{16{,}512} = \frac{1{,}960}{16{,}512} \approx 0.119 = 11.9\%$$

9. A: Experimental probability is a ratio of how many times the spinner will land on the specific letter to the total number of places the spinner can land. In this case, there are eight possible places where the spinner may land. The D is present only in one space, so the probability of landing there is 1 to 8 or $\frac{1}{8}$.

10. A: To add quadratic expressions, combine like terms. In this problem, there are three sets of like terms: the y^2-terms, the y-terms, and the constants. Set up the addition vertically, making sure to line up like terms, and then add them together:

$$\begin{array}{rrrrrrr} & y^2 & + & 9y & - & 2 \\ + & 4y^2 & - & y & - & 5 \\ \hline & 5y^2 & + & 8y & - & 7 \end{array}$$

11. C: Since Joshua has to earn more than 92 points to qualify and each question is worth 4 points, the inequality $4x > 92$, where x is the number of questions he gets correct, best represents this situation. To solve for x, the number of questions Joshua needs to answer correctly, divide both sides of the inequality by 4. This results in the inequality $x > 23$. Since there are only 30 questions, the inequality becomes $23 < x \leq 30$.

To graph this inequality, put an open dot at 23 because there is a greater than sign and not a greater than or equal to sign. This shows that 23 is not included in the solution set. Put a closed dot at 30 to show that it is included in the solution set. Then, connect the two dots with a line.

12. A: The average number of male students in the 11th and 12th grades is 125 (calculated as $\frac{131 + 119}{2}$). The number of Hispanic students at the school is 10% of 1219, which is 122 students (rounded up from 121.9). The difference in the number of male and female students at the school is $630 - 589 = 41$, and the difference in the number of 9th and 12th grade students at the school is $354 - 255 = 99$.

13. A: 20 of 38 sophomores taking an elective are male. The probability that a male is chosen is $\frac{\text{number of males}}{\text{number of sophomores}} = \frac{20}{38} \approx 0.53$.

14. D: The sum of angles in a triangle equals 180 degrees. Therefore, solve for the remaining angle as $180 - (15 + 70) = 95$ degrees.

15. B: To factor the polynomial, find factors of the first and third term whose product can be added to get the middle term. Here, the factors 7 and –8 have a product of –56, and when added together, yield –1. Another way to find the correct answer is to multiply the answer choices and select the choice that yields the original equation. In this case:

$$(x + 7)(x - 8) = (x)(x) + (x)(-8) + (7)(x) + (7)(-8)$$
$$= x^2 - 8x + 7x - 56$$
$$= x^2 - x - 56$$

16. B: The given equation is a quadratic equation that can be solved by factorization. First, move everything to one side to get it in the correct form by subtracting 6 from both sides:

$$x^2 + 5x = 6$$
$$x^2 + 5x - 6 = 0$$

Then, factor the equation.

$$(x + 6)(x - 1) = 0$$

From here, set both factors equal to 0 and solve for the two solutions.

$$x + 6 = 0 \qquad\qquad x - 1 = 0$$
$$x = -6 \qquad\qquad x = 1$$

Thus, the two solutions to the equation are $x = -6$ and $x = 1$.

17. C: A reflection is a transformation producing a mirror image. A figure reflected over the x-axis will have its vertices in the form (x, y) transformed to $(x, -y)$. The point W at $(1, -7)$ reflects to W' at $(1, 7)$. Only Answer C shows $WXYZ$ being carried onto its image $W'X'Y'Z'$ by a reflection across the x-axis. Answer A shows a reflection across the line $y = x$. Answer B shows a 90° counterclockwise rotation about the origin. Answer D shows a reflection across the y-axis.

18. D: The perimeter (P) of the quadrilateral is simply the sum of its sides:

$$P = m + (m + 2) + (m + 3) + 2m$$

Put together like terms by adding the variables (m terms) together. Then, add the constants. This gives you: $P = 5m + 5$

In this problem, it seems that some of the variables do not have a number in front of them. However, when there is no coefficient, this means multiplication by 1. So, $m = 1m$, $x = 1x$, and so on.

19. B: When the wedges are rearranged into the rectangle, half of the wedge arcs form the top length of the rectangle and the other half of the wedge arcs form the bottom length of the rectangle. Since all of the wedge arcs combine to form the entire circumference of the circle, the length of the rectangle is half of the circumference of the circle. The formula for the circumference of a circle with radius r is $C = 2\pi r$. Half of that circumference is $\left(\frac{1}{2}\right) 2\pi r = \pi r$. Answer C is the width of the rectangle. Answer D is the area of the rectangle.

20. B: To factor the polynomial, start by finding two factors that multiply to $2x^2$ that will make up the first parts of the binomials. The two factors must be $2x$ and x.

$$(2x+?)(x+?)$$

From here, find two numbers that multiply to –15 and will give you a middle coefficient of 7 when the two binomials are multiplied together. These numbers must be –3 and 5, which will create this polynomial in factored form:

$$(2x - 3)(x + 5)$$

Pay close attention to the placement and signs of the numbers. This method may take a little guessing and checking, especially when you are trying to figure out how to get the middle term. Once you have your polynomial factored, multiply it out to make sure that it matches the original polynomial.

$$2x^2 + 10x - 3x - 15 = 2x^2 + 7x - 15$$

21. B: Since the denominator is the same for both fractions, this is simple subtraction. Start by subtracting the fractions. Since 1 is less than 5, borrow from the 3. The expression is now: $2\frac{7}{6} - 1\frac{5}{6}$. Now the fractions can be subtracted: $\frac{7}{6} - \frac{5}{6} = \frac{2}{6}$, which simplifies to $\frac{1}{3}$. Then, subtract the whole numbers: $2 - 1 = 1$. Putting these two parts together gives the final answer: $3\frac{1}{6} - 1\frac{5}{6} = 1\frac{1}{3}$.

22. D: A Venn diagram may be drawn to assist in finding the answer.

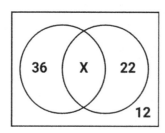

Since the set contains 75 total people, the solution is equal to $75 - (36 + 22 + 12)$ or 5 people.

23. D: Since there are 100 homes' market times represented in each set, the median time a home spends on the market is between the 50th and 51st data point in each set. The 50th and 51st data points for Zip Code 1 are six months and seven months, respectively, so the median time a house in Zip Code 1 spends on the market is between six and seven months (6.5 months), which by the realtor's definition of market time is a seven-month market time. The 50th and 51st data points for Zip Code 2 are both thirteen months, so the median time a house in Zip Code 2 spends on the market is thirteen months.

To find the mean market time for 100 houses, find the sum of the market times and divide by 100. If the frequency of a one-month market time is 9, the number 1 is added nine times (1×9), if frequency of a two-month market time is 10, the number 2 is added ten times (2×10), and so on. So, to find the average market time, divide by 100 the sum of the products of each market time and its corresponding frequency. For Zip Code 1, the mean market time is 7.38 months, which by the realtor's definition of market time is an eight-month market time. For Zip Code 2, the mean market time is 12.74, which by the realtor's definition of market time is a thirteen-month market time.

The mode market time is the market time for which the frequency is the highest. For Zip Code 1, the mode market time is three months, and for Zip Code 2, the mode market time is eleven months. Therefore, the median time a house spends on the market in Zip Code 1 is less than the mean time a house spends on the market in Zip Code 1.

24. C: The power to which 2 is raised to give 64 is 6; $2^6 = 64$. Thus, $x = 6$.

25. B: It is helpful to recall that percentages can be converted to decimals: 30% of 3300 is $0.3 \times 3300 \text{ lbs} = 990 \text{ lbs}$

26. B: The volume of a rectangular box can be determined using the formula $V = l \times w \times h$. This means that the volume of a rectangular box can be determined by multiplying the length of the base of the box by the width of the box and multiplying that product by the height of the box. Therefore, the volume of the box described in this question is equal to $5 \times 7 \times 9$, or 315 in^3.

27. D: The measure of the angle formed by the chord and the tangent is equal to one-half of the measure of the intercepted arc. Since the measure of the angle is 72°, the measure of the intercepted arc may be found by writing $72° = \frac{1}{2}x$. Dividing both sides of the equation by $\frac{1}{2}$ gives $x = 144°$. The measure of the intercepted arc may also be found by multiplying 72° by 2. Since the measure of the full circle is 360°, we subtract 144 from 360 to find that $x = 216°$.

28. B: Determine the probability of each option.

For choice A, this is the total number of students in the tea circle of the Venn diagram divided by the total number of students surveyed:

$$\frac{42 + 12 + 7 + 26}{250} = \frac{87}{250} = 34.8\%$$

For choice B, this is the total number of students in the hot chocolate circle and in at least one other circle divided by the total number in the hot chocolate circle:

$$\frac{31 + 7 + 26}{31 + 7 + 26 + 56} = \frac{64}{120} \approx 53.3\%$$

For choice C, this is the number of students in the intersection of all three circles divided by the total number in the overlap of the coffee and hot chocolate circles:

$$\frac{7}{7 + 31} = \frac{7}{38} \approx 18.4\%$$

For choice D, this is the number of students outside of all the circles divided by the total number of students surveyed:

$$\frac{11}{250} = 4.4\%$$

Choice B has the greatest probability.

29. C: To solve for x, simplify this equation through factoring.

$$x^2 + 8x + 16 = 0$$
$$(x + 4)(x + 4) = 0$$
$$x + 4 = 0$$
$$x = -4$$

30. B: We can find the area of the shaded part by viewing the target as five separate circles of various sizes, one inside the other. We add the areas of the three shaded circles and subtract the areas of the two white circles. The area of a circle is πr^2, so the area of the largest circle (the entire target) is $\pi(5a)^2$. We subtract the white circle inside it, add the shaded circle inside that one, and so on:

$$A = \pi(5a)^2 - \pi(4a)^2 + \pi(3a)^2 - \pi(2a)^2 + \pi(a)^2$$
$$= 25\pi a^2 - 16\pi a^2 + 9\pi a^2 - 4\pi a^2 + \pi a^2$$
$$= (25 - 16 + 9 - 4 + 1)\pi a^2$$
$$= 15\pi a^2$$

31. A: Candidate A's vote ratio is the number of votes that he obtained divided by the total number of votes cast. Then, multiply that decimal by 100 to convert the decimal into a percentage. Now, Candidate A's vote is: $\frac{36800}{36800+32100+2100} \times 100$. So, you have a percentage of 51.8%.

32. B: 25% off is equivalent to, $25 * \frac{\$138}{100} = \$34.50$, and therefore the sale price becomes:

$138 -$34.50 = $103.50.

33. D: When the dress is marked down by 20%, the cost of the dress is 80% of its original price; thus, the reduced price of the dress can be written as $\frac{80}{100}x$, or $\frac{4}{5}x$, where x is the original price. When discounted an extra 25%, the dress costs 75% of the reduced price, or $\frac{75}{100}\left(\frac{4}{5}x\right)$, or $\frac{3}{4}\left(\frac{4}{5}x\right)$, which simplifies to $\frac{3}{5}x$. So, the final price of the dress is three-fifths of the original price.

34. B: The percent increase is represented as $\frac{525-400}{400}$, which equals 0.3125 or 31.25%.

35. A: Since $2x + 4y = 8$ is written in standard form, use the equation to find the x- and y-intercepts. Once we know where the line passes through each axis, we can match the graph to the equation. Start by finding the y-intercept. When using the standard form of an equation to find the y-intercept, make x equal to 0 and solve for y. Start by replacing x with 0 in the equation.

$$2x + 4y = 8$$
$$2(0) + 4y = 8$$

Next, simplify the equation and solve for y. Since $2 \times 0 = 0$, rewrite the equation as $0 + 4y = 8$, which is the same as $4y = 8$.

$$0 + 4y = 8$$
$$4y = 8$$

From here, isolate the variable y by doing inverse operations. Since the opposite of multiplying by 4 is dividing by 4, divide both sides of the equation by 4.

$$\frac{4y}{4} = \frac{8}{4}$$

$4y \div 4 = 1y$ (or y), and $8 \div 4 = 2$. Therefore, $y = 2$. The line intersects the y-axis at point (0,2).

Now that we know the location of the y-intercept, find the x-intercept. When using the standard form of an equation to find the x-intercept, make y equal to 0 and solve for x. Start by replacing y with 0 in the equation.

$$2x + 4y = 8$$
$$2x + 4(0) = 8$$

Next, simplify the equation and solve for x. Since $4 \times 0 = 0$, rewrite the equation as $2x + 0 = 8$, which is the same as $2x = 8$.

$$2x + 0 = 8$$
$$2x = 8$$

From here, isolate the variable x by doing inverse operations. Since the opposite of multiplying by 2 is dividing by 2, divide both sides of the equation by 2.

$$\frac{2x}{2} = \frac{8}{2}$$

$2x \div 2 = 1x$ (or x), and $8 \div 2 = 4$. Therefore, $x = 4$. The line intersects the x-axis at point (4,0).

Now that we know that the location of the x-intercept is (4,0) and the location of the y-intercept is (0,2), look for the graph that contains both coordinate pairs. Since the graph shown in answer A contains both points, the correct answer is A.

36. A: To simplify the polynomial, group and combine all like terms.

$$4x^3 + 5x - x^3 + 2x^2 + 17 - 3x^3 + 5x - 2x^2 + 3$$
$$= (4x^3 - x^3 - 3x^3) + (2x^2 - 2x^2) + (5x + 5x) + (17 + 3)$$
$$= 0 + 0 + 10x + 20$$
$$= 10x + 20$$

37. B: The total volume of the cylinder is given by $V = h\pi r^2 = 10\pi \times 1 = 31.4$, when $\pi = 3.14$. Since the slice is a straight, 60-degree slice, its volume is one sixth of this $\left(\frac{60}{360} = \frac{1}{6}\right)$, or 5.23.

38. D: The fraction of those playing drums plus the fraction of those playing a brass instrument must total 1. The number that play drums is therefore pn, and the number playing brass must be $(1-p)n$.

39. B: A die has a total of six sides, with a different number on each side. Three of these numbers are odd, and three are even. When throwing a die, the probability of rolling an odd number is 3 out of 6 or $\frac{3}{6}$. Reducing the fraction, yields a $\frac{1}{2}$ or 50% chance an odd number will be rolled.

40. C: Start by distributing the 4, and then use inverse operations to solve for x.

$$8x - 24 = 10x - 6$$
$$-24 = 2x - 6$$
$$-18 = 2x$$
$$-9 = x$$

41. C: Angles g and c are alternate exterior angles. Thus, they are congruent.

42. C: First, write an equation to represent the word problem. This scenario can be represented by the equation $48 + 36 - 50 =$ ___. First, add the first two integers in the problem, 48 and 36. Write the problem vertically, making sure to line up the numbers according to place value. Start by adding the ones column to the right. Since $8 + 6 = 14$, write 4 in the ones place as part of the answer and carry the 1 over to the tens place column. Next, add the tens column. Since $1 + 4 + 3 = 8$, write 8 in the tens place as part of the answer. Therefore, $48 + 36 = 84$.

$$
\begin{array}{r} 48 \\ +36 \\ \hline \end{array}
\qquad
\begin{array}{r} {}^{1} \\ 48 \\ +36 \\ \hline 4 \end{array}
\qquad
\begin{array}{r} {}^{1} \\ 48 \\ +36 \\ \hline 84 \end{array}
$$

From here, subtract the next integer from the original problem, 50, from 84. Write the problem vertically, making sure to line up the numbers according to place value. Start by subtracting the ones column on the right. Since $4 - 0 = 4$, write 4 in the ones column as part of the answer. From here, move to the tens column and subtract. Since $8 - 5 = 3$, write 3 in the tens place as part of the answer. $48 + 36 - 50 = 34$. There were 34 cookies left over after the bake sale. Therefore, the correct answer is C.

$$
\begin{array}{r} 84 \\ -50 \\ \hline \end{array}
\qquad
\begin{array}{r} 84 \\ -50 \\ \hline 4 \end{array}
\qquad
\begin{array}{r} 84 \\ -50 \\ \hline 34 \end{array}
$$

43. B: To find the value of w, we will isolate the w on one side of the equation. Since 57 is being subtracted from w, to isolate w we will add 57 to both sides of the equation. On the left side of the equation, we will be left with w. On the right side, we will add 57 to –279, which is –222. Therefore, the value of w is –222.

44. C: The hypotenuse must be the longest side of a right triangle, so it must be the lengths of the other two sides that are given as 6 and 8 units. Calculate the length of the hypotenuse, H, from the Pythagorean Theorem: $H^2 = S_1^2 + S_2^2 = 6^2 + 8^2 = 36 + 64 = 100$, which yields $H = 10$ and the perimeter equals $10 + 6 + 8 = 24$.

45. C: One way to find this is to align like terms and subtract them vertically, remembering that subtraction of a term is equivalent to adding its opposite. This gives us:

$$
\begin{array}{rrrrrrr}
 & -8x^2 & +5xy & & & -4y & -10 \\
- & (-8x^2 & & +12y^2 & +5x & -6y & -10) \\
\hline
 & 0x^2 & +5xy & -12y^2 & -5x & +2y & +0
\end{array}
$$

This result simplifies to $5xy - 12y^2 - 5x + 2y$.

46. A: If the digits in a number add up to a multiple of 3, it is also divisible by 3. For instance, in the number 27, $2 + 7 = 9$, which is a multiple of 3.

47. C: There are four, equally possible places the spinner may land. The digit 2 is only present in one space, so the probability of landing there is 1 out of 4 or $\frac{1}{4}$.

48. D: Recall that area (A) is length (l) times width (w):

$$A = l \times w$$
$$A = 4 \text{ ft} \times 6 \text{ ft}$$
$$A = 24 \text{ ft}^2$$

49. B: Start by creating a table that shows the relationship between minutes jogged (m) and distance (d).

Minutes jogged (m)	Distance in miles (d)
0	0
10	1
20	2
30	3

As you can see, the table represents the equation $d = \frac{1}{10}m$. The independent variable is minutes (m), and the dependent variable is the distance (d). From here, we can use the data from the table to graph points on the coordinate plane. The x-axis represents the independent variable, which is minutes jogged, and the y-axis represents the dependent variable, which is distance run in miles.

Rewrite the data from the table as points on the coordinate plane, (x, y): (0,0), (10,1), (20,2), (30,3). Although all answer options contain the point (0,0) on their coordinate planes, the only graph with all four coordinate pairs is answer B. Therefore, the correct answer is B.

50. B: If l and w represent the length and width of the enclosed area, its perimeter is equal to $2l + 2w$; since the fence is positioned x feet from the lot's edges on each side, the perimeter of the enlarged garden is $2(l + 2x) + 2(w + 2x)$. Since the extra amount of money spent by fencing the larger area is $36, and since the fencing material costs $1.50 per linear foot, 24 more feet of material are used to fence around the garden than would have been used for the original. This can be expressed as the equation:

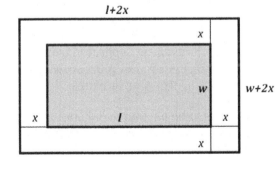

$$2(l + 2x) + 2(w + 2x) - (2l + 2w) = 24$$
$$2l + 4x + 2w + 4x - 2l - 2w = 24$$
$$8x = 24$$
$$x = 3 \text{ ft}$$

The difference in the area of the lot and the enclosed space is 34 yd^2, which is the same as 306 ft^2. So, $(l + 2x)(w + 2x) - lw = 306$. Substituting 3 for x,

$$(l + 6)(w + 6) - lw = 306$$
$$lw + 6l + 6w + 36 - lw = 306$$
$$6l + 6w = 270$$
$$6(l + w) = 270$$
$$l + w = 45 \text{ ft}$$

This is the original length and width, so we add 6 to each, or 12 total, for a new length and width of $l + w = 57$ ft. Therefore, the perimeter of the enclosed space, $2(l + w)$, is $2(57) = 114$ ft. The cost of 114 ft of chicken wire is $114 \times \$1.50 = \$171$.

Language

1. D: "Sonja works very hard" and "she is tired all the time" are both independent clauses (they contain a subject and a verb and express a complete thought). It is appropriate to join two independent clauses with a semicolon. Choice A is a comma splice. Choice B is a run-on sentence. Choice C incorrectly uses a comma to precede the conjunctive adverb *however*.

2. A: *Answer* (present tense form of the verb) maintains the parallel structure of the sentence and matches the verb tense of the words *get* and *read*. The other answer choices represent the present participle (*answering*), infinitive (*to answer*), and future tense (*will answer*).

3. B: The correct spelling of the word is *deleterious*.

4. D: A stele is a large, upright stone that typically has writing on it. Steles were commonly used as monuments in ancient cultures in the Middle East.

5. D: This is an example of a compound-complex sentence. A simple (A) sentence contains a subject and a verb and expresses a complete thought. Its subject and/or verb may be compound (e.g., "John and Mary" as subject and "comes and goes" as verb). A complex (B) sentence contains an independent clause and one or more dependent clauses. The independent and dependent clauses are joined by a subordinating conjunction or a relative pronoun. A compound (C) sentence contains two independent clauses—two simple sentences—connected by a coordinating conjunction. A compound-complex (also called complex-compound) sentence, as its name implies, combines both compound and complex sentences: it combines more than one independent clause with at least one dependent clause. In the example sentence given, the first two clauses, joined by "however," are independent, and the clause modifying "actual test questions," beginning with "which cover," is a relative, dependent clause.

6. D: This sentence contains a prepositional phrase and an independent clause separated from the main sentence via a semicolon. This is the only choice that uses correct grammar. A prepositional phrase starts with a preposition and usually ends with a gerund, noun, pronoun, or clause.

7. B: A semicolon links two (or more) independent clauses. It can also be used to avoid confusion when listing items. Choice B is listing items and using the semicolon to avoid a misunderstanding. Choices A and C combine a dependent and independent clause. Choice D incorrectly mixes commas and semicolons in the list.

8. C: The statement "And even the name of the legendary King Arthur" is not a complete sentence and thus cannot stand on its own. The period that is placed before the word *And* should be removed and the two statements combined.

9. C: The meaning of *lachrymose* is "mournful" or "tearful." The context of the sentence shows that the girls are upset (they are crying and comforting each other) in connection with the unpleasant subject (bad haircuts) of the stories.

10. A: This is an example of a conditional adverbial clause; it acts like an adverb and usually starts with words like *if* or *unless*. This talks about a situation that could happen. The other choices do not make sense in this situation; it's clear from the second part of the sentence that a consequence is coming. Choices B and C are independent clauses, and choice D is a clause of manner.

11. A: A semicolon is used to connect two independent clauses that are closely related. A comma should not be used to separate independent clauses, as a comma is more for a pause in the text. The sentence needs some punctuation, so choice C is incorrect. Choice D uses a colon, which should be used to show a list or provide an explanation.

12. B: The student used the present-tense verb forms go instead of went and have instead of had in describing actions that took place in the past. The student also used the idiomatically incorrect preposition on instead of in. The student did not make any other errors.

13. C: *Acrimonious* means "bitter" or "vitriolic," and is very similar in meaning to *rancorous*.

14. A: This version is correctly punctuated because it is a compound-complex sentence, consisting of two independent clauses and a dependent/subordinate (relative) clause. Independent clauses should be separated by a semicolon. In (B) and (D), the two independent clauses have no punctuation separating them, creating a run-on sentence; additionally, (B) has an incorrect comma between the first independent clause and the subordinating conjunction "that," which introduces the relative clause. (If "that" were omitted, it would be correct with or without the comma.) Version (C) incorrectly separates the independent clauses with a comma instead of a semicolon.

15. B: This question deals with being able to identify different meanings or parts of speech through patterns in words. The first and second blanks require nouns; the third blank requires a verb. Choice A provides noun, verb, verb. Choice C provides verb, noun, noun. Choice D provides all nouns.

16. B: The sentence portrays a scenario where it seems as though the floor supervisor has knowledge about everything that is happening and is ready to step in to keep things from going wrong. While the supervisor may also be cautious, eager, or a micromanager, the meaning and use of *omniscient* in this context is "all-knowing".

17. A: This sentence offers the most effective revision. The syntax is clearer than the other answer choices. The writer achieves maximum impact by holding Mary Shelley's achievement, the creation of Dr. Frankenstein and his hideous monster in her novel *Frankenstein*, for the end of the sentence.

18. D: It is appropriate to use a colon to introduce a list. It is not appropriate to use a colon following a preposition (choice B), or after the phrases "including" and "for example" as used in choices A and C, which make the use of a colon redundant.

19. B: The word *arbitrary* means that an outcome is not determined by predictable rules, so a random drawing fits this meaning. The sentence should read: The selection of the winning lottery numbers is entirely arbitrary, with numbers being drawn at random out of a large ball.

20. C: "I am going to buy a new car" and "it is a blue sedan" are independent clauses (they each contain a subject and a verb and express a complete thought). It is appropriate to join two independent clauses in a single sentence with a semicolon. Choice A is a run-on sentence. Choice B is a comma splice. Choice D uses a comma to precede the conjunctive adverb *therefore*, which is incorrect.

21. A: This choice is the only one that is punctuated correctly.

22. A: Choice A is correct because it changes *forced*. The word *forced* is out of place here because it suggests that every employee without a badge is physically made to check in. The intended meaning of the sentence seems to be that there is a rule regarding badge-less employees: they must check in at the main entrance. Presumably, this rule could be broken, resulting not in the use of force but in a warning or reminder. This rule would be accurately indicated by *required*. The other choices are all plausible changes that would not introduce additional problems. However, none of them would address the issue that *forced* presents.

23. B: This sentence correctly capitalizes the place name of Washington, D.C., a proper noun. The word "president" is incorrectly capitalized in (A): it should only be capitalized when used as a proper noun, e.g., "President Obama." But when a civil title is used instead of a name as it is here, it is not capitalized. The word "south" is incorrectly capitalized in (C). Compass directions are not capitalized, as in "coming south" or "going south." They are capitalized only when referring to actual regions, as in "We live in the South." The words "science" and "math" are incorrectly capitalized in (D). Academic subjects are not capitalized. It is correct to capitalize "English" because it is derived from the proper noun "England." *Specific* titles of classes or courses, like "Elementary Algebra" or "Math 101" should be capitalized, but general nouns like "science" and "math" should not.

24. B: The key to an effective concluding statement is a concise summary of the argument's main points. Such a conclusion leaves the opponent and audience with a clear and organized understanding of the argument. The introduction of new points, or a detail added merely to lighten mood, would weaken the argument by straying off point at the last minute. Introducing contradictory perspectives would work against the argument's effectiveness.

25. A: The first sentence introduces an argument against complete freedom of speech. The second sentence makes an argument in favor of it. The second argument opposes the first one, so the two sentences should be linked with the adverb *however*. *Therefore* and *so* would be used only if the sentences supported each other.

26. D: This statement mentions the death of William Shakespeare, effectively indicating his end. It also refers to the importance and continued relevance of his work in the years to come, which is integral to any general essay about the playwright. This statement offers a stronger conclusion to an essay on William Shakespeare than stopping short with the cause and date of his death. In addition, this choice does not stray from an authoritative tone by presenting personal opinion about Shakespeare's best play or a random detail about the theaters that staged his work.

27. C: The first sentence explains how television once was criticized. The second sentence shows how contemporary shows are now being praised. They require a linking sentence indicating that an attitude change toward television has occurred over time. Explaining the premise of *Mad Men* or the variety of shows on television is not the best way to link these sentences. Stating, "Today's television shows prove that the medium has not changed much," contradicts the second sentence.

28. D: This sentence is written correctly. Choice A is wrong because the introductory prepositional phrase needs a comma. Choice B is not correct because the verb needs to stay in singular form. Choice C is incorrect because *healthy* is spelled correctly.

29. B: Items in a series need commas between each item. Choice A is wrong because there are no commas for this series. There is no need to capitalize the name of a disease. So, choice C is incorrect. There is an error in the sentence. So, choice D cannot be correct.

30. D: This sentence is a run-on. The sentence has two independent clauses. So, you can place a period between them and capitalize the word *for*. Choice A is wrong because the original sentence is not correct. Choice B is wrong as well. The reason is that a comma between two independent clauses does not correct the problem. Choice C is wrong because a colon cannot be used to separate independent clauses.

31. A: The sentence does not need an adverb. Instead, it needs a predicate adjective to modify the subject *researchers*. Choice B is incorrect because SAD is an acronym that should have capital letters. The sentence is not a question. So, choice C is wrong because it does not need a question mark. Choice D is not correct because there is a mistake in the sentence.

32. D: The sentence is written correctly. So, choice A is not correct because the adjectives are not coordinate. Choice B is not correct because the sentence is making a comparison to months that are not during the winter. In other words, the body makes less melatonin in the summer months. Choice C is wrong because *melatonin* does not need to be capitalized.

33. A: The question tests on the use of *effect* and *affect*. In this sentence, you are looking for the verb that means *influence*. So, affect is the correct word in this sentence. Choice B is wrong because the prepositional phrase should not come after *serotonin*. Choice C is incorrect because *Less* is for amounts which is true for this sentence. *Fewer* is for numbers and applies to things that can be counted. So, the correct adverb is being used in this sentence. Choice D is wrong because the sentence has an error.

34. D: Again, *fewer* is for numbers and applies to things that can be counted. Sunlight cannot be counted. *Less* is for an amount which is true for this sentence. Also, making the change brings back the intended parallelism of the sentence. Choice A is incorrect because the subject and verb agree as they are written. Choice B is also incorrect because the word is not a proper noun and does not need capitalization. Choice C is incorrect. The reason is given in the explanation above for choice D.

35. D: *Factors* is plural and needs a plural verb. The verb *has* is singular. So, this makes a disagreement between subject and verb. *Have* is the plural form of *has* and needs to be used here. Choice A is incorrect because the sentence has an error with subject-verb agreement. Choice B is wrong because removing the capital letter causes another error. Choice C is incorrect. The change simply switches the problem in agreement rather than eliminating it.

36. C: The sentence has a problem with parallel structure. The verbs *tough* and *wait* need to be parallel. Choice A is incorrect because SAD is an acronym and needs capital letters. Choice B is also incorrect. There is an attempt to correct the problem of parallelism. However, *toughing* needs an auxiliary verb. Choice D is wrong because there is an error that needs to be corrected.

37. B: The sentence is not interrogative; it is declarative. In other words, it needs a period at the end, not a question mark. Choice A is incorrect because *well* is an adverb, and the noun *news* needs an adjective modifier. Choice C is incorrect because the seasons are not capitalized. Choice D is wrong because there is an error that needs to be corrected.

38. A: Choice A is correct because the word is not being used in a different way from a dictionary definition. Choice B is not correct because readers need an explanation of the word *temp*. Choice C is wrong because *temporary* is spelled correctly. Choice D is incorrect because a comma is not needed.

39. D: This question is about parallel structure. *Employs* and *generating* are verbs that need to be changed to be parallel. The best way to make them parallel is by putting both in the present tense. Choice A is incorrect because *the staffing industry* is a single unit. So, it does not need the plural form. Choice B is incorrect because the noun is singular and needs a singular verb. Choice C cannot be done without adding more words.

40. D: The problem in the sentence is the wrong homonym. The word *their* is possessive and is needed in this sentence. *They're* is a contraction of *they are*. So, this is the wrong word. In this sentence, *because* is used correctly. So, this makes choice A incorrect. Choice C makes *skills* singular; however, this is not the correct choice. After all, an employer wants a worker who has more than one skill.

41. B: The problem in this question is with antecedent agreement. The pronoun *they* needs a plural noun: *employees*. Choice A is incorrect because of the problem with antecedent agreement. Choice C is incorrect because it has disagreement between subject and verb. Choice D is also wrong. The hyphen in *full-time* does not need to be removed. Also, choice D has disagreement between subject and verb. So, choice D is not correct.

42. C: The problem with the sentence is a comma splice. A semicolon shows that the thoughts of both sentences are related. So, the problem is corrected with the semicolon. Choice A cannot be correct because the original has a comma splice. Choice B is also wrong. The reason is that it has a pronoun-antecedent agreement problem. Choice D is incorrect because it creates a subject-verb agreement problem.

43. D: Adding a comma eliminates the problem of the run-on sentence. Choice A is wrong because there is an error in the sentence. Choice B is also incorrect because it creates a problem with subject-verb agreement. Choice C is incorrect because it creates a subject-verb disagreement in a different part of the sentence.

44. C: The problem in this sentence is a misspelling of valuable. Choice A is wrong because a hyphen is not needed to connect the two words. Choice B cannot be correct because *you're* is the right homonym. Choice D is not correct because there is an error in the sentence.

45. A: The sentence is declarative, not interrogative. So, the sentence needs a period as the end mark. Choice B is not correct because the apostrophe is needed to show possession. Choice C is incorrect because it does not solve the problem, and it creates a problem of agreement. Choice D is incorrect as well. The reason is that the sentence has an error that needs to be corrected.

46. C: The sentence contains a disagreement between the compound subject, which is considered plural, and the singular verb. Changing *is* to *are* solves the problem. Choice A is incorrect; the comma is needed for items in a series. Choice B is not correct; the word is correctly spelled as written. Choice D, likewise, is incorrect; it offers only a cosmetic change, not a solution to the problem of subject-verb agreement.

47. D: The problem in the sentence as written is one of subject-verb agreement and colloquial or substandard English. *Some* indicates that more than one apartment complex is being discussed. It, therefore, is necessary to change both the subject and verb to plural. Choice A is incorrect; the sentence as written clearly contains an error to be remedied. Choice B is not correct; choosing an alternative spelling for the homonym does not solve the problem. Choice C is incorrect as well; it creates instead a different subject-verb agreement problem.

48. C: The problem in this sentence is a dangling modifier. To correct the problem, you can write the independent clause as *"you need to consider the other issues about keeping your pet at your apartment."* Choice A is wrong because the comma needs to come after the introductory prepositional phrase. Choice B is not correct because the word is spelled correctly. Choice D cannot be correct because there is an error in the sentence.

Reading

1. C: The first paragraph gives the information to correctly answer this question.

2. B: This passage in arranged by problem and solution. The author states a problem that the cotton farmers were having: "Eventually, cotton will no longer grow on this land." The author then presents a solution: "Carver told farmers to rotate their crops: plant cotton one year, then the next year plant peanuts and other soil-restoring plants, like peas and sweet potatoes. It worked! The peanut plants grew and produced lots of peanuts."

3. D: The second paragraph discusses the problem the cotton farmers were facing. The cotton crops had depleted the nutrients from the soil.

4. A: The last paragraph answers this question. "Carver told farmers to rotate their crops: plant cotton one year, then the next year plant peanuts and other soil-restoring plants, like peas and sweet potatoes. It worked! The peanut plants grew and produced lots of peanuts."

5. B: Answer choice (B) best summarizes what this passage is mainly about. Choices (A), and (C) are not even discussed in this passage. Paragraph 5 does discuss choice (D), but it is not the main focus of the passage.

6. A: Answer choice (A) best defines "crop rotation." The passage gives the definition in the last paragraph.

7. D: In the first paragraph, Miss Lucas states that "so very fine a young man, with family, fortune, every thing in his favour, should think highly of himself. If I may so express it, he has a *right* to be proud." Basically, she feels he deserves to be proud because he is physically attractive, comes from a good family, has money, and is successful. The best choice is (E).

8. A: This question is asking you to make an inference about Elizabeth's feeling towards the gentleman. In paragraph 2, Elizabeth is "mortified" by the gentleman's actions towards her. From this statement, you can make the inference that she was offended by his actions.

9. C: Theme is a message or lesson conveyed by a written text. The message is usually about life, society or human nature. This particular excerpt is exploring pride as it relates to human nature. Mary's observations on pride are the best summary of the theme of this passage. "By all that I have ever read, I am convinced that it is very common indeed, that human nature is particularly prone to it." The best answer choice is (C).

10. C: Paragraph 3 gives the answer to this question. According to Mary, pride is an opinion of yourself, and vanity is what we want others to think of us.

11. B: As set out in section 1.0, Purpose and Scope, the document describes a procedure for identifying hazards associated with one or more jobs (in this case Tank Operations) or encountered by visitors and for instituting controls to mitigate (or minimize) the dangers that they present.

12. D: The methods to be used to mitigate hazards are given in section 4.1 of the text, which indicates that they are specified in descending order of use. Protective clothing is an example of the last method listed, personal protective equipment, so this is the last strategy to be tried to protect the workers from the hazardous chemical.

13. D: Section 4.2 indicates that safety procedures ("controls") that fall within the scope of normal training for workers do not need to be discussed in the work instructions for operations that are performed frequently.

14. A: The document is intended as a guide for those writing work instructions for jobs to be performed at the site. These work instructions are prepared by management. Workers and laborers would read those documents as part of their training.

15. D: Section 4.5 indicates that safety procedures that are not within the qualification and training of the workers for hazards should have detailed instructions for how the workers are to mitigate the hazard.

16. D: The main argument is stated in paragraph 4: "With the progression and extreme convenience of technology, printed books are going to soon become a thing of the past." The other choices are either supporting details or extra information not related to the main argument.

17. C: Paragraph 1 explains the progression of storytelling, beginning with oral tradition and going past the invention of the printing press. In context with the rest of the essay, this paragraph is needed to explain how storytelling has evolved, as well as how stories are shared within society.

18. A: In paragraph 1, it is stated that oral tradition was the main medium for storytelling before the invention of the printing press.

19. B: It is not a fact that "sliding a finger across the screen (or pressing a button) to move onto the next page is just as satisfying to the reader." Satisfaction is not something universal that can be proven for every reader. This statement is an opinion. All other choices are factual in nature.

20. A: The author makes the argument in paragraph 5 that devices such as the iPad and Kindle are "therefore better than books because they have multiple uses." All other choices reflect either supporting details or misrepresentation of the statements made by the author.

21. A: Gorkhi is described in line 5 as a bit bombastic. A bombastic individual is one who is overbearing and pretentious.

22. C: Lines 10–11 tells us that Zakov found the student on the floor.

23. D: Nasadev is described as whining, with his eyes red from crying, and concerned that his troubles will affect his family.

24. C: Zakov tries to understand how the student must have felt about Olga's rejection. His "heart went out" to the student, and later, when he leaves, he feels a deep sadness for him.

25. A: The student regards Zakov with an imploring look. To implore is to beg.

26. B: The passage describes his voice as "practically inaudible", which means "unable to be heard", but does not describe it as a whisper.

27. C: Olga's rejection of the student provides a reasonable motive, but there is nothing in the passage to suggest that Zakov had proof of Nasadev's guilt or innocence.

28. C: The author states what he believes to be the current state of the planet's environment and makes practical suggestions for making better use of its resources in the future, so choice C is correct. The author does not express expectations for improvement or regression, nor does the author condemn, complain, or make accusations in his descriptions.

29. B: As the passage states: "Locally grown food and other products manufactured within your community are the best choices. The fewer miles a product traveled to reach you, the fewer resources it required." This is summarized by choice B. The passage does not mention whether buying locally grown food supports community members, uses less packaging, or is healthier to eat, so choices A, C, and D are incorrect.

30. C: The author describes global warming and the depletion of natural resources as constant threats and makes suggestions that can slow or prevent the effects of these threats. This implies that if the author's suggestions are not followed, then these threats will continue. The author does not mention running out of resources in a specific time period, the cost of water and energy, or the possibility of hardship for local farmers.

31. D: The passage states: "You should try to be aware of your consumption of water and energy." The passage then gives examples for decreasing one's use of water and energy. The contexts of these sentences indicate that consumption means the depletion of goods. The passage instructs readers to be aware of their consumption of water and energy, but it does not suggest anything about using the greatest or least amount of water and energy. There also is no information about an illness of the lungs in the passage, so consumption does not refer to lung disease in this context.

32. C: To reduce water and energy, the author suggests that the reader turn off the water when brushing his or her teeth, limit showers to five minutes, turn off lights, and unplug appliances and chargers that are not being used. Choice C includes an item from this list, so it is correct. Choices A and B are statements related to conserving other types of resources, and choice D is a statement that applies to general conservation practices.

33. C: The Constitution overrides state law in some cases. Answer choices B and D are quite obviously factually incorrect. The last choice, A, is also not stated or implied in the passage, but this answer might seem correct to someone who hadn't read the passage carefully.

34. A: Although state courts exercised judicial review prior to the ratification of the Constitution, the doctrine is most often traced to the landmark U.S. Supreme Court decision Marbury v. Madison (1803), which struck down an act of Congress as unconstitutional. This sentence means that laws passed by Congress must comply with the Constitution. None of the other choices do.

35. A: This is an informational passage about history, so *historical* could be used to describe its contents. None of the other words fit this passage. *Transcription* refers to a passage that is a written text of a spoken communication. *Prospective* refers to the future. And *demonstrative* refers to expressing feeling or emotion.

36. A: When the 13 colonies ratified the Constitution, they endorsed it.

37. D: When Oliver Wendell Holmes dissented from many opinions, it meant he disagreed with the majority on the court. So his opinion was *different*.

38. C: As the passage explains, the Supreme Court's ruling in the 1803 case of *Marbury v. Madison*, which invalidated a law passed by Congress on the grounds that it violated the Constitution, is the foundation of the legal concept of judicial review.

39. C: According to the passage, after a period in which the Supreme Court struck down over 200 laws as unconstitutional, FDR threatened to "pack" the Court, which led to fewer laws being struck down. This is in reference to FDR's plan to add additional justices to the Supreme Court, who would have probably have been supporters of his who could be counted on to uphold the constitutionality of laws FDR got Congress to pass.

40. A: According to the passage, during the Lochner Era, the Supreme Court struck down nearly 230 laws. None of the other answer choices are supported by the passage.

41. B: The passage was written to analyze the works by Chang-rae Lee and the themes presented in his most famous novels.

42. A: The author of this passage uses the first line of the novel to provide an example of one of the themes of the novel.

43. D: Espionage is part of the plot of the novel *Native Speaker*, but it is not a theme that recurs in Lee's works.

44. C: The passage states that Lee's interests in cultural identity and race emerge from his own experiences with these subjects as a young immigrant to America.

45. A: The tone of the last paragraph suggests concern over the preservation of cultural identities in an increasingly mixed and expanding world.

46. C: The sweet potato could be stored, providing a source of food during the winter, when other food-gathering activities were difficult.

of food during the winter, when other food gathering activities were difficult.

47. A: The sweet potato provided a winter food source through storage, allowing the population to increase.

48. D: The moa were flightless birds, so they could not easily escape when humans came to hunt them.

49. D: Personification is a metaphor in which a thing or abstraction is represented as a person. Personification is used throughout this poem. However, of the answer choices given, line 11 is the best choice. The author personifies spring as a female.

50. A: The fifth stanza gives clues to whom "we" refers.

"Not one would mind, neither bird nor tree

If mankind perished utterly"

"We" is referencing mankind.

51. B: This is an example of a rhymed verse poem. The last two words of each line rhymes in every stanza. A sonnet is a poem of fourteen lines following a set rhyme scheme and logical structure. Often, poets use iambic pentameter when writing sonnets. A free verse poem is written without using strict meter or rhyme. A lyric poem is a short poem that expresses personal feelings, which may or may not be set to music.

52. A: Answer choice A gives the best summary of the poem. The poem imagines nature reclaiming the earth after humanity has been wiped out by a war. The poet imagines how little the human race will be missed.

53. C: The passage is expository because it communicates information about the mysteries of the Bermuda Triangle and what researchers have studied and now believe. The author includes facts to inform the reader, which is the goal of expository writing. The passage does not tell a story or describe one event, so it is not a narrative. The passage also does not seek to lead the reader to take action or accept a particular conclusion, so this passage is not persuasive. The passage also does not give technical information and does not aim to help the reader understand a technical concept, so this passage is not technical.

54. D: This sentence is the best summary statement for the entire passage because it clearly describes what the author is saying about the results of studies on the Bermuda Triangle. Each paragraph in the passage includes details that support the statement that researchers have never found anything truly mysterious about the Bermuda Triangle. Choices A, B, and C are all details found in the passage, but none of these answer choices give a summary of the whole passage. Each of these answer choices support the statement in choice D, as do the rest of the details in the passage. Choice D is the best summary of these choices.

CHSPE Practice Test #3

Mathematics

1. Which of the following expressions is equivalent to $-5x(x-1)^2$?

    a. $-5x^3 + 10x^2 - 5x$
    b. $-5x^3 - 10x^2 - 5x$
    c. $-5x^2 + 5x$
    d. $-5x^3 + 10x^2 + 5x$

2. Which of the following represents the expected value of the number of tails Adam will get after tossing a coin 6 times?

    a. 2
    b. 3
    c. 6
    d. 12

3. $\frac{3}{7} \div \frac{2}{3} =$

    a. $\frac{11}{14}$
    b. $\frac{3}{7}$
    c. $\frac{8}{7}$
    d. $\frac{9}{14}$

4. Simplify $\left(8 \times 10^3\right) + \left(1 \times 10^3\right)$.

    a. 8×10^3
    b. 8×10^6
    c. 9×10^3
    d. 9×10^6

5. In a game of chance, 3 dice are thrown at the same time. What is the probability that all three will land with a 6?

    a. 1 in 6
    b. 1 in 18
    c. 1 in 216
    d. 1 in 30

6. Which of the following values is closest to the diameter of a circle with an area of 314 square inches?

    a. 20 inches
    b. 10 inches
    c. 100 inches
    d. 31.4 inches

7. Solve this quadratic equation by factoring: $x^2 + 5x = -6$.

    a. $x = -3$ and $x = -2$
    b. $x = 2$ and $x = 3$
    c. $x = -1$ and $x = 6$
    d. $x = -6$ and $x = 1$

8. Which of the following expressions is equivalent to $-3x(x - 2)^2$**?**

    a. $-3x^3 + 6x^2 - 12x$
    b. $-3x^3 - 12x^2 + 12x$
    c. $-3x^2 + 6x$
    d. $-3x^3 + 12x^2 - 12x$

9. Solve: $\$8.45 - \$0.56 =$

    a. $7.45
    b. $7.99
    c. $7.89
    d. $8.11

10. $156 \div 4 =$

    a. 27
    b. 35
    c. 13
    d. 39

11. A man standing on a flat, level surface casts a shadow that is 6.2 ft in length. The man is 5.8 ft tall. Which of the following best represents the distance from the top of his head to the end of the shadow?

    a. 7 ft
    b. 7.5 ft
    c. 8 ft
    d. 8.5 ft

12. Use factoring to simplify the following:

$$x^2 + 7x + 12$$

    a. $(x + 6)(x + 2)$
    b. $(x + 4)(x + 3)$
    c. $(x + 6)(x + 1)$
    d. $(x + 5)(x + 2)$

13. What is the sum of 0.77 and 0.54?

    a. 0.131
    b. 0.20
    c. 1.31
    d. 2.00

14. Evaluate the product $3\sqrt{11} \times 4\sqrt{14}$. Simplify your answer as much as possible.

    a. $24\sqrt{38}$
    b. $12\sqrt{154}$
    c. $24\sqrt{39}$
    d. 60

15. A sheriff's office in a small town creates a chart of violent crimes in the area for the year of 2005. Based on the chart below, which prediction for 2006 seems the most appropriate?

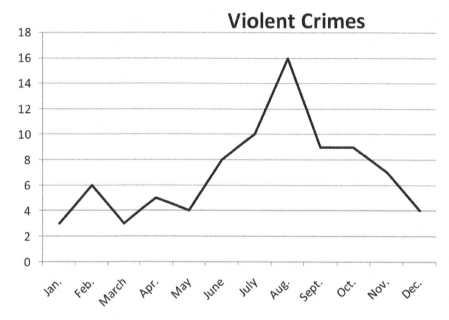

    a.   The winter months are likely to see a spike in violent crime rates.
    b.   Holiday months will likely see an increase in personal theft.
    c.   Violent crimes will be greatest when the weather is the warmest.
    d.   The number of violent crimes per month will continue to grow throughout the year.

16. If $f(x) = \frac{x^3+3x+2}{2x}$, what is $f(-1)$?

    a. -2
    b. $\frac{1}{2}$
    c. 1
    d. -1

Refer to the following for question 17:

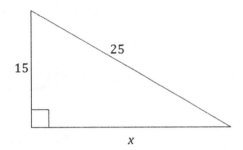

17. **Find the length of the side labeled x. The triangle is a right triangle.**
    a. 18
    b. 20
    c. 22
    d. 24

18. **Which of the following pairs of shapes may tessellate a plane?**
    a. Regular pentagons and squares
    b. Regular pentagons and equilateral triangles
    c. Equilateral triangles and regular hexagons
    d. Regular octagons and equilateral triangles

19. **$783 - 124 =$**
    a. 584
    b. 559
    c. 619
    d. 659

20. **$0.164 + 0.972 =$**
    a. 0.808
    b. 1.136
    c. 8.080
    d. 11.36

Refer to the following for question 21:

This data shows the number of students at a high school who are enrolled in various electives.

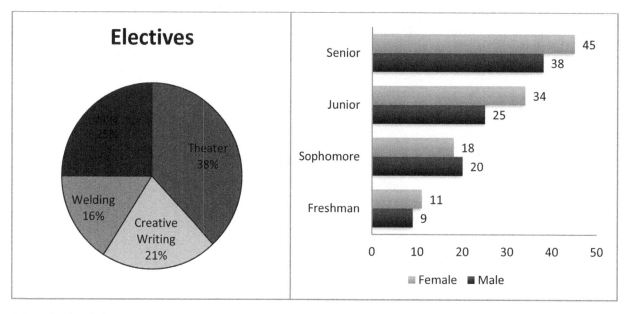

21. Which of these is the greatest quantity?

a. The number of students taking welding
b. The number of male sophomores taking an elective
c. The difference in the number of male and female students taking an elective
d. The difference in the number of 11th and 12th graders taking an elective

22. Which graph represents the linear equation $-6x + 3y = 15$?

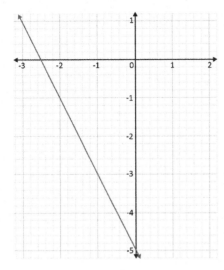

a.

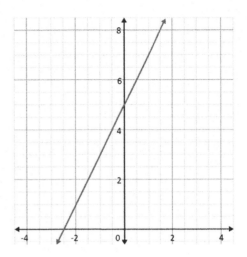

c.

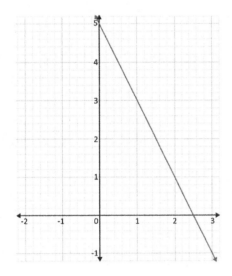

b.

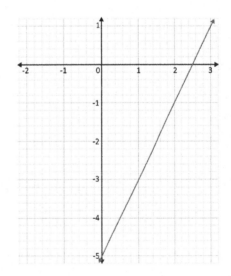

d.

23. Which of these is NOT a net of a cube?

a.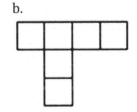

b.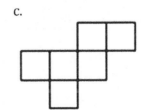

c.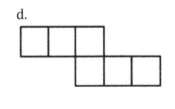

d.

24. Maria buys $\frac{1}{5}$ of a pound of grapes and $\frac{3}{4}$ of a pound of berries. How many total pounds of fruit did Maria buy?

    a. $\frac{4}{20}$

    b. $\frac{4}{9}$

    c. $\frac{5}{8}$

    d. $\frac{19}{20}$

25. Given this stem and leaf plot, what are the mean and median?

Stem	Leaf	
1	6	8
2	0	1
3	4	
4	5	9

    a. Mean = 28 and median = 20

    b. Mean = 29 and median = 20

    c. Mean = 29 and median = 21

    d. Mean = 28 and median = 21

Refer to the following for question 26:

Kyle bats third in the batting order for the Badgers baseball team. The table shows the number of hits that Kyle had in each of 7 consecutive games played during one week in July.

Day of Week	Number of Hits
Monday	1
Tuesday	2
Wednesday	3
Thursday	1
Friday	1
Saturday	4
Sunday	2

26. What is the mode of the numbers in the distribution shown in the table?

    a. 1

    b. 2

    c. 3

    d. 4

27. If c is to be chosen at random from the set {1, 2, 3, 4} and d is to be chosen at random from the set {1, 2, 3, 4}, what is the probability cd will be odd?

    a. $\frac{1}{4}$

    b. $\frac{1}{3}$

    c. $\frac{3}{4}$

    d. 4

28. Identify the cross-section polygon formed by a plane containing the given points on the cube.

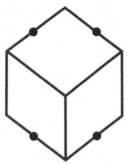

a. Rectangle
b. Trapezoid
c. Pentagon
d. Hexagon

29. Find the length of c based on the right triangle below.

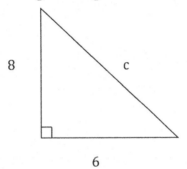

a. 7 cm
b. 10 cm
c. 14 cm
d. 20 cm

30. If the *x*-axis in the scatter plot below represents the number of miles Cyndi drives and the *y*-axis represents the gallons of gas left in her car's tank, which of the following is the *best* estimate for the number of gallons that will remain when she has driven 250 miles?

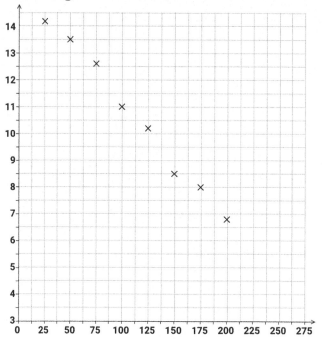

  a.   3.5 gallons
  b.   4.5 gallons
  c.   5.5 gallons
  d.   6.5 gallons

Refer to the following for question 31:

The box-and-whisker plot displays student test scores assessed throughout a semester to see if students were improving.

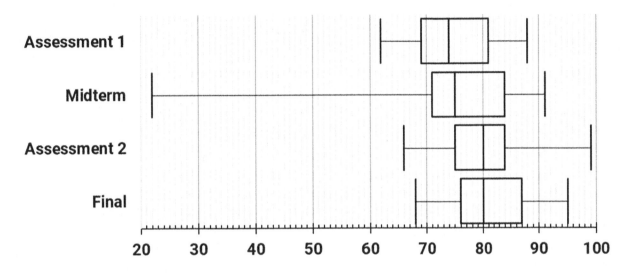

31. **Which of the following statements is necessarily true of the data?**
   a. The mean better reflects student performance at the Midterm than the median.
   b. The mean test score for assessment 2 and the final is the same.
   c. Assessment 1 had the highest median grade.
   d. The median test score is below the mean for Assessment 2.

32. $19 + 23 + 81 + 4 =$
   a. 123
   b. 104
   c. 113
   d. 127

33. **Which of the following expressions is equivalent to** $-2x(x + 6)^2$**?**
   a. $-2x^3 + 12x^2 - 36x$
   b. $-2x^3 - 24x^2 - 72x$
   c. $-2x^2 + 36x$
   d. $-2x^3 - 12x^2 - 72x$

34. **Find the volume of a cube with the length of each side as 12 cm.**
   a. 36 cm³
   b. 650 cm³
   c. 1,728 cm³
   d. 2,421 cm³

35. Ms. Elliott asks her fifth-grade students, "Do you prefer chocolate or vanilla ice cream?" If the probability of her students preferring chocolate ice cream is 0.6, what is the probability of her students preferring vanilla ice cream?

    a. 0.6
    b. 0.4
    c. 0.3
    d. 0.5

36. Which of the following expressions is a factor of the polynomial $x^2 - 4x - 21$?

    a. $(x - 4)$
    b. $(x - 3)$
    c. $(x + 7)$
    d. $(x - 7)$

37. Three rectangular gardens, each with an area of 48 square feet, are created on a tract of land. Garden A measures 6 feet by 8 feet; Garden B measures 12 feet by 4 feet; Garden C measures 16 feet by 3 feet. Which garden will require the least amount of fencing to surround it?

    a. Garden A
    b. Garden B
    c. Garden C
    d. All gardens will require the same amount of fencing

38. Maddie is creating a garden in her backyard. The area of her garden is 15 meters. The length of the garden is 2 meters more than its width. Using this information, write a quadratic equation that represents this scenario, and solve to identify the length and width of the garden.

    a. The length is 15 meters, and the width is 0 meters.
    b. The length is -3 meters, and the width is -5 meters.
    c. The length is 5 meters, and the width is 3 meters.
    d. The length is 3 meters, and the width is 5 meters.

39. Lex charges $25 to mow a lawn. He spends $80 a week on fuel for his lawn mower. Which equation can be used to model this situation, where x is the number of lawns Lex mows in one week and y is the total amount of money that he makes in one week?

    a. $x = 25y - 80$
    b. $x = 80y - 25$
    c. $y = 25x - 80$
    d. $y = 80x - 25$

Refer to the following for question 40:

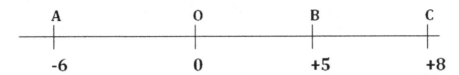

40. In the figure, A, B, and C are points on the number line. Also, O is the origin. What is the ratio of the distance *BC* to distance *AB*?

    a.   3:5
    b.   8:5
    c.   8:11
    d.   3:11

41. Which graph represents the linear equation $y = -6$?

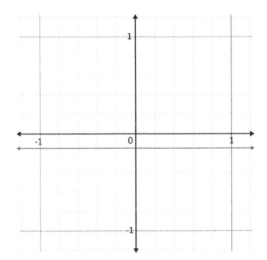

a.

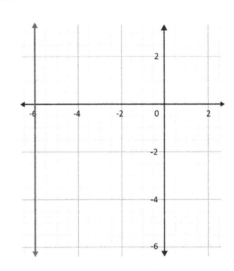

c.

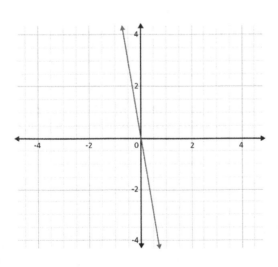

b.

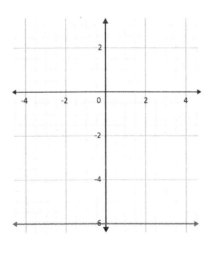

d.

Refer to the following for question 42:

An MP3 player is set to play songs at random from the fifteen songs it contains in memory. Any song can be played at any time, even if it is repeated. There are 5 songs by Band A, 3 songs by Band B, 2 by Band C, and 5 by Band D.

42. What is the probability that the next two songs will both be by Band B?
   a.   1 in 25
   b.   1 in 3
   c.   1 in 5
   d.   1 in 9

Refer to the following for question 43:

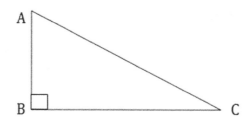

43. △ABC is a right triangle, and ∠ACB=30°. What is the measure of ∠BAC?
   a.   40°
   b.   50°
   c.   60°
   d.   45°

44. A bag contains 14 blue, 6 red, 12 green and 8 purple buttons. 25 buttons are removed from the bag randomly. How many of the removed buttons were red if the chance of drawing a red button from the bag is now $1/3$?
   a.   0
   b.   1
   c.   3
   d.   5

45. If the midpoint of a line segment graphed on the xy-coordinate plane is $(3, -1)$ and the slope of the line segment is -2, which of these is a possible endpoint of the line segment?
   a. $(-1,1)$
   b. $(0,-5)$
   c. $(7,1)$
   d. $(5,-5)$

46. Juan walks $(x - 10)$ meters west and x meters south to get to the park. On a neighborhood map which has a scale of 1 cm : 20 m, the distance between Juan's house and the park is 2.5 cm. How far did Juan walk to the park?

   a. 30 m
   b. 40 m
   c. 50 m
   d. 70 m

47. The equation $\frac{y}{17} = 22$ is given. What is the value of y?

   a. $y = 5$
   b. $y = 39$
   c. $y = 110$
   d. $y = 374$

48. The equation $y - 14 = 63$ is given. What is the value of y?

   a. $y = 49$
   b. $y = 57$
   c. $y = 71$
   d. $y = 77$

49. A circle is inscribed within a square, as shown. What is the difference between the area of the square and that of the circle, where r is the radius of the circle?

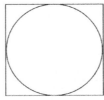

   a. 2π
   b. $\frac{4}{3}\pi r^3$
   c. $r^2(4 - \pi)$
   d. $2\pi r$

50. Which of the following is the percentage equivalent of 0.0016?

   a. 16%
   b. 160%
   c. 1.6%
   d. 0.16%

Language

1. Which of the following choices best completes the sentence?

When at last Amber was able to _____ the numerous difficulties associated with the task, she concluded the that wisdom of her grandfather was not only desirable, but absolutely necessary.

a. perceive
b. perception
c. perceptive
d. perceived

2. Which of the following words best completes the sentence?

The plan seemed flawless until its execution. The flames from the modified grill licked the bottom portion of the new wooden deck. Emil's elation warped into horror as he began to sweat. His grandparents had been extremely angry with the experiment on their car and his grandfather's red face hung before his eyes like a dark vision: "Before you _____ some other wild plan, talk to me first so we don't need to bring in the fire department."

a. concoct
b. invent
c. make
d. design

3. Which of the following sentences shows the correct usage of the hyphen?

a. Miriam was a real-estate-broker with Hendry and Henderson, so she understood the importance of a well-cared-for home.
b. Felipe dialed Joyce's number since it was easy-to-remember and listened with bated breath.
c. Although Biraju was not an accident-prone person, he knew his older brother did not share this trait.
d. James and Henry, both twenty-one year old students, had been able to pass the difficult test for medical school.

4. A number of verb forms are used in headlines. These include simple tenses, infinitive forms, and auxiliary verbs dropped in the passive voice. Which headline below uses a simple tense?

a. LOST DOG RETURNS
b. GOVERNOR TO VISIT CITY
c. GRADUATE NAMED VALEDICTORIAN
d. HERO GIVEN AWARD

5. Choose the sentence that most effectively follows the conventions of standard written English:

   a. Betty MacDonald became famous for her first novel, *The Egg and I*, which chronicles her adventures in chicken farming.
   b. *The Egg and I*, a book written by Betty MacDonald, made the book's author famous and chronicled her adventures in chicken farming.
   c. Betty MacDonald wrote *The Egg and I*, and became famous chronicling her adventures in chicken farming.
   d. *The Egg and I* chronicles the author's adventures in chicken farming, and made Betty MacDonald famous.

6. Which of the following is the best way to write the sentence?

   a. Any person who uses a cell phone in a movie theater has little respect for the other audience members.
   b. Any people who use a cell phone in a movie theater has little respect for the other audience members.
   c. Any persons who uses a cell phone in a movie theater has little respect for the other audience members.
   d. Any person who use a cell phone in a movie theater has little respect for the other audience members.

7. Which of the following versions of the sentence is written correctly?

   a. To repeat ideas in an essay unnecessarily is to commit the mistake of redundant.
   b. To repeat ideas in an essay unnecessarily is to commit the mistake of redundantly.
   c. To repeat ideas in an essay unnecessarily is to commit the mistake of redundancy.
   d. To repeat ideas in an essay unnecessarily is to commit the mistake of redundance.

8. Which version of the sentence is written correctly?

   a. We stopped for extended visits in Indiana, Kansas, Nevada and California during our cross country trip.
   b. We stopped for extended visits, in Indiana, Kansas, Nevada and California during our cross-country trip.
   c. We stopped for extended visits in Indiana, Kansas, Nevada and California, during our cross-country trip.
   d. We stopped for extended visits in Indiana, Kansas, Nevada, and California during our cross-country trip.

9. Which version of the sentence is written correctly?

   a. The two-year-old was just learning how to walk.
   b. The two-year old was just learning how to walk.
   c. The two year-old was just learning how to walk.
   d. The two year old was just learning how to walk.

10. Choose the word that correctly fills the blank in the following sentence:

> Joanne still needs to finish her homework: revise her essay, _____ the next chapter, and complete the math problems.

a. reading
b. to read
c. read
d. will read

11. In the sentence below, the expressions "to reflect" and "to enlighten" are examples of which of the following types of verbals?

> While set in the ancient and mythical world of Camelot, Tennyson's *Idylls of the King* often do more to reflect the Victorian issues of his day than to enlighten the reader about the world of King Arthur.

a. adverb
b. gerund
c. participle
d. infinitive

12. Choose the word that best fills the blank in the following sentence:

> Peter is so talented with horses that the skittish colt became _____ once Peter took over his training.

a. frantic
b. docile
c. lucid
d. prudent

13. Choose the words that best fill the blanks in the following sentence:

> King George III was _____ to have the American colonists _____ taxes to Britain on items such as tea and paper.

a. devious, remand
b. prudent, attribute
c. detrimental, tribute
d. determined, pay

14. Choose the words that best fill the blanks in the following sentence:

> Susan B. Anthony was _____ that women were _____ the same rights as men, such as equal pay and the right to vote.

a. glad, written
b. outraged, denied
c. determined, have
d. credulous, given

15. Which version of the sentence is written correctly?
   a. Veronica was contemptible of the noisy construction workers who made it hard to concentrate on her work.
   b. Veronica was contemptuous of the noisy construction workers who made it hard to concentrate on her work.
   c. Veronica was contempt of the noisy construction workers who made it hard to concentrate on her work.
   d. Veronica was contemptful of the noisy construction workers who made it hard to concentrate on her work.

16. Choose the word set that best fills the blanks in the following sentence:
   As a student council _____, Travis endeavored to _____ his peers to the best of his ability.
   a. represent, representational
   b. representative, represent
   c. representation, represent
   d. represent, representative

17. Choose the words that best fill the blanks in the following sentence:
   Harper Lee wrote *To Kill a Mockingbird* as an _____ of social _____.
   a. argument, dance
   b. incident, class
   c. exposé, injustice
   d. ulterior, inequalities

18. Which of the following versions of the sentence is best?
   a. Because she wanted to reduce unnecessary waste, Cicily decided to have the television repaired instead of buying a new one.
   b. Cicily decided to have the television repaired because she wanted to reduce unnecessary waste instead of buying a new one.
   c. Cicily decided to have, because she wanted to reduce unnecessary waste, the television repaired instead of buying a new one.
   d. Because Cicily decided to have the television repaired instead of buying a new one she wanted to reduce unnecessary waste.

19. Based on how it is used in this sentence, what does the word *reminiscent* mean?
   The melody in that pop song is reminiscent of the one Beethoven used in the first movement of his ninth symphony.
   a. Superior
   b. Suggestive
   c. Situated
   d. Synonymous

20. As used in the sentence, "Julie and I made tentative plans to go to the park because she might have to study that day," what does the word *tentative* mean?
   a. Specific
   b. Uncertain
   c. Absolute
   d. Unlikely

21. Based on how it is used in this sentence, what does the word *translucent* mean?

Although the street could not be seen through the translucent curtains, sunshine still flowed through them.

a. Flimsy
b. Transitory
c. Semitransparent
d. Opaque

Refer to the following for questions 22 - 27:

(1) The observance of Halloween (All Hallow's Eve) on October 31 has long been associated with images of witches, ghosts, devils and hobgoblins. (2) The holiday dates back to the Celtic festival of Samhain thousands of years ago. (3) The Celts believed that at the time of Samhain the ghosts of the dead were able to mingle with the living. (4) Because that was when the souls of those who had died during the year traveled into the otherworld.

(5) Over the years Halloween customs and rituals have changed. (6) Today, many Americans celebrate the traditions of Halloween by dressing in costumes and telling tales of witches and ghosts. (7) Pumpkins are carved and children go from house to house, knocking on doors and calling out "trick or treat" hoping to have their bags filled with candy. (8) Many communities also celebrate Halloween by holding local parties and parades.

22. Which is the best version of sentence 1 (reproduced below)?

The observance of Halloween (All Hallow's Eve) on October 31 has long been associated with images of witches, ghosts, devils and hobgoblins.

a. (As it is now)
b. The observance of Halloween (All Hallow's Eve), on October 31 has long been associated with images of witches, ghosts, devils and hobgoblins.
c. The observance of Halloween (All Hallow's Eve) on October 31 has long been associated with images of witches, ghosts', devils and hobgoblins.
d. The observance of Halloween (All Hallow's Eve) on October 31 has long been associated with images of witches, ghosts, devils and hobgoblin.

23. Which is the best version of sentence 2 (reproduced below)?

The holiday dates back to the Celtic festival of Samhain thousands of years ago.

a. (As it is now)
b. The holiday dates back to the Celtic Festival of Samhain thousands of years ago.
c. The holiday date back to the Celtic Festival of Samhain thousands of years ago.
d. The holiday dates back to the Celtic festival of Samhain thousands, of years ago.

24. What is the best way to write the underlined part of sentences 3 and 4 (reproduced below)?

The Celts believed that at the time of Samhain the <u>ghosts of the dead were able to mingle with the living. Because that was when the souls of those who had died during the year traveled into the otherworld.</u>

a. (As it is now)
b. ghosts of the dead were able to mingle with the living, because that was when the souls, of those who had died during the year, traveled into the otherworld.
c. ghosts of the dead were able to mingle with the living, because that was when the souls of those who had died during the year traveled into the otherworld.
d. ghosts of the dead were able to mingle with the living, because that was when the souls of those who had died during the year travel into the otherworld.

25. In context, which is the best version of sentence 5 (reproduced below)?

Over the years Halloween customs and rituals have changed.

a. (As it is now)
b. Over the years, Halloween customs, and rituals have changed.
c. Halloween customs and rituals have changed, over the years.
d. Over the years, Halloween customs and rituals have changed.

26. What is the best way to write the underlined part of sentence 7 (reproduced below)?

Pumpkins are carved and children go from house to house, <u>knocking on doors and calling out "trick or treat" hoping to have their bags filled with candy.</u>

a. (As it is now)
b. knocking on doors and calling out trick or treat, hoping to have their bags filled with candy.
c. knocking on doors and calling out "trick or treat," hoping to have their bags filled with candy.
d. knocking on doors, and calling out "trick or treat" hoping to have their bags filled with candy.

27. Which would be the best sentence to use before sentence 8 (reproduced below)?

Many communities also celebrate Halloween by holding local parties and parade.

a. There are lots of adults that enjoy celebrating Halloween just as much as children.
b. There are lots of adults which enjoy celebrating Halloween just as much as children.
c. Just as much as children there are lots of adults who enjoy celebrating Halloween.
d. There are lots of adults who enjoy celebrating Halloween just as much as children.

Refer to the following for questions 28 - 34:

(1) A new car is second only to a home as the most expensive purchase that many consumers make. (2) According to the National Automobile Dealers Association, the average price of a new car sold in the United States as of February 2010 was $28,400. (3) That's why it's important to know how to make a smart deal.

(4) Think about what car model and options you want and how much you're willing to spend. (5) Do some research. (6) If you do, you'll be less likely to feel pressured

making a hasty or expensive decision at the showroom and more likely to get a better deal.

(7) To get the best possible price by comparing models and prices in ads and at dealer showrooms shop around. (8) You also may want to contact car-buying service and broker-buying service to make comparisons.

(9) Plan to negotiate on price. (10) Dealers may be willing to bargain on their profit margin which is often between 10 and 20 percent. (11) Usually, this is the difference between the manufacturer's suggested retail price (MSRP) and the invoice price.

(12) Because the price is a factor in the dealer's calculations regardless of whether you pay cash or finance your car — and also affects your monthly payments — negotiating the price can save you money.

28. Which is best added to the beginning of sentence 1 (reproduced below)?

A new car is second only to a home as the most expensive purchase many consumers make.

   a. However
   b. Although
   c. Increasingly
   d. For example

29. In context, which is the best version of sentence 2 (reproduced below)?

According to the National Automobile Dealers Association, the average price of a new car sold in the United States as of February 2010 was $28,400.

   a. (As it is now)
   b. The average price, according to the National Automobile Dealers Association, of a new car sold in the United States as of February 2010 was $28,400.
   c. According to the National Automobile Dealers Association a new car sold in the United States as of February 2010, was $28,400, the average price.
   d. Sold in the United States as of February 2010 was $28,400, accordingly to the National Automobile Dealers Association, the average price of a new car.

30. What is the best way to write the underlined part of sentence 6 (reproduced below)?

If you do, <u>you'll be less likely to feel pressured making a hasty or expensive decision at the showroom</u> and more likely to get a better deal.

   a. (As it is now)
   b. you'll be less likely to feel pressures making a hasty or expensive decision at the showroom
   c. you'll be less likely to feel pressured into making a hasty or expensive decision at the showroom
   d. you'll be less likely to feel pressured into making an hasty or expensive decision at the showroom

31. In context, which is the best version of sentence 7 (reproduced below)?

To get the best possible price by comparing models and prices in ads and at dealer showrooms shop around.

   a. (As it is now)
   b. By comparing models and prices in ads and at dealer showrooms, shop around, to get the best possible price.
   c. To get the best possible price in ads and at dealer showrooms shop around by comparing models and prices.
   d. Shop around to get the best possible price by comparing models and prices in ads and at dealer showrooms.

32. Which is the best version of sentence 8 (reproduced below)?

You also may want to contact car-buying service and broker-buying service to make comparisons.

   a. (As it is now)
   b. You also may want to contact car-buying services and broker-buying services to make comparisons.
   c. You also may want to contact car-buying services, and broker-buying services, to make comparisons.
   d. You'll also may want to contact car-buying services and broker-buying services to make comparisons.

33. In context, which is the best version of sentence 10 (reproduced below)?

Dealers may be willing to bargain on their profit margin which is often between 10 and 20 percent.

   a. (As it is now)
   b. Dealers may be willing to bargain on their profit margin, which is often between 10 and 20 percent.
   c. To bargain on their profit margin dealers may be willing, often between 10 and 20 percent.
   d. Often between 10 and 20 percent dealers may be willing to bargain on their profit margin.

34. What is the best way to write the underlined part of sentence 12 (reproduced below)?

Because the price is a factor in the dealer's calculations regardless of whether you pay cash or finance your car — and also affects your monthly payments — negotiating the price can save you money.

   a. (As it is now)
   b. Because the price is a factor in the dealer's calculations regardless of whether you pay cash or finance your car, and also affects your monthly payments,
   c. Because the price is a factor in the dealer's calculations, regardless of whether you pay cash or finance your car (it also affects your monthly payments),
   d. Because the price is a factor in the dealer's calculations, regardless of whether you pay cash or finance your car, and also affects your monthly payments —

Refer to the following for questions 35 - 40:

(1) New rules limit the fees that banks and other financial institutions can charge on some services, so it's possibly that the costs of other services could go up. (2) In the spring 2010 issue of FDIC Consumer News, we discussed how to avoid potential interest rate and fee increases for credit cards. (3) And here, from expectations that banks will be adding new fees or requirements on bank accounts — such as by

299

discontinuing or limiting free checking services — we focus on ways that careful consumers can avoid unnecessary costs on their deposit accounts.

(4) Comparison shop so you don't pay more for accounts than you have to. (5) Look at what is being offered by your bank and a few competitors. (6) If your bank is among those that eliminates its free checking services, you may still be able to find another bank offering them, especially if you sign up for direct deposit or electronic statements, or if you conduct a certain number of transactions each month.

(7) In today's low-interest rate environment, it must be better to choose a free account that pays no interest or only a small amount of interest instead of selecting an account that pays a modest interest rate but imposes a monthly fee. (8) Similarly, it may be better to maintain a balance and avoid a monthly fee rather than putting that money in an account and paying a modest interest rate. (9) In both cases, any interest you would earn will probably be a lot less than the monthly fee, which can be $10 or higher.

35. What is the best way to write the underlined part of sentence 1 (reproduced below)?

New rules limit the fees that banks and other financial institutions can charge on some services, so it's possibly that the costs of other services could go up.

    a. (As it is now)
    b. so it's possible that the costs of other services could go up.
    c. so it's possible that the costs of other services can go up.
    d. so it's possibility that the costs of other services could go up.

36. Which is the best way to write the underlined part of sentence 3 (reproduced below)?

And here, from expectations that banks will be adding new fees or requirements on bank accounts — such as by discontinuing or limiting free checking services — we focus on ways that careful consumers can avoid unnecessary costs on their deposit accounts.

    a. (As it is now)
    b. And here, from expectations that banks will be adding new fees or requirements within bank accounts
    c. And here, with expectations that banks will be adding new fees or requirements on bank accounts
    d. And then, with expectations that banks will be adding new fees or requirements on bank accounts

37. Which is the best version of sentence 4 (reproduced below)?

Comparison shop so you don't pay more for accounts than you have to.

    a. (As it is now)
    b. Comparison shop so you don't paying more for accounts than you have to.
    c. Comparison shop so you don't pays more for accounts than you have to.
    d. Comparison shop so you didn't pay more for accounts than you have to.

38. What is the best way to write the underlined part of sentence 6 (reproduced below)?

If your bank is among those that eliminates its free checking services, you may still be able to find another bank offering them, especially if you sign up for direct deposit or electronic statements, or if you conduct a certain number of transactions each month.

a. (As it is now)
b. If your bank is among those that eliminates its free checking services;
c. If your bank is within those that eliminates its free checking services,
d. If your bank is among those that eliminate its free checking services,

39. What is the best way to write the underlined part of sentence 7 (reproduced below)?

In today's low-interest rate environment, it must be better to choose a free account that pays no interest or only a small amount of interest instead of selecting an account that pays a modest interest rate but imposes a monthly fee.

a. (As it is now)
b. In today's low-interest rate environment, it might be better to choose a free account that pays no interest
c. It might be better to choose a free account that pays no interest, in today's low-interest rate environment,
d. In today's low-interest rate environment, it might be better to have chosen a free account that pays no interest

40. In context, which is the best version of sentence 9 (reproduced below)?

In both cases, any interest you would earn will probably be a lot less than the monthly fee, which can be $10 or higher.

a. (As it is now)
b. Any interest you would earn is probably a lot less than the monthly fee, which can be $10 or higher, in both cases.
c. In both cases, any interest you would earn will probably be a lot less then the monthly fee, which can be $10 or higher.
d. In any cases, any interest you would earn will probably be a lot less than the monthly fee, which could be $10 or higher.

Refer to the following for questions 41 - 44:

(1) The United States Department of Agriculture Forest Service has reached a milestone. (2) It now protects more than two million acres of private forests threatened by development. (3) *The Forest Service's Northeastern Area helped the agency reach the milestone* when the state of Ohio purchased a 15,494-acre property as the new Vinton Furnace State Experimental Forest approximately 90 miles south of Columbus. (4) The milestone was achieved through public-private partnership *using federal and leveraged funds of approximately $1.1 billion through the Forest legacy program.* (5) The Legacy program has leveraged the federal investment of more than 50 percent of project costs. (6) To date, through non-federal matching funds, to these efforts, more than $630 million has been contributed.

(7) The Forest Legacy program works with private landowners, states and conservation groups to promote sustainable, working forests. (8) Roughly 57 percent of the nation's forests are privately owned, yet the country has lost 15

million acres of private working forests in the last 10 years, with an additional 22 million acres projected to be at risk in the next decade. (9) The Forest Legacy has protected millions of acres of privately owned forests that could have been turned into strip malls and housing developments, say Forest Service experts. (10) They say there have been many success stories, which they are proud of.

41. Which is the best version of sentence 2 (reproduced below)?

It now protects more than two million acres of private forests threatened by development.

 a. (As it is now)
 b. It now protect more than two million acres of private forests threatened by development.
 c. It now has protected more than two million acres of private forests threatened by development.
 d. It now has been protecting more than two million acres of private forests threatened by development.

42. Which is the best version of the underlined part of sentence 3 (reproduced below)?

The Forest Service's Northeastern Area helped the agency reach the milestone when the state of Ohio purchased a 15,494-acre property as the new Vinton Furnace State Experimental Forest approximately 90 miles south of Columbus.

 a. (As it is now)
 b. The Forest Services Northeastern Area helped the agency reaching the milestone
 c. The Forests' Services Northeastern Area helped the agency reach the milestone
 d. The Forest Services Northeastern Area helped the agency reach a milestones

43. Which is the best version of the underlined part of sentence 4 (reproduced below)?

The milestone was achieved through public-private partnership using federal and leveraged funds of approximately $1.1 billion through the Forest legacy program.

 a. (As it is now)
 b. using federal and leveraged funds of approximately $1.1 billion through the forest legacy program.
 c. using federal and leveraged funds of approximately $1.1 billion through The Forest legacy program.
 d. using federal and leveraged funds of approximately $1.1 billion through the Forest Legacy program.

44. In context, which is the best version of sentence 6 (reproduced below)?

To date, through non-federal matching funds, to these efforts, more than $630 million has been contributed.

 a. (As it is now)
 b. To date, more than $630 million has been contributed to these efforts through non-federal matching funds.
 c. Through non-federal matching funds, to these efforts, more than $630 million, to date, has been contributed.
 d. To these efforts, through non-federal matching funds, more than $630 million has been contributed, to date.

45. Which of the following word choices best completes the sentence?

Matthew posted the notice in the main hall, and then proceeded to pass out the rest of the invitations to the _____ until his backpack was empty.

a. receive
b. reception
c. receivable
d. receiving

46. Which of the following would best support the idea that "fracking," shooting water and chemicals into the ground at a high pressure to gain access to underground gas stores, may be hazardous to the environment?

a. A letter in the science journal *Climatic Change* that includes results from research on fracking showing that it may be more damaging to the environment than burning coal
b. A letter to the editor of the *Chicago Tribune* from an activist who secretly taped what was going on at fracking locations throughout the US
c. A feature-length movie developed by a former politician that uses special effects to highlight the effects of fracking on climate change
d. An article in a newspaper discussing the impact of fracking on the local community, noting that all of the people interviewed were nervous about the issue

47. Read the claim below. Which of the following supports a counterclaim?

Schools need to provide year-round education for students. Since the evolution of our society has moved us from an agrarian population to a largely urban one, there is no longer any need for the two-month break during the summer. It is, in fact, a waste of students'—and society's—precious time.

a. The prospect of a year-round education for students is akin to an endless prison sentence; however, the inmates, in this case, cannot speak for themselves. They are the most vulnerable among us, and there is no one who will be their voice in this debate. Let's face it. This debate isn't about longer school days to help children. It's about providing more funding to the school staff.
b. There's a reason teachers are fleeing the public school system. It's broken. Teachers often work long hours in difficult conditions—imagine having the occupant of your office throw a paper airplane at you while you are working—and get paid little. A longer school day punishes teachers who are already sweating blood over their occupation. Teachers not only work through the school day, but often spend hours at home, developing curricula, grading papers, and preparing for the following day.
c. The limitations of this view are clear: there are no scientifically backed works establishing that students perform better if they spend more time in school. However, there is significant research establishing the idea that learners do require time for creative pursuits and thinking. This supports the necessity of a summer break. In fact, it may be necessary to provide longer semester breaks so children have more time for their own creative pursuits.
d. In the interests of fairness, we must consider the possibility of a longer school day.

48. Which choice best completes the sentences below?

Our energy needs are not being adequately met, and in only a few short decades, we will be unable to satisfy the growing demand. _____, no one has developed a plan to address those needs. Both sides of the argument have facts, science, and history to back their claims. _____, fossil fuels are widely used and available. _____, there is a limited supply of them and they damage the environment.

a. So it seems, Similar to other claims, However
b. However, On one hand, On the other hand
c. On one hand, However, Similarly
d. Strangely, First of all, Second of all

Reading

Refer to the following for questions 1 - 5:

[In 1906, Elinore Pruitt Stewart moved to Denver for housework to support her daughter, Jerrine. Her employer in Denver was Mrs. Juliet Coney. A few years later, she moved to Wyoming to be a housekeeper for a rancher. The following passage is one of many letters that Stewart wrote to Mrs. Coney on life as a homesteader in Wyoming.]

A Letter of Elinore Pruitt Stewart

January 23, 1913

When I read of the hard times among the Denver poor, I feel like urging them every one to get out and file on land. I am very enthusiastic about women homesteading. It really requires less strength and labor to raise plenty to satisfy a large family than it does to go out to wash, with the added satisfaction of knowing that their job will not be lost to them if they care to keep it. Even if improving the place does go slowly, it is that much done to stay done. Whatever is raised is the homesteader's own, and there is no house-rent to pay. This year Jerrine cut and dropped enough potatoes to raise a ton of fine potatoes. She wanted to try, so we let her, and you will remember that she is but six years old.... Any woman strong enough to go out by the day could have done every bit of the work and put in two or three times that much, and it would have been so much more pleasant than to work so hard in the city and be on starvation rations all winter.

To me, homesteading is the solution of all poverty's problems, but I realize that temperament has much to do with success in any undertaking, and persons afraid of coyotes and work and loneliness had better let ranching alone. At the same time, any woman who can stand her own company, can see the beauty of the sunset, loves growing things, and is willing to put in as much time at careful labor as she does over the washtub, will certainly succeed; will have independence, plenty to eat all the time, and a home of her own in the end.

Experimenting need cost the homesteader no more than the work, because by applying to the Department of Agriculture at Washington he can get enough of any seed and as many kinds as he wants to make a thorough trial, and it doesn't even cost postage. Also one can always get bulletins from there and from the Experiment Station of one's own State concerning any problem or as many problems as may come up. I would not, for anything, allow Mr. Stewart to do anything toward improving my place, for I want the fun and the experience myself. And I want to be able to speak from experience when I tell others what they can do. Theories are very beautiful, but facts are what must be had, and what I intend to give some time.

1. **The writer of this letter is suggesting that women should own land and farm rather than**
   a. cook in a restaurant.
   b. open a bed and breakfast.
   c. do laundry for others.
   d. teach in a one-room schoolhouse.

2. What do you think Mrs. Coney's reaction to the letter might have been?

    a. She was probably glad to be rid of such a lazy worker.

    b. She may be glad to know that Mrs. Stewart is enjoying her time with homesteading.

    c. She may have been sorry that she too did not homestead.

    d. She was likely angry that Mrs. Stewart had written.

3. Which of the following does Stewart NOT give as an advantage of homesteading?

    a. It takes less strength and work than doing laundry for others

    b. The worker cannot lose her job if she wants to keep it.

    c. No one has to pay rent.

    d. One can always find good company.

4. Which of the following is a risk for the poor in Denver?

    a. the possibility of losing their jobs

    b. the likelihood of a strike

    c. the probability of a landslide

    d. their shacks and apartments will burn

5. The tone of the letter is

    a. complaining and bitter.

    b. sad and lonely.

    c. positive and encouraging.

    d. hopeless and despairing.

Refer to the following for questions 6 - 8:

NOTE: The instructor of a history class has just finished grading the essay exams from his students, and the results are not good. The essay exam was worth 70% of the final course score. The highest score in the class was a low B, and more than half of the class of 65 students failed the exam. In view of this, the instructor reconsiders his grading plan for the semester and sends out an email message to all students.

Dear Students:

The scores for the essay exam have been posted in the online course grade book. By now, many of you have probably seen your grade and are a little concerned, since this accounts for 70% of your final grade. (And if you're not concerned, you should be—at least a bit!) At the beginning of the semester, I informed the class that I have a strict grading policy and that all scores will stand unquestioned. With each class comes a new challenge, however, and as any good instructor will tell you, sometimes the original plan has to change. As a result,

I propose the following options for students to make up their score:

1. I will present the class with an extra credit project at the next course meeting. The extra credit project will be worth 150% of the point value of the essay exam that has just been completed. While I will not drop the essay exam score, I will give you more than enough of a chance to make up the difference and raise your overall score.

2. I will allow each student to develop his or her own extra credit project. This project may reflect the tenor of option number 1 (above) but will allow the student to create a project more in his or her own line of interest. Bear in mind, however, that this is more of a risk. The scoring for option number 2 will be more subjective, depending on whether or not I feel that the project is a successful alternative to the essay exam. If it is, the student will be awarded up to 150% of the point value of the essay exam.

3. I will provide the class with the option of developing a group project. Students may form groups of 3 to 4 and put together an extra credit project that reflects a stronger response to the questions in the essay exam. This extra credit project will also be worth 150% of the point value of the essay exam. Note that each student will receive an equal score for the project, so there is a risk in this as well. If you are part of a group in which you do most of the work, each member of the group will receive equal credit for it. The purpose of the group project is to allow students to work together and arrive at a stronger response than if each worked individually.

If you are interested in pursuing extra credit to make up for the essay exam, please choose one of the options above. No other extra credit opportunities will be provided for the course.

Good luck!

Dr. Edwards

6. Which of the following describes this type of writing?

 a. Technical
 b. Narrative
 c. Persuasive
 d. Expository

7. Which of the following best describes the instructor's purpose in writing this email to his students?

 a. To berate students for the poor scores that they made on the recent essay exam
 b. To encourage students to continue working hard in spite of failure
 c. To give students the opportunity to make up the bad score and avoid failing the course
 d. To admit that the essay exam was likely too difficult for most students

8. Which of the following quotes offers the best summary for the instructor's motive in sending the email to the students?

 a. By now, many of you have probably seen your grade and are a little concerned, since this accounts for 70% of your final grade. (And if you're not concerned, you should be—at least a bit!)
 b. With each class comes a new challenge, however, and as any good instructor will tell you, sometimes the original plan has to change.
 c. The purpose of the group project is to allow students to work together and arrive at a stronger response than if each worked individually.
 d. At the beginning of the semester, I informed the class that I have a strict grading policy and that all scores will stand unquestioned.

Refer to the following for questions 9 - 13:

In the United States, the foreign language requirement for high school graduation is decided at the state level. This means the requirement varies, with some states deciding to forego a foreign language requirement altogether (www.ncssfl.org). It is necessary that these states reconsider their position and amend their requirements to reflect compulsory completion of a course of one or more foreign languages. Studying a foreign language has become increasingly important for the global economy. As technology continues to make international business relations increasingly easy, people need to keep up by increasing their communication capabilities. High school graduates with foreign language credits have been shown to have an increased college acceptance rate. In addition, students who have mastered more than one language typically find themselves in greater demand when they reach the job market. Students who did not study a foreign language often find themselves unable to obtain a job at all.

9. What is the main idea of this passage?

   a. Studying a foreign language will help graduating students find jobs after high school.
   b. Studying a foreign language should be a mandatory requirement for high school graduation.
   c. Studying a foreign language helps students gain an understanding of other cultures.
   d. Studying a foreign language is essential if a student hopes to get into college.

10. Which of the following statements represents the best summary of the claims made in this passage?

   a. Studying a foreign language is important if you want to graduate from high school and get a job.
   b. Studying a foreign language is important for the global economy because of the technological advances that have been made in international communications.
   c. Studying a foreign language is important for the global economy, college acceptance rates, and becoming a sought-after candidate in the job market.
   d. Studying a foreign language is important for college acceptance rates and obtaining a job after college.

11. Which of the following statements represents an exaggerated claim in support of the argument presented in this passage?

   a. In the United States, the foreign language requirement for high school graduation is decided at the state level.
   b. Studying a foreign language has become increasingly important for the global economy.
   c. High school graduates with foreign language credits have been shown to have an increased college acceptance rate.
   d. Students who did not study a foreign language often find themselves unable to obtain a job at all.

12. Which of the following would be a useful source of information to determine the validity of the argument presented in this passage?

   a. A survey of high school students' preferences with regard to foreign language requirements
   b. A comparison of the correlation between a second language introduced at home and subsequent college acceptance rates
   c. A survey that asks parents to select the foreign language they would like their children to study in high school
   d. A comparison of the correlation between high school students' study of a foreign language and subsequent college acceptance rates

13. Which of the following would be the best concluding statement for this passage?

  a. States should consider how important foreign languages are for the global economy when making their policies regarding foreign language requirements for graduation from high school.

  b. Policies regarding a foreign language requirement for graduation from high school should take into account the importance of foreign languages for the global economy and the correlation between foreign languages and increased college acceptance rates and employment opportunities.

  c. High school graduation requirements should include a foreign language class because of the influence knowledge of a second language has on college acceptance rates.

  d. Policies regarding a foreign language requirement for graduation from high school should take into account how difficult it is to obtain a job in today's economy for those who do not have knowledge of more than one language.

Refer to the following for questions 14 - 16:

> Jo's face was a study next day, for the secret rather weighed upon her, and she found it hard not to look mysterious and important. Meg observed it, but did not trouble herself to make inquiries, for she had learned that the best way to manage Jo was by the law of contraries, so she felt sure of being told everything if she did not ask. She was rather surprised, therefore, when the silence remained unbroken, and Jo assumed a patronizing air, which decidedly aggravated Meg, who in turn assumed an air of dignified reserve and devoted herself to her mother. This left Jo to her own devices, for Mrs. March had taken her place as nurse, and bade her rest, exercise, and amuse herself after her long confinement. Amy being gone, Laurie was her only refuge, and much as she enjoyed his society, she rather dreaded him just then, for he was an incorrigible tease, and she feared he would coax the secret from her.

(*Little Women* by Louisa May Alcott)

14. What can you infer about Laurie?

  a. He was stoic.
  b. He was taciturn.
  c. He was unruly.
  d. He was uncanny.

15. From what point of view is this passage written?

  a. First person
  b. Second person
  c. Third person
  d. Fourth person

16. The phrase "was a study" implies that

  a. Jo looked jubilant.
  b. Jo looked secretive.
  c. Jo looked disheveled.
  d. Jo looked angry.

Refer to the following for questions 17 - 26:

In ancient times, the people hunted the buffalo on the Great Plains. These huge animals were their source of food and clothing. With stone-tipped spears, they stalked the great beasts through the tall grasses. It was difficult and dangerous work, but they were forced to do it in order to survive.

At that time, there were many crows flying above the plains, as there are today. But unlike the crows we see now, these birds were white. And they were friends to the buffalo, which caused the hunters no end of travail. The white crows flew high above the plains, where they could see all that was happening below. And when they saw that hunters were approaching the herd, they would warn the buffalo. Swooping down low, they would land on the heads of the great beasts and call out to them: "Beware! Beware! Hunters are coming from the south! Caw, caw. Beware!" And the buffalo would stampede, leaving the hunters empty-handed.

This went on for some time, until the people were hungry, and something needed to be done. A council was convened, and the chief of the people spoke to them. "We must capture the chief of the crows, and teach him a lesson, he said. If we can frighten him, he will stop warning the buffalo when our hunters approach, and the other crows will stop as well."

The old chief then brought out a buffalo skin, one with the head and horns still attached. "With this, we can capture the chief of the crows," he said. And he gave the skin to one of the tribe's young braves, a man known as Long Arrow. "Disguise yourself with this, and hide among the buffalo in the herd," the chief told Long Arrow. "Then, when the chief of the crows approaches, you will capture him and bring him back to the tribe."

So Long Arrow donned the buffalo skin disguise and went out onto the plains. Carefully, he approached a large herd of buffalo and mingled among them, pretending to graze upon the grasses. He moved slowly with the herd as they sought fresh food, and he waited for the great white bird that was the chief of the crows.

The other braves made ready for the hunt. They prepared their stone-tipped spears and arrows, and they approached the grazing herd of beasts, hiding in ravines and behind rocks to try to sneak up on them. But the crows, flying high in the sky, saw everything. The chief of the crows saw the men in the ravines and tall grasses, and eventually he came gliding down to warn the buffalo of the approaching hunters.

Hearing the great white crow's warning, the herd ran from the hunters. All stampeded across the plains except Long Arrow, still in his disguise. Seeing that Long Arrow remained, and thinking that he was a buffalo like all the others, the great white crow flew to him and landed upon his head. "Caw, caw. Hunters are approaching! Have you not heard my warning? Why do you remain here?" But as the great bird cried out, Long Arrow reached from under his disguise and grabbed the bird's feet, capturing him. He pushed him into a rawhide bag and brought him back to the tribal council.

The people debated what to do with the chief of the crows. Some wanted to cut his wings, so that he could not fly. Some wanted to kill him, and some wanted to remove his feathers as punishment for making the tribe go hungry. Finally, one brave strode forward in anger, grabbed the rawhide bag that held the bird, and before anyone could prevent it, threw it into the fire.

As the fire burned the rawhide bag, the big bird struggled to escape. Finally, he succeeded in getting out of the bag and managed to fly out of the fire, but his feathers were singed and covered with black soot from the fire. The chief of the crows was no longer white; he was black – as crows are today.

And from that day forward, all crows have been black. And although they fly above the

310

plains and can see all that transpires below,
95 they no longer warn the buffalo that hunters
are approaching.

17. According to the passage, the people used stone spears to hunt the buffalo because
  a. They had no metal.
  b. They had no horses.
  c. They needed to eat.
  d. They were plentiful.

18. The word *travail* (Line 14) means
  a. Travel.
  b. Difficulty.
  c. Anger.
  d. Fear.

19. Which statement best describes what the chief of the crows represents in this passage?
  a. He symbolizes all that is evil.
  b. He is a symbol representing all crows.
  c. He represents the animal kingdom.
  d. He represents other predators who compete with the tribe.

20. Which of the following best describes the people's motivation for wanting to capture the chief of the crows?
  a. They hated birds.
  b. They wanted to turn him black.
  c. They wanted to eat him.
  d. They were hungry.

21. Long Arrow's activities among the herd while disguised imply that he
  a. Had time to kill.
  b. Wanted to fool the buffalo.
  c. Wanted to fool the crows.
  d. Had forgotten his stone-tipped spear.

22. In this tale, the rawhide bag and stone-tipped spears are both details that
  a. Are important for the outcome of the tale.
  b. Paint a picture of the primitive culture of the people.
  c. Make it clear that the people were dependent upon the buffalo.
  d. Show how the people hunted.

23. Why might the chief of the crows have landed upon Long Arrow's head after seeing the other buffalo stampede away?
  a. He thought his warning had not been heard.
  b. He wanted to see the disguise.
  c. He thought that Long Arrow was an injured buffalo.
  d. He had no fear of men.

24. Once the bird has been caught, what emotions are revealed by the people's deliberations about how to deal with him?

   a. Anger
   b. A calm resolve to change the birds' behavior
   c. A feeling of celebration now that the bird has been caught
   d. Hunger

25. What does the story tell us about why Long Arrow was selected for this task?

   a. He was the bravest man in the tribe.
   b. He was related to the chief.
   c. He was able to act like a buffalo.
   d. The story says nothing about why he was selected.

26. What does this story suggest that the American Indians thought of crows?

   a. They were dirty animals.
   b. They were clever animals.
   c. They were selfish animals.
   d. They disliked the people in the tribe.

Refer to the following for questions 27 - 28:

> Physically, at least, Hal seemed a most unlikely burglar. He looked more suited to the life of a professional athlete, the practitioner of some brutal contact sport. His legs were the trunks of ancient trees and his white shirts – he always wore white shirts – spread across is belly like the winter snow on an Alberta meadow. And yet, at night, he moved across the glistening rooftops on cat's feet, a passing shadow, dropping unseen to the topmost landing of fire escape or outside stairway. There, by starlight, his soft hands found whatever open window had been left unguarded and, in a matter of seconds, he would disappear inside.

27. The reference to tree trunks shows that

   a. Hal's legs were brown
   b. Hal's wore pants the color of bark
   c. Hal's legs were very large
   d. Hal's skin was wrinkled

28. The passage describes Hal as moving on cat's feet. This means that

   a. he had fur-lined shoes
   b. he moved very quietly
   c. he was disguised
   d. he moved on all fours

Refer to the following for questions 29 - 34:

> In the United States, where we have more land than people, it is not at all difficult for persons in good health to make money. In this comparatively new field there are so many avenues of success open, so many vocations which are not crowded, that any person of

either sex who is willing, at least for the time being, to engage in any respectable occupation that offers, may find lucrative employment.

Those who really desire to attain an independence, have only to set their minds upon it, and adopt the proper means, as they do in regard to any other object which they wish to accomplish, and the thing is easily done. But however easy it may be found to make money, I have no doubt many of my hearers will agree it is the most difficult thing in the world to keep it. The road to wealth is, as Dr. Franklin truly says, "as plain as the road to the mill." It consists simply in expending less than we earn; that seems to be a very simple problem. Mr. Micawber, one of those happy creations of the genial Dickens, puts the case in a strong light when he says that to have annual income of twenty pounds, per annum, and spend twenty pounds and sixpence, is to be the most miserable of men; whereas, to have an income of only twenty pounds, and spend but nineteen pounds and sixpence, is to be the happiest of mortals.

Many of my hearers may say, "we understand this; this is economy, and we know economy is wealth; we know we can't eat our cake and keep it also." Yet I beg to say that perhaps more cases of failure arise from mistakes on this point than almost any other. The fact is, many people think they understand economy when they really do not.

—Excerpted from *The Art of Money-Getting* by P.T. Barnum

29. Which of the following statements best expresses the main idea of the passage?
   a. Getting a job is easier now than it ever has been before.
   b. Earning money is much less difficult than managing it properly.
   c. Dr. Franklin advocated getting a job in a mill.
   d. Spending money is the greatest temptation in the world.

30. According to the author, what is more difficult than making money?
   a. managing money
   b. traveling to a mill
   c. reading Dickens
   d. understanding the economy

31. Who is the most likely audience for this passage?
   a. economists
   b. general readers
   c. teachers
   d. philanthropists

32. What is the best definition of *economy* as it is used in this passage?
   a. Exchange of money, goods, and services
   b. Delegation of household affairs
   c. Efficient money management
   d. Less expensive

33. Which word best describes the author's attitude towards those who believe they understand money?

   a. supportive
   b. incriminating
   c. excessive
   d. patronizing

34. This passage is most likely taken from a(n) _____.

   a. self-help manual
   b. autobiography
   c. epistle
   d. novel

Refer to the following for questions 35 - 40:

Selection of "The Gettysburg Address" *by Abraham Lincoln*

Four score and seven years ago our fathers brought forth, upon this continent, a new nation, conceived in Liberty, and dedicated to the proposition that all men are created equal.

Now we are engaged in a great civil war, testing whether that nation, or any nation so conceived, and so dedicated, can long endure. We are met here on a great battlefield of that war. We have come to dedicate a portion of it as a final resting place for those who here gave their lives that that nation might live. It is altogether fitting and proper that we should do this.

But in a larger sense we cannot dedicate - we cannot consecrate - we cannot hallow this ground. The brave men, living and dead, who struggled here, have consecrated it far above our poor power to add or detract. The world will little note, nor long remember, what we say here, but can never forget what they did here.

It is for us, the living, rather to be dedicated here to the unfinished work which they have, thus far, so nobly carried on. It is rather for us to be here dedicated to the great task remaining before us - that from these honored dead we take increased devotion to that cause for which they here gave the last full measure of devotion - that we here highly resolve that these dead shall not have died in vain; that this nation shall have a new birth of freedom; and that this government of the people, by the people, for the people, shall not perish from the earth.

35. What is the main message of this speech?

   a. Those who died in this battle honor this land we are dedicating today better than anyone else.
   b. As we honor those who died in this battle, we should move forward with renewed dedication to ensuring the nation our founding fathers created continues to function the way they intended.
   c. We need to put the regrets of the past aside, without remembering the sacrifices of those who gave their lives for our country.
   d. The war we are fighting is far from over, as evidenced by the number of lives lost in this battle.

36. The phrase "the world will little note" means what?

a. The world will not soon forget.
b. The world will record what we say here.
c. The world will not pay much attention.
d. The world will recall what we do with perfect accuracy.

37. There were nearly 100 years between the American Revolution and the Civil War. The speech connects ideas about these two conflicts by saying that the ideas of the Civil War

a. threaten those of the Revolution.
b. are similar to those of the Revolution.
c. are newer than those of the Revolution.
d. are better than those of the Revolution.

38. Why does Lincoln most likely talk about the past before he talks about the present?

a. to incite listeners of his message to protest
b. to remember what has been lost in the past
c. to establish context for his main message
d. to try to get listeners to side with his position

39. What is the following sentence addressing?

Now we are engaged in a great civil war, testing whether that nation, or any nation so conceived, and so dedicated, can long endure.

a. whether or not a nation based on ideas of freedom and equality can survive for any significant length of time
b. whether or not the Union will be able to preserve the existing structure of the United States by preventing the Confederacy from seceding
c. whether or not the Confederacy will be successful in seceding from the United States and surviving on its own
d. whether or not Lincoln should continue dedicating troops to the war

40. In paragraph 4, the word "vain" most nearly means:

a. decisive
b. frivolous
c. momentous
d. practical

Refer to the following for questions 41 - 46:

How to Choose and Purchase an Automobile

Choosing and purchasing an automobile in a volatile market is not simply a function of color or engine preference; on the contrary, consumers need to treat the purchase of an automobile as the investment that it is—they need to research the pros and cons of owning various automobiles, and they need to make an informed decision before arriving at the dealership. Failure to properly prepare for such an investment can result in an unnecessary economic loss for the consumer.

While there are many pros and cons associated with automobile ownership, many consumers do not adequately research the specific benefits and <u>detriments</u> associated with purchasing a particular vehicle. One of the most common concerns is economic: how much does it cost to own a particular vehicle over time? The cost of ownership is not limited to purchase price; it also includes things like insurance prices, repair costs, and gas consumption. While a given vehicle may have a higher sticker price, its low cost of ownership may, over time, offset this expense. Conversely, a vehicle may have a low sticker price but a high cost of ownership over time. Accordingly, consumers should thoroughly research vehicles before they visit an automobile dealership.

There are numerous ways for consumers to research the cost (defined broadly) of a vehicle before they ever step inside that vehicle. Most simply, there are a number of publications that list the relative depreciation of automobiles over time. Consumers can use these publications to track how a particular model tends to lose value over time and choose that vehicle that best retains its value. Consumers can also go directly to a manufacturer's website to compare gas mileage or the cost of replacement parts. Furthermore, insurance agents can provide insurance quotes for customers before a purchase is made. Awareness of factors such as these can also simplify the purchasing process.

When a consumer is finally ready to purchase a vehicle, he or she is less likely to be pressured by a salesperson if he or she is equipped with the relevant data for that purchase; if a consumer knows the long-term costs of a particular vehicle, he or she is less likely to be swayed by short-term or cosmetic benefits. Arriving at a dealership unprepared can result in an impulse purchase, which, in turn, may result in increased automotive expenditure over time. Conducting even a modicum of research, however, can potentially save the average automotive consumer thousands of dollars in the long run.

41. Why should consumers treat an automobile purchase as an investment?
  a. Automotive stock is traded on various stock exchanges.
  b. If consumers do not treat it as an investment, they may unnecessarily lose money.
  c. Vehicles may appreciate over time.
  d. Owning a vehicle has potential risks and rewards.

42. Based on the passage, which of the following is another word for the underlined word *detriments*?
  a. Purchases
  b. Cons
  c. Benefits
  d. Investments

43. According to the passage, which of the following is true?
  a. Vehicles with a higher sticker price always cost the most over time.
  b. SUVs are always expensive to own.
  c. Red automobiles are more expensive because their insurance rates are higher.
  d. Sticker price does not determine the overall cost of a vehicle.

44. What does the cost of ownership of a vehicle include?

a. Purchase price
b. Gas consumption
c. Cost of repairs
d. All of the above

45. If a consumer conducts research before going to an automobile dealership, he or she is:

a. More likely to be swayed by high-pressure sales techniques
b. Less likely to be swayed by the short-term benefits associated with a particular vehicle
c. More likely to be dismissive with, or rude to, salespeople
d. Less likely to be concerned with insurance rates associated with a particular vehicle

46. According to the passage, what information can consumers find on a manufacturer's website that can help them make a sound financial decision?

a. The gas mileage of a particular vehicle
b. The different colors offered for a particular vehicle
c. The cost of replacement parts
d. A and C

Refer to the following for questions 47 - 54:

Daylight Saving Time

Daylight Saving Time (DST) is the practice of changing clocks so that afternoons have more daylight and mornings have less. Clocks are adjusted forward one hour in the spring and one hour backward in the fall. The main purpose of the change is to make better use of daylight.

DST began with the goal of conservation. Benjamin Franklin suggested it as a method of saving on candles. It was used during both World Wars to save energy for military needs. Although DST's potential to save energy was a primary reason behind its implementation, research into its effects on energy conservation is contradictory and unclear.

Beneficiaries of DST include all activities that can benefit from more sunlight after working hours, such as shopping and sports. A 1984 issue of *Fortune* magazine estimated that a seven-week extension of DST would yield an additional $30 million for 7-Eleven stores. Public safety may be increased by the use of DST: some research suggests that traffic fatalities may be reduced when there is additional afternoon sunlight.

On the other hand, DST complicates timekeeping and some computer systems. Tools with built-in timekeeping functions, such as medical devices, can be affected negatively. Agricultural and evening entertainment interests have historically opposed DST.

DST can affect health, both positively and negatively. It provides more afternoon sunlight in which to get exercise. It also impacts sunlight exposure; this is good for getting vitamin D, but bad in that it can increase skin cancer risk. DST may also disrupt sleep.

Today, daylight saving time has been adopted by more than one billion people in about 70 countries. DST is generally not observed in countries near the equator because sunrise times do not vary much there. Asia and Africa do not generally observe it. Some countries, such as Brazil, observe it only in some regions.

DST can lead to peculiar situations. One of these occurred in November 2007, when a woman in North Carolina gave birth to one twin at 1:32 a.m. and, 34 minutes later, to the second twin. Because of DST and the time change at 2:00 a.m., the second twin was officially born at 1:06, 26 minutes earlier than her brother.

47. According to the passage, what is the main purpose of DST?
   a.   To increase public safety
   b.   To benefit retail businesses
   c.   To make better use of daylight
   d.   To promote good health

48. Which of the following is NOT mentioned in the passage as a negative effect of DST?
   a.   Energy conservation
   b.   Complications with timekeeping
   c.   Complications with computer systems
   d.   Increased skin cancer risk

49. The passage states that DST involves:
   a.   Adjusting clocks forward one hour in the spring and the fall
   b.   Adjusting clocks backward one hour in the spring and the fall
   c.   Adjusting clocks forward in the fall and backward in the spring
   d.   Adjusting clocks forward in the spring and backward in the fall

50. Which interests have historically opposed DST, according to the passage?
   a.   Retail businesses and sports
   b.   Evening entertainment and agriculture
   c.   7-Eleven and health
   d.   Medical devices and computing

51. According to the passage, increased sunlight exposure:
   a.   Is only good for health
   b.   Is only bad for health
   c.   Has no effect on health
   d.   Can be both good and bad for health

52. What is an example given in the passage of a peculiar situation that DST has caused?
   a.   Sleep disruption
   b.   Driving confusion
   c.   Twin birth order complications
   d.   Countries with DST only in certain regions

53. For what purpose did Benjamin Franklin first suggest DST?
   a.   To save money for military needs
   b.   To save candles
   c.   To reduce traffic fatalities
   d.   To promote reading

54. The article states that DST is observed only in some regions in which of the following?
   a.   The equator
   b.   Asia
   c.   Africa
   d.   Brazil

Essay Question

1. A study conducted by a non-profit foundation examined teenagers' socializing on the Internet. The study found that most teenagers turn on their computers as soon as they return home from school every day, and that they use social media sites, as well as text messaging, to stay in touch with their circle of friends almost constantly throughout the day. Since many parents believe that internet socializing is a waste of time, the teenagers were subject to many restrictions, but they usually found ways to circumvent these rules.

In your essay, select either of these points of view, or suggest an alternative approach, and make a case for it. Use specific reasons and appropriate examples to support your position and to show how it is superior to the others.

Answer Key and Explanations

Mathematics

1. A: The expression $(x - 1)^2$ may be expanded as $x^2 - 2x + 1$. Multiplication of $-5x$ by this expression gives $-5x^3 + 10x^2 - 5x$.

2. B: The number of tails he can expect after 6 coin tosses is equal to the product of the probability of getting tails on one coin toss and the number of coin tosses. Thus, the expected value is $\frac{1}{2} \cdot 6$, or 3.

3. D: When dividing fractions, remember the phrase, "Keep, change, flip." *Keep* the first fraction the same. *Change* the division sign to a multiplication sign and *flip* the second fraction.

$$\frac{3}{7} \times \frac{3}{2}$$

Then, multiply across.

$$\frac{3}{7} \times \frac{3}{2} = \frac{9}{14}$$

4. C: Because both expressions share the factor 10^3, we can simply factor and add the ones places. $(8 \times 10^3) + (1 \times 10^3) = (1 + 8)(10^3) = 9 \times 10^3$.

5. C: For each die there is a 1 in 6 chance that a 6 will be on top. The reason is that the die has 6 sides. The probability that a 6 will show for each die is not affected by the results from another roll of the die. In other words, these probabilities are independent. So, the overall probability of throwing 3 sixes is the product of the individual probabilities: $P = \frac{1}{6} \times \frac{1}{6} \times \frac{1}{6} = \frac{1}{6^3} = \frac{1}{216}$

6. A: The area A of a circle is given by $A = \pi \times r^2$, where r is the radius. Since π is approximately 3.14, we can solve for $r = \sqrt{\frac{A}{\pi}} = \sqrt{\frac{314 \text{ inches}^2}{3.14}} = \sqrt{100 \text{ inches}^2} = 10$ inches. Now, the diameter d is twice the radius, or 2×10 inches $= 20$ inches.

7. A: Since we need to factor to solve the quadratic equation, first set the equation equal to zero.

$$x^2 + 5x = -6$$
$$x^2 + 5x + 6 = -6 + 6$$
$$x^2 + 5x + 6 = 0$$

Factor the quadratic on the left hand-side and solve both equations for x.

$$x^2 + 5x + 6 = 0$$
$$(x + 3)(x + 2) = 0$$

$$x + 3 = 0 \qquad\qquad x + 2 = 0$$
$$x = -3 \qquad\qquad\qquad x = -2$$

8. D: The expression $(x - 2)^2$ may be expanded as $x^2 - 4x + 4$. Multiplication of $-3x$ by this expression gives $-3x^3 + 12x^2 - 12x$.

9. C: Start by writing the problem vertically, making sure to line up the digits in each number according to place value. To subtract, begin with the hundredths column on the right. Since $5 - 6$ results in a negative number, we need to borrow from the tenths place. Cross out 4 in the tenths place and replace it with 3 since we are taking 1 away. Next, write the borrowed 1 in front of the 5 in the hundredths place to get 15. Since $15 - 6 = 9$, write 9 in the hundredths place as part of the answer. From here, move to the tenths column and subtract. Since $3 - 5$ results in a negative number, we need to borrow from the ones place. Cross out the 8 in the ones place and replace it with 7 since we are taking 1 away. Next, write the borrowed 1 in front of the 3 in the tenths place to get 13. Since $13 - 5 = 8$, write 8 in the tenths place as part of the answer. Finally, move to the ones column and subtract. Since $7 - 0 = 7$, write 7 in the ones place as part of the answer. Therefore, $\$8.45 - \$0.56 = \$7.89$, so the correct answer is C.

$$
\begin{array}{r}
8\ .45 \\
-0\ .56 \\
\hline
\end{array}
\qquad
\begin{array}{r}
{\scriptstyle 3\ 15} \\
8\ .4\!\!\!/5 \\
-0\ .56 \\
\hline
9
\end{array}
\qquad
\begin{array}{r}
{\scriptstyle 13} \\
{\scriptstyle 7\ \ 3\ 15} \\
8\!\!\!/\ .4\!\!\!/5 \\
-0\ .56 \\
\hline
.89
\end{array}
\qquad
\begin{array}{r}
{\scriptstyle 13} \\
{\scriptstyle 7\ \ 3\ 15} \\
8\!\!\!/.4\!\!\!/5 \\
-0\ .56 \\
\hline
7\ .8^{9}
\end{array}
$$

10. D: The correct answer is 39. This can be found by using long division.

$$
\begin{array}{r}
39 \\
4\overline{)156} \\
-12 \\
\hline
36 \\
-36 \\
\hline
0
\end{array}
$$

11. D: The Pythagorean theorem may be used to find the diagonal distance from the top of his head to the base of the shadow. The following equation may be written and solved for c: $5.8^2 + 6.2^2 = c^2$. Thus, $c \approx 8.5$. The distance is approximately 8.5 ft.

12. B: The expression $x^2 + 7x + 12$ can be simplified by using the factors $(x + 4)(x + 3)$. To check the answer, multiply the first, outside, inside, and last terms (FOIL), then combine like terms to simplify.

$$x^2 + 3x + 4x + 12$$

$$x^2 + 7x + 12$$

13. C: To find the sum of two numbers with decimals, we will line the numbers vertically with the decimal and add. We will bring the decimal down into the answer where it is lined up. For this problem, when we line the numbers vertically with the decimal and add, we start by adding 7 and 4, which is 11, 1 gets carried over to the next column. Then we add 7, 5 and 1, which is 13, the 1 gets carried over again. Lastly, we add 1, 0 and 0, which is 1. Then we will bring the decimal down where it lines up with the answer, and we find that the sum of 0.77 and 0.54 is 1.31.

$$
\begin{array}{r}
\overset{1}{0}.\overset{1}{7}7 \\
+\,0\,.54 \\
\hline
1\,.3\,^1
\end{array}
$$

14. B: Applying the rule that $\sqrt{a}\sqrt{b} = \sqrt{ab}$ when $a, b \geq 0$, we get $3\sqrt{11} \times 4\sqrt{14} = 3 \times 4 \times \sqrt{11} \times \sqrt{14} = 12\sqrt{154}$. Since the radicand, 154, has no perfect square factors, we cannot further simplify this answer.

15. C: If the rate of violent crimes per month is anything like it is the year before, it will be greatest in the summer months, as there is a spike in the data on the 2005 graph during the summer months. While there is some fluctuation up and down throughout the entire year, these months are well beyond the numbers of the other months and represent the only upward trend in the graph.

16. C: Substituting –1 for each x-value gives $f(-1) = \frac{(-1)^3+3(-1)+2}{2(-1)}$. To simplify, follow the order of operations. Start by simplifying the exponent in the numerator.

$$f(-1) = \frac{-1 + 3(-1) + 2}{2(-1)}$$

From here, simplify the multiplication in both the numerator and denominator.

$$f(-1) = \frac{-1 - 3 + 2}{-2}$$

Then, simplify the numerator by adding and subtracting in order from left to right.

$$f(-1) = \frac{-4 + 2}{-2} = \frac{-2}{-2}$$

Finally, divide to simplify the expression completely.

$$f(-1) = 1$$

17. B: The figure is a right triangle. So, the Pythagorean Theorem can be used. The side that is 25 units long is the hypotenuse. Its square will equal the sum of the squares of the other two sides. That is $25^2 = 15^2 + x^2$. Solve for x^2 by subtracting 15^2 from each side of this equation. Then, take the square root to find x.

$$x = \sqrt{25^2 - 15^2} = \sqrt{625 - 225} = \sqrt{400} = 20$$

18. C: Equilateral triangles and regular hexagons may tessellate a plane. Each triangle may be attached to each side of a hexagon, leaving no gaps in the plane.

19. D: First, place 783 on top of 124 to subtract vertically. Then, subtract from right to left. $3 - 4$ is negative, so borrow from the 8 to make 3 become 13 and 8 is reduced to 7. $13 - 4 = 9$, so write a 9 under the 4. $7 - 2 = 5$, so write a 5 under the 2. $7 - 1 = 6$, so write a 6 under the 1. This gives a final answer of 659.

$$
\begin{array}{r}
783 \\
-124 \\
\hline
9
\end{array}
\qquad
\begin{array}{r}
{}^{+10} \\
773 \\
-124 \\
\hline
9
\end{array}
\qquad
\begin{array}{r}
{}^{+10} \\
773 \\
-124 \\
\hline
59
\end{array}
\qquad
\begin{array}{r}
{}^{+10} \\
773 \\
-124 \\
\hline
65\,{}^{9}
\end{array}
$$

20. B: To find the sum of 0.164 and 0.972, we will write the two numbers vertically with the decimals lined up. We will start by adding 4 and 2, which is 6. Then we add 6 and 7, which is 13. Write down 3 and carry over 1. Then we add 9, 1, and 1, which is 11. Write down 1 and carry over the second 1 to the next column, then add 1, 0, and 0. Therefore, the value of the expression $0.164 + 0.972$ is 1.136.

$$
\begin{array}{r}
{}^{1}\quad{}^{1}\quad\ \\
0.164 \\
+0.972 \\
\hline
1.13\,{}^{6}
\end{array}
$$

21. A: The total number of students taking electives is 200, as seen in the chart on the right, and 16% of these are taking welding, so the number of students taking welding is $0.16(200) = 32$. The number of male sophomores taking an elective is 20. The difference in the number of male and female students taking an elective is $108 - 92 = 16$, and the difference in the number of 11th and 12th grade students taking an elective is $83 - 59 = 24$. The greatest quantity of these is 32, the number of students taking welding.

22. A: Since $-6x + 3y = 15$ is written in standard form, use the equation to find the x- and y-intercepts. Once we know where the line passes through each axis, we can match the graph to the equation. Start by finding the y-intercept by setting x equal to 0 and solve for y.

$$
\begin{aligned}
-6x + 3y &= 15 \\
-6(0) + 3y &= 15 \\
0 + 3y &= 15 \\
3y &= 15 \\
y &= 5
\end{aligned}
$$

The line intersects the y-axis at point (0,5).

Now that we know the location of the y-intercept, find the x-intercept. When using the standard form of an equation to find the x-intercept, make y equal to 0 and solve for x.

$$
\begin{aligned}
-6x + 3y &= 15 \\
-6x + 3(0) &= 15 \\
-6x + 0 &= 15 \\
-6x &= 15 \\
x &= -2.5
\end{aligned}
$$

The line intersects the x-axis at point (-2.5,0).

Now that we know that the location of the x-intercept is $(-2.5,0)$ and the location of the y-intercept is $(0,5)$, look for the graph that contains both coordinate pairs. Since the graph shown in answer A contains both points, the correct answer is A.

23. B: A cube has six square faces. The arrangement of these faces in a two-dimensional figure is a net of a cube if the figure can be folded to form a cube. If this is folded, the bottom square in the second column will overlap the fourth square in the top row, so the figure does not represent a net of a cube. The other figures represent three of the eleven possible nets of a cube.

24. D: Since we are finding the total pounds of fruit, we will add $\frac{1}{5}$ and $\frac{3}{4}$. To add the two fractions, we must first find the common denominator, which we will do by multiplying the first fraction by $\frac{4}{4}$ and the second fraction by $\frac{5}{5}$. We will then evaluate the expression $\frac{4}{20} + \frac{15}{20}$, by keeping the denominator and adding the numerators to get $\frac{19}{20}$. Therefore, the total amount of fruit that Maria bought is $\frac{19}{20}$ of a pound.

25. C: The mean is the average of the data and can be found by dividing the sum of the data by the number of data: $\frac{16+18+20+21+34+45+49}{7} = 29$. The median is the middle data point when the data are ranked numerically. The median is 21.

26. A: The mode is the number that appears most often in a set of data. If no item appears most often, then the data set has no mode. In this case, Kyle had one hit for a total of three times. There were two times that he had two hits. Also, on one day, he had three hits. Then, on another day, he had four hits. One hit happened the most times. So, the mode of the data set is 1.

27. A: There are 4 members of the first set and 4 members of the second set, so there are $4(4) = 16$ possible products for cd. cd is odd only when both c and d are odd. There are 2 odd numbers in the first set and two in the second set, so $2(2) = 4$ products are odd and the probability cd is odd is 4/16 or 1/4.

28. D: The cross-section is a hexagon.

29. B: Use the Pythagorean Theorem to solve this problem: $a^2 + b^2 = c^2$

$$8^2 + 6^2 = c^2$$
$$64 + 36 = c^2$$
$$100 = c^2$$
$$\sqrt{100} = 10$$

30. B: The points may be entered into a graphing calculator or Excel spreadsheet to find the least-squares regression line. This line is approximately $y = -0.044x + 15.59$. Substituting 250 for x gives $y = -0.044(250) + 15.59$, or $y = 4.59$. Thus, 4.5 gallons is a good estimate for the amount of gas that will be left after 250 miles. If a line of best fit is predicted visually using the points (25,14.2) and (100,11), the slope between points near that line is approximately –0.043, and the line passes through the y-axis around 15. Thus, another good estimate would be 4.25. This estimate is also close to 4.5.

31. D: The box plot for Assessment 2 is skewed to the right, which means that the mean is above the median.

32. D: Add from left to right. $19 + 23 = 42$, then $42 + 81 = 123$, and finally, $123 + 4 = 127$.

33. B: To simplify this expression, start by expanding the squared term using the FOIL method.

$$(x + 6)^2 = (x + 6)(x + 6) = x^2 + 6x + 6x + 36 = x^2 + 12x + 36$$

The expression now becomes $-2x(x^2 + 12x + 36)$. From here, distribute the $-2x$ to each term in the set of parentheses.

$$-2x \cdot x^2 - 2x \cdot 12x - 2x \cdot 36$$

$$-2x^3 - 24x - 72$$

34. C: The formula for the volume of a cube is $V = L^3$.

$$12^3 = 1{,}728 \text{ cm}^3$$

35. B: Since the events are mutually exclusive, the sum of their individual probabilities is 1.0. Subtracting 0.6 from 1.0 yields 0.4. Therefore, the correct choice is B.

36. D: The polynomial can be factored as $(x - 7)(x + 3)$. Thus, $(x - 7)$ is a factor of the given polynomial.

37. A: To solve, find the perimeter (sum of all sides) of each garden:

Garden A: 6 ft by 8 ft rectangle, 6 ft + 8 ft + 6 ft + 8 ft = 28 ft

Garden B: 12 ft by 4 ft rectangle, 12 ft + 4 ft + 12 ft + 4 ft = 32 ft

Garden C: 16 ft by 3 ft rectangle, 16 ft + 3 ft + 16 ft + 3 ft = 38 ft

The smallest perimeter, Garden A, will require the least amount of fencing.

38. C: First, write an equation that represents the scenario. Use n to represent the width. Since the length is 2 meters more than the width, use $n + 2$ to represent the length. Since $A = lw$, multiply n and $n + 2$ to get a product of 15.

$$n(n + 2) = 15$$

Next, convert the quadratic equation to standard form. To do so, distribute n to each term inside the parentheses. Move all the terms to the left side and set it equal to 0 by doing inverse operations. Subtract 15 from both sides of the equation.

$$n^2 + 2n = 15$$
$$n^2 + 2n - 15 = 15 - 15$$
$$n^2 + 2n - 15 = 0$$

Next, factor the left side of the equation.

$$(n + 5)(n - 3) = 0$$

From here, set each factor to 0 and solve for the variable, starting with $n + 5 = 0$. Use inverse operations, and subtract 5 from both sides of the equation.

$$n + 5 = 0$$
$$n + 5 - 5 = 0 - 5$$
$$n = -5$$

Finally, solve $n - 3 = 0$. Use inverse operations, and add 3 to both sides of the equation.

$$n - 3 = 0$$
$$n - 3 + 3 = 0 + 3$$
$$n = 3$$

The solution set is $\{-5, 3\}$. Since measurements of length and width use positive integers, omit –5 in this scenario. Therefore, the width of the garden is 3 meters, and the length is 5 meters.

$$\text{width} = n = 3$$

$$\text{length} = n + 2 = (3) + 2 = 5$$

39. C: The equation that can model this situation would have to have the amount of money Lex spends each week as the constant, or y-intercept, and the rate, or the slope, would be the amount of money he charges for each lawn he mows. Therefore, the best equation to model this situation is $y = 25x - 80$.

40. D: The figure is a number line. So, the distance from point A to point B will be the difference of B − A. This is $5 - (-6) = 11$. Also, the distance from point B to point C will be the difference of C − B. This is $8 - 5 = 3$. So, the ratio BC:AB will be 3:11.

41. D: In the linear equation $y = -6$, the value of y is –6 for every value of x. The graph for $y = -6$ looks like a horizontal line intersecting the y-axis at point $(0, -6)$. Therefore, the correct answer is D.

42. A: Since 3 of the 15 songs are by Band B, the probability that any one song will be by that band is $\frac{3}{15} = \frac{1}{5}$. The probability that two successive events will occur is the product of the probabilities for any one event or, in this case $\frac{1}{5} \times \frac{1}{5} = \frac{1}{25}$.

43. C: The internal angles of a triangle always add up to 180°. Since $\triangle ABC$ is a right triangle, then $\angle ABC = 90°$ and $\angle ACB$ is given as 30°. The middle letter is for the vertex. By using the triangle addition theorem, the answer must be: $\angle BAC = 180 - (90 + 30)$. This equals 60°.

44. B: Add the 14 blue, 6 red, 12 green and 8 purple buttons to get a total of 40 buttons. If 25 buttons are removed, there are 15 buttons remaining in the bag. The chance of drawing a red button is now $\frac{1}{3}$. So, you divide 15 into thirds to get 5 red buttons remaining in the bag. The original total of red buttons was 6; so $6 - 5 = 1$: one red button was removed, choice (B).

45. D: The point $(5, -5)$ lies on the line segment that has a slope of -2 and passes through $(3, -1)$. If $(5, -5)$ is one of the endpoints of the line segment, then the other would be $(1,3)$.

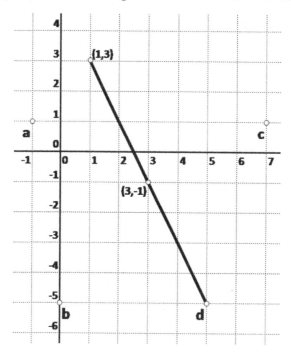

46. D: If the distance is 2.5 cm on the map, then the actual distance is 50 m. To find x, use the Pythagorean theorem:

$$x^2 + (x - 10)^2 = (50)^2$$
$$x^2 + x^2 - 20x + 100 = 2{,}500$$
$$2x^2 - 20x - 2{,}400 = 0$$
$$2(x^2 - 10x - 1{,}200) = 0$$
$$2(x - 40)(x + 30) = 0$$
$$x = 40 \quad x = -30$$

Since x represents a distance, it cannot equal –30. Since $x = 40$, $x - 10 = 30$. Juan walks a total of 70 m to get to the park.

47. D: To find the value of y, we will start by isolating the y on one side of the equation. Since y is being divided by 17, we will multiply both sides of the equation by 17. On the left side of the equation, we will be left with y. On the right side of the equation, we will multiply 22 by 17 to get 374, which is the value of y.

48. D: To find the value of y, we ask the question, what is happening to y? The answer is that 14 is being subtracted from y, so we do the opposite operation, which is addition. We will add 14 to both sides of the equation. On the left side we will be left with y, and on the right side we will add 63 and 14 to get 77, which is the value of y.

49. C: The side of the square is equal to the diameter of the circle, or twice the radius, that is, $2r$. The area of the square is this quantity squared, or $4r^2$. The area of the circle is, πr^2. Subtracting gives the difference between the two areas, $\Delta A = 4r^2 - \pi r^2 = r^2(4 - \pi)$.

50. D: To find a percentage from a decimal, multiply by 100: $0.0016(100) = 0.16\%$.

Language

1. A: This is the correct form of the word for the sentence.

2. A: While the words are all very similar in meaning (denotation), *concoct* best matches the tone of the passage: Emil is prone to developing wild ideas that result in disaster. The other three verbs have more neutral or positive connotations.

3. C: One use of hyphens is to join up a descriptive phrase before a noun, as in choice C ("accident-prone person"). Choice A uses hyphens where none are necessary ("real estate broker" is correct), although it does use hyphens correctly in "well-cared-for home." Choice B also uses hyphens unnecessarily because the descriptive phrase, "easy to remember," comes after the noun, "number." Choice D needs additional hyphens because the entire phrase, "twenty-one-year-old," describes the noun "students."

4. A: This headline uses the simple tense. In this case, it's the simple present tense. B uses the infinitive form, while C and D both drop the auxiliary verb in the passive voice.

5. A: This sentence best conveys the information without using too many words or having an awkward construction.

6. A: The subject *person* is singular and must use the singular verbs *uses* and *has*. The subjects *people* and *persons* are both plural and must be paired with the plural verbs *use* and *have*. Only choice A correctly matches the subject with both verbs.

7. C: In the context of this sentence, the word *redundant* should appear in its noun form, which is *redundancy* (meaning "unnecessary repetition"). *Redundant* is an adjective, and *redundantly* is an adverb. *Redundance* is a nonstandard variant of *redundancy* and is not widely accepted.

8. D: The comma that comes after the next-to-last item in a list (in this case, Nevada) is called the serial comma. It is okay to include it (choice D) or not (the other three choices). But choices B and C each include an extra comma where it does not belong. Choice A misses the essential hyphen that should join the adjective phrase *cross-country*.

9. A: Adjective phrases consisting of more than one word (compound modifiers) should be hyphenated, even if the person, place, or thing they're describing is only implied. The word *child* is only implied in this sentence, but the adjective phrase describing it—"two-year-old"—still needs to be fully hyphenated in order for it to be correct.

10. C: *Read* (present tense form of the verb) maintains the parallel structure of the sentence and matches the verb tense for *revise* and *complete*. The other answer choices represent the present participle (*reading*), infinitive (*to read*), and future tense (*will read*) of the word.

11. D: The clue for identifying infinitives is the word *to* before a verb. In this case, *to reflect* and *to enlighten* are excellent examples of infinitives, which are a type of verbal, or a verb form that actually function as a different part of speech. Infinitives (and gerunds) function as nouns.

12. B: The word *docile* means "easily taught" or "ready to be taught." The sentence should read: Peter is so talented with horses that the skittish colt became docile once Peter took over his training.

13. D: The sentence should read: King George III was determined to have the American colonists pay taxes to Britain on items such as tea and paper.

14. B: The sentence should read: Susan B. Anthony was outraged that women were denied the same rights as men, such as equal pay and the right to vote.

15. B: *Contempt* is a feeling of scorn or disdain, and to be *contemptuous* is to experience or express that feeling. *Contemptible* refers to something that inspires contempt, which in Veronica's case, would be the noisy construction workers. *Contemptful* is not a word in standard English.

16. B: *Representative* acts as a noun and *represent* as a verb. The sentence should read: As a student council representative, Travis endeavored to represent his peers to the best of his ability.

17. C: The sentence should read: Harper Lee wrote *To Kill a Mockingbird* as an exposé of social injustice.

18. A: The syntax of this sentence is correct. It uses a comma to offset the subordinate clause ("Because she wanted to reduce unnecessary waste") from the independent clause ("Cicily decided to have the television repaired instead of buying a new one"). Placing the independent clause, which is the most important idea in the sentence, at the end for emphasis also makes the sentence stronger.

19. B: The sentence compares the melody of a pop song to that of the first movement in Beethoven's ninth symphony. Therefore, concluding that they probably are similar is logical. The pop song reminds the speaker of the Beethoven piece, which means the pop song suggests the melody of the Beethoven piece. *Reminiscent* and *suggestive* are synonyms in this context.

20. B: Julie may have to study on the day she and the speaker consider going to the park, which means their plans are uncertain. The plans might happen, but they also might not happen. Based on this context, you can conclude that the word *tentative* means "uncertain." Because the speaker does not indicate that either the plan to go to the park or the possibility Julie may have to study is more likely, *unlikely* is not the best answer choice.

21. C: According to the sentence, while certain things could not be seen through the curtains, light could. The curtains are not transparent enough to show the street, yet they are transparent enough to show sunshine. The prefix *semi-* means "partially." Based on this context, you can conclude that *translucent* and *semitransparent* share the same meaning. Although something that is flimsy may be transparent, this is not always the case, so the words are not synonyms. *Transitory* shares the root *trans-*, meaning "through," but *transitory* means "not lasting." Something that is opaque does not allow light to pass through it at all.

22. A: Choice B incorrectly uses a comma after the parenthesis. Choice C uses an apostrophe with "ghosts" where it is unnecessary because it is not a possessive form. Choice D uses a singular "hobgoblin" when it should be plural with all the other items in the list.

23. B: "Celtic Festival of Samhain" is a title, and so all the key words should be capitalized. Choice A is incorrect because "Festival" is not capitalized. Choice C has an incorrect form of the verb "date," using a plural when the subject is singular. Choice D is also incorrect because it does not capitalize "festival" and uses a comma incorrectly after "thousands."

24. C: Choice A is not correct because sentence 4 is incomplete. Choice B is wrong because there are unnecessary commas after "souls" and "year." And in choice D, the present tense "travel" does not agree with the past tense verb "had died."

25. D: "Over the years" is an introductory phrase and needs to be set off by a comma, so choice A is incorrect. Choice B incorrectly places a comma after "customs." Choice C is incorrect because the comma after "changed" does not belong there.

26. C: Choice C correctly uses a comma after "trick or treat." Choice A is not correct because there is no comma after "trick or treat." Choice B is not the correct choice because it does not have quotation marks around "trick or treat" to identify what the children are calling out. Choice D incorrectly places a comma after "doors."

27. D: Choice D correctly uses the pronoun "who," which agrees with "adults." Choices A and B respectively use the incorrect pronouns "that" and "which." Choice C is not correct because a comma would be needed after the opening phrase "just as much as children."

28. C: Choice C makes sense in terms of the statement. Choices A and B suggest an opposite relationship, which does not fit in with the first sentence. Choice D would create an example before establishing the thought necessary for explanation and is thus incorrect.

29. A: The ideas in choice A follow logically. Choice B is awkward. Choices C, and D do not make sense.

30. C: By adding the preposition "into" in choice C, the sentence makes sense. Choice A is not correct because it does not use a preposition. Choice B incorrectly uses the word "pressures." Choice D is not correct because the word "hasty" does not require the article "an" in front of it.

31. D: The main idea is "shop," so putting it at the beginning of the sentence makes it flow the best. Choice A puts it at the end, which dilutes its importance. Choice B has incorrect use of commas before and after "shop around." Choice C would require a comma after "showrooms" to make it correct.

32. B: This choice conveys the correct meaning of the sentence. Choice A uses singular "service," when plural is needed. Choice C incorrectly places commas after both of the words "services." Choice D has the contraction "You'll" together with "may." There can be one or the other, but not both.

33. B: This choice places the comma correctly between "margin" and "which." Choice A needs a comma before "which." Choice C make no sense, and choice D is awkwardly worded.

34. C: By putting the secondary idea of a monthly payment in brackets, thereby omitting the "and" from the sentence and using a pronoun, the sentence reads very well. Choices A, B and D use dashes, commas, or a combination of the two, all of which result in poor readability.

35. B: This choice is correct because it replaces the incorrect adverb "possibly" with the correct adjective "possible." Choice A incorrectly uses the adverb "possibly." Choice C uses the correct adjective, but the verb "can" does not go with the sense of possibility because it is too definite. Choice D is incorrect because the article "a" is not placed before the noun "possibility."

36. C: This choice is correct because it uses the preposition "with," which indicates "as a result." Choice A incorrectly uses the preposition "from," which indicates a starting place. Choice B uses the incorrect prepositions "from" and "within." Choice D incorrectly uses "then," which indicates "next" rather than a possibility.

37. A: This choice uses the correct verb form. Choices B, C and D all use incorrect forms of the verb.

38. D: This choice uses a singular verb that agrees with the subject. Choice A is not correct because the plural verb does not agree with the singular "bank." Choice B incorrectly uses a semicolon after "services." Choice C uses the wrong preposition "within."

39. B: The verb "might be" indicates a probability. Choice A is not correct since the verb "must be" means something is necessary and has to be done, which is not the case here. Choice C is awkwardly written. In Choice D, the verb "have chosen" does not agree with the verb tense of the earlier verb "might be."

40. A: This choice is correct because it uses "In both cases" at the beginning, rather than at the end as choice B does. Choice C incorrectly uses the adverb "then" instead of the preposition "than." And choice D incorrectly uses the adjective "any" when the previous sentences have two subjects.

41. A: Choice A is the only option with the correct verb form. Choice B uses a plural verb form rather than a singular. Choice C has a verb in a past tense, when the "now" makes it clear that the sentence is in the present tense. Choice D has an incorrect verb form as well.

42. A: Choice A uses the possessive of "service's" correctly. Choice B has no possessive and also has an incorrect verb form. Choice C uses an incorrect possessive form and choice D has a plural noun "milestones" with a singular article "a."

43. D: Choice A does not have "legacy" capitalized as it should be. Choice B does not have the proper name "forest legacy" capitalized. Choice C incorrectly capitalizes "the" and does not capitalize "legacy."

44. B: Choice B has a logical flow of ideas. Choices A, C, and D are all awkwardly written.

45. B: The sentence requires a noun. In this case, *reception* is the only word that correctly completes the sentence.

46. A: Only choice A uses science-based research to back up an argument. All of the other choices involve emotional or inconclusive approaches to the issue.

47. C: Only this choice develops and supports a counterclaim. Choice A provides a counterclaim but does not give support. Choices B and D focus on related but separate issues (length of the school day, teacher salaries).

48. B: This is the best choice because the first blank shows a change in direction. The second blank indicates that an initial point will be made. The final blank indicates a counterargument.

Reading

1. C: The question asks which job is less desirable than homesteading according to the writer. Choice C is correct because Stewart speaks of going out to wash as less preferable than homesteading. Choice A is incorrect because the letter does not mention cooking or restaurants. Choice B is also incorrect. The reason is that there is no mention of opening a bed and breakfast in the letter. Choice D is also wrong because the letter shares nothing about teaching.

2. B: Stewart mentions the hard work of laundry, but she does not speak of any enjoyment of it as she does about homesteading. Choice A cannot be correct because Stewart does not seem to be lazy. Choice C is possible, but there is no evidence to support that idea. Choice D cannot be correct because no reason for anger is given.

3. D: Stewart says that homesteading is a lonely task. For example, she mentions that "persons afraid of ...loneliness had better let ranching alone." Stewart explains in the letter that her work uses less strength than washing. So, choice A is wrong. Choice B is also incorrect because it is addressed in the first paragraph of the letter. Choice C is incorrect because it is mentioned as an advantage in the first paragraph.

4. A: Stewart directly states that women would have "the added satisfaction of knowing that their job will not be lost to them if they care to keep it." Although going on strike was common at the time, Stewart does not mention it. So, choice B is incorrect. Denver is in the Rocky Mountains, but landslides are not mentioned as a risk. So, choice C cannot be the correct answer. Fire is always a risk, but Stewart does not bring it up in the letter. So, choice D is not the correct answer.

5. C: The letter is very positive and full of reasons on why homesteading is a good choice. Choice A is incorrect. The reason is that there is no complaint of hard work, weather, or loneliness. Choice B is also not correct because the letter does not speak of sadness or loneliness. Instead, Stewart rejoices in the good success of the homestead. Also, choice D is not correct because there is no hopelessness expressed in the letter.

6. A: Technical passages focus on presenting specific information and have a tone of formality. They also usually prompt a response from their recipient. Expository passages reveal information to the reader. This passage does give information, but the information is specific, technical, and meant to prompt action from the students receiving the email. Therefore, choice A, technical, is the best answer. Narrative writing focuses on telling a story, and the passage offers no indication of this. Persuasive writing attempts to persuade the reader to agree with a certain position; the instructor offers the students information and advice but leaves the decision up to each student.

7. C: Choice C fits the tone of the passage best. The instructor is simply offering students the chance to make up the exam score (which is worth 70% of their grade) and thus avoid failing the course. The instructor does not berate students at any point, nor does the instructor admit that the exam was too difficult. Additionally, the instructor offers encouragement to the students should they choose to complete an extra credit project, but that is not the primary purpose of this email.

8. B: This question asks for the best summary of the instructor's motive. In the opening paragraph, the instructor notes that his original grading plan has to change to reflect the exam scores. Because they were low, he now wants to give students a chance to make up for their low scores. Choice B thus summarizes his motive effectively by stating that he recognizes the need for a change in the policy. The instructor introduces his email with the notes about the scores being posted, but given the information that is provided in the message, this is not the sole motive for his writing, so choice A is incorrect. Choice C limits the motive to the details about the group project, but the instructor provides three options. Choice D overlooks the instructor's further note about how the grading policy sometimes has to bend to reflect circumstances.

9. B: The passage argues that high schools should require that students study a foreign language and gives reasons to support this argument. Choice B accurately describes the main idea of the passage. The passage does say that studying a foreign language is helpful for college acceptance and finding a job, but neither of these points are the main idea of the passage. They are both supporting details. The passage does not say that studying a foreign language will help students gain an understanding of other cultures.

10. C: The passage includes claims that studying a foreign language is helpful for participating in the global economy, being accepted into college, and being a desirable candidate for various jobs. These points are summarized in choice C, making it the best summary of the passage. The passage argues that studying a foreign language should be mandatory, but it does not claim that studying a foreign language is currently essential to high school graduation, so choice A is incorrect. Choices B and D represent claims made in the passage, but do not include all of the claims made.

11. D: Although students may find knowledge of a foreign language helpful for obtaining a job, it is clearly an exaggeration to claim that students who did not study a foreign language are unemployable. Choice A simply lists a fact that can be verified, so it cannot be an exaggeration. Choices B and C include statements that the importance of knowing a foreign language and the acceptance rates for students who have studied a foreign language have increased. These statements simply describe the direction of a trend, so while they can be incorrect, they cannot be exaggerations.

12. D: Choice D can confirm the author's claim that high school graduates who studied a foreign language are more likely to be accepted to college, so it is correct. Choices A and C would provide information regarding the opinions of students and parents, but not actual evidence regarding the influence of studying a foreign language on future success. Choice B specifies a second language taught at home, whereas the passage focuses specifically on a foreign language taught in high school.

13. B: Choice B emphasizes the passage's argument and includes a summary of the main supporting details used to defend it. This makes choice B the best conclusion. Choices A, C, and D each emphasize the passage's main argument, but each one only mentions one supporting detail. These are not effective conclusions, so they are incorrect.

14. C: The last sentence states that Laurie was "an incorrigible tease." From this statement you can infer that Laurie was unruly or unmanageable. Stoic means not showing passion or emotion. Taciturn means silent. Uncanny means supernatural. There is nothing in the passage to imply he had any of these characteristics.

15. C: Point of view refers to the vantage point from which a story is written. First person uses the pronoun *I*. Second person uses the pronoun *you*. Third person uses the pronouns *he/she/they*. There is no fourth person point of view. This passage was written in the third person.

16. B: The words "mysterious" and "important" used in the sentence help the reader deduce that Jo looked secretive. Jo neither looked jubilant, or joyful; disheveled, or disarrayed; or angry.

17. C: The passage makes no mention of metals or horses. Although we may infer that they hunted the buffalo because they were plentiful, that is not stated in the passage.

18. B: Travail means work, or effort, and shows that the crows made it more difficult for the people to kill buffalo during the hunt.

19. B: The story tells us that after the great white crow turned black, all the other crows were black as well. Thus, he is a symbol for all these birds.

20. D: Lines 29–30 tells us that the tribe planned to frighten the chief of the crows to prevent the crows from warning the buffalo about the hunts. The passage does not suggest that they hated all birds or that they planned to eat this one.

21. C: Long Arrow acted like the buffalo in the herd so that the chief of the crows would approach, making it possible to capture him. Although we may infer that he had to fool the buffalo in the herd as well, this is secondary to his need to fool the birds.

22. B: These details help us to see how the people lived. Although they hunted with the stone tipped spears, the rawhide bag was not a part of the hunt.

23. A: As he lands, he asks "have you not heard my warning?" (Lines 68–69).

24. A: The suggestions included several for killing or mutilating the bird, which does not suggest a calm resolve. And there is no suggestion that they were either celebrating or hungry at this time.

25. D: There is no characterization of Long Arrow in the passage, and we know nothing about him or why he was chosen.

26. B: The birds in the story are able to observe the actions of hunters, to interpret them as potentially harmful for their buffalo friends, and to act for the protection of the buffalo. They do not appear to do this for their own benefit, nor do they seem to act specifically to harm the tribe, but rather to help the buffalo.

27. C: The passage describes Hal as a very large man suited to contact sports, and this metaphor indicates that he had massive legs the size of tree trunks.

28. B: Cats are known to move very quietly. Here, Hal's massive size is being contrasted with his ability to move as quietly as a cat.

29. B: The author asserts that earning money is easy, but what often challenges people is managing money. This is the main idea of the passage. Choice B says that earning money is less difficult than managing money, so it is correct. Getting a job and the temptation to spend money are both mentioned in the passage as details. However, neither of these are the main idea, so choices A and D are both incorrect. The quote from Franklin does not advocate for working at a mill and does not summarize the main idea, so choice C is also incorrect.

30. A: The author insists that many people who have no trouble earning money waste it through lavish spending, along with several other statements that show the reader that the author believes managing money is more challenging than making it.

31. B: This passage is clearly intended for a non-expert adult readership.

32. C: In this passage, the author is speaking of money management on a personal or household level. In this context, economy refers to efficient money management, so choice C is correct. While this definition of economy is relevant to households, it is not related to delegation within a household, making choice B incorrect. Economy in the context of the exchange of money, goods, and services is more applicable beyond personal or household finances, so choice A is incorrect. This passage uses economy to describe wise money management, not simply goods that are less expensive than others, so choice D is incorrect.

33. D: The author suggests that many people who believe they understand economy in fact do not.

34. A: It seems clear that the author is about to describe the correct means of personal economy.

35. B: Lincoln begins this speech by discussing the founding of the U.S. and what the original purpose of the U.S. was. Then, he goes on to talk about how the U.S. is currently engaged in a war intended to fracture the nation, and he states that the battle being discussed was one large tragedy that came out of the war. Next, Lincoln says that his speech and even the memorial itself can't truly honor those who died, and that it's up to those who survived to continue the fight to ensure the nation does not break apart. Answer B best communicates this message.

36. C: The sentence in which this phrase is found is: The world will little note, nor long remember, what we say here, but can never forget what they did here. In this context, the phrase "the world will little note" means that no one outside of those in attendance or possibly those outside the country will pay attention to the speech or the ceremony. This eliminates all of the answer choices except C.

37. A: The ideals of the revolution are addressed in the first paragraph: Four score and seven years ago our fathers brought forth, upon this continent, a new nation, conceived in Liberty, and dedicated to the proposition that all men are created equal. This introduces the point that Lincoln is trying to make about the battle at hand and the war as a whole: the Civil War is threatening the ideas upon which the nation was created.

38. C: There is a comparison between the ideas of the Revolution and the Civil War in this speech. To facilitate understanding of this comparison, Lincoln has to set the stage by telling his audience about the past event he is referencing. This establishes the context of his message.

39. A: This line directly references the idea in the previous paragraph, which is that the U.S. is a nation that was created to ensure liberty and equality. This sentence talks about how the Civil War is testing whether or not a nation that was created to ensure liberty and equality can really survive.

40. B: When President Lincoln argues that the people who died at Gettysburg did not die in vain, he asserts that their passing was not frivolous or unimportant or meaningless.

41. B: This question basically asks for the main idea of the passage as a whole. Choice A is inappropriate because the passage does not discuss automotive stock. Choice B is a good choice because the final sentence of the first paragraph says exactly the same thing. Choice C is not only inappropriate, it is also only true for a very limited number of vehicles. Choice D is so general that it does not really say anything at all. The best choice is, therefore, Choice B.

42. B: Even if the meaning of "detriments" is unclear, the sentence it is used in provides some clues: "While there are many pros and cons associated with automobile ownership, many consumers do not adequately research the specific benefits and <u>detriments</u> associated with purchasing a particular vehicle." The sentence's structure makes it probable that there is an identification of "pros and cons" with "benefits and detriments." Leaving this aside, if it is clear that "pros" and "benefits" are the same thing, then it is likely that "cons" and "detriments" are the same thing. The best answer, then, is B, "Cons."

43. D: This is a detail question with tricky wording in the answer choices. The use of the term "always" should make the reader suspicious. In the real world, things are almost never "always" *x* or *y*. For example, choice A is explicitly contradicted in the second paragraph. Choice B is doubly inappropriate because of its use of "always" and its irrelevance to the passage (SUVs are not discussed in the passage). While choice C does not use "always," it is not a good choice because the relationship between color and cost is not discussed in the passage. Choice D is supported by the second paragraph and is the best overall choice.

44. D: Because this is an "all of the above question," if the reader can confirm two of the answer choices, he or she need not examine the third. Choice A is a good one because the second paragraph says that the cost of a vehicle is not limited to purchase price alone. Choices B and C are included in the passage as additional costs of ownership Since A has already been confirmed, confirming either B or C means that the correct answer is D.

45. B: According to the passage, choice A is inappropriate because if the consumer has done research, he or she will be less likely to be swayed by less important concerns. Choice B is explicitly stated in the final paragraph. Choice C is inappropriate because the passage says nothing about the consumer's attitude towards salespeople. Choice D is directly contradicted in the third paragraph. Thus, choice B is the best answer.

46. D: This is a difficult question because it is easy to make a simple mistake. The passage explicitly says that choices A and C can be explored on a manufacturer's website. While it seems likely that one could visit a manufacturer's website and find information on a vehicle's color, two things should be noted. First, the passage does not discuss a vehicle's color with reference to a manufacturer's website. Second, the passage does not discuss the relationship between a vehicle's color and its cost. For both of these reasons, choice B is a poor choice; thus, the best answer is choice D.

47. C: The first paragraph states that the main purpose of DST is to make better use of daylight.

48. A: Energy conservation is discussed as a possible benefit of DST, not a negative effect of it.

49. D: The first paragraph states that DST involves setting clocks forward one hour in the spring and one hour backward in the fall.

50. B: The last sentence in paragraph four notes that agricultural and evening entertainment interests have historically been opposed to DST.

51. D: The passage gives examples of both good and bad effects extra daylight can have on health.

52. C: The last paragraph of the passage notes that DST can lead to peculiar situations and relays an anecdote about the effect of DST on the birth order of twins.

53. B: In the second paragraph, the author asserts that Benjamin Franklin suggested DST as a way to save candles.

54. D: The sixth paragraph notes that DST is observed in only some regions of Brazil.

Thank You

We at Mometrix would like to extend our heartfelt thanks to you, our friend and patron, for allowing us to play a part in your journey. It is a privilege to serve people from all walks of life who are unified in their commitment to building the best future they can for themselves.

The preparation you devote to these important testing milestones may be the most valuable educational opportunity you have for making a real difference in your life. We encourage you to put your heart into it—that feeling of succeeding, overcoming, and yes, conquering will be well worth the hours you've invested.

We want to hear your story, your struggles and your successes, and if you see any opportunities for us to improve our materials so we can help others even more effectively in the future, please share that with us as well. **The team at Mometrix would be absolutely thrilled to hear from you!** So please, send us an email (support@mometrix.com) and let's stay in touch.

> **If you'd like some additional help, check out these other resources we offer for your exam:**
> **http://MometrixFlashcards.com/CHSPE**

Additional Bonus Material

Due to our efforts to try to keep this book to a manageable length, we've created a link that will give you access to all of your additional bonus material:

mometrix.com/bonus948/chspe